CALIFORNIA POLITICS

Shifting Majorities, Emerging Minorities

REVISED FIRST EDITION

EDITED BY **ROBERT STANLEY ODEN**

CALIFORNIA STATE UNIVERSITY - SACRAMENTO

cognella® | ACADEMIC PUBLISHING

Bassim Hamadeh, CEO and Publisher
Kassie Graves, Director of Acquisitions
Jamie Giganti, Senior Managing Editor
Miguel Macias, Senior Graphic Designer
Carrie Montoya, Acquisitions Editor
Natalie Lakosil, Licensing Manager
Allie Kiekhofer and Kaela Martin, Associate Editors
Kat Ragudos, Interior Designer

Cover image copyright © Jamison Wieser (CC by 2.0) at https://commons.wikimedia.org/wiki
         File:CACourt_protest.jpg.
         copyright © Depositphotos/rudyumans.

Printed in the United States of America

ISBN: 978-1-5165-1064-1 (pbk) / 978-1-5165-1065-8 (br)

cognella® | ACADEMIC PUBLISHING

CONTENTS

CHAPTER THREE—
CRITICAL ISSUES OF INCLUSION IN CALIFORNIA   217

In memory of Arlene and Percy Slaughter.

Acknowledgments

Upon publication of this anthology, I want to acknowledge the many people who have helped me throughout my journey as an academic and an activist. First and foremost, I want to thank my parents, Allie Mae and Clyde Oden Sr., who were inspirational lifelines for my personal achievement and my love of life. To my brothers, Rev. Dr. Clyde Oden, whose steadfast dignity and faith provide with me constant sustenance, and Douglas Oden, Esq., whose constant prodding and positive support for my endeavors have been vital in my success: I thank you both immeasurably for your support. Additionally, I want to thank members of my family, especially my sons, Marcus and Kofi, and their wives and children, and their mom Maddy Oden, for being there for me, as well as my other close relatives and friends who also celebrate this publication.

This academic endeavor would not have occurred unless some perceptive, progressive-minded individuals had opened some gates for me. I want to deeply thank my mentor and great friend, Dr. Hardy Frye, Sociology Professor Emeritus, U.C. Santa Cruz, for his friendship and guidance throughout my graduate study and beyond. I will never forget all he has given. And to my other great professors and friends at U.C. Santa Cruz, too many to name here, a thank you for assisting me throughout my Ph.D.

work to help get me to the starting line, which ultimately led to producing this anthology. I also want to greatly thank former chair of the CSUS Department of Government, Dr. Mignon "Mimi" Gregg, for her confidence in me and for her guidance. As well, to all my colleagues in the Government Department, a thanks for the opportunity to teach the course on which this anthology is based, "The Politics of the Underrepresented." I want also to thank the professors who taught this course before me; most especially, the late Mayor of Sacramento, Joe Serna, whose untimely death due to cancer in 1999 was a great loss to us all. Additionally, my writing and my academic career would not be where it is today without the support and kindness of Dr. Wendy Martyna, whose editorial assistance over the years has been greatly appreciated. I also want to thank my dear friend, Ms. Regina Wander, for assisting in editing this introduction and for her continual support of my academic success.

Finally, I want to thank the staff at Cognella Publishers and University Readers, for their outstanding efforts and cooperation in assembling this anthology. I particularly want to thank Brent Hanify, Production Assistant, and Amy Wiltbank, Graphics Designer, for their technical assistance. I want to give a special thanks to Melissa Accornero, Acquisitions Editor, who discovered my course curriculum and presented me the valuable opportunity to produce this anthology.

And lastly, this anthology is in memory of the many fighters for social justice and equality in California including my late aunt and uncle, Arlene and Percy Slaughter who in their generation created the political and social space for myself and many others to pursue fighting for social justice and equality in California.

Introduction

In the early morning of New Year's Day 2009 in Oakland, California, a fatal altercation occurred between a white Bay Area Rapid Transit (BART) police officer and a young African American man, Oscar Grant III. The BART police officer meant to pull out his Taser weapon to apprehend Grant, his suspect, who was facedown. Instead of pulling out his Taser weapon, the officer took out his service revolver "by mistake" and shot and killed Grant. This fatal incident occurred at the Fruitvale BART station in Oakland. The BART police officer, Johannes Mehserle, had arrested the twenty-two-year-old Grant after he was allegedly involved in a fight on the BART train. In a videotaping of the incident by someone with a phone camera at the scene, Mehserle is seen pulling out his service revolver and kneeling over Grant, who is prone and facedown. Mehserle shoots Grant in the back with one bullet.

Due to shock and anger by some Oakland and other East Bay residents—mostly youth—the initial response was to start fires in downtown Oakland and loot stores along Broadway and other downtown streets. The violent reaction by the youth, who were composed of multiple races and cultures, was decried by Oakland mayor Ronald Dellums and others who helplessly saw the scattered burning and looting in downtown Oakland. This reaction occurred in a city that has, for the past forty-plus years, been at the forefront of political change; despite that, it never experienced riots and rebellions during the 1960s due to the presence of the Black Panther Party, which was founded in Oakland in 1966.

In July 2010, a jury in Los Angeles (the trial was moved to Los Angeles County due to the publicity of the incident) found that Officer Mehserle was guilty of involuntary manslaughter, and on November 5, 2010, he was sentenced to two years in prison, to the outrage of the Grant family and many in the Bay Area. Outside of Oakland City Hall that day, as the sentence was being handed down, more than five hundred people rallied to denounce the sentence. Later in the evening, a number of youths smashed windows and looted stores in anger in a residential area south of Lake Merritt. In their eyes, the youths were reacting to another unjustifiable killing of a black man by a white police officer. In the words of Grant's family attorney, John Burris, "life can be taken from you with no just cause and price to pay" (*San Francisco Chronicle*, November 6, 2010, p. A10). During the sentencing phase of the trial, Mehserle was very remorseful and claimed that it was a mistake that he pulled his gun instead of the Taser. This historic moment has been memorialized in the movie *Fruitvale Station*, released in 2013 and directed by Ryan Coogler with Michael B. Jordan playing Oscar Grant III.

This incident reflects the continued tensions between the police and black youth in California. This is a continuation of the memories of the Watts rebellion in Los Angeles in 1965, which began with an altercation between a white police officer and a black male motorist. The memories continue with the beating of Rodney King by four Los Angeles police officers in 1991. The acquittals of the police officers after the beatings led to a rebellion by thousands of people in Los Angeles and elsewhere. In Los Angeles, this resulted in fifty-three deaths and billions of dollars in property damage.

Most did not realize that moment in Oakland was the impetus for the beginning of the Black Lives Matter movement. After the death of Oscar Grant III, thousands of young people and many other activists rallied to protest the murder of this young man. Much like the vanguard militancy of the Black Panther Party (begun in October 1966 with Huey P. Newton and Bobby Seale), the conditions for a national movement to again protest the police brutality and murder of black people were taking shape again forty-three years later. Locally, community-based organizations in Oakland began to emerge as accusations of police brutality and excessive force by Oakland and Bay Area law enforcement agencies were increasing. Two years later, Occupy Wall Street demonstrations and encampments sprang up in all major cities in the United States. Zuccotti Park next to Wall Street in lower Manhattan served as the spiritual center of this incipient movement of mostly young white people and community activists of color. In Oakland as well as Los Angles, encampments were erected. In Oakland, dozens of people set up camp next to Oakland City Hall. Occupy Oakland emerged as a flashpoint as the encampment was besieged by the City of Oakland and Alameda County law enforcement officers dressed in riot gear. "What began as just another anti-Wall Street protest 'occupation' in a mid-size California city has grown into a global phenomenon and turned

Oakland into the epicenter of the Occupy Wall Street movement" (*Sacramento Bee*, October 29, 2011, p. A5, quoted in Oden, 2012, p. 3)

Following the demise of Occupy Oakland and other encampments in California and nationally, the murder of Trayvon Martin occurred a year later on February 26, 2012, in Sanford, Florida. Martin, who was African American and nineteen years old, was unarmed and walking home in a condominium development when he was confronted by George Zimmerman, a self-described neighborhood watch coordinator. Zimmerman immediately engaged Martin physically, which resulted in a tussle and the shooting death of Martin. The subsequent arrest and trial of Zimmerman—who can be described as white, although he came from mixed Latino heritage—was quite controversial, particularly when Zimmerman was acquitted of the charge of second-degree murder. Zimmerman's acquittal set off demonstrations in Florida, California, New York, and elsewhere, and the Black Lives movement was born. The subsequent shooting death of Michael Brown in Ferguson, Missouri, touched off violent protests and arrests that lasted several days. The choking death of Eric Garner in Staten Island, New York; the death of Freddie Hayes in Baltimore, Maryland; and numerous other murders of unarmed black men have fueled the fury and activated a new generation of black activists.

In California, this movement has been formed to prevent police shootings of unarmed individuals who in the majority are black. The Black Lives Matter movement has been active in Oakland with continued demonstrations and coordination led by several groups, including Bay Area Solidarity Action, the Blackout Collective, and other organizations. The Black Lives Matter movement in San Francisco just recently led the movement to oust San Francisco police chief Greg Suhr, who resigned on May 20, 2016, after the fatal shooting of an African American woman by a police officer—the third controversial police shooting since December 2015. The national demonstrations and continued shootings by law enforcement around the country has caused President Obama to push for legislation and actions requiring body cameras with all police personnel as well as other reforms to address the scourge of police shootings of unarmed black people.

These events symbolize the continuing political and economic struggle African Americans have in a state of great promise and dreams that elude millions who are not white: immigrants from Third World countries, African Americans who migrated to California from the South, and native people and the Mexicans who lived here prior to the discovery of gold in 1848. The discovery of gold brought white settlers who ravaged the native population, stole much of the lands of Mexican land grantees, and imposed a white antiforeigner state government that formed the basis for California to become a state dominated by whites in agriculture, business, and politics.

California has proven to be the most economically viable state in the union with an economy that makes the state the seventh richest country in the world. During the twenty-first century, there have been great changes in the population, culture, economy, and politics that speak to shifting majorities and emerging minorities. This anthology is a compilation of writings from accomplished, esteemed scholars and writers who have analyzed the ethnic, racial, and cultural realities of California in the twenty-first century. They provide a political and sociological view of multicultural relations in a state where the demographic environment has shifted tremendously. According to the California State Department of Finance in their Race/Ethnic Population Estimate,

> The race/ethnic distribution in California shifted substantially during the 1990s. By 2000, the white Non-Hispanic's share of the population decreases from 57 percent to about 47 percent at the same time that Hispanics' portion of the state population grew from about a quarter to a third of the total. The Asian and Pacific Islander Non-Hispanic population's share also increased to 12 percent from 9 percent. Over the same period, the proportion of the Black or African American Non-Hispanic population remained just about constant at 7 percent while the share of American Indian Non-Hispanics grew to just over 1 percent. (California Department of Finance, August 2005, p. 1)

The Department of Finance projects that by the year 2020, the Hispanic population will be 40 percent; the white population will be 36 percent; the Asian, non-Pacific Islander at 12 percent; and the African American population at 5 percent. The projected nonwhite population would be 64 percent to the white population of 36 percent. A more predictive statistic indicating the shift in majorities and emerging minorities is in the K–12 school population figures of 2009–2010 by the State of California Board of Education. These show the enrollment of Hispanic or Latinos at 50.38 percent; white, non-Hispanic, 27.03 percent; Asian, 8.51 percent; African American, 6.83 percent; Filipino, 2.53 percent; American Indian, 0.73 percent; and Pacific Islander, 0.60 percent. The non-white school enrollment, including populations with two or more races and with non-reported is 73 percent, compared with 27 percent white. While this statistic is for public school enrollment, the shift from the 1960s to 2010 in California is indeed dramatic.

The population shift has been just as proportionally dramatic in the political sphere, where Latinos have taken over the leadership mantle in many of the key legislative positions in Sacramento in both the State Assembly and State Senate. African American political leaders forged the political pathway in the 1960s, 1970s, and 1980s with legislators such as Assembly member Byron Rumford (Berkeley, 1948–1966); Assembly member, State Senator, and Lieutenant Governor Mervyn Dymally (Los Angeles, 1962–2004); Assembly member and Speaker of the Assembly Willie Brown (San Francisco, 1964–1996); and Yvonne Brathwaite Burke (Los Angeles, 1966–1972) among many other stellar African American legislators. African American legislators formed the Black Caucus and presently have eight members: six in the Assembly and two in the State Senate. The last African American to hold a key legislative post was Assembly member Karen Bass, who was speaker of the State Assembly from 2007–2009.

While the African American representation in the state is holding steady or slightly declining, the Latino political representation has increased substantially. Currently, the number of Latinos in the State Assembly and State Senate is twenty-five. Between 1960 and 1980, there were only nine Latino legislators. The political clout of Latinos has been on a steady, if not dramatic, increase. Immense obstacles still lie ahead for Latino political incorporation in state and local politics, including a high percentage of Latinos under the age of thirty—a high nonvoting population—and immigration and naturalization laws, continued immigrant bashing, and racism. These obstacles keep the registered Latino voter population under the population total in the state. The Latino political clout, however, is seen throughout California in electoral races as well as nationally. The recent governor's race in California between billionaire Meg Whitman and former governor Jerry Brown may have turned on the revelation that Whitman hired and fired an undocumented housekeeper. Whitman's denials and aspersions directed at the undocumented housekeeper enraged many Latinos and other voters and assisted in the sound defeat of Whitman by Brown to capture the governor's seat once again in 2011.

Additionally, the Asian American and Pacific Islander communities have increased their representation in the state legislature. In the 2009–2010 legislative year, there were ten members representing the Asian and Pacific Islander Legislative Caucus, with eight in the State Assembly and two in the State Senate. In 1998, there was only one Asian American representative, Mike Honda of San Jose. Moreover, with the exception of San Diego, every major city in California has elected a nonwhite person to the mayor's position. Most recently, Jean Quan was elected in November 2, 2010, to become the first Asian American mayor in Oakland's history.

Not only has the nonwhite population emerged to become politically powerful and active, but another emerging minority has been the gay and lesbian community. This community, kept in the closets and closed doors of a homophobic society, began to emerge in the 1950s and 1960s as an identifiable group. The Stonewall Inn rebellion in New York City in 1969 created the political environment for the beginning of the gay liberation movement, which surfaced in the Castro district of San Francisco as a gay and lesbian political stronghold. This came to fruition with the election of Harvey Milk, a Castro district business owner and the first openly gay member of the Board of Supervisors, who propelled himself and the issues of the lesbian, gay, bisexual, and transgendered (LGBT) community to the forefront of political considerations in San Francisco. Milk successfully helped beat back Proposition 6 in 1978, which would have prevented homosexuals from teaching in public schools. Milk's advocacy, however, cost him his life as well as the life of Mayor George Moscone, when Milk was gunned down with Moscone in November 1978 by Dan White, a deranged former member of the Board of Supervisors. Milk's death, as he predicted, "opened the closet door" for many in the LGBT community. Using Milk's legacy, gays and lesbians became politically powerful in San Francisco and elsewhere in the state. Following Milk, there have been strong gay and lesbian political figures, including present San Francisco state legislators State Senator Mark Leno and Assemblyman Tom Ammiano. Also, there have been a number of lesbian legislators, including past State Assembly member Jackie Goldberg and former State senator Sheila Kuehl. In November 2008, California voters rejected same-sex marriage by voting for Proposition 8, which stated that marriage is a union between a man and a woman only. This vote was challenged in the federal courts, and the federal judge in the case decided in favor of same-sex marriage. The case is now before the ninth circuit court of appeals. This issue is now national in scope, along with the political decision by the

Congress and the Obama administration to end the military's "Don't Ask, Don't Tell" edict, which has discriminated against gays and lesbians in the military and in many cases caused gay and lesbian military personnel to be "outed" and removed from military service.

This is the cultural and political environment these selections in this anthology will address. The economic picture in the state has been severely altered by the global economic recession, which had its epicenter in the California housing market. The bursting of the housing bubble saw home values in some cases go bottoms-up, with the majority of the home mortgages losing between 30 percent and 80 percent of their market value. Thousands of foreclosed homes now dot the California and national suburban and urban landscapes with no change in sight. Many of these foreclosures originate in nonwhite households. The unemployment rate statewide is around 12 percent, with an even higher rate for Latinos and African Americans.

The economic, political, and cultural environment in California is multifaceted and evolving. This anthology hopes to capture that dynamic impacted by demographic, political, and cultural shifts that are reshaping California, making California the destination for individuals over the past two centuries.

This anthology is divided into three chapters: the first chapter details the impact of immigration from Mexico and the political impact it has had in California. The second chapter focuses on the city and region of Los Angeles. This area has the greatest population in the state and is home to a sizable Latino population. The impact of the politics of that region will dictate much of the politics in the rest of the state. Finally, the anthology analyzes crucial issues in race and ethnicity in the state and how these issues affect the proponents and opponents of racial inclusion in California.

The first selection, "Building the Immigrant Movement," is by Randy Shaw, who details the historical trajectory of the immigrant movement. From a chapter in *Beyond the Fields: Cesar Chavez, the UFW, and the Struggle for Justice in the 21st Century*, Shaw carefully acknowledges the groundbreaking work of Cesar Chavez and the United Farm Workers movement in the undocumented immigrant issue. Chavez challenged the use of undocumented as strikebreakers, while maintaining a need for farm workers' rights and dignity even for undocumented farm workers. Shaw provides the framework in which immigrant community-based organizations and labor unions and the religious community united using UFW-based organizing strategies to create an immigrant movement. This first selection lays out the basis for understanding the most crucial issues in the twenty-first century in California, among which is the immigration from Latin America, principally Mexico. Shaw presents the electoral potential of organizing and mobilizing immigrant workers and how conservative forces are arrayed to oppose pathways for the naturalization and citizenship of undocumented immigrants.

The conceptualization of Latino immigrant inclusion into the political process becomes operationalized in Kim Geron's selection "The Salinas Valley," a chapter from *Latino Political Power* (2005). Geron provides a historical political analysis of the emergence of Chicano political power in the city of Salinas, California. This city historically has been the home of intense agricultural production, known as the "salad bowl of the United States." This city was the setting of several John Steinbeck novels describing the hardships of migrant farming and life in the Salinas/Monterey areas. Geron demonstrates how Latinos used the movement of the UFW to challenge the at-large voting structure of the city. This challenge and the increased political awareness of Chicanos in Salinas led to the increase in political incorporation of Chicanos in Salinas. This expanded political clout, according to Geron, helped low-income persons in Salinas—mostly Chicanos—obtain affordable housing, greater social services, and ultimately a Chicano-controlled city government.

The final selection in the first chapter is "They Keep Coming" by Daniel Martinez HoSang from his book *Racial Propositions: Ballot Initiatives and the Making of Postwar California*. In this selection, HoSang presents a detailed historical analysis of the development of Proposition 187, the voter-initiated ballot measure that eliminated public services such as education and public health to undocumented immigrants in California. This selection by HoSang frames the debate on immigration that has been raging since the passage of this measure. Proposition 187 became the vessel for anti-Mexican and anti-Latino sentiments that created the sweeping victory of Proposition 187, which won by a vote of 59 percent to 41 percent. This overwhelming victory was temporary and was challenged by immigrant rights' organizations as well as the American Civil Liberties Union. Their court challenge was successful, and Proposition 187 was never fully implemented. However, as a result of the court decision, immigrant rights organizing increased and a new social movement was created. Concomitantly, anti-immigrant sentiment has increased, with conservative Republican legislators in Washington, DC, voting down any attempt for comprehensive immigration reform to bring the more than 11 million undocumented individuals out of the shadows of suspicion and deportation to genuine legal status and citizenship. This selection by HoSang details the political organizing on both sides of the issue and provides an understanding of why this is the seminal domestic issue in California and the United States. This matter has become central to the 2016 presidential race, with Republican nominee Donald Trump declaring his intent to deport 11 million undocumented immigrants and proposing to build a wall across the 1500-mile Mexican-US border to keep these immigrants and others out of the United States. Final resolution of the immigration issue is seemingly years away, with chaos looming in the future if Donald Trump is elected president.

The second chapter in the anthology focuses on Los Angeles and the region of the Los Angeles Basin. Los Angeles is highlighted in this anthology for obvious reasons. It is the second largest city in the United States, and its region has close to 40 percent of the population in California. Economically, politically, and culturally, Los Angeles sets the tone for the entire state and in many cases, the United States. The influence in Los Angeles in the late twentieth century as a multicultural, mega-metropole with an enormous Latino population is highly significant. Kenneth Burt's essay "Latino Los Angeles: The Promise of Politics" from *City of Promise: Race and Historical Change in Los Angeles* edited by Martin Schiesl and Mark Dodge (2006), discusses the historical emergence of Latino electoral politics in Los Angeles. The efforts of the groundbreaking political work of Edward Roybal and the community organization efforts led by him and the Community Service Organization (CSO) helped elect Roybal as the first Latino to the city council since the Gold Rush days are discussed.

Moreover, Burt assiduously details the role Roybal and others played in creating a Latino political machine in Los Angeles. The political machine, which incurred defeats as well as victories, eventually created opportunities for many prominent Chicanos to get elected to political office in Los Angeles and surrounding areas. Burt points to the election of former mayor Antonio Villaraigosa as evidence of the Latino-labor coalition forged by the late Miguel Contreras, former head of the powerful Los Angeles County Federation of Labor.

The Los Angeles Basin is a tapestry of multiracial enclaves and multicultural interactions. With this immense transracial mix, Los Angeles has experienced strife and tension, which came to a boil in 1992. The next selection, "The Multicultural Nature of Los Angeles Unrest in 1992," is by Kwang Chung Kim. It dramatizes the grief, anger, and violence that exploded in Los Angeles after the verdict exonerating the four Los Angeles police officers in the beating of Rodney King in 1991, which was caught on videotape. In Kim's view, the violence that occurred during the rebellion that was directed against Korean American business owners by a mixture of multiracial rioters illustrates the misplaced anger of inner-city blacks and Latino youth and adults against Korean American entrepreneurs, as opposed to white corporate and financial interests that have historically neglected black and Latino inner-city areas such as South Central Los Angeles. Kim provides a theoretical framework to understand the victimization from whites from both the African American and Korean American perspectives. Kim's chapter from *Koreans in the Hood* (1999) provides a view of the most destructive urban rebellion in US history and how multicultural relations in Los Angeles were left hanging in the balance as a result of white-dominated economic and political processes which enabled a divide-and-conquer dynamic to take place between communities of color in Los Angeles.

The multicultural tensions that occasionally play a significant role in Los Angeles politics is the topic of the next two selections in the anthology, both written by Nicolas C. Vaca and taken from his provocative and revealing book *The Presumed Alliance: The Unspoken Conflict Between Latinos and Blacks and What It Means for America* (2004). In the first selection, "The Folly of Presumption: Black Voters and the Los Angeles 2001 Mayoral Elections," Vaca critically discusses the political dynamics between the African American and Latino communities in Los Angeles and how the perceived link of ideological and economic conditions between both groups fails to materialize in several political instances. The primary focus of Vaca's critique of Los Angeles's black political structure is the 2001 Los Angeles mayoral race, in which former Chicano assemblyman Antonio Villaraigosa sought to defeat in the runoff mayoral race a member of a well-known family legacy in Los Angeles politics, the Hahn family. The late Los Angeles Board of Supervisors' Kenneth Hahn had been the main public official responsible for getting public funding for various programs and projects for South Central Los Angeles. Vaca analyzes the political discourse from the African American community and their refusal to join in a black-Latino coalition to elect Villaraigosa over Hahn. Vaca accurately portrays the conflicts of interests and power between the African American community and the Latino community during this historic moment.

The second selection by Vaca in this anthology, "When Blacks Rule: Lessons from Compton," provides another illustration of the lost opportunities for a black-Latino coalition in a community in which there are common issues such as education, housing, jobs, crime, etc., which would unite both communities. However, Vaca charges that African Americans, once they became politically incorporated in the municipal government and school district, were highly resistant to give up their established political positions to include Latinos. This dynamic occurred despite a demographic shift in 1988 that brought the Latino population in Compton eight years earlier from 21.6 percent to 32 percent. The turf wars occurred in the political arena of city council and school board races and meetings as well as in the employment of Latinos in both bureaucracies. Vaca points out how the adult-world conflicts cascaded into youth violence, with fights erupting in the high schools between black and brown youth. African American control and apparent refusal, according to Vaca, to share power in a once white-dominated city has made the black-brown coalition difficult if not improbable in Compton and indicates the difficulties and realities of making multiracial coalitions viable in twenty-first-century California.

The multicultural fabric of California is captured by the emergence of gay and lesbian enclaves in local communities to include the Castro district in San Francisco, the Hillcrest district in San Diego, the West Hollywood community in Los Angeles, and many other areas in the state. In her selection "Inclusion and Exclusion in West Hollywood" from *Mapping Gay L.A.* (2001), Moira Rachel Kenny explores the contours of place naming and the politics of political incorporation and development as the gay male community in West Hollywood evolved in the 1970s. Kenny presents a historical analysis of the development of West Hollywood in its "pre-incorporation years," in which the city revolved around the Hollywood celebrity environment of boom-and-bust dynamics. The evolution of a gay presence and the political movement toward incorporating the area from the county govern-ment into a city gave West Hollywood a sense of gay power with a greater feeling of community and economic development that uplifted its residents. The desire to evolve as an inclusive city for all community residents poses conflicts in a white, male-dominated—albeit gay—community. Moira effectively situates West Hollywood as a focal point in Los Angeles for greater gay and lesbian political incorporation as well as a continued haven for alternative sexual appetites.

The last chapter of the anthology focuses on some of the key political issues that have affected the pace of multicultural and multiracial inclusion in California. One issue that has caused much controversy in California (and continues to be an issue) is that of affirmative action and the impact of Proposition 209, passed by voters in 1996. In the selection "Proposition 209 and Its Implications" from *Impacts of Affirmative Action* (1999), Paul Ong analyzes the attack on affirmative action in California by conservative forces and the use of the initiative process to pursue racially charged causes against laws seeking to end race and gender discrimination. Ong provides the economic and demographic factors which created a zero-sum mentality of many whites in California, who viewed their livelihoods threatened by the social demands of people of color and the increased immigration of nonwhites into the state. The racial reaction of whites, Ong points out, produced a majority supporting Proposition 209, a measure that essentially ended affirmative action in California. Ong presents evidence of the effectiveness of affirmative action and the deleterious effects Proposition 209 had on employment, business, and educational opportunities for African Americans and Latinos in California.

After the end of affirmative action in California in 1996, the main proponent in ending affirmative action in California and nationally was Ward Connerly, an African American appointed by Republican governor Pete Wilson to the Board of Regents to the University of California. Connerly joined with conservative forces who propelled Proposition 209 to victory. In 2002, Connerly launched an initiative campaign to ban the collection of data based on race and ethnicity. This ban of information would cover the areas of health, education, law enforcement, and civil rights enforcement. This initiative, initially dubbed "The Racial Privacy Act," was a successor to Proposition 209 in that it would have made racial distinctions disappear statistically by creating a false sense of a "color-blind" society, without any substantiation that the race and ethnic differences in California had been breached. The author of this anthology, Robert Stanley Oden, wrote an account and analysis of the defeat of Proposition 54, the measure to ban information based on race and ethnicity. In "The Rebirth of the Rainbow Politics in California," Oden provides insights on how political forces representing communities of color organized labor, education, and health and other communities of concern created a rainbow coalition of support that overcame the highly financed Yes on 54 campaign. Oden demonstrates how social action tactics such as rallies and pickets and grassroots organizing helped fuel a resurgence in social justice at a time when the Proposition 209 victory by conservative forces demoralized the proponents of social justice and racial equality in California. It shows that with great organizing and a common message, conservative initiatives can be defeated by a coalition of political forces from communities of color and other forces.

The final selection in this anthology is "The Third World Left Today and Contemporary Activism" by Laura Pulido from her book *Black, Brown, Yellow and Left: Radical Activism in Los Angeles* (2006). In this final selection, Pulido analyzes the fallout of Third World left organizing in Los Angeles. She recounts the effects and influences of left-oriented organizations such as the Black Panther Party and Asian American and Chicano organizations. She provides an understanding of the difficulties and obstacles in organizing both internally and externally to endure the fight for revolution by defending themselves against an aggressive, unrepentant state police apparatus. Pulido provides lessons and guidance for multicultural organizing that reflects gender and sexual orientation equality, which is essential in such a diverse environment as Los Angeles. This final selection provides a perspective for future organizing in urban settings in the twenty-first century in California that links the struggles of people of color and working-class whites to accomplish the mission of seeking social and economic justice in California and in the United States as well.

CHAPTER ONE

LEGACY OF THE FARM WORKER'S MOVEMENT

Building the Immigrant Rights Movement

Sí Se Puede!

RANDY SHAW

I n 2006, millions of Latino immigrants and their allies marched through America's streets to demand legalization for the nation's undocumented immigrants. Protests occurred in more than two hundred cities, with huge turnouts not only in cities such as Los Angeles and Chicago but also in small cities and rural towns across the country. This unprecedented public outpouring stunned many Americans, who had been largely unaware of the nation's growing immigrant rights movement.

Beginning with community-based immigrant advocacy groups in the mid-1950s, the movement had expanded to include labor and church groups in central roles. Its ranks quickly swelled after the passage of the Sensenbrenner bill, HR 4437, in December 2005, a bill strongly backed by President Bush and House Republicans. The measure would have made undocumented immigrants, and those who provided services to them, guilty of felonies. Opposition to the bill sparked a series of mass protests from March to May of 2006, and activists vowed to boost citizenship applications, Latino voter registration, and Latino voter turnout in the November 2006 midterm elections.

The marchers' rallying cry in cities large and small was the same: the farmworkers' chant, *"sí se puede!"* That millions would identify the cause of immigrant rights with Cesar Chavez and the UFW is fitting, as the union helped to lay the ground-work for today's immigrant rights movement. Such UFW veterans as Eliseo Medina, Fred Ross Jr., Miguel Contreras, and others played an important role in building the labor-clergy-community alliance that had once been key to the UFWs success and now was the vehicle for bringing millions to march, apply for citizenship, register to vote, cast ballots, and otherwise work on behalf of America's increasingly powerful immigrant rights movement more than thirty years later.

Chavez, The UFW, and Immigrants: Setting the Record Straight

Although the UFW strongly backed the 2006 marches, some still hold misconceptions about the union's stance on the issue of immigration over the years. Many who recall Chavez's support for crackdowns on immigration in the 1960s and early 1970s are not aware of his battles with the Immigration and Naturalization Service in the 1950s. Nor do his critics appreciate the historical context of the UFW's pro-enforcement position, adopted at a time when growers routinely brought in undocumented immigrants to break farmworker strikes. In fact, by the mid-1970s, Chavez had become a strong supporter of immigrant rights.

When Chavez worked for the Community Services Organization in the 1950s, organizing in the small town of Madera, near Fresno, one of his duties was to help immigrants become citizens. He quickly confronted a problem. The Immigration and Naturalization Service citizenship examiner for the area would not give the tests in Spanish, even though federal law authorized him to do so. When Chavez confronted the INS official, the man told him, "If they can't speak English, they shouldn't become citizens." He then implied that Chavez was a communist. This charge from a government official was taken seriously by the CSO's Madera board, which held a sort of "trial" of Chavez to determine whether he was in fact a communist. When Chavez learned that the board was holding a public meeting about his background, he rushed to the event and denounced the INS as "Gestapos." He then succeeded in electing new officers to the board, all of whom were farmworkers who supported his tough approach to INS abuses of immigrant rights.[1]

In 1958 and 1959, Chavez's organizing took him to Oxnard, California, which had the biggest bracero camp in the country. The bracero program had begun during World War II; because of labor shortages, growers won federal legislation allowing them to bring workers from Mexico to pick crops. But the program continued after the war, enabling growers to employ braceros rather than paying higher wages to local workers. Braceros were also used as strikebreakers. Given the impact of these Mexican workers on the local labor market, experts believed that killing the program was a prerequisite for improving the wages and living conditions of farmworkers. Chavez described the bracero program as "a vicious racket of the grossest order." As he saw it, "The jobs belonged to local workers. The braceros were brought only for exploitation. Braceros didn't make any money, and they were forced to work under conditions the local people wouldn't tolerate. If the braceros spoke up, if they made the minimal complaints, they'd be shipped back to Mexico."[2]

During his time in Oxnard, Chavez was struck by the community's overwhelming demand "to get those jobs from the braceros," and he believed that this desire represented the potential organizational base for a union. He spent much of the next year waging a grassroots campaign to get growers in Oxnard and the surrounding county to hire local farmworkers rather than braceros. Through marches, demonstrations, and sit-ins, he won a major but temporary victory, when the growers began to hire local workers directly from the CSO offices. But when Chavez proposed that it form a union and essentially operate a hiring hall, the CSO did not want to invest the necessary resources. Chavez later recalled, "If I had had the support of CSO, I would have built a union there." He moved on to organize in Los Angeles, and the progress he had made in Oxnard soon fell apart in his absence. After two years of trying to persuade the CSO to take up the cause of organizing farmworkers, Chavez left the group and, at age thirty-five, moved to Delano to take up the challenge.[3]

The beginning of the farmworkers movement coincided with the demise of the bracero program, so the union did not have to address the issue. But two lessons from Chavez's CSO days would come to shape his views of undocumented immigrants. First, he could not support workers being brought from Mexico, or anywhere else, for use as strikebreakers. The issue was not their illegal status—the UFW had undocumented immigrants within its ranks for years—rather, it was their key role in helping growers deny labor rights to local workers. Second, he saw the importation of these Mexican workers as a "vicious racket," in which the undocumented workers themselves were left in abject poverty while jobs were eliminated for local workers, who were Mexican nationals legally living in the United States.

Both principles came into play in October 1966, a year after the start of the grape boycott, when the farmworkers union was involved in supporting melon workers along the Rio Grande border in Texas who were striking for better conditions. The strike had failed to produce a union contract because growers were importing strikebreakers from Mexico. In response, the melon workers and their UFW supporters began stopping vehicles that were carrying workers across the border. A struggle with a local sheriff ensued, and in protest the UFW blocked traffic on the international bridge at the border for over an hour. The resulting public controversy led Mexican unions to set up their own picket line on their side of the border, aimed at dissuading workers from crossing to break the strike. With the UFW and its Mexican counterparts demonstrating cross-border solidarity, and growers demanding legal and political action to halt the strike, it was clearer than ever that the UFW was not anti-immigrant, only anti-strikebreaker.[4]

During the grape strike and boycott, the UFW held ongoing demonstrations against the INS for its failure to stop growers from bringing in Mexican immigrants to break the strike. Chavez continually demanded that the INS enforce the federal law prohibiting employers from recruiting green card holders (who had legal status) as strikebreakers. The INS refused, and the Justice Department eventually ruled that it lacked sufficient evidence to prosecute. Convinced that the UFW could not raise wages and improve working conditions for farmworkers so long as immigrant strikebreakers were freely available, Chavez testified before a U.S. Senate committee in support of sanctions for those employing illegal immigrants and fines for green card holders who acted as strikebreakers. He made it clear to the committee that all the UFW was asking for was "some way to keep the illegal and green carders from breaking our strikes."[5]

In 1973, the UFW adopted a new constitution that provided a bill of rights for all members and committed the union to uniting "all individuals employed as agricultural laborers, regardless of race, creed, sex or nationality." The constitution made no distinction based on a worker's legal status. The UFW had never sought to exclude or penalize farmworkers who were undocumented. But pushing for the enforcement of laws to prevent undocumented immigrants from working as strikebreakers was another matter. This became clear in Yuma, Arizona, in 1973, when growers brought workers across the border to undermine a UFW strike over a contract dispute. The union began monitoring the border to prevent strikebreakers from coming in and asked the INS to stop the entries. When the INS took no action, some UFW members took the law into their own hands and physically attacked those trying to cross the border. Several strikers were arrested for assaulting undocumented immigrants, prompting civil rights groups to denounce the UFW and embarrassing a movement that was publicly committed to nonviolence. Activists affiliated with Latino civil rights groups also expressed anger that year when the UFW endorsed tough new immigration restrictions proposed in Congress.[6]

In 1974, with the UFW still battling grape growers after ending a bitter and violent strike, Chavez publicly stated that there were "more than 2,200 illegal aliens working on ranches in the Fresno area." Just as he felt that the INS had intentionally failed to stop strikebreakers from crossing the border in Yuma, he saw the pro-grower agenda of the Nixon administration behind the government's effort "to make sure this flood of desperately poor workers continued unchecked."[7]

While the UFW held protests against the INS throughout 1974, a national coalition of Latino groups criticized Chavez for his support of strict border controls. But when the Justice Department announced late that year that it would begin a massive deportation drive, Chavez wrote a letter to the *San Francisco Examiner* denying charges that the UFW supported any plans to deport millions of immigrants. The letter reiterated his long-held position that the INS was siding with growers by failing to prevent the use of undocumented immigrants as strikebreakers. Significantly, the letter expressed support for an amnesty that would lead to the legalization of undocumented workers. The public commitment of Chavez and the UFW to legalization and the union's longtime willingness to include undocumented immigrants as members refute the often repeated but erroneous views about where Chavez and the union stood on immigrant rights.[8]

As Richard Griswold del Castillo and Richard Garcia observe, "The hard realities of farm-labor organizing compelled Chavez and the UFW to support immigration restrictions that were not popular with Chicano activists." These activists were focused on building a movement based on ethnic and nationalist unity, and they saw this unity being undermined by immigration restrictions. But, unlike many of the union's critics, Chavez had to live in a world where people's livelihoods depended on preventing an unrestricted flow of immigrant labor. Whereas today's immigration opponents care little about Latino workers, Chavez and the UFW made empowering Latino workers their top priority; the farmworkers movement saw undocumented immigrants as jeopardizing the jobs, wages, and working conditions of Latinos already *in* the United States. In other words, seeking border restrictions as part of a strategy to build the power of Latino workers represents a much different agenda than attacking undocumented immigrants on the basis of racism and xenophobia, as some do today.[9]

In 1986, the UFW joined with other labor unions in supporting the Immigration Reform and Control Act (IRCA). Opposed by both immigrant rights advocates and Latino civil rights groups because it increased employer sanctions and strengthened border enforcement, the bill also had a far-reaching (and largely unanticipated) impact on the process of building Latino political power, because it created a path to citizenship for millions of undocumented immigrants. Chavez believed that the measure would encourage these immigrants to unionize, as their path to legalization created rising expectations for improved wages and working conditions. Referring to these soon-to-be-legalized farmworkers, he observed, "I think they'll always support, if not our union, the idea of a union.... When a work force is not afraid, it bargains for itself." When Chavez made these comments, few saw undocumented immigrants as a future source for new union members. Those were the days when such immigrants were still considered "unorganizable," a perception that UFW alumni such as Steven Lerner of Justice for Janitors would begin to change by decade's end.[10]

Throughout the 1980s, the percentage of the UFW's Mexican-born membership increased. Chavez became more involved in Mexican politics, and in 1990 his lobbying won legislation that encouraged Mexican immigrants to join the UFW by allowing UFW members living in the United States to receive Mexican social security benefits. He continued to form relationships with Mexican unions and government officials, and by the 1990s the UFW was seen as one of America's few "binational" unions. Some attribute Chavez's adoption of a more international perspective to his increasing alignment with civil rights groups on immigration issues, but a more significant factor may have been that the UFW had largely abandoned the strike strategy by the 1980s. Since the UFW's problems around immigration arose entirely from the use of undocumented workers as strikebreakers, the lack of strikes reduced the importance of the issue.[11]

Laying The Groundwork: The Active Citizenship Campaign

In the two decades that preceded the public emergence of a broad-based immigrant rights movement in 2006, UFW veterans forged some key alliances. Through Neighbor to Neighbor (described in chapter 2), Fred Ross Jr. and other former UFW activists helped strengthen links between labor unions, religious groups, nonprofits, and Central American solidarity organizations. In 1986, the passage of the Immigration Reform and Control Act, which offered a route to citizenship for nearly

2.7 million undocumented immigrants who entered the United States before January 1, 1982, provided another opportunity to build support for immigrant rights. To seize this chance, immigrants would have to navigate the notorious complexities of the Immigration and Naturalization Service. It soon became clear that immigrants would need assistance in becoming citizens, and Ross and other UFW veterans were again there to help facilitate Latino citizenship and support the broader political movement for immigrant rights.

IRCA imposed a five-year waiting period on applications for citizenship, and immigrants also had to take courses in English and U.S. civics before they could get permanent visas. So the law's impact in boosting citizenship was delayed. At first, there was no sense of urgency in applying for citizenship, and only forty-seven thousand applications were filed in Los Angeles County when the first wave of IRCA-eligible immigrants could apply for citizenship in 1992. Nor was there a steep rise in applications in 1993.[12]

In 1994, however, California governor Pete Wilson qualified the anti-immigrant Prop 187 for the November ballot, an initiative that punished undocumented immigrants by denying them access to medical care and public schools. Its harsh provisions and its passage by a resounding 59 percent to 41 percent spurred Latino immigrants to seek citizenship. The governor's aggressively anti-immigrant stance had particular significance: more than two million of those affected by IRCA were from Mexico, and California became their main state of residence. As it turned out, 53.5 percent of all IRCA applications came from California; Los Angeles alone included eight hundred thousand applicants.[13]

Understanding that California and the Los Angeles region would be the focus of any citizenship drive, four faith-based groups in Los Angeles that were affiliated with the Saul Alinsky-created Industrial Areas Foundation launched the Active Citizenship Campaign in 1995. The ACC's goals were threefold: to help immigrants apply for citizenship, to end the two-and-a-half-year backlog in processing applications at the INS, and to register voters and reach out to the newly naturalized Latino immigrants. The third component was critical, as there was a widespread feeling in the community that only increased voting by Latino immigrants could defeat future anti-Latino measures. As ACC director Father Miguel Vega put it, "The campaign is not about making citizens. It's about making active citizens."[14]

To spearhead what became a critical drive for immigrant rights throughout Los Angeles County, one of the four IAF groups—the Valley Organized in Community Efforts (VOICE), based in the San Fernando Valley—hired Fred Ross Jr. as its executive director. The Ross family had a long history with the IAF, as Fred Ross Sr. had been an organizer with the IAF's CSO when he became a mentor to Cesar Chavez. Ross Jr. became the ACC's chief organizer and political strategist, using skills he had developed with the UFW to boost the ACC's political clout. When he began working with VOICE in 1994, the San Fernando Valley was primarily a conservative white enclave. According to Ron Kaye, who was then managing editor of the San Fernando Valley-based *Los Angeles Daily News,* "Ross got the wealthy white portions of the community to support VOICE's agenda, which gave the group broader credibility. He translated the group's message in such a way that even the valley's insulated white leadership supported 'citizenship' as a worthy goal."[15]

Ross and the ACC faced two immediate challenges: the immigrants' need for assistance in applying for citizenship, and the huge backlog of completed applications at the INS. To address the first problem, VOICE requested on June 9, 1995, that its site at Mary Immaculate Catholic Church, in the suburb of Pacoima, be officially designated an INS outreach location. The other three ACC groups, located in such heavily Latino areas as East Los Angeles, South Central, and the Pomona and San Gabriel Valleys, sought similar designation, which would make it far more convenient for Latinos to apply for citizenship. They predicted that opening these sites would also speed up the citizenship process from its current twelve to fourteen months to four months.

Citizenship as Political Empowerment

Ross approached the campaign with the same focus on grassroots organizing that he had employed during the UFW boycott days. Cecilia Barragan, a VOICE leader, recalled that she and Ross walked block by block through San Fernando Valley neighborhoods, talking to people about the campaign and encouraging residents to get involved. Much of Ross's time was devoted to training and developing the leadership skills of VOICE volunteers. Barragan described herself as a "little Mexican girl from a small mining town in Arizona" who was convinced by Ross that "she could have a say in what was going on." Ross taught Barragan and other volunteers "how to speak to the powers that be," and he inspired VOICE members to believe that the campaign would achieve its goals.[16]

Richard K. Rogers, the INS district director, was the person who had to approve the four satellite outreach sites. Rogers initially claimed that the INS "liked to see CBOs [community-based organizations] get real heavily involved," because these groups could "educate applicants and bring the fear out of the process." But efforts by VOICE to set up a meeting with Rogers continually faltered. He finally agreed to meet with seven members of the group at his downtown office, refusing requests that he come out to Mary Immaculate Church. Ross figured that "since Mr. Rogers would not come to our neighborhood, we thought we would go to his." Translation: VOICE brought three hundred members to INS headquarters for the meeting. Consuelo Valdez, who was associate director of the ACC, recalls that INS staff members were not suspicious about the large crowd of Latinos, assuming that they were there to apply for citizenship. The group proceeded to Rogers's fifth-floor office and occupied the hallways, holding American flags. Rogers was not pleased by the turnout and told Barragan, "All you want to do is cause trouble." It became clear that VOICE would have to seek out higher authorities to get its needs met.[17]

As Ross and the ACC pressed the INS to reduce the backlog, the troubled agency was undergoing a "reengineering" to expedite the citizenship process. In August 1995, this led INS chief Doris Meissner to launch a new INS initiative, Citizenship USA, targeting INS districts in Chicago, Los Angeles, New York City, San Francisco, and Miami—areas that accounted for 75 percent of the pending application caseload. The program's goal was to ensure a maximum six-month turnaround on naturalization applications by the summer of 1996. Its implementation was accompanied by a 20 percent increase in funding.[18]

Unfortunately, Meissner's initiative did not account for the zeal with which Ross and the ACC were getting immigrants to file citizenship applications. The sheer volume of applicants recruited by the ACC quickly overwhelmed the bolstered INS staff, and by late January 1996, the backlog was worse than before. This led Father Vega to publicly announce that "INS incompetence will stop 300,000 California new citizens from voting in the 1996 presidential election."[19]

On January 30, 1996, Ross, Barragan, other Los Angeles ACC leaders, and representatives of the IAF's Active Citizenship Campaigns in New York, San Francisco, and Chicago joined Representative Xavier Becerra from Los Angeles at a Washington, D.C., meeting with INS commissioner Meissner. The Los Angeles ACC submitted a memo to Meissner setting forth in detail what the group could accomplish to fulfill the expectations of immigrants applying for citizenship pursuant to IRCA. The tasks included producing thousands of volunteers to process applications and help the INS screen applicants, with a specific pledge to submit at least 1,200 applications per month. The ACC was also committed to registering 26,000 new citizens to vote, turning out 52,000 occasional voters by focusing on 960 underrepresented precincts, conducting 5,000 house meetings, and creating voter interest around issues of affirmative action and the minimum wage. The memo echoed Father Vega's cautionary words, warning that "INS inaction will deny 300,000 Latinos the right to vote in the 1996 presidential election in California." The document pledged that the IAF's ACC was willing to "fight along side the Clinton Administration in efforts to maximize INS efficiency and effectiveness and to decrease massive backlogs while increasing the number of New Americans."[20]

This detailed and number-filled work plan, along with the focus on house meetings, was right out of the UFW playbook. The memo also made an explicit connection between citizenship and Latino political empowerment; these new citizens were going to be *active* participants in the elections that shape city, state, and national policies. Ross and others had effectively transformed a 1986 legalization bill into a potentially powerful long term vehicle for greatly boosting Latino political power and immigrant rights. But the 1996 presidential election was rapidly approaching, and this would be California Latinos' first opportunity to respond to 1994's Prop 187 campaign. Time was of the essence, and the ACC believed that it was imperative that its applicants become eligible to vote.

Vice President Gore Enters the Fight

When ACC's meeting with Meissner, who had spent five years as a top INS official in the Reagan administration, did not resolve its concerns, Ross and his allies went over Meissner's head and contacted Henry Cisneros, secretary of the Department of Housing and Urban Development (HUD), and Leon Panetta, White House chief of staff. Both men forwarded ACC's concerns to Vice President

Al Gore, who also received a letter from Cardinal Roger Mahony of Los Angeles expressing a "sense of urgency" over the INS backlog. Ross's longtime relationship with Mahony, who had been an associate bishop in Fresno and a close ally of Cesar Chavez, came in handy, as it would on many occasions in future years.[21]

In addition to turning to political allies, Ross organized a protest by VOICE and the Southern California Organizing Committee (SCOC) outside Rogers's office in the Federal Building in downtown Los Angeles on February 28, 1996. Members waved American flags, chanted "We want to vote," and demanded to meet with Rogers. Father Pat Murphy of Our Lady of the Holy Rosary Church accused Rogers of "not completing his promise" and said that the group was still praying to "get four more outreach teams." According to VOICE and SCOC, Rogers had promised a three-month turnaround for citizenship interviews when he approved the satellite outreach locations, but the process was instead taking eleven months. Rogers told the media that he had never made such a promise— and never would have, given the overwhelming number of applications. In case the Clinton administration was not sufficiently troubled by Cardinal Mahony's letter, Rogers was now essentially accusing some of Mahony's parishioners of lying about the INS's commitment.[22]

On March 8, 1996, Vice President Al Gore extended his California schedule so that he could meet with Ross, Barragan, Vega, and other Los Angeles ACC representatives. At the meeting, Gore pledged the Clinton administration's full cooperation with their efforts to expedite citizenship applications and reduce the backlog. He promised that the INS would hire more temporary workers, increase office space, and address the unexpectedly large volume of applications. When Gore's commitment was not promptly followed by action, Elaine Kamarck of the vice president's staff sent a memo on March 21 to Doug Farbrother of the National Performance Review (the agency working to use its "reinventing government" principles to address the INS backlog). The memo said, "The President is sick of this and wants action. If nothing moves today we'll have to take some pretty drastic measures." Results soon followed. By early April, Gore's intervention, along with pressure from Panetta, swayed Rogers, who had been avoiding a meeting with the ACC all year. On May 1, Rogers announced at an ACC meeting at Our Lady of Lour-des Church in East Los Angeles that the INS would process 220,000 applications by the end of September. He even claimed that the agency, which until recently had been hostile to the ACC, had a "duty to apply every resource to process every application."[23]

To avoid any doubt about this commitment, Rogers signed his name to a pledge on a giant card while the crowd of eight thousand immigrant rights activists cheered. The pledge included the ninety-day turnaround that Rogers had previously claimed could not be achieved. ACC leader Orinio Opinado of the SCOC in South Central again highlighted the chief purpose of the citizenship campaign, telling the crowd, "We don't count unless we vote. We don't count unless we're active citizens. We don't count unless we are organized." The Reverend George Schukze was even more specific, saying that only through political involvement could the nation's anti-immigrant sentiment be reversed.[24]

From Citizens to Activists

The ACC's successful pressuring of the Clinton administration to end the INS backlog did not slow Ross's efforts to build grassroots support for the citizenship drive. On July 14, 1996, the IAF held its first West Coast convention at the Grand Olympic Auditorium, which was attended by more than 5,000 low-income and working-class people. The keynote speaker was HUD secretary Cisneros, who had helped get Gore's attention on ACC's concerns about the INS. Richard Rogers, the INS district director, was among the speakers, showing the agency's willingness to turn onetime adversaries into allies. VOICE turned out more than 1,500 people for the event, which included the introduction of 750 soon-to-be citizens who had been helped by the ACC. ACC leader Rosalinda Lugo of the East Los Angeles-based United Neighborhoods Organization described the meeting as a "Get Out to Vote" campaign. Lugo asserted that people were coming "because they want to take back the election process" and that they realized that if they did not get involved, "then our communities are in danger of being neglected." Lugo's comments demonstrated the ACC's clear linkage between achieving citizenship and getting Latino immigrants to exercise their civil right to vote.[25]

ACC's grassroots campaign to increase Latino voting in Los Angeles County coincided with Miguel Contreras's efforts to implement the UFW's successful Latino voter outreach model at the Los Angeles County Federation of Labor (LACFL) (described in chapter 7). While the media largely ignored the ACC's connection to organized labor, the ACC's voter outreach efforts benefited greatly from the support of both Contreras and Eliseo Medina. Medina had headed SEIU's San Diego local since 1986 and won election as a national officer with SEIU in 1996. Ross recognized the value of Medina's national connections, and since Medina was also spending time working to strengthen SEIU's Los Angeles locals, Ross contacted him and reunited with his longtime UFW ally.

Medina was attracted to the ACC for two reasons. First, he was eager to promote civic engagement among immigrant workers. Second, he saw the ACC's work as "empowering immigrant workers to have political power and create a much more progressive electorate in the state." As is often the case with Medina's contributions, there is little public record of his role with the ACC. But VOICE leader Cecilia Barragan recalled that Medina "was very involved" in the ACC; "Eliseo," she commented, "was someone who cared about our community and was always there for us." Medina was a frequent speaker at VOICE events and helped secure critical financial assistance for the campaign from SEIU's state and national offices. With Contreras's labor federation providing local financial support for ACC's voter registration and outreach efforts and Medina bringing in state and national resources, organized labor played an important role in the citizenship campaign.[26]

While Contreras was assembling a grassroots Latino voter outreach team of unionized workers through LACFL, Ross was building a similar Latino voter mobilization operation through VOICE. Many of Ross's precinct walkers were recent citizens, who were fulfilling Father Vega's pledge to become "active" in the community. Among them was Augustina Garcia, a single parent of two, who became a citizen in April 1996. On October 5, she was among 3,000 volunteers out knocking on doors, registering people to vote, and encouraging noncitizens to apply for naturalization. Garcia told the *Los Angeles Daily News* that she was "determined to fight for my rights. I don't want to be anonymous anymore." Garcia was among many who would meet at weekly workshops at Mary Immaculate Catholic Church to receive training from Barragan and other leaders before going out to hit the streets. ACC's Latino voter outreach campaign included members from eighty churches and synagogues, who had committed to cover 960 precincts and reach 96,000 voters for the November 1996 election.[27]

As a result of securing INS approval to use churches, school cafeterias, and community centers for conducting citizenship interviews, rather than requiring immigrants to go to the INS's downtown offices, the ACC generated historic increases in the number of new citizens. VOICE alone processed more than 3,000 citizenship applications through election day. In August 1996, 60,800 applicants were granted citizenship in Los Angeles, the district's highest one-month total ever. By September 30, the INS had processed 1.3 million naturalization applications and approved 1.1 million, more than double the prior year. The ACC's efforts had forced the INS to clear the backlog of 225,000 citizenship applications, and 25,000 immigrants had become citizens by 1998. The impact of the combined efforts of LACFL and the ACC became clear on election day, when Latino turnout in Los Angeles reached record levels and Tony Cardenas became the first Latino elected to the state assembly from the San Fernando Valley. According to an election night survey by Professor Chuck Hotchkiss of California Polytechnic State University in Pomona, the ACC's get out the vote efforts in 140 targeted precincts turned out an estimated 16,500 voters.[28]

How did the ACC do it? The organization employed the same approach that Fred Ross Jr. had used with the UFW in the 1970s and that Miguel Contreras brought to the LACFL in 1995. Father Pat Murphy of Our Lady of the Holy Rosary Church, one of the churches affiliated with VOICE, described it as a "door-to-door, neighbor-to-neighbor" recruitment effort that involved citizenship classes, voter registration drives, and phone banks, all aimed at Latinos and other ethnic groups in the 140 precincts. Murphy claimed that watching Latino voters go to the polls on election day was a "joyous exercise."[29]

As the media hailed VOICE's successful citizenship drives and Latino voter turnout, Fred Ross Jr. remained out of the limelight. But Cecilia Barragan, Consuelo Valdez, and Ron Kaye all noted that Ross had been the chief strategist and organizer of the ACC campaign. Valdez noted that it was Ross who understood "the big picture" and who had inspired and trained a single working mother like Barragan and hundreds of other VOICE members to become committed and skilled organizers for social change. Cesar Chavez and Fred Ross Sr. had created a model for this process of leadership development, and what worked among farmworkers in the 1960s and 1970s was proving successful among the urban immigrants in the San Fernando Valley and elsewhere in the 1990s.[30]

The Anti-ACC Backlash

While the ACC's citizenship drive won broad support by appealing to the American spirit of civic engagement, the Republican Party was not happy about the group's success in expediting citizenship applications. A week prior to election day, Republican congressional representative William Zeliff of New Hampshire called for the appointment of an independent counsel to investigate how the Clinton administration had allegedly used the Citizenship USA program to benefit its reelection campaign. Zeliff charged Clinton and Gore with putting "enormous pressure on the INS to naturalize as many new citizens as possible, regardless of the consequence."[31]

Particularly targeted were "private contractors" such as VOICE, who Zeliff claimed were responsible for an "alarming" pattern of fraud in the citizenship application process. Zeliff had held hearings in September 1996 on the many "violent criminals" who had allegedly been rushed into citizenship with insufficient INS review. California governor Pete Wilson expressed his own alarm that "perhaps thousands of criminal aliens" had wrongfully been granted citizenship as a result of the Clinton administration's "rush to naturalize new voters before Election Day." Wilson's concerns, however, were never substantiated.[32]

Foreshadowing the party's shift to a strong anti-immigrant stance in 2005, Republicans continued challenging the Clinton administration's processing of citizenship applications long after the November 1996 election. In fact, three years after the election, Vice President Gore responded to a detailed list of questions from the special counsel to the inspector general at the Justice Department about his role in the Citizenship USA program and his meetings with the ACC. The inspector general sought specific information about Gore's meeting with Father Vega and the ACC's widely publicized claim—included in a February 14, 1996, letter to Gore—that the backlog would "deny 300,000 Latinos the right to vote in the 1996 presidential election." This letter had also hinted that the backlog could lead to a perception of the Clinton administration as "anti-Latino," which Republicans claimed was evidence that the Clinton administration had illegally expedited the citizenship process for political reasons.[33]

Although nothing ever came of the Justice Department investigation, the notion that "Gore pressured the INS" to win the 1996 election and that Citizenship USA "turned criminals into citizens just in time to vote" remained articles of faith among Republican anti-immigrant activists. This helps to explain the Bush administration's inadequate response to a later citizenship backlog in 2007 and 2008: expediting applications from Latino immigrants was likely seen as bringing more Democratic voters to the polls in November 2008 (see chapter 9).[34]

Welfare Reform And The Attack On Legal Immigrants

After Fred Ross Jr. and Eliseo Medina reconnected during the ACC citizenship drive, Medina urged Ross to join him at SEIU in Los Angeles. But Ross's mother in Marin County was in poor health, and he was committed to moving back to the San Francisco Bay Area after the 1996 election. Once there, Ross became the top district aide to his good friend Representative Nancy Pelosi. Almost immediately, he became involved in fending off a major attack on immigrants' rights.[35]

In order to fulfill his 1992 campaign pledge to "end welfare as we know it," President Clinton had signed into law a "welfare reform" bill on August 22, 1996, at the height of the ACC citizenship and voter registration drive. Most of the discussion concerning the measure focused on how to address poverty among low-income families. But the bill also included little-noticed provisions denying legal immigrants such critical federal benefits as Supplemental Security Income (SSI) and food stamps. Nancy Pelosi's San Francisco congressional district included thousands of elderly Chinese and Filipino immigrants who had entered the country legally decades earlier but had never bothered to become citizens. For many, their entire income, even their food budget, was now at stake. Ross joined with San Francisco's immigrant rights groups to change the provisions affecting legal immigrants before the law was implemented.

From his work with the Clinton administration during the ACC effort, Ross knew who to contact about this new struggle. Initiated by a broad coalition of San Francisco-based Asian American and immigrant civil rights groups, a national campaign quickly emerged to protect vulnerable elderly immigrants. This campaign, like the ACC, created another bridge between immigrant rights groups nationwide that would later help to build a broader movement.[36]

As activists generated sympathetic news stories about the plight of elderly immigrants facing the loss of all their benefits, the congressional Republicans who had insisted on inserting the anti-immigrant provisions in the bill found themselves on the defensive. The political demands for a resolution required action with record speed in order to beat the deadline for the law's implementation. The coalition that Ross helped organize eventually won a new law that prevented existing legal immigrants from losing benefits but maintained the ban on food stamps and SSI for future legal immigrants. The short-term battle was won, but Congress's backroom elimination of benefits for legal immigrants as part of the welfare bill showed that building immigrant political power to avoid such bills in the future was imperative.

The AFL-CIO Joins The Immigrant Rights Movement

Although the AFL-CIO was among the key groups pushing to reinstate public benefits to legal immigrants in 1996, this stance ran counter to its history. Since the early 1900s, the AFL-CIO had consistently supported restricting immigration, claiming that the entry of foreign workers suppressed wages and slowed the growth of union membership. While labor's reasons for opposing immigration may have differed from the often race-based anti-immigrant attitudes of political conservatives, the AFL-CIO's alignment with such forces created a powerful political base against progressive immigration reform. For example, in 1985, the AFL-CIO endorsed employer sanctions for hiring undocumented workers, a provision of the 1986 Immigration Control Reform Act that was strongly opposed by immigrant rights groups. The AFL-CIO was so proud of its support for IRCA that it passed a resolution in 1987 calling the bill "the most important and far-reaching immigration legislation in 30 years." The UFW's primarily Latino immigrant workforce, and its refusal to distinguish between undocumented and legal immigrants in its membership, may have moderated the AFL-CIO's anti-immigrant rhetoric, but even Cesar Chavez could not alter the federation's official policy at that time.[37]

Starting with organizing drives among immigrant workers by HERE and SEIU in the 1980s, however, union attitudes began to change. Unions that were organizing undocumented immigrant workers no longer blamed immigrants for lowering wages or taking union jobs. As a result, with UFW veterans playing important roles, the AFL-CIO's historical anti-immigration stance began to shift. The federation's 1993 convention adopted a resolution praising immigrants for helping build America and criticizing efforts to make immigrants "scapegoats for economic and social problems." The resolution also urged affiliated unions "to develop programs to address the special needs of immigrant members and potential members" and to work with "immigrant advocacy groups and service organizations" to protect the interests of new immigrants.[38]

In 1994, organized labor aggressively opposed California's anti-immigrant Prop 187, and the Los Angeles County Federation of Labor, which had rarely backed community struggles in the past, helped mobilize a massive rally of seventy thousand people at Los Angeles city hall to protest the measure. When the U.S. Commission on Immigration Reform (CIR) recommended greater immigration restrictions in a 1995 report, the AFL-CIO spoke out against all the proposed changes. At its 1995 convention, the labor federation passed a resolution that declared: "The notion that immigrants are to blame for the deteriorating living standards of America's low-wage workers must be clearly rejected." According to Vernon M. Briggs Jr., "rather than immigration reform," the resolution "proposed increasing the minimum wage, adopting universal health care and enacting labor law reform as the remedies for the widening income disparity in the nation." When Congress sought to enact many of CIR's punitive recommendations in 1996, the AFL-CIO joined immigrant rights groups in killing the key proposals.[39]

Although organized, labor's stance toward immigration had changed by the mid-1990s, Eliseo Medina and others recognized that simply stopping bad proposals was not enough. Medina believed that labor should help lead the fight for immigrant rights, and he saw immigrant workers as the future of organized labor. Medina himself was an immigrant, whose family had come to Delano from Mexico in 1956. He began picking grapes at the age of ten and began organizing with the UFW in 1965. Medina learned from Chavez and the union that people working in the fields could challenge the growers and be treated with respect. Describing years later what the UFW meant to him and others, Medina observed, "For the first time, people actually felt we have some rights, we can stand up for ourselves, we can fight, and we can win." He believed from his early UFW days that the surest route for Latino immigrants to win respect, fair wages, and decent working conditions was by joining a union.[40]

After leaving the UFW in 1978, Medina worked briefly for the American Federation of State, County, and Municipal Employees (AFSCME) and then moved on to organize public employees in Texas for the Communication Workers of America from 1981 to 1985. Despite the state's restrictions on collective bargaining, Medina boosted the membership of CWA's Texas State Employees Union from about six hundred to more than four thousand. Medina then joined fellow UFW alumni Stephen Lerner in leaving CWA for SEIU. Marshall Ganz had been working on some projects for SEIU, and, after seeing Medina in Houston, Ganz suggested to SEIU organizing director Andy Stern that the union should consider hiring Medina to run its troubled San Diego local. In 1986, Medina went to SEIU's Washington, D.C., headquarters to be interviewed by President John Sweeney and Stern. But the UFW veteran was asking his own questions: Medina wanted to know about Sweeney's commitment to fund organizing efforts, and he wanted assurances that he would get the resources he needed to succeed. Having spent the previous years organizing in Texas, Medina told the SEIU president, "I [am] not interested in going to San Diego to get a suntan, because I already have one."[41]

Sweeney and Stern agreed to provide the necessary organizing resources, and Medina took up the challenge. When he arrived in San Diego, his former UFW colleagues Marshall Ganz and Scott Washburn were both there, trying to clean up the mess left by Medina's predecessor. Medina quickly turned the situation around. He helped the union's primarily Latino janitors to win pay raises of 40 percent and successfully organized paramedics, health care workers, and other county staff. In just five years with Medina's leadership, the membership of the San Diego local increased from seventeen hundred to ten thousand.[42]

Medina was eager to change the AFL-CIO's anti-immigration policy, but he did not believe that it was possible until longtime AFL-CIO leader Lane Kirkland was replaced. In October 1995, John Sweeney was elected to succeed Kirkland as president of the AFL-CIO. His election gave Medina and others the opportunity to align the federation with the immigrants' cause and to unite the power of the labor and immigrant rights movements. Medina saw Sweeney as a strong supporter of immigrant rights but knew that the new president liked to operate by consensus: Sweeney would not change AFL-CIO immigration policy until a broad consensus was organized from below. Medina took up the task of creating this popular groundswell. As the newly elected executive vice president of SEIU and the highest-ranking Latino in the labor movement, he used his new base in Los Angeles to make it happen.[43]

When Medina arrived in Los Angeles in 1996, the city had a pro-business Republican mayor and a weakened though recovering labor movement. SEIU's Justice for Janitors had begun to revitalize labor in 1990 with its historic Century City campaign (later profiled in the film *Bread and Roses*), and Miguel Contreras, Medina's former UFW ally, had become political director of the county federation of labor in 1994. But there was much work left to be done. Medina told his assistant, Ben

Monterroso, who had been the Los Angeles regional director of SEIU, that they had to launch the "L.A. project." Monterroso had no idea what Medina was talking about and asked what "the project" involved. Medina replied that he "wanted Los Angeles to be as labor-friendly as San Francisco" and that Monterroso would be responsible for making sure this happened. Having frequently been asked by Cesar Chavez to run campaigns without being given detailed directions, Medina clearly thought he was giving Monterroso a great opportunity to display his talents. While Monterroso met with Los Angeles union heads to discuss how to fulfill this goal, Medina set out to ensure that Contreras would be elected to head the county federation. SEIU was the largest affiliate of the LACFL, and Medina secured enough additional support to allow Contreras to take over the reins.[44]

Medina had a vision of unifying labor with community, religious, and immigrant rights groups; he spent 1997 and much of 1998 discussing this vision and how to implement it in Los Angeles with Contreras, UNITE HERE president Maria Elena Durazo, the UFW, and the United Food and Commercial Workers. By late 1998, when Sweeney had been in power for three years, the group decided that it was time to offer a resolution to the 1999 AFL-CIO convention to shift the labor federation's immigration policy, Medina "had his doubts whether they could change it" that year, but two factors worked in the group's favor.[45]

First, the October 1999 convention was held in Los Angeles, and there was not a more dramatic illustration of the importance of labor supporting immigrant rights. Union officials from across the country could see firsthand how a city's growing union-immigrant alliance was expanding labor's political clout. Immigrant janitors, drywallers, home health care workers, and hotel workers had become the face of the city's labor movement. Second, HERE president John Wilhelm was achieving great success boosting his union's membership in the Las Vegas hotel industry. He was close enough to Los Angeles to have attended some of the reform group's strategy meetings. With Wilhelm and Andy Stern, now president of SEIU, increasing their influence and both backing a new pro-immigrant policy, a shift in the AFL-CIO's longstanding position was at hand.

Medina took the lead in debating the resolution on the convention floor. He told the assembled leaders that his recent experience working with Los Angeles's unionized janitors showed the importance of aligning labor with the cause of immigrant rights. "While we do everything to bring justice and dignity to janitors in the workplace, the minute they leave the worksite, they revert to their undocumented status." Medina knew that Sweeney was in full support of the resolution and accepted his strategy of forming a special committee on immigration that would study and recommend changes to the AFL-CIO's policy. Since Wilhelm chaired the committee and Medina was a member, the outcome of its deliberations was not in doubt. But the committee's formation gave union leaders from every sector the opportunity to assess the proposed new policy and provide input, moving toward the broad consensus that Sweeney sought.[46]

In February 2000, on the committee's recommendation, the AFL-CIO executive board met in New Orleans and reversed its 1985 policy favoring employer sanctions for hiring undocumented immigrants. Since the AFL-CIO had extolled its support for this policy as recently as 1987, this reversal was dramatic. The labor leaders justified the shift on the grounds that some employers were circumventing the sanctions and the federal government's lack of enforcement made the current system unfair and unworkable. The federation also called for a new system that ensured a level play-ing field for all employers and urged amnesty for the nation's estimated six million undocumented workers. Wilhelm was among those who argued that standing up for the rights of immigrants was good for workers, unions, and communities. "We weren't trying to do anything special—we just wanted to do what was right," he said. Reflecting the increasing number of union members who were undocumented, the AFL-CIO urged strong penalties against employers who abused workers' immigration status to deny them job rights and labor protections.[47]

The AFL-CIO's new policy immediately changed the longstanding political calculus around legalization for undocumented workers. The federation's action also showed how the Los Angeles labor movement, with Medina and Contreras playing key roles, was helping to transform organized labor nationally. While some labor supporters argued that unions would regret their support for increased immigration, immigrant workers had been in the forefront of America's labor movement from the fight for the eight-hour day in the 1880s to the passage of the National Labor Relations Act in the 1930s. Backers of the new, pro-immigrant policy pointed out that much of labor's historical opposition to immigration from Mexico and Asia had been based on racism and a fear of foreigners, which helped split the labor movement, to the benefit of employers. The AFL-CIO highlighted the example of Cesar Chavez as someone who had helped the union movement understand that it must accept the responsibility to represent all workers regardless of their immigration status. But neither his example nor the UFW's successes had been able to change the AFL-CIO's immigration policy; instead, it had taken years of effort by individuals such as Medina, Contreras, Ross, Stephen Lerner, and Chava Bustamante, along with other farmworker veterans and labor activists, to move immigrant rights to the forefront of the American labor movement.[48]

Building A Powerful Alliance For Immigrant Rights

The AFL-CIO accompanied its February 2000 policy shift with a request that unions hold forums across the country where immigrant workers could explain their struggle to find a better life through union membership. Most unions expected these events to involve around three hundred people. But Medina, Contreras, and the Los Angeles labor movement had a broader vision. Medina saw the Los Angeles forum as an opportunity for organized labor to solidify its partnerships with church, community, and immigrant rights groups. He had sensed the potential power of the immigration issue when, after returning to Los Angeles after the AFL-CIO's policy shift, he scheduled a news conference with church, community, and immigrant rights groups to discuss the decision. He was shocked to see at least ten television stations and a huge number of newspaper and radio staff at the event. Even in comparison to the UFW's high-profile press events, Medina "had never seen so much media coverage." The media turnout told him that labor and immigrant rights activists were not the only ones who saw the AFL-CIO's policy shift as a "huge deal"—the "outside world" did as well.[49]

After getting the SEIU international to cover most of the cost of a larger event, Medina went to the participating groups and asked them to contribute according to their ability to pay. He wanted to convey the message that labor was looking for a "true partnership" in fighting for immigration reform and wanted the broader community to "feel ownership" of the event. The response to Medina's overtures exceeded his highest expectations. The "community forum" on June 10 became a massive rally in the Los Angeles Sports Arena, with seventeen thousand people in the arena and three thousand more outside. Contreras described the crowd as representing "the birth of a powerful new alliance." Medina was "blown away by the number of people who had shown up" and credited labor's organizational partners and the Latino media with generating the huge turnout. Medina believed that the crowd demonstrated the huge untapped potential of the immigrant rights movement, and he also felt that the event signaled a willingness on the part of the religious community to wage a major fight for immigration reform.[50]

The speakers at the Sports Arena rally included Antonio Villaraigosa and other prominent Latino politicians and labor officials. Longtime activist Bert Corona gave the keynote address. Corona had begun organizing with the International Longshoremen's and Warehousemen's Union in 1937; in 1960, he was among those who formed the Mexican American Political Association. Corona and MAPA had provided support to workers during the UFW's Delano grape strike in 1965 against DiGiorgio farms. As Corona later stated, "MAPA unconditionally endorsed the farmworkers' cause. It inspired and energized us." Corona was also inspired by Chavez's leadership and particularly appreciated the UFW leader's success in fusing the symbols of Mexican nationalism with a broader, class-based approach.[51]

But in the late 1960s, Corona ran into conflict with Chavez and the UFW over the union's policies toward undocumented immigrants. Corona had been organizing these immigrants in Los Angeles on behalf of the Hermandad Mexicana Nacional (a group formed by union members in 1951 to support the rights of Mexican residents working in Southern California), and he opposed the UFW's support for deporting undocumented immigrants who were working as strikebreakers. Chavez and the UFW had no sympathy for such "scabs," but Corona and the Hermandad believed that they should be organized rather than deported. Corona understood and sympathized with the UFW position, and his disagreement with Chavez's stance did not diminish his support for the UFW cause. He later pointed out that by the 1970s, Chavez and the union supported positive immigration reforms and that "in the main, we have agreed on ninety percent of what the farmworkers have done or advocated."[52]

Since the 1970s, Corona had focused on battling anti-immigrant legislation at the state and federal level. His selection as keynote speaker for labor's high-profile event symbolized the AFL-CIO's new strategy and sent a powerful message that the labor movement was now on the side of immigrants. Although eighty years old and physically frail, Corona had lost none of his fire, as he delivered an inspiring speech at the June 10 event: "There is no mine, no bridge, not a row in the fields or a construction site in all the United States that hasn't been watered with the tears, the sweat, and blood of immigrants. We demand an amnesty for the workers who have made the wealth of this country possible. Amnesty is not a gift, but a right, for those who have contributed so much."[53] Corona's lifelong dream of labor-immigrant unity had been fulfilled in Los Angeles, and this alliance would soon spread across the nation. Those whose organizing experience had begun with Cesar Chavez and the UFW were the driving force in transforming Corona's vision into reality.

After the event, Medina scheduled a concert and fundraiser for immigrant rights, which was also held at the Sports Arena. News of the remarkable June 10 rally in Los Angeles had spread nationally, and Medina made a special effort to invite labor officials from across the country to be part of the second event so that they could view the power of the emerging labor-clergy-community alliance firsthand. The successful concert and fundraiser further confirmed that a model for the American labor movement was being created in Los Angeles and that momentum for immigrant rights legislation was growing.[54]

During 2000, many AFL-CIO unions, especially those in the food, service, and building trades, began restructuring their organizing efforts to include immigrant workers. In April 2000, the benefits of immigrant organizing became even clearer, as Medina worked with SEIU 1877's Los Angeles janitors to win the largest wage increases in the history of the union's Justice for Janitors campaign. This victory was another step in the process of transforming Los Angeles into a pro-union town, and it sent a powerful message nationally about the power of the labor-immigrant alliance.

In April 2001, Medina followed up this success by securing a historic agreement between SEIU and Catholic Healthcare West to facilitate union representation in the largest nonprofit health care system in the western United States. SEIU had been engaged in high-profile conflicts with CHW over its attempts to unionize hospitals since 1997, and CHW had fought back with full-page newspaper ads attacking SEIU's "corporate campaign" and "disruptive activities." This conflict between labor and a Catholic institution disturbed Medina, a deeply spiritual man whose UFW experience had taught him the importance of labor-church unity. In 1999, Medina reached out to a former UFW supporter, Los Angeles cardinal Roger Mahony, to help resolve the dispute.

Although Mahony had been a close ally of Cesar Chavez and the UFW, he had backed away from involvement in labor causes since 1989–90, when his diocese successfully defeated efforts by the Amalgamated Clothing and Textile Workers Union to organize the church's cemetery workers. Some union activists accused Mahony of hypocrisy, but Medina understood how to approach Mahony, assuring him that the labor movement needed, and would appreciate, his support. Mahony worked behind the scenes to pressure CHW, which reached a settlement with SEIU in 2001. By 2002, SEIU had won contracts covering nine thousand workers at more than twenty CHW hospitals. This "peace accord" between SEIU and the hospital operator would have dramatic implications for the immigrant rights movement, as it repaired a rift and reunified two powerful forces supporting the immigrant community. In addition, Cardinal Mahony would prove to be a critical ally of the labor and immigrant rights movements in the years ahead.[55]

As support for immigration reform grew throughout 2000, among both the public and policy makers, Eliseo Medina joined Randall Johnson of the U.S. Chamber of Commerce and other business, labor, and political leaders from both the United States and Mexico on an immigration reform panel convened by the Carnegie Endowment for International Peace. Mexico's involvement on the panel became key in 2001, as its newly elected conservative president, Vicente Fox, seemed to have a good relationship with President George W. Bush. Fox supported increased migration to the United States—money flowing back to Mexico from undocumented immigrants in America, in the form of remittances, was Mexico's biggest source of income—and many assumed that the Bush administration would want to boost a conservative ally by supporting his immigration reforms. With the AFL-CIO and the Fox government supporting legalization for undocumented immigrants, and key business groups such as the U.S. Chamber of Commerce believing that "we were on a roll," as Randall Johnson put it, there was a growing sense in 2001 that a progressive immigration measure was on the horizon. This sense of momentum continued through the day that Johnson presented the panel's recommendations to a U.S. Senate committee—the Friday before September 11, 2001.[56]

The September 11 tragedy stopped this momentum in its tracks. Although the attacks on the World Trade Center and the Pentagon had no connection to undocumented Latino immigrants, new fears were raised about foreigners who might be in the country illegally. Unions and immigrant rights groups tried their best to counter rising anti-immigrant feelings. They highlighted the large number of immigrant workers in New York City's UNITE HERE Local 100—headed by UFW alumni Bill Granfield—who had died in the collapse of the World Trade Center and the essential role played by unionized firefighters and police officers in rescue efforts. Eliseo Medina argued that "the terrible events of September it should serve to unite Americans, not to divide us between immigrants and native-born." Citing the many SEIU and UNITE HERE members who had rushed to help people get out of the fallen buildings, Medina noted, "Nobody asked the people who were helping them what their immigration status was." He correctly pointed out that 9/11 actually demonstrated the human tragedy of America's immigration policy: undocumented families of 9/11 victims were left "totally unprotected because of their legal status" and had to continue "to live in the shadows, fearful that, if they go and ask for public help, they could be deported."[57] Nonetheless, it was clear that efforts to implement progressive immigration reform had ground to a halt. An issue that had seemed ripe for resolution suddenly shifted off the political radar screen, and there was no choice but to wait out the aftereffects of the attacks.

In 2002, however, reform efforts were revived with the launch of the "Reward Work" campaign, a brainchild of Eliseo Medina. This was an effort by the AFL-CIO and more than four hundred religious, community, political, student, and immigrant organizations to collect signatures on one million postcards urging legalization for undocumented immigrants who work and pay taxes. The campaign, also known as "One Million Voices," brought an important new element into the burgeoning immigrant rights movement: the notion of civic participation.[58]

Medina's faith in the power of civic engagement came from his UFW days, when he saw how the union negotiated contracts that included a provision for grower-funded "Citizen Participation Days." Workers received a paid holiday for participating in voter registration, campaign work, or other acts of civic engagement. A worker who chose not to participate could sign over the amount of the paid day to the UFW's citizen participation fund, which then used the money to advance the union's political agenda. According to Bill Carder, who negotiated some of the UFW's first grape contracts in 1970 and spent over three decades negotiating contracts for a wide range of unions, such provisions "are extremely uncommon. I cannot think of another union contract that included a civic participation clause."[59]

A 1972 study of the impact of the UFW's civic participation drive found that UFW members had a much greater sense that voting was a civic duty and had much more faith in democratic institutions than farmworkers who supported the union but were not members or those who opposed the union. Interviews with 244 farmworkers in and around the Central Valley city of Fresno supported the assertion that "the UFW has served as a mobilizing agent for its members, inducing them to new and expanded citizenship roles." Based on his experience while working for the UFW, Medina strongly believed that Latino immigrants must advocate for themselves in the political arena. He also argued that this was the lesson of immigrant empowerment throughout U.S. history. Noting the examples of the Irish, the Jews, and the Italians, Medina described how "they organized and made their issues an important part of the American agenda. We're trying to do the same."[60]

Cesar Chavez used to tell workers that they had two contracts—a collective bargaining contract that covered them at work, and a "social contract" that covered them outside the workplace. This latter protection, reflected in the UFW's civic participation days, required union members to be involved with community organizations and churches and to work to ensure fair treatment of farmworker children at school. UFW members also used civic participation days to organize voter registration drives in the many small, rural California towns where the farmworker population dominated numerically but had no political power. As Latino voting in these communities increased, local governments became more accountable to farmworkers. Medina was deeply troubled that even though unions could achieve equality and fairness for undocumented immigrants in the workplace, many of these workers felt they had to avoid public engagement because of their legal status. He conceived his civic participation plan as a way to send a message to undocumented immigrants that they had the right to circulate petitions, attend rallies, and otherwise engage in American civic life. Such participation would bring them out of the shadows and allow them to positively shape policies that affected their lives.[61]

Medina, Ben Monterroso, Maria Elena Durazo, and Miguel Contreras had created a model for civic participation for immigrant workers in Los Angeles when they founded the Organization of Los Angeles Workers (OLAW) in 2000. But that group's activities primarily involved elections. Now

Medina was using the One Million Voices campaign to expand immigrants' participation from elections and union meetings to local and national advocacy campaigns, particularly those involving immigrant rights. And his plan was to expand this project nationally as a strategy for engaging hundreds of thousands, if not millions, of undocumented immigrants in the fight for legalization.

The New York Civic Participation Project (NYCPP) was an early example of how Medina's strategy could be successfully implemented. The NYCPP was created in 2003 as a collaboration between SEIU 32BJ, the nation's largest janitors' local; HERE Local 100; District Council 37, New York City's public employees union; Make the Road by Walking, a community organization based in Bushwick (Brooklyn); and the National Employment Law Project, an immigrant advocacy group. Confirming its strong identification with the legacy of Cesar Chavez and the UFW, a quotation from Chavez appeared in both English and Spanish in the center of the original home page of NYCPP's website (http://nycpp.org): "We don't need perfect political systems; we need perfect participation." The page was headed with multiple photos of immigrants carrying banners with the UFW rallying cry, *"sí se puede!"*

According to Gouri Sadhwani, NYCPP's executive director until 2007, the group was created "because there was a big vacuum among New York City community organizations in having a way for immigrant workers to be engaged in civic participation." Unlike OLAW, NYCPP does not focus on electoral politics. Rather, the group seeks to "change the framework about how immigrant workers could contribute to civic life." NYCPP accomplishes this by involving immigrants in local campaigns around such issues as ensuring language access in city services and protecting libraries in immigrant neighborhoods from proposed budget cuts. The group also focuses on national immigration reform, with its participants collecting tens of thousands of signatures for the national Reward Work campaign. In its first three years, NYCPP created an active base of more than one thousand active new immigrants, both union and community members. As the project expands to several other states, the potential activist base for local, state, and national immigrants rights advocacy will grow exponentially.[62]

In addition to working with NYCPP, SEIU 32BJ makes a separate effort to get union members involved in civic participation through its American Dream Fund. The fund uses voluntary donations from union members to back legislation and candidates and brings union members into these campaigns. Under the leadership of Secretary-Treasurer Hector Figueroa, the union has used its campaign to "Stand Up for the American Dream" to double the wages of state-contracted workers in New Jersey and to expand the workplace rights of building service staff. In the 2006 election, the American Dream Fund helped SEIU 32BJ put more than three thousand members on the streets during the campaign season and more than one thousand on election day.[63] Many of the union's members are immigrants, and their growing electoral participation creates the opportunity for an East Coast version of California's powerful Strengthening our Lives voter mobilization organization (described in chapter 7).

Having rebounded from 9/11 with a series of campaigns to reenergize the drive for legalization, the AFL-CIO sought to renew efforts for progressive federal immigration reform by linking immigrant rights to the 1960s civil rights movement through the Immigrant Workers Freedom Ride. The IWFR became a critical vehicle for refocusing the debate around immigration away from domestic terrorism and toward enacting legislation that would meet the needs of America's millions of hardworking undocumented immigrants.

Immigrant Workers Freedom Ride

The Immigrant Workers Freedom Ride was a nationwide event chiefly organized and sponsored by UNITE HERE, SEIU, and the AFL-CIO. UNITE HERE and SEIU played a leading role in building a broad coalition of religious groups, students, immigrant rights organizations, and community groups in support of the event. The IWFR largely escaped national consciousness at the time, and many labor allies questioned the allocation of union resources for the event. I was at a meeting of national organizers in December 2002, when the proposed IWFR was discussed. The group of veteran labor allies was incredulous that, after major Republican gains in the November 2002 elections, so much union staff time and money would be devoted to an event that involved neither a labor election nor a political election. I shared this skepticism and was encouraged when I learned that the IWFR had been delayed and might never happen. But all of us were wrong. We failed to foresee how the IWFR would reenergize and broaden America's immigrant rights movement as well as building and deepening labor-clergy-community alliances.

The IWFR was named after the 1961 Freedom Rides of the U.S. civil rights movement, in which student activists rode buses in the Deep South to challenge segregation on interstate transportation and in bus and train terminals. The chief organizer of the IWFR was Dave Glaser of UNITE HERE, who later went on to head the national Hotel Workers Rising boycotts. The national chair of the IWFR was Maria Elena Durazo, who then headed UNITE HERE's Los Angeles local. Durazo believed that the IWFR would "take the fight for immigrant rights to a new level of unity and strength" and would show that "immigrants are also fighting for good jobs, access to health care and rights on the job—the same issues all workers are seeking." The LACFL showed its commitment by donating $100,000 to offset the cost of the Freedom Ride.[64]

A critical aim of the IWFR was to strengthen working relationships between labor unions and the many community, civil rights, religious, and student groups that collectively made up the nation's immigrant rights movement. The Freedom Riders included immigrants themselves, both documented and undocumented, as well as union and community allies, who planned to promote the need for immigration reform when stopping in dozens of communities across the country. The IWFR also hoped to return immigration issues to the national political agenda a year before the 2004 elections and to encourage greater civic participation by immigrants. IWFR organizers planned to emphasize that immigrants were also workers, and part of the U.S. working class.

"Immigrants built this country and the union movement," said HERE president John Wilhehn, chair of the AFL-CIO executive council's committee on immigration. "Today, millions of immigrants are working hard at jobs many of us don't want to do, paying taxes, and playing by the rules. They deserve the same freedom and equality we all strive for in America." Laborers president Terence O'Sullivan echoed this, noting, "Exploiting any group of workers is an attack on the living standards of all workers."[65]

As the start of the IWFR approached, key relationships were being forged that would expand and strengthen the immigrant rights movement. In Chicago, a crowd of fifteen hundred rallied in support of immigration reform on August 9 before marching to the Congress Hotel, whose primarily immigrant workers had been on strike for eight weeks (see chapter 2). Seattle unions used the IWFR to reach out to diverse community groups, with Steve Williamson, executive secretary-treasurer of the King County Labor Council, noting, "Labor is saying that immigrant issues are union issues, and other groups are talking about unions as never before. The energy is growing exponentially." Houston's Central Labor Council also sought new alliances in support of immigrant rights. "We are building ties with groups that have never had a relationship with the union movement before," said Richard Shaw, secretary-treasurer of the Harris County (Texas) Central Labor Council.[66]

The religious community was also gearing up. In Maryland and Washington, D.C., Labor in the Pulpits programs emphasizing immigrant rights were held at 125 religious services over Labor Day. "Just as the Freedom Rides in the 1960s set the stage for a national movement to secure the rights of African Americans in this country, the Immigrant Workers Freedom Ride can create the platform for a real national dialogue about immigration reform," noted Fred Mason, president of the Maryland State and D.C. AFL-CIO. More than *160* religious groups, including affiliates of Interfaith Worker Justice, endorsed the IWFR. Throughout the rides, meetings and rallies were often held in churches, just as they were during the UFW grape boycott.[67]

Buses carrying more than nine hundred activists began departing on September 23, 2003, from ten major cities—Boston, Chicago, Houston, Las Vegas, Los Angeles, Miami, Minneapolis, Portland, San Francisco, and Seattle—with plans to converge in Washington, D.C, and New York City in early October. Glaser described the buses as "traveling freedom schools," which would "enable workers to share personal experiences and discuss the need for immigrants to gain legal status, have a clear road to citizenship, reunite their families, be free to form unions without regard to legal status, and enjoy full civil rights protection."[68]

The IWFR got off to a rousing start. In Los Angeles, an estimated ten thousand people gathered on September 23 to send the riders off. Cardinal Roger Mahony held a service in the city's cathedral and offered his blessing to the riders and the event. This inspirational start came in handy when, on September 26, the Los Angeles Freedom Ride delegation was detained for over three hours while immigration officials interrogated some of the riders at a border checkpoint eighty-eight miles east of El Paso, Texas. The riders braved the threat of deportation by refusing to disclose their immigration status and singing "We Shall Overcome." Protests over the INS action poured in to the Bush administration from union presidents, members of Congress, and bishops from around the country. At the bus's next scheduled stop, in San Antonio, hundreds of people outside city hall chanted *"sí se puede!"* while awaiting the arrival of the buses from Los Angeles that had been "routinely detained." Faced with resistance by the riders and the national outcry, immigration officials finally gave up and released them.[69]

Although no one expected the riders to be brutally beaten, as had occurred in the 1961 bus trips, the INS did not ignore the IWFR. In another incident, two buses that left from Las Vegas encountered about two hundred anti-immigrant protesters when they arrived in Little Rock, Arkansas. The protesters surrounded the buses, and although police had been notified about the buses' arrival, no officers were present at the scene. Legal observers accompanying the ride contacted a hotline staffed by the Los Angeles chapter of the National Lawyers Guild, who in turn contacted the police. The officers soon arrived to defuse the situation.[70]

The journey east gave Freedom Riders a great opportunity to meet local supporters and build alliances along the route. When Houston's delegation of about ninety-five riders reached Atlanta, they joined with five thousand supporters in what was the state's largest immigrant rights demonstration ever. The Houston delegation visited churches, community centers, and union halls in fifteen southern cities. In Selma, Alabama, the group marched across the Edmund Pettis Bridge, where local and state police had viciously attacked civil rights activists in 1965 as marchers sought to reach Montgomery. Overall, the riders visited 103 cities. Various delegations attended a rally in Sacramento, a march in downtown Palm Springs, a welcome event in Phoenix, a mass in Tucson, and rallies at the Bureau of Citizenship and Immigration Services in Reno, Nevada. They heard rousing speeches at St. Joseph's Catholic Church in Yakima, Washington, and a boisterous crowd welcomed them to Denver. Immigrant rights supporters in St. Louis welcomed riders at a city hall rally with gospel music and held a memorial in honor of a rider's son, a legal immigrant who died while in INS custody. In Toledo, bus riders and a group of farmworkers met at the headquarters of the Farm Labor Organizing Committee.[71]

The IWFR highlighted the diversity of cities in which a burgeoning immigrant rights movement was taking root. Neither Tulsa, Oklahoma; Knoxville, Tennessee; Birmingham, Alabama; Grove Springs, Florida; Charleston, South Carolina; nor Des Moines, Iowa, had been well known for immigrant rights activism, yet riders were warmly received by local supporters in each of these cities. At one level, the stops in more than a hundred cities were simply a function of logistics: riders needed places to eat and sleep. And it was only logical that they would meet local supporters from labor, the religious community, and student and community groups while staying in or passing through town. But beyond the practical necessity, the plan represented a brilliant strategy for laying the groundwork for a national immigrant rights movement. This proved particularly true in the smaller cities in the Midwest and the South, where little infrastructure for such a movement existed.

The riders converged in Washington, D.C., to lobby Congress on October 1. The delegations urged representatives to support three legislative goals: creating a path to legalization and citizenship for all immigrants, making it easier to reunite the families of undocumented immigrants, and protecting immigrants' workplace rights. But the IWFR was less about pushing specific legislation and more about announcing the emergence of a larger movement. Eliseo Medina captured the broader vision of the IWFR, saying, "We need to organize and use the power of our vote. That's the next step in the struggle. It's not just about immigrant workers' rights, but about living wages, about decent education. This is the beginning of us taking back America." IWFR national director Dave Glaser echoed Medina's assessment of the broader implications of the Freedom Ride. He felt that the experience of organizing the Freedom Ride had changed the labor movement and the immigrant communities; and he predicted that "employer resistance to organizing is going to have to reckon with the deep passion for justice we saw as we traveled across the country," as immigrant workers were increasingly seeing unions as a vehicle for achieving that justice.[72]

After leaving Washington, D.C., eighteen buses carrying the Freedom Riders headed for New York City, where they were met by hundreds of additional buses sent by churches, unions, and student organizations on October 4. The ride concluded with a rally of more than a hundred thousand people. Speakers included numerous representatives of the religious community. Cardinal Edward M. Egan, the archbishop of the Catholic archdiocese of New York, was warmly received by the crowd and spoke of how "shameful advantage is being taken of men and women in the work force who do not have proper papers." Bishop Nicholas DiMarzio of Brooklyn echoed Egan, condemning the way that immigrants are "often ridiculed, exploited, and abused. This must stop, and this immoral system must be changed." Congressman John Lewis, Democrat from Georgia, a Freedom Rider in the 1960s, declared, "Martin Luther King would be very proud. We are white, Black, Hispanic, Native American—we are one family, in one house, and we are not going to let anybody turn us around."[73]

Maria Elena Durazo, IWFR national chair, summed up the essence of the organizers' strategy when she told the crowd that the Immigrant Workers Freedom Ride was not an event, "but the creation of a new movement. Immigrants now understand we are not alone, we have allies.... Whether you are second generation, or fourteenth," she said, "we have to build a new movement in the United States of America." By setting a movement in motion and building a framework for future action, the Freedom Ride helped pave the way for the mass immigrant rights marches of 2006.[74]

Notes

1. Jacques E. Levy, *Cesar Chavez: Autobiography of La Causa* (New York: W. W. Norton, 1975), p. 118.
2. Dick Meister and Anne Loftis, *A Long Time Coming: The Struggle to Unionize America's Farm Workers* (New York: Macmillan, 1977), pp. 75–76; Levy, *Cesar Chavez*, pp. 12.9, 130.
3. Levy, *Cesar Chavez*, pp. 143, 144.
4. Richard Griswold del Castillo and Richard Garcia, *Cesar Chavez: A Triumph of Spirit* (Norman: University of Oklahoma Press, 1995), pp. 159, 160.
5. Ibid., p. 162.

6. Ibid., pp. 159, 160, 167, 168.

7. Ibid., p. 162.

8. Ibid.

9. Ibid., pp. 167, 170.

10. Ibid., p. 168; Steven Lerner, interview with author, September 26, 2006.

11. Griswold del Castillo and Garcia, *Cesar Chavez*, pp. 168–69.

12. Luz Villarreai, "Group Seeks to Join INS Outreach Effort," *Los Angeles Daily News,* June 30, 1995.

13. Douglas S. Massey, Jorge Durand, and Nolan J. Malone, *Beyond Smoke and Mirrors: Mexican Immigration in an Era of Economic Integration* (New York: Russell Sage Foundation, 2002), p. 90; Viliarreal, "Group Seeks to Join INS Outreach Effort"; Matt Barreto, Ricardo Ramírez, and Nathan Woods, "Are Naturalized Voters Driving the California Latino Electorate? Measuring the Effect of IRCA Citizens on Latino Voting," *Social Science Quarterly* 86, no. 4 (December 2005): 797, 798.

14. Viliarreal, "Group Seeks to Join INS Outreach Effort."

15. Ron Kaye, interview with author, January 22, 2007. The other IAF groups were the United Neighborhoods Organization, the Southern California Organizing Committee, and the East Valleys Organization.

16. Cecilia Barragan, interview with author, January 21, 2007.

17. Ibid.; Consueio Valdez, interview with author, January 22, 2007; Villarreal, "Group Seeks to Join INS Outreach Effort."

18. See David Schippers, "Gore Pressured INS to Win in 1996" www.american-patrol.com/INDUSTRIAL-AREAS-FOUNDATION/SchippersGoreCitUSAooo82.8.html. This article is excerpted from Schippers's book *Sellout: The Inside Story of President Clinton's Impeachment* (Washington, D.C.: Regnery, 2000). See also Thomas McArdle, "Al Gore's Voter Mill," *National Review,* March 24, 1997.

19. Ibid.; Father Vega is quoted in Dick Kirschten, "The Politics of Citizenship," GovernmentExecutive.com, January 1, 1997, http://govexec.com/features/0197s4.htm.

20. Schippers, "Gore Pressured INS"; Schippers's article links to the full memo, which is available at www.americanpatrol.com/INDUSTRIAL-AREAS- FOUNDATION/IAFMemooo1105Show.html.

21. Fred Ross Jr., interview with author, July 2.5, 2006; Kirschten, "The Politics of Citizenship."

22. Luz Villarreal, "Activists Stage Protest," *Los Angeles Daily News,* February 28, 1996.

23. Rick Orlov, "INS Sets Goal for Processing Applications," *Los Angeles Daily News,* May 2, 1996; Schippers, "Gore Pressured INS," p. 3.

24. Orlov, "INS Sets Goal."

25. Luz Villareal, "Activist Groups Plan Convention to Get Out Vote," *Los Angeles Daily News,* July 13, 1996.

26. Eliseo Medina, interview with author, February 13, 2,007; Barragan interview.

27. Luz Villarreal, "Volunteers Hit Streets to Register New Voters," *Los Angeles Daily News,* October 6, 1996.

28. Dennis Love, "Latinos Look to Build on Record Vote," *Los Angeles Daily News,* November 11,1996; Yvette Cabrera, "60,800 Naturalized in L.A. in One Month," *Los Angeles Daily News,* August 19, 1996; Luz Villarreal, "Registering Their Power," *Los Angeles Daily News,* November 17, 1996.

29. Love, "Latinos Look to Build on Record Vote."

30. Kaye interview; Valdez interview; Barragan interview.

31. Kirschten, "The Politics of Citizenship."

32. Ibid.

33. Gore's responses to the Office of the Inspector General's questions are available online at www.usd0j.gov/0ig/special/0007/dappendix.htm.

34. Schippers, "Gore Pressured INS"; Schippers, *Sellout.*

35. Ross interview.

36. Ibid.

37. Vernon M. Briggs Jr., "Immigration Policy and American Unionism: A Reality Check," *Briggs Papers and Speeches,* Vernon M. Briggs Jr. Collection, Kheel Center for Labor-Management Documentation and Archives, School of Industrial Relations, Cornell University, 2004, vol. 4, p. 16. This paper is available for downloading at http://digitalcommons.ilr.cornell.edu/briggsIV/13.

38. Ibid., pp. 17, 18.

39. Ibid., p. 19.

40. Eliseo Medina, "On Hope and Activism," in Studs Terkel, *Hope Dies Last: Keeping the Faith in Difficult Times* (New York: New Press, 2003), www.commondreams.org/scriptfjles/views03/1111–09.htm.

41. Medina interview; Marshall Ganz, interview with author, February 28, 2007.

42. Medina interview; Ganz interview.

43. Medina interview.

44. Ben Monterroso, interview with author, February 14, 2007.

45. Medina interview.

46. Ibid.

47. James Parks, "Recognizing Our Common Bonds," www.aflcio.org/aboutus/thisistheaflcio/publications/magazine/commonbonds.cfm.

48. On the AFL-ClO's new policy, see "A Nation of Immigrants," 2001 AFL-CIO Convention Resolution, www.aflcio.org/aboutus/thisistheaflcio/convention/resolutions_ecstatements.cfm#immigration. The text of the 2000 resolution is not available online.

49. Medina interview.

50. Ibid. Contreras is quoted in Lloyd Billingsley, "Union Card for Green Card: The Radical Vanguard in the Los Angeles Labor Movement," August 2000, www.americanpatrol.com/RECONQUISTA/NUNEZ-FABIAN/UnionCdGreenCd000800Nunez.html. Billingsley is militantly anti-immigrant, and his article reflects this.

51. Mario Garcia, *Memories of Chicano History: The Life and Narrative of Bert Corona* (Berkeley: University of California Press, 1995), pp. 2.46, 247.

52. Ibid., pp. 249–50, 290–91.

53. Billingsley, "Union Card for Green Card."

54. Medina interview.

55. Ibid.; Arthur Jones, "Catholic Hospital Organization Signs Accord with Union," *National Catholic Reporter,* April 20, 2001.

56. Luis Alonso Lugo, "Remittances Are Mexico's Biggest Source of Income, Says Fox," Associated Press, September 24,2003, *San Diego Union-Tribune,* www.signonsandiego.com/news/mexico/20030924–205r-us-mexico.html; Susan Ferriss, "Surprising Allies on Immigration," *Sacramento Bee,* May 8, 2006. On the composition and recommendations of the Carnegie panel, see U.S.-Mexico Migration Panel, "Mexico-U.S. Migration: A Shared Responsibility," Carnegie Endowment Report, February 14, 2001, www.carnegieendowment.org/publications/index.cfrn?fa-view&id=623&prog=zgp.

57. Eliseo Medina, keynote address, Democratic Socialists of America convention, November 9, 2001, www.dsausa.org/convention2k1/eliseo.html.

58. Medina interview.

59. Ibid.; Bill Carder, interview with author, February 15, 2007; e-mail from Marshall Ganz, February 17, 2007; Daniel Weintraub, "A Union's New Focus Is on Immigrants and Voting," *Sacramento Bee,* November 14, 2002.

60. Michael Denney, "Participant Citizenship in a Marginal Group: Union Mobilization of California Farm Workers," *American Journal of Political Science* 23, no. 2 (May 1979): 330–37; Weintraub, "A Union's New Focus."

61. Medina interview; "Roberto De La Cruz 1971–1991" interview by Anamaría De La Cruz, Farmworker Movement Documentation Project, www.farmworkermovement.org/essays/essays/109 %2oDe%2oLa% 20Cruz_Roberto.pdf.

62. Gouri Sadhwani, interview with author, February 12, 2007; Hilary Russ, "Making Change: Union Schmooze," *City Limits* magazine, February 2003.

63. See "Election Day 2006," www.seiu32BJ.org.

64. James Parks, "Immigrant Workers Freedom Ride," www.aflcio.org/aboutus/thisistheaflcio/publications/ magazine/o9O3_iwfr.cfm. Parks provides an invaluable account of the IWFR.

65. Ibid.

66. Ibid.

67. Ibid.

68. Ibid.

69. Ibid.; Victor Narro and Dan Gregor, "People's Lawyering on the Bus: How a Small Band of NLG Members Became the Legal Vanguard for Immigrant Freedom Riders," *Guild Practitioner* 63, no. 2 (Spring 2006): 65–72; Steven Greenhouse, "Immigrants Rally in City, Seeking Rights," *New York Times,* October 5, 2003, http://query.nytimes.com/gst/fullpage.html?res=9Do6E5D6123CF 936A35753C1A9659C8B63.

70. Narro and Gregor, "People's Lawyering on the Bus."

71. Roy Van Dyke, *The Immigrant's Journal,* www.immigrantjournal.com; Parks, "Immigrant Workers Freedom Ride"; Maya Raquel Anderson, "Immigrant Workers' Freedom Ride: 'Somos Uno, We Are One,'" *Peacework* magazine, November 2003, www.peaceworkmagazine.org/pwork/0311/031106.htm.

72. Judith Le Blanc, "Immigrant Workers Freedom Ride: A New Movement Is Born," *People's Weekly World,* October 11, 2003, www.pww.org/article/view/4106/1/184.

73. Ibid.; Greenhouse, "Immigrants Rally in City, Seeking Rights."

74. Greenhouse, "Immigrants Rally in City, Seeking Rights."

A Surge of Representation in the Salinas Valley

KIM GERON

The city of Salinas, California, is a model of how a well-organized predominantly Mexican-origin community can achieve a fairly high level of political incorporation within a short period of time. From 1980 to 2001, Latinos went from zero representation in local political offices to winning a number of significant electoral empowerment victories, including the majority on local school boards and the Salinas City Council, the first Mexican American Monterey County supervisor in the twentieth century, and the first state assembly member from the Salinas-Watsonville-Hollister area. They were also successful in both establishing district elections for local judges and electing a progressive Chicano judge to the Superior Court. The rapid transformation to visible Latino representation at the local level occurred after many years of hard work by a dedicated group of Chicano community activists and offers lessons for how to build Latino political power at the local level.

This chapter is a case study of these group efforts; in particular, it focuses on the potential to expand policy benefits through substantive political representation. Unlike large urban communities, where a viable biracial or multiracial coalition was viewed as a necessary requirement for minority political incorporation in the 1960s and 1970s, Salinas's Latinos have achieved strong electoral representation largely through their own political efforts. After gaining political control, Latino political leaders have addressed issues of growth, housing, and quality of life, helping reallocate policy benefits to the Mexican American community in ways that had not been possible under all-white local administrations. How this occurred, and why, is important for the study of racial coalition politics.

Salinas is also important because in most large urban contexts ethnic and racial groups are constantly jockeying for greater political influence with white voters and among themselves, but in the majority of Southwest locations where Mexican Americans reside, the main demographic groups in close proximity to one another are Anglos and Latinos. It is in these suburban and rural communities that Mexican Americans have an excellent opportunity to advance politically as their numbers increase. In most cases they do not have to compete with another racial minority group, such as African Americans, for political influence and electoral positions. In many of these communities, they are the majority population, and as more Mexican Americans undergo naturalization, register to vote, and become politically active, the possibility of increasing the ranks of Latino elected officials will grow exponentially. For example, in Los Angeles, California's largest city, five of the fifteen council members as of 2004 were Latino. Even if Latinos were to win another two or three seats over the next few years, this would not substantially change the overall numbers and clout of Latinos nationally. However, if Latinos can get elected in other suburban and regional center cities such as Salinas, the total number of Latino elected officials will grow dramatically. Not only is the Salinas case study significant for its local transformative value, but it offers important lessons for similarly situated communities in the Southwest and in other regions where Latino population growth has surged dramatically but where there is virtually no political representation, such as small cities in the South, Northeast, and Midwest. The Latino populations of many of these communities are mostly first-generation immigrants, yet with grassroots organization, electable leaders, and sufficient economic resources to run effective campaigns, the Salinas experience could be repeated.

Urban governments provide most government functions, especially those that directly affect the lives of residents. Basic local services such as police, fire, and social services are as necessary as those provided by the federal government. In addition, it is at the local level that the type and quality of housing, jobs, and education are contested. It is therefore important to study how policy benefits were distributed before and after Mexican Americans ascended to political leadership of Salinas, a regional agricultural center. As Latinos become a major presence in many parts of the nation, their process of political incorporation is instructive of how politics operates in cities with large Latino communities. It provides insights into the racial dynamics that have begun to unfold in the new millennium.

Salinas is the county seat of Monterey, California. This city had an estimated population of more than 129,900 people in 1996 and more than 151,000 people by 2000 (see Table 2.1).[1] It is located one hour's drive south of San Jose and thirty minutes inland from the coastal city of Monterey. Salinas was born out of *rancho* lands awarded to settlers by the Mexican government. A town was established in 1856, and the city was incorporated in 1874. Salinas is the food processing and shipping center of the Salinas Valley, which is internationally known for its mass production of vegetables and fruits. In fact, it is known as "the salad bowl of the world."

TABLE 2.1 Latino Population of Salinas

Year	General Population	Latino Population	% of Total Population
1890	2,339	n/a	
1900	3,304	n/a	
1930	10,263	n/a	
1940	11,586	n/a	
1950	13,917	n/a	
1960	28,957	2,586[a]	9.8
1970	58,896	4,760[b]	8.0
1980	80,479	30,577	38.0
1990	108,777	54,428	50.6
2000	151,060	96,880	61.1

Source: U.S. Bureau of the Census, various years.

Notes: a. No specific information on Spanish-surname or Latino population is available; however, the total foreign-born population was 2,838. Of this number, 252 were of Asian origin. The majority of the remaining 2,586 were of Latino or Portuguese origin.

b. This number represents the number of foreign born or of mixed parentage from Mexico. Another table lists a similar number of Spanish-language or Spanish-surname residents. This number is significantly higher—21 percent. However, since Salinas has a relatively high percentage of both Portuguese- and Spanish-surnamed Filipinos, I have used the smaller number of foreign born from Mexico.

A famous native of Salinas, John Steinbeck, used the city as the setting for his novels *Tortilla Flats,*[2] *Of Mice and Men,*[3] and *East of Eden.*[4] These fictionalized accounts of life in this community reflect the agricultural roots of the region. The agricultural character of Salinas drew migrants from the East, including Oklahomans during the Great Depression, and immigrants from Mexico. The waves of migrant labor since the 1930s has created a growing Latino community constituting more than 61 percent in 2000 (see Table 2.1).

A Brief History of Salinas

The roots of Latino political incorporation efforts can be traced back to the decades of discrimination and inequality faced by migrant farm-workers who labored in the Salinas Valley fields to produce fruits and vegetables for consumers but received poor compensation and little opportunity for advancement. The landowning elites who founded the city of Salinas in the nineteenth century tightly controlled the political and educational systems.

Efforts to improve the conditions of Chicanos began in the agricultural fields and in the educational arena. In the late 1960s, young Chicanos demonstrated in the streets of Salinas to demand the right to celebrate their history and culture. The inspiration for the young Chicanos was *campesinos* (farmworkers) who had been stirred into action by the organizing of the United Farm Workers of America (UFW). The UFW had a profound impact on the city of Salinas.

In 1970, the UFW was drawn to the city after the Teamsters Union unilaterally signed contracts with most of the lettuce growers in the area.[5] Having just completed the successful organization of grape workers in the San Joaquin Valley in 1965–1970, the UFW moved most of its leaders to Salinas to oversee what was to become one of the largest agricultural strikes in California's history and a nationwide lettuce boycott.

In 1970, when the UFW began to organize in the Salinas and Pajaro valleys, people of Mexican descent were in the process of establishing permanent roots in and around Salinas. Previously, the population of Mexicans had been small, made up mostly of migrant farmworkers. In 1950, only a small percentage of the population of Salinas was Mexican. These numbers did not begin to change until the ending of the Bracero Program in 1964, which enabled many Mexican workers to bring their families and settle in the area. Many workers lived outside the city limits in the East Alisal area.

The history of Salinas, similar to that of many cities in the Southwest, is closely linked to Mexico. After Mexico seceded from Spain in 1822, two ranchos in the Salinas Valley were granted to Mexican settlers: Sausal and Nacional. The ranchos were sold to white settlers following the Gold Rush of 1849. These early settlers formed the town of Salinas in the 1850s, which soon became the county seat of Monterey County, after a vote where Salinas' 150 new residents swung the election.[6] Many of the early ranchers wanted to make sure the county seat was moved out of the city of Monterey, which they viewed as "too Mexican" and too far off the north-south travel route. The city was incorporated in 1874.

From being only a small way station between Los Angeles and San Francisco, Salinas grew to 25,000 by 1960.[7] This population growth was fueled by the introduction of lettuce in the early 1900s and later artichokes and broccoli, which were the main agricultural crops and the dominant focus of the local economy. The development of a variety of crops and the start of the Great Depression in the 1930s drew large numbers of poor migrants, including a large number from the Dust Bowl of Oklahoma.

Mexican migrant workers also came to Salinas. In 1936, a lettuce strike organized by the Fruit and Vegetable Union erupted into a conflict between the new migrants and the townspeople, who were backed by the shed owners. A combination of local guards, vigilantes, and state and local law-enforcement forces attacked four thousand workers and sympathizers.[8] Workers were left beaten and bloody from this confrontation. The new settlers were not deterred, however, and more people continued to arrive. A huddle of shacks became Alisal, an unincorporated part of Monterey County.

In 1960, the Salinas population was 28,000, and the Alisal area contained an additional 18,000 people, with a sizable percentage from Mexico. Salinas and Alisal had a combined population of 46,000, making it the largest agricultural center in the region. Under the city of Salinas's general plan, the Alisal area was annexed into Salinas in 1963. This area was physically an integral part of Salinas, with almost as many people as north and south Salinas combined.

Beginning in the 1930s, the Mexican population grew rapidly, especially with the advent of the Bracero Program during World War II, when a shortage of farm laborers led the U.S. government to create a seasonal worker agreement with the Mexican government to bring temporary workers to pick vitally needed crops.[9] Following World War II, however, there were still very few Mexicans who lived in Salinas on a year-round basis.

Historically, a triumvirate of Anglo and Japanese agricultural interests, downtown banking and financial interests, and real estate developers controlled economic development in Salinas. During World War II, local Japanese farmers, along with all other West Coast Japanese Americans, were rounded up and placed in internment camps. The incarceration of Japanese farmers enabled other growers to purchase some of their land and limited the influence of Japanese farmers following the war. In the 1950s and 1960s, Salinas grew from solely an agricultural community into a manufacturing and retail center for the region. A Firestone tire and rubber plant opened, along with other major plants owned by Peter Paul Cadbury, Nestle, Shilling, and J. M. Smucker companies. Thousands of Chicanos and Mexicans who had been drawn to the area for agricultural work were now being employed in the manufacturing and food-processing industries.

The impact of the United Farm Workers on Monterey County Politics

The economic story of the early 1970s was the struggle in the fields to unionize farmworkers. As mentioned previously, in 1970 the UFW made it a top priority to organize thousands of lettuce and other agricultural workers in the Salinas and Pajaro valleys. For several years these farmworkers had been calling for the UFW to come and support them.[10] Lettuce growers in the Salinas and Santa Maria valleys, anticipating that they would be the next target of a UFW organizing campaign, had secretly signed contracts with the Teamsters to represent their field-workers, without even consulting with the mainly Mexican workers.[11] After intense negotiations between the two unions, a peace agreement was reached whereby any Teamster contracts would switch to the UFW.

When the 170 lettuce growers refused to switch unions, a general strike was called, and all lettuce was boycotted. More then 7,000 men, women, and children walked off their jobs in the lettuce and strawberry fields.[12] In one of the most dramatic episodes of the UFW organizing drive, Cesar Chavez refused to abide by a court order to stop the boycott against Bud Antle, the largest lettuce grower, who became the target of the UFW (even though it had signed a separate union contract with the Teamsters a decade earlier). A local judge ordered Chavez arrested in the Monterey County

Courthouse in Salinas. Chavez went on a hunger strike. An around-the-clock vigil began, with thousands of farmworkers surrounding the courthouse. Finally, on Christmas Eve, some twenty days later, the judge relented and freed Chavez.[13] This incident received national publicity when Robert Kennedy's widow, Ethel Kennedy, traveled to Salinas to support Chavez, and it helped to galvanize more public support for the farmworkers' campaign in the Salinas area.

For most of the 1970s, Salinas was polarized as the powerful agricultural interests sought to prevent farmworkers from choosing the union to represent them. The Chicano and Mexican community was largely in support of the UFW, as many of these families included members who were farmworkers. However, politically the Chicano community was not organized, and in some respects there were contradictions in the community's response to the UFW. As noted earlier, the Teamsters Union had cut a deal with Bud Antle in 1961 and had unionized more than 1,000 workers, almost exclusively Mexican migrants who were sent back and forth between Salinas and Yuma, Arizona, during the dual harvesting seasons to prevent them from being organized by the Agricultural Workers Organizing Committee, a forerunner to the UFW.[14] Many of these workers were sympathetic to the UFW, yet they received better wages and benefits than nonunionized farmworkers.[15] The UFW was unable to secure strong union contracts within the lettuce industry, and the Teamsters Union let most of its contract lie dormant and did not enforce its provisions. The low level of unionization in the fields weakened organized labor's presence and kept the Mexican community without political power. The growers' power to control the fields meant that they continued to control the politics of the Salinas Valley as well. Without the strong presence of an active union like the UFW, farmworkers and their families had little hope of gaining a political voice in their employment terms and in their communities.

In addition to the power of the growers, the political inexperience of the Chicano community limited Chicano economic progress in the 1970s, and the lack of unionization meant that farmworker families were paid poorly. There was only a very small Chicano middle class, as few families were able to move from the working-class into middle-class professions and small businesses. The economic difficulties of the Latino community were reflected in its early attempts to gain political incorporation.

Initial Efforts Toward Political Incorporation

Historically, a large number of Mexicans lived outside the city limits in the Alisal area. In 1963, the Alisal area was annexed to the city of Salinas; this action by the city helped prompt a movement for political inclusion for the Chicano community. An early political activist, Sally Gutierrez, was the first Latina to run for local office in 1970. While her campaign was unsuccessful, Gutierrez's attempt was an important first step in the Latino community's efforts to win political representation.[16] In addition to traditional electoral participation efforts, the UFW campaign to organize farmworkers exposed a broader lack of political power for all Latinos in the Salinas area. Many local residents began their involvement in local political issues by supporting the UFW and the lettuce boycott.

The Monterey County chapter of the League of United Latin American Citizens (LULAC) was founded in 1973. Also in the mid-1970s, Willie Velasquez, the founder of the Southwest Voter Registration Project, visited Salinas and discussed the need to build a local organization to do voter registration and education. From 1976 to 1978, a local community activist, Jesse Sanchez, developed a Salinas-based Southwest Voter Registration Project. By 1980, these efforts converged to begin running local Chicanos for office. Sanchez was elected to the Alisal Union School Elementary School Board in 1981. In 1982, Bill Melendez ran for Monterey County school superintendent and placed second. The effort to get Melendez elected showed the potential power Latinos had in the county, if they were organized and mobilized.[17]

While Latinos were beginning to be elected to school boards, the city council and mayor's seat remained firmly in the hands of Anglos. From 1970 to 1985, Latinos tried unsuccessfully four times to get elected to the city council. Each time, there was polarized voting, with Chicanos voting in large numbers for the Chicano candidate but white voters overwhelmingly rejecting Chicano candidates. As long as Latinos were a minority population, they would face an uphill battle to elect one of their own in citywide elections.

Finally, in 1985, a Cuban American businessman, Ralph Portuondo, became the first Latino elected under the at-large electoral system. Portuondo, a real estate developer, had the support of the white political establishment, a combination of agricultural interests and developers, that had governed Salinas for decades. Community activist Jesse Sanchez ran unsuccessfully in the same race. Sanchez received 70 percent of the vote in Chicano precincts but only 9 percent of the vote in white precincts.[18] The Sanchez defeat in 1985, coupled with the filing of a lawsuit in Watsonville (twenty miles away in Santa Cruz County) the same year to challenge that city's electoral system, had a big impact on Salinas's community activists. Their strategy now shifted toward exploring legal options to challenge the citywide electoral system.

In early 1987, when a federal district court judge ruled that Watsonville's at-large electoral system did not discriminate, the reaction of local Salinas Chicano activists was to point out differences between Watsonville and Salinas: "In Salinas, it's very clear that you would have a majority of Hispanics in some districts, if the city was broken down into districts."[19] Three elements are needed to prove that at-large election systems are discriminatory. Sanchez pointed out that in Salinas "voting is polarized, Hispanics are geographically compact, and Hispanics are politically cohesive.... I think we can show that there is a legacy of discrimination and that a Hispanic from East Salinas could win if the city were broken into districts."[20]

On June 2, 1987, mayoral and council elections were held, and although no Chicano candidates ran from the East Salinas area, a grassroots organization, the Alisal Betterment Committee (ABC), endorsed three white candidates, including Al Styles, a resident of East Salinas. East Salinas contributed 21 percent of the total votes, including over 1,000 votes delivered through the efforts of ABC.[21]

The actions of ABC grew out of a larger vision of local Chicano community activists, who decided not to run their own candidate but to endorse other candidates and continue to build their own grassroots organization. Later that year, an official of the Department of Justice came to Salinas to investigate local politics and determine whether there was discriminatory voting.[22]

In 1988, hiring practices in Salinas came under fire, as local Latino community leaders, including the LULAC, criticized the city for failing to hire and promote minorities and women. A member of the City's Affirmative Action Commission, Juan Oliverez, charged, "Even though we are making some strides, there's still not any hiring at management levels.... I'm not convinced there is a real commitment to Chicanos." Local LULAC chapter president Bill Melendez said, "Unless feet are held to the fire, they won't hire Latinos and minorities." Demands were raised to hire more bilingual public contact people, including recreation staff, police, fire, library, and building inspectors.[23]

Citywide Effort Wins District Elections

In late August 1988, following the path taken by community activists in Watsonville, Joaquin Avila, the attorney in the Watsonville case, filed a class action suit to end Salinas' at-large election system on behalf of three Chicano activists: Fernando Armenta, Simon Salinas, and Marta Nava (who had been the first Chicana to win office in Salinas when she was elected trustee of the Alisal Union School Elementary School Board following Sanchez's election). Avila filed a lawsuit charging that the city of Salinas's at-large electoral system diluted Latino voting strength and prevented Chicanos from being elected. As Sanchez noted later, "We could prove that voting was polarized. We could prove that when a Chicano was placed on the ballot, there was a higher Chicano voter turnout. If the elections were held by districts, a Chicano could win."[24]

Fearing the high cost of a court trial and the real possibility of defeat, city officials agreed to settle the matter through a local election.[25] According to Salinas city manager Roy J. Herte, "We watched what was happening in Watsonville.... We had no insurance policy to cover the costs of a suit, and no estimate of what it would cost, and we knew that once the precedent had been set over there, our chances of winning would have been remote."[26] The political establishment counted on being able to defeat the citywide measure, just as it had defeated eastside Chicano candidates previously.

Elections were scheduled for December 6, 1988. The election proved difficult for several reasons. First, proponents of district elections had to win an at-large election. This would require a heavy turnout in Chicano precincts (as Chicanos were not yet officially the majority population) and a substantial sympathy vote by Anglos. Second, there was very little time to prepare, as the elections were scheduled four months after the lawsuit was filed. Third, proponents of district elections had to urge voters to pass not one but three measures: measure one would establish district elections with six council seats; measure two would expand the size of the city council from five to seven members, and measure three would amend the process by which vacancies on the city council were filled.[27]

Local grassroots organizations used a combination of voter education and get-out-the-vote efforts. They were up against a Salinas City Council that gave "tepid support" and hoped the three measures would fail.[28] Using experience gained in previous elections, the Chicano community had developed an effective vote-generating operation. Volunteers went door to door throughout East Salinas, explaining the measures on the ballot. Supporters of district elections organized rides to the polling places on election day. While Chicano community sentiment ran high in favor of the three measures, the Anglo community overwhelmingly opposed district elections. When the votes were counted, district elections had won by only 107 votes, 3,507 to 3,400.[29]

The majority of the margin of victory came from the high Chicano voter turnout, accounting for 35 percent of all votes cast. Voting was polarized along racial lines, as Chicano activists had consistently charged. Chicano precincts voted 85 percent in favor of the three measures, while white precincts voted 75 percent against it. Nevertheless, the small white vote in favor of district elections, combined with votes of Filipinos, who made up 5 percent of total voters and also favored the measure, were sufficient to tip the scales. After the votes were tallied, Sanchez commented, "The vote makes it clear that Chicanos are now a force in this community. What's really impressive is that we won this in only six months.... Now, we're finally going to have a Chicano on the city council."[30]

As the votes were counted, affirming the establishment of district elections in the city, a fierce battle erupted within the Chicano community. Two Chicano candidates emerged to seek the same seat on the council. Simon Salinas, a thirty-three-year-old schoolteacher in East Salinas and a plaintiff in the initial lawsuit against the city, faced two other opponents: Chicano attorney Juan Uranga and a non-Latina, Deloris Higgins, who owned a small business in East Salinas. Uranga was supported by the Central Coast Democratic Club and elected city officials. He also had worked for fourteen years as an attorney for the California Rural Legal Assistance and advocated for the rights of farmworkers. The differences between Salinas and Uranga reflected less their political differences than differences about who and how the community would select its elected leaders. Veteran community activists, many of who had worked since the early 1970s for the opportunity to elect a Chicano representative to the city council through the Alisal Betterment Committee, expected to discuss who would be the best candidate and then unite to work for that person's election. When Uranga decided to run without their endorsement and rely on the local Democratic leadership, some Chicano activists were angered. According to then attorney and now municipal court Judge José Velásquez, "We were shocked to find the Democratic leadership attempting to impose their hand-picked leader on our community."[31]

Simon Salinas said he was concerned with local issues—"my priority is not going to be pleasing Democratic higher-ups in Sacramento"—and that Uranga had too much "outside" support from as the Central Coast Democratic Club and other political leaders. Uranga, who used his fourteen-year experience with the California Rural Legal Assistance as evidence of his concern for East Salinas residents, was shocked by the tenor of the campaign: "Using negative campaigning as a strategy at this level of politics really surprises me."[32]

The competition between two viable Chicano community candidates sparked increased voter registration and participation. Lydia Villareal, Uranga's campaign manager, predicted a heavy voter turnout in District 2. "It's because of district elections," she said. "Everything flows from that.... The interest is much more immediate."[33] Signs from one camp or the other were visible in every store window on East Alisal Street. By election day, the differences between the two candidates' camps reached such an intense level that authorities had to be called in to keep the peace in eastside precinct polls. There was chanting, insults were exchanged, and there was even pushing in line as Chicano residents anxiously waited to vote for the candidate of their choice.[34] In the words of Monterey County voter registrar Ross Underwood, "Poll officers were forced into the role of yard-duty teacher. It was almost a carnival-like atmosphere."[35]

When the votes were tallied, 2,375 persons, or 43 percent of the 5,519 registered voters living in the city's newly created heavily Latino District 2, had showed up to vote. This was the highest voter turnout percentage in the city. In 1987, before district elections were approved, 966 voters, only 23 percent of the area's 4,132 registered voters, had cast votes for mayoral and council candidates. In that election, there had been three white council candidates and one Latino candidate.[36]

In the District 2 election in 1989, the clear victor in a hard-fought race was Simon Salinas, who captured 62.4 percent of the ballots cast. The election of the first Latino to the Salinas City Council, under the district election system, occurred just as Latinos were becoming the majority population. The 1990 census revealed what Chicano activists had been saying for some time: Latinos had become the majority population in the city (see Table 2.1). Their numbers had risen dramatically between 1980 and 1990. This demographic change, along with the change in the political structure, proved to be the winning combination for the election of Latinos. To change the electoral structure in a racially polarized environment such as Salinas, there must be sufficient numbers of Latinos present, and they must vote in large numbers.

In addition to a change in the structure, other ingredients are necessary to achieve Latino incorporation. The disenfranchised group must be organized, viable candidates developed, and issues clearly articulated. In Salinas, these conditions were met. Latinos had built grassroots community organization, and they had run electoral campaigns for school boards, superintendent of schools, city council, and other races. They had a community presence in these campaigns. There were identifiable community candidates with the potential to be elected, if the rules were changed to enable Chicanos to select a candidate who would represent their interests on the council. They had a captivating issue—the documented history of racialized voting. The citywide vote to change the electoral rules was historic, as it enabled wider participation by Salinas residents and greater opportunities to be elected through neighborhood campaigns.

The election of a community resident from East Salinas was a reflection of the strong ties and support that local community organization had constructed. The white businesswoman in the race, though an eastside resident, was no match for the mandate from the community for local Chicano representation. The contest between two well-qualified and well-known candidates indicated that already there were divisions within the Chicano community between various camps, not necessarily around major policy differences but rather regarding from whom they received initial support. Since neither Salinas nor Uranga had held elective office previously, this election came down to who was best able to register and organize new and existing voters.

Latinos Achieve Political Control, 1989–2001

Since 1989, Latinos have been elected on a regular basis to the Salinas City Council. The second section of this chapter discusses the progress of Latino political incorporation and examines whether the inequalities in benefit distribution to the Latino community that prompted the movement for political representation are affected by different political rule. While, as some scholars note, "equality is a complex and uncertain guide to public policy,"[37] the dominant paradigm in government since the Great Depression is to address societal inequalities with social programs. Yet most broad social programs have been the jurisdiction of the federal government. At the local level, there are numerous constraints that limit cities.[38] This section of the chapter will study the results of seven years of gradual Latino incorporation in Salinas, during which Latinos gained a majority presence on the city council.

We will review the first two years, 1989–1991, then briefly examine the years 1991–1993, when two additional Latino representatives were elected. Next, we will examine the period 1993–1997, when four out of seven city council members elected were Latinos. Finally, we will assess the 1998–2002 period, when the first Chicana mayor was elected. The latter period transformed Salinas into the largest California city with a majority-Latino city council.

Salinas represents an excellent case to examine this book's basic question: does electing Latinos to political office make a difference for the Latino community that elects them? The issue of equality underlying this study is complex. Are there group entitlements that flow from organizing a group's power to achieve electoral success? Are there observable differences in how social policy and policy benefits are distributed before and after Latinos take power? In addition, this chapter includes an analysis of the role of government bureaucrats to affect the setting of policy and the distribution of resources.

The First Two Years, 1989–1991

An inequality of services and benefits for the Chicano community, such as a lack of low-cost housing, a lack of parks and recreational activities for youth, and little hiring of minorities in city government, prompted the drive for Chicanos' political empowerment. These issues began to receive more concerted attention from the city council after Simon Salinas took office. One of the first actions of the new city council was to form a citizen task force with broad representation from various segments in the city, with the responsibility to recommend an affordable housing program and funding to meet the General Plan's goal of making 10 percent of all new units affordable to lower-income households. There were 13,200 households, or 40 percent of all city households, estimated to be lower income in 1990. For a family of four, "lower income" was defined as an annual income of less than $23,000.

During 1980–1990, virtually all of the city's single-room occupancy housing and group farmworker housing was lost to building closures or abandonment.[39] The groundbreaking work of the task force was to bear fruit with several housing projects in later years.

Also, the new council hired the city's first Latino city manager, David Mora, who brought experience and an ability to work with different forces to provide a fresh perspective to the city's administration. Mora came from the city of Oxnard, another community with a high percentage of Latinos. One of his accomplishments as Salinas city manager was the hiring of Latino, Asian, and black people to head six of the city's departments. In 1992 Mora noted, "When I was hired as city manager two years ago, I said I would go out and find the best qualified candidates and I also said that these would include more minorities.... I have always been convinced that there are qualified minority candidates out there. I hired the best people available."[40]

The hiring of an experienced Latino city manager and other people of color in management positions, in addition to the election of Latinos, may account for a change in policy benefits for the Latino community. The Robert Lineberry argument that it is primarily changes in government bureaucracy that affect the delivery of services, rather than elections of new public officials, is a serious challenge to the argument that it is primarily the political actor's relationship to the community that determines to what degree benefits are returned to the community.[41] If full-time bureaucrats distribute policy benefits in a colorblind fashion, rather than politicians who serve only on a part-time basis, does electoral empowerment matter? This question will be addressed after the changes in Salinas's government have been explored.

By 1991, a growing gang problem, which had been swept under the rug by previous councils, was addressed by the new city council. The council called a community meeting to hear testimony and gather insights on what to do about the problem. The head of LULAC, Juan Oliverez, spoke to the city council and called for action by the city to address the problem: "One thing's for sure, after the June election, there's going to be more Chicanos up there," which was a reference to the need for a more diverse council.[42]

LULAC, the Alisal Betterment Committee, and other community organizations continued to monitor city government and to fight for issues of concern in the Mexican American community. The election of Simon Salinas to the council of a rapidly growing Latino community, along with the involvement of experienced organizations and leaders, were signs that Salinas' Chicano community was well positioned to further advance Latino political empowerment.

Growing Empowerment, 1991–1993

In 1991, during the next round of elections, a Chicano and a Chicana were added to the Salinas City Council. Fernando Armenta, a Monterey County Medical social worker, ran unopposed in the city's District 1, with a Chicano/Mexican population of 85 percent. The fact that he ran unopposed led some outside the Chicano community to ask pointedly whether there was an "east Salinas political machine and one of its leaders a godfather."[43] This perspective, common among many white voters, did not take into account that Chicano activists had worked together for many years in a careful construction of political campaigns, voter registration drives, and political organization. As Armenta's campaign manager, Jesse Sanchez, commented, there are practical reasons for getting community leaders together: "If you include all of those who are active in the decision-making process, they will support the person who comes out of that process. Everyone had a hand in selecting the person—by everyone, I mean those who are politically active, who walk precincts, who are volunteers.... Because they are a part of the process, they will defend their decision and that's a source of strength."[44]

Armenta was well qualified to be the next Chicano councilperson. He had worked for more than a decade on various campaigns, supporting Simon Salinas's campaign in 1989. He was born and raised in Salinas and had graduated from area schools, including Hartnell Community College. He had returned to the community after obtaining a master's degree in social work in San Jose. The fact that no one ran against him indicated that he commanded broad support from various groups in the community.

Anna Caballero, meanwhile, won in District 6, with a Latino population of only 25 percent. Her election had not been nearly as certain as Armenta's. Caballero, a well-known local attorney, had worked for several years for California Rural Legal Assistance before entering private practice in 1982. She was appointed to the city's planning commission from 1985 to 1989, becoming the first Chicana in any of Salinas's governing bodies. In 1989 she had worked to elect her husband, Juan Uranga, to city council, against Simon Salinas. The 1989 campaign had caused a split among Chicano activists. By 1991, Caballero had moved to another district, the wealthier and more diverse District 6. District 6 had a 10 percent Filipino population in addition to its 25 percent Latino population. Caballero ran a racially inclusive campaign, focusing on issues local residents had in common rather than accentuating the historical exclusion of Latinos from city politics. Caballero said, "This is the beginning of a bridging for Salinas. This is a diverse community. It was an opportunity for Salinas and even though we didn't say that, I think a lot of voters understood it. I think it appealed to many voters, casting a vote for a harmonious town."[45]

Caballero had traveled a distinctly different path to electoral office than that of the other two Chicano council members. Her campaign message was not the Salinas campaign message that a racist power structure controlled local politics and excluded Chicanos. Unlike Armenta and many other community activists, she did not grow up in Salinas; rather, she had come to Salinas to work in the CRLA in the late 1970s. She had witnessed firsthand the mistreatment of farmworkers and worked to defend their rights on the job and in the community. She became involved in politics less for reasons of Chicano empowerment than to bring communities together. Her campaign message was one of racial and class harmony.

For the next two years, these three Chicanos agreed that they would work together on issues of common concern such as affordable housing, the youth and gang problem, and the underrepresentation of Latinos in local government. While at first there were hard feelings and a lack of trust left over from the 1989 election, some of these differences were ameliorated over time in the context of a city council that was still predominantly white, with three white councilmembers elected through the district election system and a white mayor elected citywide.

A Chicano Majority on the City Council

In 1993, Chicanos became the majority on the Salinas City Council, making Salinas the largest city in California with a majority-Latino city council. The biracial electoral coalition that generally leads to the strongest political incorporation was less evident in Salinas than in the cities studied by Rufus Browning, Dale Marshall, and David Tabb,[46] but the results were more substantial. In Salinas, in contrast to the Browning, Marshall, and Tabb model, Chicano activists achieved a council majority by organizing within their neighborhoods and electoral districts to elect progressive Chicanos to office with virtually no support from white voters—except in District 6, where Caballero ran and white voters were the predominant voters. The Latino council majority would not have been possible without Caballero's election in a non-Latino-majority district. Her election proved that Latinas could win office in non-Latino-majority sections of the city and broke down some stereotypes that Latinos could win only in Latino-majority districts and that non-Latinos would not vote for Latinos. This became important later in the decade, when Caballero ran for mayor.

In early 1989, there were no Latinos on the city council; the change in representation within just four years was unprecedented. This change in leadership, which had occurred only after a change in the electoral structure, indicated the symbiotic relationship between structure and agency. Once the structural impediment to change was removed, there was a tangible reason to organize: to win electoral seats. Winning a council majority for Chicanos was achieved not by incumbents winning reelection but rather by the election of two new members. Gloria Reyes won in a close race in District 4, defeating an appointed incumbent, Deloris Higgins. Roberto Ocampo won in District 2, the seat vacated by incumbent Simon Salinas, who decided to seek election to the board of supervisors. The city council now included Caballero, Armenta, Reyes, and Ocampo. Fernando Armenta commented, "I think it will broaden the sensitivity to the Latino community … and the sensitivity to all minorities and all walks of life."[47]

Over the next eight years, Latinos retained their council majority. From 1993 to 1997, only Reyes left the council, and Juan Oliverez, a longtime community activist and professor of ethnic studies at a local college, replaced her in District 4. Mayor Allan Styles continued in the position he had won in 1991, until he stepped down to run for a state assembly seat in 1998.

Latinos and County Offices

In addition to Latino community efforts to win in several district elections in the city, their sights were expanded to other electoral contests, including a campaign to redistrict boundaries for county supervisor seats. Since 1991, Chicano activists had pressured for a redrawing of supervisory boundaries to reflect demographic changes. They were successful in delaying three of five district elections. Chicano community pressure—especially from the La Raza Redistricting Committee, composed of Simon Salinas, Local 890 Teamster Union president Frank Gallegos, and other area activists—was exerted through a united front in numerous hearings and meetings to "review about three dozen maps, a lawsuit, a federal study of various plans, and a ballot measure."[48] The board of supervisors finally caved in, recognizing that they could not hold back the demographic and political changes taking place in the county. A new Monterey County district map for supervisors was drawn up in 1993, and elections were set for later that year.

Chicano community activists, as they had done since the early 1980s, met to discuss who should run for supervisor in District 1, the seat that would afford Chicanos the best opportunity to win election, with a Latino population of 68 percent (see Table 2.2). After the majority of local activists decided to support Jesse Sanchez, the principal organizer and architect of the Chicano empowerment, Salinas decided to run for the same seat. Once again, as in 1989, there was disunity in the Chicano community over whom to support to secure the first seat for a Latino, this time on the board of supervisors. Many longtime activists felt that Salinas had allowed individual advancement to overshadow the community unity needed to achieve Latino political empowerment. Nevertheless, the campaign began, with both sides hurling charges and countercharges.

By the time of the June elections, when the city of Salinas was electing Gloria Reyes and Roberto Ocampo to the city council, the two other Chicano candidates, Salinas and Sanchez, were battling for support and endorsements. Salinas garnered the support of organized labor (including the Central Labor Council, Communication Workers of America Local 9490, and the Building and Construction Trades Council of Monterey and Santa Cruz Counties), the Monterey County Prosecutors Association, North Monterey county growers, and several Chicano community leaders. Sanchez, who was an outspoken voice for farmworkers' rights, carried the support of most of the Chicano activists who formed the core of the Alisal Betterment Association and who believed it was Sanchez's turn to seek higher office.

Following the June primary, a runoff was set for August 3, 1993. After initially planning to run, Sanchez decided to withdraw from the race, citing the divisive nature of the campaign in the Chicano community. Salinas went on to win, thereby becoming the first Mexican American to hold a board of supervisors seat in the twentieth century. Chicano activists who had sought to change the face of not only city government but county government as well were cognizant of the progress that had been made; however, they wondered, at what cost? How significant was the division that had developed between Salinas and Sanchez? Did this represent the end of the Chicano community's efforts to work together for Latino empowerment, or was it a reflection of the diversity of candidates and views within the Chicano political community?

TABLE 2.2 Monterey County Supervisor Districts

District	Total Population	% Latino	% Black	% NativeAmerican	% Asian/Pacific	% White
1	67,095	68	2	1	3	26
2	71,634	22	6	0	8	63
3	72,165	62	4	0.4	1	32.6
4	72,540	12	8	1	0.2	78.8
5	72,125	7	10	1	5	77
Total	335,560	34	6	1	3	59

Source: Salinas Californian (August 21, 1992), p. 1.

Chicano activists were not content with electing one of their own to the board of supervisors. Another arena that did not reflect the changing demographics in the county was the judicial system. A key issue was to change the boundaries for municipal court judges, since while 33 percent of the county was Latino at the time, all nine municipal court judges were white. As community activist Jesse Sanchez commented, "Any institution, at least in our form of government, must reflect the community in which it functions.... Only when that happens do people truly feel it represents them."[49] The issue arose because Monterey County consolidated two municipal court and seven justice court districts into a single municipal court. Judges in the resulting court were elected on an at-large basis and served the entire community.

A lawsuit was filed in 1991 that claimed that Monterey County had violated the federal Voting Rights Act. The plaintiffs argued that the system robbed minorities of their voting strength and that none had been elected for decades. Their legal argument, however, was that Monterey County had failed to seek the approval of the U.S. Justice Department before consolidating the districts. Under the Voting Rights Act, Monterey County is one of four California counties required to clear any voting practice changes. It had become subject to federal oversight after under 50 percent of its voters took part in the 1968 presidential election (Yuba, Merced, and Kings counties were also subject to this ruling).

In October 1993, the board of supervisors agreed to split the 1994 judicial elections among seven districts. Civil rights attorney Joaquin Avila, who had been instrumental in challenging Salinas's city wide electoral system and redrawing the Monterey County Board of Supervisors district lines to reflect changing demographics in the county, viewed the board's decision to establish district elections of municipal court judges "the first victory in a statewide battle to reshape judicial elections."[50]

The issue of district elections for judges remained controversial. In 1994, there were no people of color on the municipal court bench. In 1995, Lydia Villarreal was appointed to the municipal court bench by then governor Pete Wilson. She was an attorney for eight years with the California Rural Legal Services in the 1980s; she then worked for the Monterey County District Attorney's Office from 1989 until her appointment. But Judge Villarreal was forced to run for office almost immediately after her appointment, as part of the settlement of a suit alleging that the county had discriminated against Hispanic voters by consolidating a multiplicity of municipal and other local courts into a countywide court of limited jurisdiction.[51]

In 1995, in a court-ordered special election in a Latino-majority single-judge district, longtime Chicano community activist attorney Jose Angel Velasquez defeated Villarreal in a tight race. Velasquez was the first Latino to be elected to the county's municipal court (in 2000, he became a superior court judge following the unification of all county courts). He has remained on the bench and continues to advocate for farmworkers, the poor, and youth. Villarreal was later appointed to another seat on the bench in Monterey County in 2001 by then Governor Grey Davis.

City Jobs and Affirmative Action

The argument put forward by Marshall, Browning, and Tabb that following the ascent to power of minorities, the spoils of power, including the power to hire and appoint for city jobs, pass into the hands of those in power,[52] is substantiated in the city of Salinas. Salinas has had a long and controversial history of not hiring and appointing people of color and women. In 1980, after pressure by Chicano activists, the mayor and city council adopted the city's first formal affirmative action plan (AAP). The AAP included the following guidelines: "1) flexible and narrowly-tailored hiring/promotion goals designed to remedy prior discriminatory employment practices that had caused it to underutilize women and minority group members; and 2) EEO [Equal Employment Opportunity] policies designed to achieve a work environment free of discrimination on the basis of disability, race, national origin, sex, or age."[53]

Even though there was an AAP in place, Chicano activists filed several civil rights and employment discrimination complaints regarding the lack of hiring of minorities, particularly in positions not traditionally held by minorities, such as professionals, key management staff, and department heads. In one instance reflecting the vestiges of institutional discrimination, the city paid out $453,000 in 1993 to four firefighters to settle a civil rights lawsuit. The firefighters were of different races and genders, but the common charge was that discriminatory behavior and sexual harassment were not being dealt with by the city's fire department.

When Dave Mora was hired as city manager in 1990, he became the first person of color in this critical position. Mora vowed to hire more minorities in city government. By 1992, Mora had made good on his promise by hiring Latinos, Asians, and blacks to head six departments. He also hired Latinos for the positions of fire marshal and police captain.[54] Table 2.3 illustrates the change in demographics of city employment between 1975 and 1996.

It is apparent from the figures in Table 2.3 that Latinos, Asians, and women have benefited from the change in city hiring policies, whereas white males have seen their percentage share of the total workforce decrease dramatically. In 1994, the city's workforce was composed of 39.8 percent women and minority employees. This reflects a 13 percent increase of women and minorities hired and/or promoted since 1980.[55]

What types of jobs, however, have Latinos and women obtained? In 1994, the city of Salinas undertook a revision of its affirmative action plan. Based on local civilian labor force statistics in the 1990 U.S. census, the city had an overall goal of 45.4 percent representation of women and minorities. The 1994 report noted, "Despite its EEO progress in the last 13 years, the City's evidence shows that prior discrimination continues to have an adverse impact upon the selection of women and minorities for employment and promotion."[56]

In the broad categories of office/clerical, paraprofessional, service/maintenance, and skilled craft, there was minority representation of 43–59 percent. However, these numbers are deceiving when it comes to Latino representation, the majority population in the city. In the skilled craft and technician categories, Latinos were 25 and 26 percent respectively; thus some activists pointed out that Latinos were still underrepresented in the higher-paying skilled positions in the city. Also, Latinos held only three positions, or 15 percent, of the top-level administrator positions, albeit two of these were the key positions of city manager and assistant city manager. Thus Latino political power in the city bureaucracy had brought advances in total overall hiring; however, their political power was concentrated at the top, in the city manager and assistant city manager positions.

The hiring of those historically underrepresented for city jobs will continue to be controversial, particularly since the passage of California's anti-affirmative action law in 1996 that banned implementing hiring goals based on race, sex, or other categories. An affirmative action officer had attempted to aggressively challenge the hiring practices and institutional discrimination but faced a wall of indifference by other city officials; this person's departure in the mid-1990s did not bode well for quick solutions. Further, Salinas is governed by a civil service system that protects job security, so it is extremely difficult to remove high-ranking administrators from office, except for major malfeasance.

TABLE 2.3 **Salinas Workforce Comparison**

	1976		1984		1996		Percentage + or -, 1976–1996
	Number	Percent	Number	Percent	Number	Percent	
Latino	72	13.32	93	18.00	177	30.5	+17.18
African American	13	2.40	14	2.5	17	3.00	+0.60
Asian	27	4.99	47	8.50	20	3.45	+4.01
White	425	78.62	368	69.00	327	56.40	-22.22
Indian	3	0.55	5	1.00	6	1.00	+0.45
Total	540	100.00	528	100.00	580	100.00	
Male	432	80.00	412	78.00	411	59.00	-21
Female	108	20.00	115	22.00	169	41.00	+ 21

Source: Personnel director, City of Salinas (1996).

These institutional factors are difficult to change; however, in the years since the inclusion of Latinos, both elected and appointed, in city government, the dynamics of Salinas's city government *have* changed. More bilingual and bicultural staff have been hired, particularly in positions where there is direct public contact. Previously, Spanish-speaking members of the community had a difficult time communicating when they needed city services. In addition, there was diversity training for all city employees in 1994. The city's affirmative action commission had told the city council that the city's growing multiculturalism makes it important for city employees to understand different cultures and ethnicities. Commission members pointed out that the more city employees know about the public and each other, the more effective they can be. Chairwoman Helen Sicalbo said, "Salinas is what all of California's going to be by the end of the century, our diversity is going to impact our services.... It makes good business sense."[57]

Besides hiring goals and diversity training, there was more scrutiny to make sure that the process of hiring and promotions is fair. The city's affirmative action commission (now equal employment opportunity commission) has been proactive in overseeing the hiring process to make sure that there is no bias in the selection process. Yet institutional changes in non-elected positions can be slower than the process of electoral change. Salinas had an almost all-white administration in the 1980s. By the mid-1990s, there had been dramatic changes; but change has not come quickly enough for many in the Latino community, who believe that the face of government is only the start of real changes that must occur. Nevertheless, in the year 2000, according to the city's Equal Employment Opportunity Plan, the workforce "is now composed of 59.8% women and minority employees. This reflects a 24.8% increase in women and minorities hired and/or promoted since ... 1984 when the City workforce was only 35% women and minorities."[58]

Economic Development Efforts and Latinos

The case of Salinas indicates that though there has been political progress, local economic development for the Latino community has not traveled a parallel track. Should a local government have a role in economic development? Does the election of a particular segment of a city—in this case Latinos—mean that this segment will benefit in terms of economic development?

Political power and economic power are not the same. The thesis of this chapter is that grassroots politicians will be able to return more benefits to their constituents than will politicians, who are primarily concerned with their own political and economic interests. In Salinas, by all accounts, the Chicanos elected in the first wave of Latino electoral empowerment were liberal to progressive in their politics; all of them ran grassroots campaigns and had strong ties to their community. They were not from the business community and did not run expensive, limited-voter-contact campaigns. An assessment of the actions of the new political leaders in Salinas is important to determine whether in fact grassroots politicians have provided benefits to the Mexican American community that it would not have received under an administration that did not have Latino representation.

In the context of an economy that is based primarily on agriculture, with large numbers of mostly Latino seasonal farm labor and tourist industry workers, what role does local government play in relation to the local economy? Specifically, was there a change in local economic development policy following the changes in local government after Latinos ascended to power? An examination of land usage, housing, and redevelopment indicates that in the 1990s the city council was active in shaping a direction for the city's economic development that directly benefited the Latino community.

The Salinas Redevelopment Agency (SRA) is directed by the Salinas City Council, which acts as the agency's board. The agency and council set goals that clearly reflect a concern for the needs of Salinas's Latino community. In 1996 these goals included working with the Hispanic Chamber of Commerce and the Alisal Merchants Association, using a central city tax increment and other inter-fund transfers, to develop an economic development plan for the East Salinas area and to develop farmworker housing in Salinas in cooperation with agricultural and other private interests.[59]

An analysis of the work of the SRA indicates that redevelopment has been used, as in many other cities, to improve a blighted downtown area, with funding for an updated intermodal transportation center and the construction of a tourist and educational museum dedicated to John Steinbeck. In addition, the SRA established funding for annexation and development of a retail shopping area in the Boronda section, which lies outside of the city's boundaries. However, in contrast to the usual focus on downtown development, the Salinas SRA helped eliminate blight in the heavily Mexican community of East Salinas, using public and private investment to improve the exterior facade of the area and supporting local community development without tearing down badly needed existing housing. What began in 1970 as a small redevelopment project on one block of Sunset Avenue in East Salinas was expanded in the 1990s into a broader program of community revitalization. This expanded role for East Salinas's redevelopment was directed by the Latino-majority city council. The SRA was also involved with implementing a farmworker housing assistance program, using $1 million set aside by the city council in 1993.

Redevelopment, in the hands of a liberal to progressive Chicano-majority city government, has redirected tax increment funds to improve predominantly Latino East Salinas, as well as to more traditional redevelopment projects. This kind of redevelopment was not undertaken by administrations of the 1970s and 1980s. This is a significant and observable change from the programs of previous probusiness city councils, whose development was carried out haphazardly, with no attempt to improve the economic well-being of the Latino community.

While the use of city resources to benefit the Latino community was evident during the Latino-majority era, the systemic problem of low wages endemic to the agricultural, tourist, and retail industries was not challenged. Instead, elected officials sought other means to improve the lives of the working poor. One means to address this problem was to build more affordable housing.

Building Affordable Housing in a Hot Housing Market

In 1993, following the election of a Latino council majority, $2 million out of the $5.4 million in housing funds obtained was directed toward farmworker and large family housing. The goal was to build more housing for low-income farmworker families. The city council consciously directed the housing funds toward those in greatest need. As one member said, "Who are the people with the greatest need? I think we should be giving to that greatest need."[60] Where in the 1980s the priority of the probusiness council was the building of expensive new subdivisions, the new council focused on building housing for low-income farmworker families. The result has been the approval of more affordable-housing money and the building of more units than at any other time. The building of more affordable housing units that accommodate large low-income families is directly related to the change in the composition of the city council, as new Chicano members made this issue a high priority and made sure that resources were directed toward those in need.

However, the demand for affordable housing in the city still exceeds the supply. Even with strenuous efforts, there is not nearly enough housing for farmworkers and other low-wage workers who have been drawn to the region. As Frank Brunings, Monterey County housing coordinator, said, "There is an incredible need for low-income housing based on the kind of industries growing in Monterey County. If you take a look at the kind of industries we have, they are all predicated on low-wage workers."[61] To illustrate the lack of affordable housing in this city, in 1998 the Monterey Housing Authority, which uses federal funds to provide low-income housing, had a 7,000-name waiting list. Also, the Monterey County nonprofit housing developer, the Community Housing Improvement Improvement Systems and Planning Association (CHISPA), which began in 1980, had built 460 units in Salinas by 2001 and received more than 12,000 applications for residency in these units. By 2004, CHISPA had constructed 1,600 affordable housing units in Monterey County, Watsonville, and Santa Cruz, many of them in rural, heavily farmworker communities. The need for affordable housing is illustrated by the fact that Salinas is one of the least affordable housing markets in the nation. According to the Monterey County Association of Realtors, local residents earn a median income of $55,600 a year, meaning that they can afford only 49 percent of a medium-priced home of $460,000.[62]

The directing of city funds to address the affordable-housing needs of large families, farmworker families, and the elderly involved new programs. These programs reflected increased city government awareness of the urgency of meeting Salinas's affordable-housing problem. The change in policy direction toward greater efforts at constructing more affordable housing began in 1990, with the establishment of a citizen housing task force that was spearheaded by Chicano community activists.

Voter Registration and Grassroots Participation, 1998–2002

Starting in 1998, a number of important changes have had long-term significance for local Latino and regional politics in Salinas. In 1998, Anna Caballero ran for mayor of Salinas and was victorious. Caballero was the first Latina elected mayor in the city's history. Her image as a consensus builder with good relations with the different segments of the city enabled her to win this office easily. She was conscious of her role as a woman in the campaign; as she said, "It's been a challenge for women to put themselves in leadership positions, and it's been a challenge for me."[63]

With the demise of ABC in 1993, there was no central grassroots organization to unite community activists to work out who would run for various electoral offices. The emergence of several potential qualified candidates, with limited loyalties to one another, and the lack of a strong local political machine to keep candidates and officeholders in check have led to a more fluid process, with new challengers emerging to compete against veteran politicians as seats open up. The new dynamics were evident in the campaign of Latina Sandra Pizarro for an open state assembly seat against the highest-ranking local Latino official, County Supervisor Simon Salinas. Pizarro, the daughter of a local restaurant owner, had lived outside the area for many years and built a political career in Sacramento. She returned to run for this seat with the backing of the Latino caucus of the California state legislature. Simon Salinas's strong ties to a local base of support brought defeat to Pizarro in the Democratic Party primary, but her candidacy indicated that people outside the local area now viewed the city of Salinas's politics as important enough to attempt to influence its outcome.

This competitive trend within Latino politics had begun with the race for the first district election for Salinas City Council in 1989, when two Latinos, Uranga and Salinas, competed for the same seat, and continued in 1993, with the competition for the Monterey County supervisor seat between two Latino community activists, Sanchez and Salinas. Today individuals deciding to run for office do so of their own volition, without a local political organization that decides who, among all potential candidates, would best represent the community's interests. Instead, individual political leaders may serve as informal mentors to those who seek elected office.

In the absence of ABC, new organizations have emerged to participate in Latino politics. One organization was launched in the mid-1990s as an outgrowth of a local Teamsters union. As noted earlier, the Teamsters Union Local 890 has had a long presence in the Salinas Valley, with food-processing and farmworker contracts dating back decades. In the 1980s the Latino-majority rank and file, led by Frank Gallegos, elected their own leaders. In 1995, the Central Coast Citizenship Project was launched by the Teamsters Local to help its members become citizens. The citizenship project soon expanded and has been instrumental in assisting thousands of Salinas-area immigrants who have become naturalized citizens.[64] The citizenship project has spawned several other organizations, including a youth group, an organization of ex-braceros, a women's group, and Vote, a membership-based Latino political action committee that combines policy work with advocacy. Vote does voter registration work and endorses candidates for local and state office as well as state propositions.

An important labor group active in Latino politics is the UFW; while it continues to organize workers, it also endorses candidates who support its members' issues and concerns. More important, it employs sophisticated electoral campaign operations using experienced local operatives who were instrumental, for example, in helping to elect prolabor candidate Fernando Armenta for Monterey County supervisor in 2000 against a well-funded Republican candidate. In the same year, they worked for the election of Simon Salinas for the Twenty-eighth Assembly seat.

Salinas's election was another milestone for the Latino community. After defeating Pizarro in the primary, Salinas won the general election against a well-funded Republican opponent. This seat had been held for the previous six years by a conservative Republican rancher, Peter Frusetta. The district spanned the tricounty region of San Benito, Monterey, and Santa Cruz and included the cities of Hollister, King City, and Watsonville, where large numbers of Latinos resided, but also rural areas where Republican voting was strong. Salinas defeated Jeff Denham by a 52 to 43 percent margin. Assembly member Salinas is the highest-ranking Latino from this region and demonstrates the growth of Latino political power in elected office.

The systemic problems of low wages, limited affordable housing, and economic control by agribusiness and tourism industries will not be solved overnight. Achieving political power and gaining control over economic resources are not the same. Finding ways to use government influence to challenge economic elites to provide better pay and working conditions and convince surrounding wealthy communities to redistribute economic resources to provide housing and badly needed social services is a new phase in a long struggle for social justice in the Salinas community.

Conclusion

Salinas is a case study of how a well-organized and determined community of people with popular candidates and salient issues has been effective in achieving political representation and political power in a short period of time. Through community effort, observable changes in nearly every facet of city government life have taken place. In the experience of Salinas Chicanos, local grassroots political actors have indeed been able to return greater policy benefits and resources to the community than did the previous all-white administrations.

Also, this study recognizes that movement toward political incorporation is a dynamic and complex process that ebbs and flows. The internal strife that developed within the Alisal Betterment Committee in 1993 over support for different candidates for county supervisor has not healed. The ABC has not been replaced by a comparable community organization of activists. Other community-based organizations and unions, including LULAC, Vote, Teamsters Local 893, UFW, and the Service Employees International Union (SEIU), have stepped up their political activities. Further advances in political incorporation in the Salinas area hinge on the ability of local Mexican American political actors to continue working together on policy that benefits the Latino community. Differences among political actors over who can best represent the community will remain a sore point, but they need not overshadow the political gains made since the late 1980s. The political incorporation efforts by a diverse group of communtiy activists are a model for how to achieve political power and then expand to win a wide range of elected and appointed positions at different levels of government. Collectively, they have transformed the political landscape in the region and in doing so have taken a small step toward the broader goal of full inclusion of the U.S. Latino community.

The experience of local political activists in Salinas is not unique to this community; rather, it reflects the potential of Latino politics in similarly situated communities. Efforts to build and achieve strong political incorporation are being undertaken in countless communities around the United States where Latinos are a growing segment of the population. The efforts of Chicano activists to become community leaders and civic leaders within local governing coalitions is instructive for practitioners of Latino politics elsewhere.

Notes

1. California (2002a).
2. J. Steinbeck (1937a).
3. J. Steinbeck (1937b).
4. J. Steinbeck (1952).
5. J. Levy (1975); R. Taylor (1975); M. Wells (1996).
6. Salinas (1960), p. 1.
7. U.S. Bureau of the Census (1960).
8. C. Guerin-Gonzales (1994), p. 129; J. Gomez Quinones (1994), p. 139.
9. R. Acuña(1988).
10. R.Taylor (1975), pp. 251–253.
11. C. E. Daniels (1995), pp. 392–393.
12. R.Taylor (1975), p. 259.
13. Ibid., p. 261.
14. C. E. Daniels (1995), p. 392.
15. Mike Johnston, business agent, Teamsters Local 890, personal interview (September 19, 1998).
16. "Latinos at Last Get Foot in Political Door," *Monterey Herald*, September 7, 1992, p. 2c.
17. Ibid.
18. W. Flores (1992).
19. *Salinas Californian*, February 2, 1987, p. 1.
20. Ibid.
21. *Salinas Californian*, June 3, 1987, p. 1.
22. *Salinas Californian*, July 10, 1987, p. 1.
23. *Salinas Californian*, April 22, 1988, p. 1.
24. "Latinos at Last Get Foot in Political Door," *Monterey Herald*, September 7, 1992, p. 2c.
25. W. Flores (1992).
26. Ibid.

27. *Salinas Californian,* October 12, 1988, p. 1.

28. *Salinas Californian,* November 22, 1988, p. 1.

29. *Salinas Californian,* December 7, 1988, p. 1.

30. W. Flores (1992).

31. W. Flores (1992).

32. *Salinas Californian,* May 26, 1989, p. 1.

33. *Salinas Californian,* June 5, 1989, p. 1.

34. W. Flores (1992).

35. *Register Pajaronian,* June 8, 1989, p. 1.

36. *Salinas Californian,* September 15, 1992, p. 1.

37. R. Lineberry (1977).

38. P. Peterson (1981).

39. Salinas (1991).

40. "Latinos at Last Get Foot in Political Door," *Monterey Herald,* September 7, 1992, p. 2c.

41. R. Lineberry (1977).

42. *Salinas Californian,* January 29, 1991, p. 1.

43. *Salinas Californian,* April 20, 1991, p. 1.

44. Ibid.

45. *Salinas Californian,* June 5, 1991, p. 1.

46. R. Browning, D. Marshall, and D. Tabb (1984).

47. *Salinas Californian,* June 12, 1993, p. 1.

48. *Salinas Californian,* May 6, 1993, p. 1.

49. *Salinas Californian,* October 7, 1993, p. 1.

50. Ibid.

51. *Metropolitan News-Enterprise,* October 3, 2001, p. 3.

52. R. Browning, D. Marshall, and D. Tabb (1990).

53. Salinas (1994).

54. "Latinos at Last Get Foot in Political Door," *Monterey Herald,* September 7, 1992, p. 2c.

55. Salinas (1994).

56. Ibid.

57. *Salinas Californian,* September 7, 1994, p. 1.

58. Salinas (n.d.), p. 1.

59. Salinas (1996–97).

60. *Salinas Californian,* September 29, 1993, p. 1.

61. *Coast Weekly,* January 15, 1998, p. 14.

62. *Salinas Californian,* "CHISPA Builds Dreams: Agency Celebrates 25 Years of Helping Renters Build Homes for Their Families," February 1, 2005, p. 1.

63. R. Pitnick (1998).

64. R. Crocker (2000).

They Keep Coming

The Tangled Roots of Proposition 187

DANIEL MARTINEZ HOSANG

O n January 5, 1994, readers of the *Los Angeles Times* opened their morning paper to a front-page article on the status of several initiative petitions attempting to qualify for the upcoming primary and general elections. A lagging economy, reticent donors, and the lack of substantive issues, experts agreed, had slowed the number of initiatives likely to qualify to a trickle. While some twenty initiative petitions were still in circulation, the *Times* explained, "virtually all of them appear to lack significant political and financial support." "It's a bleak year," declared Mike Arno, of American Petition Consultants. His firm's effort to qualify a measure that would sentence repeat felony offenders to life in prison had been forced to suspend its paid signature gathering after proponents ran out of cash a month earlier. A measure sponsored by former Los Angeles County supervisor Pete Schabarum to eliminate medical care for undocumented immigrants was receiving only "questionable enthusiasm." Schabarum conceded that his fundraising and political support was floundering. Buried in the article's closing paragraphs was a two-sentence mention of an initiative petition sponsored by two former high-ranking Immigration and Naturalization Service (INS) officials, Alan Nelson and Harold Ezell, to "expel illegal immigrants from public schools." Unrelated to the Schabarum effort, it also had not received any large donations. California Republican Party strategists, activists, and donors seemed to be paying little attention to these initiatives, focusing instead on the upcoming gubernatorial election—Republican incumbent Pete Wilson's approval ratings had hovered in the midthirties for the last two years—as well as trying to pry a few seats away from the Democrats solid hold on the state assembly and senate. As Tony Miller, the chief deputy secretary of state observed, as far as initiative issues were concerned, 1994 seemed to be "a light year in terms of substantive and weighty measures."[1]

The political developments that erupted over the next ten months confounded nearly every one of these predictions. While the measure sponsored by Schabarum never reached the ballot, the more far-reaching immigration restriction measure by Ezell and Nelson qualified for the November election as Proposition 187. The initiative passed by eighteen percentage points after a tumultuous and deeply polarizing campaign. Proposition 187's far-reaching mandate—to make alleged violations of federal immigration status grounds for denying all public benefits, education, and health services and to require all public employees to report anyone *suspected* of such violations to federal authorities—immediately reordered the landscape for immigration policy debates nationally. Though the courts eventually ruled that most of the measure's operating provisions were unlawful, many of the initiative's animating ideas found their way into the overhaul of federal welfare and immigration policies over the next two years. On the same ballot as Proposition 187, the criminal-sentencing initiative, Proposition 184, dubbed "Three Strikes and You're Out" won 72 percent of the vote.[2] The legislation would extend the sentences of tens of thousands of Californians over the next fifteen years, including at least 8,200 condemned to spend the rest of their lives inside one of the state's eighteen maximum-security prisons, and it further heightened enormous racial disparities within the criminal justice system.[3]

To be sure, much about California was rapidly changing as Proposition 187 marched toward the ballot: the state's job and tax base shrunk dramatically, housing values in many neighborhoods plummeted, poverty rates and income inequality skyrocketed, and the state's demographic profile changed considerably. Immigration from Latin America and Asia helped drive a 25 percent increase in the California's overall population during the 1980s, while the non-Hispanic white proportion fell from 71 to 59 percent.[4] The conflagration and turmoil in May 1992 following the acquittal of the Los Angeles police officers accused of beating motorist Rodney King and the trial of O.J. Simpson in early 1994 sharpened the sense that divisions of race, class, and opportunity in California ran deep.[5]

While a souring economy may have legitimated the resolutions offered by Proposition 187 in particular ways, these circumstances alone did not produce the measure. Nor did the initiative pass solely because of an inexorable reaction to demographic transformations. Specific political actors and institutions, armed with evolving and often contradictory ideas and political objectives, labored for many years to make immigration restriction the subject of popular debate. To be sure, many of these actors, like the proponents of the English Only ballot measures explored in chapter 5, marshaled long-standing constructions of Mexican immigrants in particular as racially and culturally subordinate.

But the effort also incorporated ideas about individual worthiness and national belonging embraced by a broad range of political figures, including many self-identified liberals.[6]

As much as any measure in this book, the Proposition 187 contest reveals how an issue shaped by an array of contradictory and ambivalent attitudes became almost singularly framed by the expectations of political whiteness through an initiative campaign. This effect was evident in remarks made by Governor Wilson in his press conference the morning after the election. Triumphantly celebrating his fifteen-point victory over Democratic challenger Kathleen Brown, but mindful of the accusations of racism and xenophobia he and other Proposition 187 supporters faced during the campaign, Wilson proclaimed, "There is no room in California for bigotry or discrimination....California remains a state of compassion and tolerance.... This is a state of opportunity." Wilson then announced he was suspending a program that provided prenatal care for low-income women without regard to their immigration status because it violated the exclusions promised by Proposition 187.[7] How did it come to be that a state that had just declared a significant portion of its residents to be civically dead—void of any publicly recognizable rights to food, education, shelter, or medicine—could simultaneously celebrate its own "compassion and tolerance"? What social, cultural, and political forces permitted this seeming paradox to be embraced by such a wide portion of the state's body politic?

The Birth of Proposition 187

The group that met on October 5, 1993, at the opulent members-only Center Club in the Orange County city of Costa Mesa to draft what would become Proposition 187 could not be easily described as a coherent or well- developed political movement. Some of the participants had long-standing relationships, but the group as a whole did not have a history of working together, nor did they share a common organizational base or even a common political affiliation, though several had ties to the state and county GOP. In fact, the group largely disbanded soon after the initiative was drafted and then publicly feuded with one another in the weeks before the election, eventually leaving the campaign more than $200,000 in debt.

The October meeting was convened by Robert Kielty, a forty-six-year-old Republican political consultant and a former chair of the Orange County Republican Party, along with his wife, Barbara Kielty, age forty-seven and the mayor of the wealthy enclave of Yorba Linda. Also at the table were Ronald Prince, a forty-six-year-old accountant from nearby Tustin who had been a registered voter for only three years; Barbara Coe, sixty, another political neophyte, who published an immigrant-restrictionist newsletter from her home in Huntington Beach; Alan Nelson and Harold Ezell, two high-ranking INS officials under President Reagan; and Richard Mountjoy, a Republican assemblyman from Monrovia, a suburb east of Los Angeles.

Prince had approached the Kieltys a few months earlier after claiming he had been defrauded of $500,000 by a business partner he contended was an "illegal alien from Canada." (Court records would later reveal that the man in question had been a legal U.S. resident since 1961.) Prince had drafted his own homespun petition, asking, "Do you believe illegal immigration is a problem in California?" and stood outside a Von's supermarket near his home in the small Orange County city of Tustin to collect signatures. Prince found the response to be overwhelming, explaining that "with each signature came a story" about how "illegal immigration" was "affecting California just about everywhere they could see."[8]

Robert Kielty, sensing a potential opportunity for his consultancy, eventually contacted Ezell, a Newport Beach businessman who had parlayed his role as a Republican fund-raiser into an appointment as the INS's western commissioner, overseeing the nation's busiest ports of entry, though he lacked any experience related to immigration policy. Ezell brought in Nelson, his former boss at the INS, who was currently working for the Federation for American Immigration Reform as a lobbyist in Sacramento, and Coe, a civilian employee of the Anaheim Police Department. Coe, described in one account as possessing "an apocalyptic vision of the world that is all exclamation points and question marks," was connected to an expanding network of grassroots immigration-restriction organizations in the area.[9]

After extensive discussions at the October 5 meeting, the group decided that a ballot initiative would be the most promising avenue for their multiple legislative priorities. A ballot measure had the advantage of generating the kind of "massive public attention" that a legislative effort could not, and it would not be subject to the same sort of compromises.[10] In addition, a ballot measure could incorporate a broader set of policies reflecting the varying priorities of those in the group. For example, Mountjoy wanted a provision regarding criminal penalties for the fraudulent use of social security cards, drivers' licenses, and other government documents. Coe insisted that the grassroots immigration-restriction activists she represented would only circulate the measure if it mandated the exclusion of undocumented children from public schools. Coe and others hoped this controversial clause would provoke a legal challenge to the 1982 Supreme Court ruling in *Plyer v. Doe,* which invalidated a Texas school district effort to enact a similar ban. Nelson, a long-standing fiscal conservative, viewed the elimination of public benefits as the top priority.[11]

Once the committee gave its final approval to the language in early November, Nelson and Ezell assumed the public face of the campaign as the authors and sponsors of the petition, though Ezell in particular contributed only a few words to the measure. The final text of the measure incorporated an ambitious set of policy proposals that just a few years earlier could only be found in the communications of FAIR and other stridently restrictionist organizations. It included additions to the state's Penal Code, Welfare and Institutions Code, Health and Safety Code, Education Code, and Government Code that would implement the specified bans on public education (including post-secondary education), health services, and public benefits, along with the new criminal penalties for document forgery. In addition, the measure required all law enforcement officers to fully cooperate with the INS and state attorney general in reporting persons suspected of immigration violations, and it required all public entities or those receiving state funding, including hospitals, schools, and social service programs, to similarly verify the immigration status of anyone attempting to use their services. Public schools were additionally obligated to check the immigration status of all students who were enrolled or were attempting to enroll, as well as the status of each of their parents or guardians; the measure required the expulsion within ninety days of any student whose status (or that of the their parents or guardians) could not be verified or who was "reasonably suspected" of being in violation of federal immigration laws. Finally, every school in the University of California, California State University, and the 109-campus California Community College systems would be required to verify the immigration or citizenship status of every student enrolled; the institutions would have to repeat such verification for all three million students at the beginning of every term or semester and prohibit any student who did not comply. No due process or appeals provisions were included; a determination of suspicion alone was adequate grounds for the denial of services and referral to state and federal authorities.[12]

The formal title of the initiative conferred by the secretary of state when it was approved for circulation in January 1994—"Illegal Aliens. Ineligibility for Public Services. Verification and Reporting"—sounded a bureaucratic tone. The proponents, however, announced their effort as the Save Our State, or S.O.S., initiative, a moniker reinforced by the opening paragraphs of the measure:

> The People of California find and declare as follows:
>
> That they have suffered and are suffering economic hardship caused by the presence of illegal aliens in this state.
>
> That they have suffered and are suffering personal injury and damage caused by the criminal conduct of illegal aliens in this state.
>
> That they have a right to the protection of their government from any person or persons entering this country unlawfully.[13]

This central narrative—the "suffering" and "hardship" of an innocent populace at the hands of lawbreaking intruders—came to singularly define the campaign over the next twelve months. It was a message that resonated powerfully and immediately with the electorate; the first polling done on the measure in late March 1994, in the midst of the signature-gathering effort, found that 62 percent of registered voters declared they would support the initiative, while only 32 percent said they would oppose it, a margin that would persist for most of the campaign.[14]

Before Proposition 187, an immigration-restriction measure had not appeared on the California ballot since 1920, when voters approved a measure to restrict "aliens ineligible for citizenship" from owning land, primarily targeting Japanese American farmers.[15] Indeed, even as the number of both authorized and unauthorized immigrants in California grew dramatically during the late 1980s and early 1990s—including an estimated 42 percent jump in the number of unauthorized residents between 1988 and 1992 alone—public opinion polls consistently found that immigration ranked relatively low in comparison to other public policy concerns. In six statewide polls conducted between May 1991 and August 1993, for example, immigration was never cited by more than 5 percent of respondents as the most important problem facing the state, far below issues such as crime, the economy, and education.[16] Yet by the November 1994 election, some 48 percent of Orange County voters would identify immigration as the most important issue shaping their voting preferences, far outpacing any other option.[17]

Restrictionist organizations like FAIR had labored since the late 1970s to find the public language, frameworks, and policy demands that would allow immigration to become a source of legitimate public debate, failing much more often than they triumphed. In Congress during the 1980s, as immigration scholar Daniel Tichenor explains, "the political processes favoring a decidedly pro-immigration regime were overwhelming."[18] Political pressure from agribusiness and manufacturing interests in the West and Southwest and from civil rights activists nationally— including a growing Latino advocacy community—rebuffed any attempts to lower aggregate immigration levels. In signing the 1986 Immigration Reform and Control Act—which implemented a limited battery of sanctions targeting employers who failed to verify the legal status of their workforce and also provided amnesty to more than two million undocumented persons already in the country—President Reagan praised the newly secured opportunities "to improve the lives of a class of individuals who now must hide in the shadows, without access to many of the benefits of a free and open society."[19] While there was certainly national media coverage focused on "illegal aliens" as a political, cultural, and economic threat, and prominent figures inside and outside Washington called for greater restriction, these efforts did not culminate in any decisive policy victories.[20]

Immigration-Control Groups Ready for Battle

During this period, it was a series of grassroots restrictionist organizations that emerged in Southern California that helped incubate the unflinching criticism of immigration that animated Proposition 187. Since Harold Ezell's and Alan Nelson's tenures at the INS in the late 1980s, these groups had become increasingly active in the white suburban communities of San Diego, Orange, and Los Angeles counties and often had loose affiliations with FAIR or other national restrictionist groups.[21] Fueled by their relative proximity to the border and long-standing commitments to "taxpayer" and "homeowner" rights, they were the first to denounce new entrants as deviant and criminal, the proverbial "bad immigrant" subjects discussed in chapter 5.

In early 1992, Bill King, who had retired from his position as Border Patrol chief under Ezell, a political ally, set out to find like-minded champions for immigration restriction. He soon met Barbara

Coe, who like many early activists cited "billions of tax dollars ... being put out to illegal aliens" in explaining her motivation. Coe and King decided to convene a meeting in nearby Costa Mesa and placed a classified ad in the *National Review* to recruit people who had "been victims of crimes either financial (welfare, unemployment, food stamps, etc.), educational (overcrowding, forced bilingual classes, etc.) or physical (rape, robbery, assault, infectious disease, etc.) committed by illegal aliens."[22]

The meetings that followed established the membership base of Citizens for Action Now. Participants, primarily white, middle-aged residents of Orange County, echoed Coe's accounts of fiscal decline elaborated through cultural alienation. Their testimonies connected stories of personal loss and injury—of medical and education benefits denied, fear of crime and violence, neighborhoods lost to "marauders"—to the racial transformation of their communities. They focused relentlessly on the suffering of law-abiding, hardworking, taxpaying citizens who were "literally being inundated" by a lawbreaking class of "illegals" whose degraded and criminal behavior they were forced to sub-sidize.[23] Often expressed in gendered terms, they fixated on Latina women as rogue reproducers and deviants whose presence threatened the cultural stability of the nation. Indeed, many of FAIR's founders emerged out of the reproductive rights and population-control movements of the 1970s and 1980s.[24] While Coe and her fellow activists were always quick to deny any racist motivations, the collective identity they invoked in framing their injury had unmistakable racial dimensions. Coe explained that the group "decided that the only way we are literally going to save our heritage is to put the focus on the illegal alien problem."[25] In this setting, political whiteness sutured a range of identities—taxpayer, homeowner, American—which made the distinctions between worthy and unworthy subjects recognizable.

Scholar Lisa Cacho suggests that these collective narratives of "white injury"—captured power-fully in Proposition 187's opening declaration that "The People of California ... are suffering"—rely on individual stories of victimhood that disavow racist intent while constructing a population of "illegals" as existing beyond the pale of civil society. From Coe's perspective, racism, defined as the illegitimate and unlawful subjugation of an otherwise rights-bearing subject, could not be fairly charged. Here, a *civil offense,* technically defined by the INS as "entry without inspection," becomes a *racial offense,* an affront to a civilization and a people and thus grounds to impeach a racialized popu-lation, evident in the transformation of the term "illegal" from an adjective to a noun. Linguist Otto Santa Ana's extensive study of the language, metaphors, and imagery used to characterize Mexican immigrants within public discourse during the Proposition 187 campaign documents the violent and dehumanizing dimensions of this collective racial project: such immigrants were metaphorically represented as animals, invaders, and vectors of degeneracy.[26]

Provocative and incendiary attacks such as these were certainly connected to a much longer history of subordination forced upon the Mexican-origin population of Southern California, rationalized by implicit and explicit claims of inevitable racial, cultural, and national hierarchies.[27] This history played a constitutive role in the region's development, evident in the formative acts of violence during and after the U.S. War against Mexico, the simultaneous importation and segregation of Mexican labor that followed, the multiple rounds of deportation launched throughout the twentieth century amid economic downturns, and the history of forced sterilizations of Mexican American women that did not end until the 1970s The steady increase in migration from Mexico during the 1980s corresponded directly to periods of high demand for low-wage labor; uniform national quotas imposed by federal immigration law (which afforded the same number of visas to Mexico as for almost every other country in the world) necessitated that authorized immigration alone would not meet this demand.[28] As some Proposition 187 critics would point out, when the logics of this hierarchy were obeyed—as when low-wage manufacturing workers, landscapers, and domestics dutifully assumed their roles— the suburban enclaves of Southern California eagerly welcomed a Latino immigrant presence, legally authorized or not. But when those underlying logics became disturbed—through perceptions that immigrants were making claims for public goods, political power, or cultural autonomy—they were met in some corners with seething anger and resentment. Here again, an underlying and largely unstated notion of apartheid—a natural understanding of social position and division mediated by race—served to rationalize acerbic group-based claims of domination and subordination.[29]

Challenges Facing Restrictionists Movements

In the early 1990s, immigration restrictionists still had few prominent supporters, even within conservative ranks. The most recent bipartisan reform to federal immigration policy, the 1990 Immigration Act signed by President Bush, actually raised the annual ceiling on visas by 40 percent.[30] Those championing greater restrictions, such as Peter Brimelow, a senior editor at *Forbes*, excoriated fellow conservatives for their participation in a "conspiracy of silence" regarding immigration policy.[31] Among national Republicans, only far-right presidential candidate Pat Buchanan attempted to make immigration an issue in the 1992 presidential election. In the midst of the Republican primary, Buchanan held a news conference along the border in San Diego and called for doubling the size of the Border Patrol, further fortifying and militarizing border crossing areas, and charging a two-dollar toll on legal crossings to fund border enforcement.[32]

Lacking support among leading conservatives, Bill King and Barbara Coe moved to expand their network among other grassroots activists. In May 1992 they announced the formation of the California Coalition for Immigration Reform (CCIR) to bring together a dozen similar groups, immediately claiming a collective membership of four thousand activists.[33] Most of the concrete initiatives they pursued failed. A proposed statewide ballot initiative requiring cities to enforce immigration law and to study the impact of immigration on the state's economy and quality of life (modest goals to be sure in comparison to Proposition 187) was entirely ignored by elected officials from both parties.[34] Alan Nelson's legislative proposals on behalf of FAIR to eliminate all social services, public benefits, and public education for undocumented immigrants were roundly defeated, and FAIR continued to complain about the marginal status afforded to immigration issues.[35]

None of these efforts reaped any tangible policy reforms. But even these failed attempts helped Coe, King, and other grassroots activists refine the narratives, symbols, and story lines they would deploy within future public debates and allowed them to assemble a set of policy proposals that would be ready when the opportunity arose. These activities also enabled them to broaden their base of support, recruiting more volunteers and developing relationships with a number of Republican elected officials willing to promote their demands in the legislative arena.

The Ambivalent Immigration Politics of Pete Wilson

Most accounts of Proposition 187's development and passage give Governor Pete Wilson almost singular credit for raising the profile and salience of immigration politics within the state during this period. Immigration, together with crime, indeed rose to the top of Wilson's political agenda as the ballot initiative was beginning to emerge in the fall of 1993, and his 1994 campaign for governor took up many of the ideas animating the measure. But Wilson's full embrace of immigration occurred *after* many other public officials, including nearly all of the state's prominent Democratic leaders, signaled that they were willing to make immigration restriction and enforcement a leading political priority.

To understand these seemingly contradictory developments, it is helpful to understand Wilson's own history regarding immigration politics. In California in the 1980s, few political-opinion leaders spoke in favor of drastically reducing immigration levels or public benefits to immigrants, certainly not Senator Pete Wilson. Wilson's almost singular focus with regard to immigration policy was guaranteeing access to migrant labor for agribusiness. He cosponsored legislation that required judges to sign warrants before the INS could conduct sweeps targeting undocumented farmworkers, arguing that such protections would ensure that "timely harvests" would not be jeopardized. And he was instrumental in the passage of a provision within the 1986 legislation to ensure that some 350,000 temporary workers would be admitted annually. Agricultural lobbies rewarded Wilson with nearly $520,000 in political contributions during the 1980s.[36] In commenting on immigration policy during his 1990 campaign for U.S. Senate, he reminded voters that "a state cannot limit immigration" and suggested that "we should celebrate our diversity as a strength and distinct cultural asset" while bearing in mind the "limit on the financial burden the federal government can equitably impose through allocation of refugees."[37]

Wilson did not imagine the Mexican workers he lobbied to admit to have rights and claims once the crops were harvested. As he was championing an expansive guest-worker program on behalf of the agricultural lobby, he announced his support for Proposition 63, U.S. English's 1986 Official English ballot proposition (see chapter 5). He also described the border region as "out of control" and suggested that migrants crossed the border not for employment but because they "want their babies born here" and sought access to public services available in the United States. He suggested that "closing (the border physically) ... with some sort of physical barrier or with armed guards" was a harsh but necessary solution to this problem.[38]

Even in the early 1990s, however, W'ilson's embrace of more restrictionist and racially charged attacks against immigrants unfolded unevenly and with considerable assistance and support from Democratic leaders; his initial overtures were not considered particularly nativist or restrictionist. In 1991, as the state's economic downturn headed into its second year and the state budget forecast looked grim, Wilson released a report claiming that California's large population of authorized and unauthorized immigrants and refugees was straining the state's fiscal capacity. Alan Nelson seized on the report to call on the governor to stop providing all employment, public benefits, college educa-tion, tax refunds, and driving privileges to unauthorized immigrants.[39]

Wilson ignored Nelson's plea and instead announced that he would travel to Washington to lobby for more than $200 million he claimed the state was owed by the federal government for provid-ing services to immigrants and refugees. While some critics accused Wilson of blaming immigrants for the state's budget woes, most Democratic leaders wholeheartedly endorsed the plan, including Assembly Speaker Willie Brown, who insisted that the "federal government should appropriate more money and assign that money to where the problems are. He (Wilson) has got to go get the money. We need it. And we are entitled to it."[40] When Wilson continued to press these claims in 1992 and 1993, for even more money, he again did so with the support of a large majority of Democrats. San Jose congressman Don Edwards, the senior member of the California delegation, declared that in seeking the funds from Washington the "governor made a point on which there is no disagreement."[41] The *San Francisco Chronicle* reported that Wilson's efforts to recover the funds "cheered immigrant rights advocates and city financing experts."[42]

During this period, only a year and a half before Proposition 187 was drafted, Wilson focused far more attention on allegedly high levels of spending on welfare programs than he did on immigra-tion restrictions or benefits. In 1992, Wilson faced a budget stalemate that forced the state to issue IOUs, sending Wilson's approval ratings plummeting. In response, Wilson drafted a ballot measure to reform the state's welfare programs and budgeting process and funded a petition drive to qualify it for the November election. The measure, Proposition 165, denied cash benefits to children born to mothers already receiving welfare, restricted the amount that could be paid to applicants who had moved from other states, and implemented a 23 percent reduction in cash benefits paid to most other recipients.[43]

Thus, as the state's budget crisis was peaking and as voter frustration was heightening, Wilson believed that welfare reform, rather than immigration, was the issue that would arouse the greatest public anger. That is, at least for Wilson and his strategists and allies, immigration was not yet regarded as an issue that offered much political advantage. In addition, in spite of conditions that seemed quite encouraging for its passage—a budget stalemate, attacks on a program often regarded as unpopular with the electorate, and a well-funded statewide media campaign—Proposition 165 failed at the polls by nearly one million votes, losing 53.4 to 46.6 percent. An opposing coalition of Democratic leaders and labor unions poured more than $1.5 million into television ads of their own, depicting the measure as a power grab by the governor at the expense of vulnerable children, seniors, and families. While their campaign largely focused on portraying Wilson as an ineffective and power-hungry leader, they did not reproduce or reiterate any of the stigmatizing caricatures of welfare recipients in their campaign.[44]

Proposition 165's failure in 1992 suggests that conditions assumed favorable to a ballot initiative's success—taxpayer anger, budget shortfalls, and racially stigmatized social programs—did not guarantee passage. The electorate may have indeed harbored many misgivings towards welfare programs and frustration over the state's economic decline, but Proposition 165's opponents successfully defended the families targeted by the measure while challenging the intentions and credibility of the measure's proponents. When the public debate turned to immigration policy however, the same coalition of Democratic and union leaders employed a dramatically different strategy.[45]

When the legislative session opened in January 1993 following Wilson's Proposition 165 defeat, immigration restriction still did not garner the support of many lawmakers beyond a group of Southern California conservatives who represented districts where the grassroots restrictionist groups were most active. Assemblyman Mountjoy failed in his legislative efforts to press FAIR-endorsed measures to bar unauthorized immigrants from all public schools, colleges, and universities and to restrict medical care.[46] Mountjoy, according to one account, regularly got "hooted down as a right-wing kook whenever he attempt[ed] to advocate one of his proposals on the Assembly floor."[47]

Immigration Comes Out of the Closet

Rather than Governor Wilson, it was Senator Diane Feinstein, who won the seat vacated by Wilson in 1992 but had to stand for reelection at the expiration of the term in 1994, who made the first public move to take "immigration out of the closet," as one newspaper columnist described it. In an op-ed piece in the *Los Angeles Times* in June 1993, Feinstein detailed the growing hardships that "illegal residents" and the lack of enforcement at the border were imposing on California: drug smuggling, increased crime, and nearly two billion dollars in school, medical, and corrections costs. Feinstein insisted that she was raising the issue in order "to avoid a serious backlash against all immigrants" and to forestall more extreme proposals emanating from the "far right." But her policy prescriptions were largely taken from those same groups—her solutions mirrored those made by Pat Buchanan just one year earlier—and focused almost entirely on punitive measures. The proposals included an expansion of the Border Patrol's personnel and budget paid for in part by a new border-crossing fee, increased federal penalties for smuggling, new policies to restrict newcomer access to Medicaid, and a crackdown on unauthorized immigrants who committed federal crimes. FAIR executive director Dan Stein was thrilled, noting that Feinstein "is in a position to be a defining figure" and calling on FAIR supporters to rally "a lot of positive reinforcement" on her behalf. Stein and other observers commented that Feinstein was the first California senator in decades to take a hard-nosed stand on immigration policy, a telling comment considering that Pete Wilson and Samuel Hayakawa occupied the seat before her. Feinstein publicized her proposals aggressively, appearing on national news talk shows.[48]

Other prominent Democrats, including Senator Barbara Boxer, President Clinton, State Treasurer Kathleen Brown, and Attorney General Janet Reno, announced their own intentions to toughen border enforcement and deal with the fiscal costs associated with immigration.[49] Longtime Democratic congressman Anthony Beilenson endorsed a proposal to revoke automatic birthright citizenship to children of unauthorized immigrants and called for a tamperproof national identification card to limit unauthorized access to public benefits. Referencing his background as an environmentalist, Beilenson explained that the reason he had "long been sensitive to immigration issues of all kinds [was that he had] long been concerned about population problems" in other countries.[50] Beilenson, representing an affluent Santa Barbara district that relied heavily on low-wage immigrant labor, was a central figure in the effort to link immigration restriction to environmental concerns, eventually becoming a member of the FAIR Board of Directors.[51]

It was not until August 1993, after considerable debate within his administration, that Pete Wilson decided to add his voice to the restrictionist chorus. Continuing to face dismal approval ratings, the governor abandoned his previous restraint and joined his Democratic counterparts in championing a new restrictionist regime. On August 9, 1993, he issued an "open letter on behalf of the people of California" to President Clinton, reproduced in full-page ads in the *New York Times, USA Today,* and the conservative-leaning *Washington Times,* declaring that "massive illegal immigration will continue as long as the federal government continues to reward it … [by] providing incentives to illegal immigrants" and leaving California "under siege." Wilson's demands included the denial of public education and health care services to unauthorized residents; the creation of a new tamper-resistant identification card for legal immigrants; the end of the country's long-standing birthright citizenship policy; and using negotiations over NAFTA to win commitments from the Mexican government to deter unauthorized border crossings. He also suggested that all legal migration be temporarily halted to reduce the demand for state services. These policies virtually replicated the demands made by Alan Nelson and FAIR two years earlier, when few politicians, Democrat or Republican, took them seriously. Now, the incumbent governor of California had decided to base his reelection campaign on the very same agenda.[52]

Though Wilson's proposals were denounced by many Latino civil rights groups as trading in "the politics of racial polarization," they were received cordially by high-profile Democratic leaders. Senator Boxer suggested that "the proposals Gov. Wilson has outlined warrant serious consideration," and Senator Feinstein thought the national identification card merited particular attention. FAIR's Orange County representative said her group was "delighted to see the governor … beginning to deal with this issue."[53] Wilson's approval ratings shot up immediately, with one opinion poll finding that more than 80 percent of respondents now believed that "illegal immigration" had become a major problem.[54]

With Wilson moving to take more aggressive restrictionist positions and with leading Democrats like Feinstein, Boxer, and Clinton all endorsing the idea that unauthorized immigration posed a serious threat to the state's well-being, it became almost impossible for Democrats to offer legitimate opposition to Wilson's policies. In late August, the California Democratic Party attempted to undercut some of the momentum Wilson seemed to have built after his announcements; the party ran television ads attacking the governor for "flip-flopping" on immigration, charging him with "opening our borders to cheap labor" during his tenure in the Senate. State Democratic political director Bob Mulholland declared that Wilson's actions "made it easier for criminal migrant networks to bring their foot soldiers into the country."[55] But once immigration became framed through the language of criminality and fiscal austerity—a move that Democrats played no small part in facilitating—"toughness" increasingly became the singular standard around which positions on immigration would be measured.

Political pragmatism alone, however, did not fully explain why various Democratic figures joined the alarmist chorus around immigration. Calls for strident restriction and law enforcement did not necessarily violate long-standing liberal positions around immigration policy. Since 1965, federal immigration policy had been structured broadly within the Hart-Cellar Act, which eliminated discriminatory national immigration quotas that had long favored northern European immigrants. Passed by a Democratic Congress and signed by President Johnson in the shadows of the Statute of Liberty, the 1965 act brought the liberal commitments of equality of opportunity and nondiscrimination driving much civil rights legislation to bear on federal immigration policy. While supporters emphasized the traditions of inclusion and American exceptionalism on which the act was founded, the legislation did not disavow the ideals of restriction altogether. Nearly all of the proponents of the 1965 act eagerly insisted that only those newcomers whose presence could be justified as beneficial to the nation would be welcomed. As Senator Ted Kennedy, a forceful champion of the 1965 law explained, "Favoritism based on nationality will disappear. Favoritism based on individual worth and qualifications will take its place." He specifically assured his colleagues "that the people who comprise the new immigration—the type which this bill would give preference to—are relatively well educated and well to do.... They share our ideals."[56]

While public discourse over immigration changed noticeably in the aftermath of the Hart-Cellar Act, stigmatizing some restrictionist demands as nativist and bigoted, the legislation also remained heavily invested in the principle that individual contribution, merit, and worthiness were defensible tests of admissibility and inclusion. Immigrants (or their advocates) had to be prepared to justify and explain how their presence benefited the nation economically, culturally, and politically. This distinction, between worthy and unworthy immigrant subjects, rehearsed in the English Only initiatives of the mid-1980s, operated powerfully within the emerging debate over immigration enforcement, allowing actors from across the political spectrum to insist that restrictionist policies were necessary to defend and protect the nation's inclusionary traditions. Thus, when President Clinton announced an effort in late 1994 to further militarize and fortify the border, he explained that the nation would "not surrender our borders to those who wish to exploit our history of compassion and justice."[57] Though the 1965 law disavowed official policies that placed immigrants from different nations into a hierarchy, race could still operate as a silent referent within this framework, helping to distinguish those who did and did not meet the criteria for worthiness. Proposition 187 would be debated within, rather than beyond, the framework of liberal immigration policy, as its proponents insisted that the nation was justified in excluding those immigrants who failed to meet these tests.

Even Democratic assemblyman Richard G. Polanco of Los Angeles, who as head of the state Latino Caucus led the legislative fights against the proposals backed by Mountjoy and FAIR earlier in 1993, felt compelled to publicly distinguish between worthy and unworthy immigrants. His *Los Angeles Times* opinion piece on August 13, 1993, endorsed Feinstein's border-crossing toll, a proposal by the Clinton administration to limit preventive and emergency health care for undocumented immigrants, and echoed Wilson's long-standing demand for Washington to reimburse the state for expenses related to immigration. Polanco described his position as "a get-tough but humane policy to tighten up our borders, while ensuring that legal immigrants are allowed to reach their potential." He also stated at a press conference with other Latino legislators and Assemblyman Willie Brown that the "Latino caucus believes we need to take a tough stance on illegal immigration."[58]

Thus, as Ronald Prince, Barbara Coe, Harold Ezell, Alan Nelson, Richard Mountjoy, Robert Kielty, Barbara Kielty, and their supporters met in Orange County to draft their ballot initiative in the fall of 1993, the bulwark that had prevented ardent restrictionists for nearly three decades from shaping the public debate over immigration had been breached. By this point, much of the taboo over addressing immigration that had long frustrated groups like FAIR had been diminished. Feinstein, Clinton, and other Democrats had faced some criticism from Latino elected officials and advocacy groups for their positions, but they proved it was possible to take openly restrictionist positions without being altogether dismissed as a racist or extremist.[59] And with the head of the Latino Caucus now adopting a "get-tough" posture, there was little to obstruct the floodwaters that would become Proposition 187.

Getting S.O.S. on the Ballot

The preliminary period of coalition building, activist recruitment, and assorted campaigns that grassroots restrictionist groups embarked upon in the early 1990s failed to yield any concrete policy reforms. But they succeeded in expanding the groups' memberships and organizing capacity, transformations that proved crucial in qualifying S.O.S. for the ballot.[60] Without a budget to hire paid signature gatherers or even funding to print and mail petitions, their prospects for qualifying initially seemed dim. The effort was sustained at first by small contributions from individual supporters and the volunteer time of local activists, drawn from the growing network of Bill King and Barbara Coe's California Coalition for Immigration Reform. The upsurge in activism eventually convinced state GOP leaders that the initiative was worth sustaining, and the state Republican Party soon provided some $86,500 worth of nonmonetary contributions to the S.O.S. petition drive.[61] Additional contributions from individual Republicans late in the qualification period finally allowed the campaign to retain paid signature gathers to collect some three hundred thousand signatures in the final two months of petitioning. Together with the three hundred thousand signatures collected by volunteers, the campaign met its mid-May qualification deadline and earned a spot on the November ballot.[62]

As the initiative circulated, Pete Wilson continued to frame his own attacks on immigration strategically. On the one hand, during the petition phase, Wilson insiders were cautious about how the S.O.S. effort would play out. Wilson did not participate in drafting the initiative nor did he contribute funding to the effort or use his campaign organization to help collect signatures. To be clear, Wilson did not harbor substantive ethical or moral concerns about the measure. Instead, it is important to remember that even a growling critic of undocumented immigration like Wilson had early doubts about how Proposition 187 would play in the arena of public opinion. Though Wilson would ultimately announce his support of the measure six weeks before the election, and tether much of his reelection campaign to the initiative's passage, at these preliminary stages his official support was measured rather than unqualified.[63]

At the same time, Wilson sharpened and explicitly racialized his own attacks on immigration. In mid-May, almost at the exact time that S.O.S. proponents submitted their signatures to the secretary of state for verification, Wilson's gubernatorial campaign released a highly controversial and inflammatory television spot. Over grainy footage of a group of figures running past cars identified by an on-screen graphic as a "Border Crossing … San Diego County" an ominous voice warned, "They keep coming. Two-million illegal immigrants in California. The federal government won't stop them at the border, yet requires us to pay billions to take care of them."[64] The ad rehearsed the same distinctions animating the S.O.S. initiative—a beleaguered body of hardworking taxpayers under siege by lawbreaking foreign invaders. Like the S.O.S. backers, Wilson made the racial and spatial dimensions of the threat easy to comprehend—the invasion was coming from Mexico, and the invaders were beyond the pale of civil society. Here, race and national identity again helped signify which potential immigrants failed to meet the test of worthiness. Wilson's concluding line, "Enough is enough," suggested that the taxpayers' tolerance and compassion had been exhausted and that only muscular and punitive action could resolve the crisis.[65]

Wilson's position on the S.O.S. initiative converged powerfully with his support for a "Three Strikes" criminal-sentencing initiative that would also appear on the November 1994 ballot, and there were strong resonances between the two measures. California had been in the midst of a historic Prison boom since the early 1980s, with the Department of Corrections' budget swelling from $728 million to $3.1 billion between 1984 and 1994.[66] Since voters had adopted a death-penalty measure in 1972, sixteen subsequent criminal-sentencing enhancements or prison-construction measures had been approved by the electorate, many driven by the same political forces (and actors) implicated in the antitax, antidesegregation, and homeowner's rights initiatives.[67] But the high-profile abduction and murder of twelve-year-old Polly Klass from a slumber party in Marin County in October 1993, and the media frenzy that followed, paved the way for more. Mike Reynolds, a photographer whose own eighteen-year-old daughter had been murdered at a Fresno restaurant the year before, was waiting in the wings with a legislative proposal to dramatically increase prison sentences for repeat felony offenders, including those convicted of nonviolent crimes. Wilson, who had ignored the Reynolds measure before the Klass murder, now became a loud defender of the far-reaching legislation. Wilson signed the law in March 1994, inaugurating what one analyst described as "the largest penal experiment in American history."[68] Wilson then joined Reynolds in championing identical legislation as a ballot measure, in order to ensure that their quest to place "career criminals, who rape women, molest innocent children and commit murder, behind bars where they belong," could not be undone by a simple majority vote of the legislature.[69] As in the Proposition 187 conflict, the Three Strikes debate depicted an angry and vulnerable populace drawing the line against an incorrigible criminal class that lay beyond the pale of society. Both the Three Strikes measure (Proposition 184) and eventually Proposition 187 helped Wilson establish himself as the singular figure defending "Californians who work hard, pay taxes, and obey the law."[70]

The Opposition Begins to Organize

Throughout the qualification period in the first half of 1994, civil rights groups, immigrant rights organizations, union and Democratic leaders, and other opponents of the measure were reluctant to call public attention to the petition, fearing that such publicity might inadvertently help proponents to further announce their effort. They regarded the initiative's sponsors as fringe organizations drawn from the most reactionary corners of Orange County politics, and they remained unconvinced that such groups had the capacity or sophistication to bring their agenda before a statewide electorate. Indeed, the signature-gathering effort received relatively little attention from the press, much to the chagrin of Ronald Prince and Barbara Coe.[71] The opponents of S.O.S mostly hoped the petition would go away.

On June 23, 1994, when the secretary of state announced that the S.O.S. initiative had qualified for the November ballot, all such illusions were shattered.[72] Only then did a coalition of leading Democratic elected officials and organizations announce the formation of a No on S.O.S. fundraising committee. The group included representatives from the Service Employees International Union, California Federation of Teachers, State Federation of Labor, and the California Medical Association as well as Assembly Speaker Willie Brown and Assemblyman Richard Polanco. All sophisticated and experienced players in state politics, they soon realized they faced a daunting task. A *Los Angeles Times* poll in late May revealed that the measure was favored by 59 percent of registered voters and opposed by only 27 percent. In addition, public denunciations of the "illegal alien" crisis had escalated dramatically during the last twelve months, culminating in Wilson's fuming "They Keep Coming" spot. Funding prospects for the opposition were not encouraging; the state Democratic Party remained officially undecided about the issue, withholding any funding until a statewide meeting in September. At the same time, the state GOP formally endorsed Proposition 187, and both the party and individual Republican candidates began to aggressively promote it. And while Proposition 187's proponents had been developing a network of grassroots supporters and refining their populist rhetoric for many years, the opponents were forced to build a fund-raising and public messaging strategy from scratch, with the election only four months away.[73]

The Taxpayers Against 187 Campaign

In early July, the No on S.O.S. committee turned to the political consulting firm of Woodward and McDowell, a veteran ballot initiative consultancy, to develop a strategy to defeat Proposition 187. Based in the tony San Francisco peninsula suburb of Burlingame, the firm's two principals, Richard Woodward and Jack McDowell, were Republicans who specialized in defeating heavily favored ballot measures, most famously two 1990 pro-environmental measures, nicknamed Big Green and Forests Forever, opposed by corporate interests. The decision by a Democratic-civil rights-labor coalition to retain a Republican consultancy to derail a deeply racialized ballot initiative spoke volumes about the limited confidence they had in their own ability to communicate with the electorate about this issue.

Woodward and McDowell quickly undertook its own survey and convened focus groups to gauge public opinion on the initiative and to test potential messages and arguments. In mid-July, the consultants produced a memo for their clients summarizing their findings. The "bad news," the memo began, was that "without a doubt, voters are eager to do something (anything) to address what they perceive to be an illegal immigration problem" and would vote yes on any measure that seemed to represent a solution. Anticipating what would become a major cleavage in the campaign, the consultants acknowledged that while "diverse groups and individuals opposing Proposition 187 differ in their views on illegal immigration," the imperative was to "make the most salient arguments necessary to move *public opinion*" and there was "no time to undertake any 'general education' on the issue." The consultants argued that it was fruitless to challenge voters' beliefs that "'our illegal immigration problem' [is caused by] ... the flow of people coming across our southern border." "You can't change that," the memo insisted. "Don't try."[74]

The good news the consultants contended, was that the measure could be defeated if the campaign obeyed a basic imperative: "RECOGNIZE THERE IS A PROBLEM AND POINT OUT HOW PROPOSITION 187 DOES NOTHING TO FIX THE PROBLEM ... [and] WOULD CAUSE A HOST OF NEW PROBLEMS." As Scott Macdonald, a Woodward and McDowell staff member who became the campaign's communications director later explained, the campaign was "trying to talk to white middle-class voters with messages that resonated with them, because they are the people who vote." Macdonald conceded that while it would certainly be better if the electorate were more diverse and broad-minded, "when you're trying to win an election campaign, you have to deal with the realities of it."[75]

Woodward and McDowell soon established Taxpayers against 187 (hereafter Taxpayers) as the statewide organization to carry this message out to the electorate, attempting to connote a reasoned, centrist profile that would persuade the proverbial median voter, and the firm pledged to raise up to $4 million in order to purchase the television and radio time necessary to do so.[76] A campaign spokesperson declared that the issue was "much deeper than the Hispanic vote" because the "real battleground will be in the San Fernando Valley and Orange County—in the white, middle-class suburban communities," where voters must be convinced that the measure would undermine their interests. And these interests were defined in subtle but unmistakable racial terms; that is, the Taxpayers campaign would seek to affirm the notion of collective white injury proposed by Proposition 187 supporters but would argue that the measure failed to effectively resolve such injuries as promised.[77]

One of the first tasks of the campaign was to draft the ballot argument for the official guide distributed by the secretary of state to all voters. The Taxpayers argument exemplified its basic assumptions and strategy. It began, "Something must be done to stop the flow of illegal immigrants coming across the border.... Illegal Immigration is a real problem, but Proposition 187 is not a real solution." It warned that the measure would "kick 400,000 kids out of school and onto the streets" but "won't result in their deportation" and would certainly create more "crime and graffiti." It declared that "every day, hundreds of thousands of undocumented workers handle our food supply in the fields and restaurants. Denying them basic health care would only spread communicable diseases throughout our communities and place us all at risk." The argument concluded with an unambiguous declaration: "Illegal immigration is illegal. Isn't it time we enforce the law?" It called for more enforcement at the border and the punishment of "employers who continue to hire illegal immigrants." The argument was signed by Los Angeles County sheriff Sherman Block and the heads of the California Medical Association and California Teachers Association.[78]

During the next four months, Taxpayers continued to appeal to the same sense of political whiteness—a shared understanding of political community, interests, and opposition—that Proposition 187 supporters had painstakingly constructed in the years leading up to the campaign. Woodward himself criticized the education ban as folly because the students would "have free time and [be] on the streets. It doesn't take too much imagination to see that it will lead to more gang activity, and more graffiti." He pledged that the Taxpayers campaign would not try "to argue that illegal immigration is good" but would instead make the case that more aggressive law enforcement was the real solution. He explained that Proposition 187 "does nothing to beef up the Border Patrol. This doesn't deport one single illegal alien. This doesn't touch the thousands of illegal aliens in prison."[79]

From one perspective, the logic of the Taxpayers campaign followed the conventional wisdom about how to defeat a controversial initiative that starts out with a sizable lead among voters: frame arguments in terms of the perceived self-interests of frequent and persuadable voters; give voters concrete reasons to reject the measure and suggest troubling unintended consequences if the measure passes; and use credible, recognizable public figures to deliver the message through mainstream television and radio advertising.[80] To be sure, the consultants at Woodward and McDowell were not the only figures insisting upon such a strategy. Many of the labor, health, and education leaders that formed the leadership of the campaign similarly believed that if the goal of the campaign was to win on Election Day, they could not afford to rehearse wide-eyed claims about immigrant rights and social justice.[81]

This line of reasoning even proved highly influential to one of the leading Washington, D.C.-based advocates for immigrant rights. Frank Sharry, the executive director of the National Immigration Forum, a leading advocacy coalition supporting immigrant rights and liberal immigration reforms, took a leave of absence from his job to work on the Taxpayers campaign as deputy campaign manager. Sharry became convinced that the strategy advised by Woodward and McDowell provided the only realistic possibility for defeating the measure; what mattered in the end was "the goal of winning 50% plus 1 of the votes on election day" and that "actions and decisions made need[ed] to flow from the priority of winning."[82]

Other seasoned advocacy organizations agreed. The Service Employees International Union, which was in the midst of its groundbreaking Justice for Janitors campaign to organize tens of thousands of immigrant workers who cleaned downtown office buildings in Los Angeles, San Jose, and other western cities, also joined the Taxpayers effort. The union loaned an organizer to serve as the campaign's deputy manager in the newly opened Los Angles office.[83]

Immigrants Rights Groups Organize

To other opponents of Proposition 187, however, the "pragmatic" decision to rehearse the most stigmatizing and degrading caricatures of immigrants was appalling. Since the passage of the Immigration Reform and Control Act (IRCA) in 1986, dozens of service and advocacy groups had formed across the state, especially in Los Angeles and the San Francisco Bay Area, to assist immigrants in taking advantage of the amnesty provisions and to help them access various social and legal services. Groups like the Northern California Coalition for Immigrant and Refugee Rights (NCCIRR), which included some sixty affiliated organizations in the Bay Area that operated such programs, also lobbied in Sacramento and Washington, D.C., in favor of inclusive public benefit programs and other immigrant rights issues. From their perspective, one of the main imperatives of immigrant rights advocacy was to challenge the demeaning language and assaults that immigrants, particularly those from Mexico and Central America, often faced in the political arena.[84]

Many local immigrant rights advocates were thus outraged when informed of the Taxpayers strategy. They were particularly mortified that the first line of the No on 187 ballot argument was an explicit attack on undocumented immigrants, essentially endorsing the proponents' claim that "illegal immigration is out of control." Ignatius Bau, an immigrant rights attorney for the Lawyers Committee for Civil Rights in San Francisco, saw in the argument "all the 'racial specters' of undocumented kids running around causing crime, undocumented immigrants spreading disease, [and] all the fear" that the Taxpayers campaign hoped to use to motivate voters. "All of us said there's absolutely no way we're going to sign off on this," Bau said in an interview. It was inconceivable to try and defeat a measure attacking immigrants by joining the attacks.[85]

Bau and other California-based immigrant rights advocates quickly concluded that there was little they could say or do to deter Taxpayers from its message or strategy. These immigrant rights groups, however, faced a severe limitation. Unlike the consultants and the unions who made up the mainstream campaign, the immigrant rights organizations had little experience organizing around a ballot initiative or participating in electoral politics more generally. "Groups interacting the most with undocumented folks [didn't] historically play in the electoral arena," explained Bau. To fight a ballot initiative meant that it was "no longer a conversation about organizing in the Mission District" of San Francisco and other immigrant- rich neighborhoods but about "what do you say in San Bernardino or Orange County to voters." A group—including Bau, NCCIRR executive director Emily Goldfarb, and others—realized they needed help to navigate this unfamiliar terrain.

They quickly turned to Jan Adams, a veteran organizer who cut her political teeth during the Berkeley antiwar movement in the late 1960s before doing Central America solidarity work in the 1980s. Adams also had important electoral experience; she had been a field organizer in her hometown of San Francisco for a campaign to defeat a 1989 ballot proposition that would have repealed the city's first domestic-partnership ordinance. Adams's employer, the Applied Research Center, an Oakland-based nonprofit focusing on racial justice issues, agreed to allow her to help establish and organize a grassroots response to Proposition 187 centered on immigrant communities in particular. Together with Goldfarb and Bau, Adams helped launch what would be one of the main grassroots efforts against the measure, Californians United against 187.[86]

Working out of a small office provided by the teachers union in San Francisco, Adams, Goldfarb, Bau, and other Californians United organizers began their work with the election only four months away. They had no difficulty generating interest or passion in the issue among their own constituents. As word spread of Proposition 187's qualification during the late summer, particularly in immigrant Latino communities, small groups in dozens of cities began to meet and organize on their own. Sometimes the groups were simply comprised of parents seeking to share and disseminate information about the measure; other groups were convened by activists based in local community organizations or college campuses. Adams later described the effort as "probably one of the most intense campaign experiences" she had ever had in more than three decades of organizing: "The quality of emotion of the people who were against it was greater than anything I've ever seen before or since.... The notion that somebody would put to a vote whether their kids should enjoy the benefits of living in this country, should be able to go to school, should be able to get health care was a moral outrage of the sort that people don't usually feel."[87]

The challenge that Adams and others faced was trying to provide basic organization and infrastructure to this upsurge of activism. To be sure, there was already deep and sophisticated political experience within many of these communities. Many immigrants and refugees who arrived from Mexico and Central America in the 1980s were politicized during the often violent civil and military struggles that raged within their countries of origin; they needed no tutoring in political analysis, the operation of power, or the importance of civil and human rights. But the nonprofit and civic organizations that had been built in these communities during the last decade had focused most of their energies on direct service and legislative advocacy rather than on overt political conflicts. Proposition 187 would be a baptism by fire.

Over the next three months, Adams and other Californians United organizers attempted to support, enhance, and expand this upsurge of activity. The San Francisco campaign eventually trained and organized more than a thousand volunteers to take on specific tasks to reach voters directly. During the weekend before the election alone, a group of more than seven hundred activists delivered some sixty thousand door hangers across the city and made more than thirty thousand calls. Phone banks were conducted in English, Chinese, and Spanish—an innovation at the time—and flyers and other publicity materials were translated into as many as eight languages.[88]

Californians United eventually expanded its work beyond San Francisco and affiliated with several other anti-187 local efforts across the state. By early September, a loose coalition of anti-187 groups based in immigrant communities was beginning to take shape, with groups actively organizing in Los Angeles, Sacramento, San Diego, Marin County, the San Francisco East Bay, Orange County, and San Diego.[89] As in San Francisco, many were built out of the emerging network of immigrant rights advocacy organizations. In Los Angeles, advocates and organizers based in nonprofit organizations such as the Central American Resource Center, One Stop Immigration, and the Coalition for Humane Immigrant Rights of Los Angeles coordinated various anti-187 activities, focusing most of their efforts in immigrant communities.[90] A coalition of Asian American groups called Asian Pacific Americans Opposed to Proposition 187 also joined the statewide alliance, though as Ignatius Bau later pointed out, "no major contributions from Asian Pacific American organizations, businesses, or individuals were made" to the opposition campaign.[91] Other groups, such as the newly founded Latino Civil Rights Network and various student organizers based at different campuses within the University of California and California State University systems, also eschewed the Taxpayers strategy of focusing solely on high-frequency white voters by affirming anti-immigrant sentiments. But the grassroots strategy also had its limitations.

Challenges Facing the Grassroots Campaigns against Proposition 187

Three critical challenges faced the grassroots campaigns, which operated independently of the Taxpayers campaign. First, the assertion by the Woodward and McDowell consultants that white voters dominated the electorate was entirely accurate. In 1994, Latinos constituted 29 percent of the California population, 26 percent of the adult population, 14 percent of the eligible voter population, and only 11 percent of registered voters. In the June 1994 primary, white voters cast 83 percent of the total ballots, compared to just 8 percent for Latinos and 4 percent each for African Americans and Asian Americans. On this point, there could be no dispute; the fate of most statewide elections was largely in the hands of the collective white electorate.[92]

The reasons that white voters dominated the electorate, and that Proposition 187 opponents lacked a political vocabulary to discuss immigration politics, however, were more complex. Historian and union organizer Kenneth Burt suggests that as the Chicano movement of the late 1960s and 1970s demobilized, an emerging bloc of Latino leaders focused attention on political incorporation within the electoral system rather than building grassroots organizations. "In the general absence of grassroots social movements," he explains, "liberal Latinos utilized the court system or formed alliances with Democratic legislative leaders. While these moves produced tactical victories in an increasingly hostile political environment, the failure to invest resources in naturalization and citizenship classes, voter registration, and get-out-the vote drives served to depress Latino working class participation in politics. It also failed to incorporate new voters among the millions of immigrants and their children who arrived in the state from Mexico and Central America during the seventies and eighties."[93]

In addition, the provisions within IRCA for obtaining citizenship were not instantaneous, and naturalization rates among Latinos in California eligible to become citizens were relatively low. And unlike restrictionist groups such as FAIR, which were constantly developing and promoting a *public* language through which to contest immigration policy, these advocates had no such experience or capacity, confining their work almost exclusively to service delivery or occasional legislative lobbying. Groups that had historically served as the repository for more robust political claims on behalf of the undocumented, such as the leftist Centros de Accion Social Autonomos (CASA), went into decline by the late 1970s.[94] As a result, even immigrant rights advocates affiliated with Californians United against 187 had little experience in making forceful demands for the rights of immigrants in general and the undocumented in particular.[95] They understood clearly what they opposed—the derogatory racial propositions that fueled both the S.O.S. and Taxpayers campaigns—but they struggled to articulate a more proactive and unified framework on behalf of immigrant rights. Even among social justice organizations, there were vigorous disputes about the most effective way to respond to Proposition 187.[96]

A second major challenge facing the various grassroots efforts against Proposition 187 involved the rapid expansion of a political discourse shaped by often violent claims that undocumented immigrants lacked any standing to assert political rights or demand civic recognition. The emergence of these dynamics was at least two decades in the making; public opinion about immigration had always been contradictory and paradoxical rather than unified and coherent.[97] But as a growing number of elected officials and opinion leaders from across the political spectrum affirmed the notion that unlawful immigration was the central policy crisis of the day—and as grassroots restrictionist groups grew in size, recognition, and influence (accelerated through the process of qualifying Proposition 187)—claims for immigrant rights became increasingly stigmatized and ridiculed within public debates. The restrictionist claim that unauthorized immigrants—constructed in racialized terms as undeserving, criminal, and degenerate—lacked any claims-making authority now moved to the center of California political culture.

This shift did not exempt the standard-bearers of the Democratic Party. While gubernatorial candidate Kathleen Brown, Senators Boxers and Fein—stein, and President Clinton all eventually came out against Proposition 187 by late October, their stance was hardly unequivocal. Feinstein continued to conduct tours of the California-Mexico border accompanied by the press to spotlight her call for greater enforcement. In July, a Feinstein campaign ad accused her Republican challenger, Congressman Michael Huffington, of failing to vote for additional border guards while declaring that Feinstein herself "led the fight to stop illegal immigration." The ad included footage similar to that used by Wilson's "They Keep Coming" ad of a shadowy mass of border crossers and a voice-over by Feinstein declaring that "three thousand illegal immigrants try to cross the border many nights." Even when Feinstein came out against Proposition 187 in late October, she championed her alternative plan of 2,100 additional Border Patrol agents, a dollar-per-person border-crossing fee, and a tamperproof work permit.[98] At a September press conference in Los Angeles, Attorney General Janet Reno announced the inauguration of Operation Gatekeeper to further fortify the San Diego sector of the Border Patrol with new agents and resources.[99] In short, while leading Democrats did not endorse Proposition 187, they fully participated in constructing unauthorized immigration as a political and economic crisis that required uncompromising action, essentially affirming the rationale that fueled Proposition 187.

Grassroots immigrant rights advocates struggled with these sentiments in their daily work. In the midst of the election in 1994, the *Orange County Register* carried a story about the nascent anti-187 organizing efforts of a group affiliated with the Delhi Community Center and the Sisters of St. Joseph in Anaheim. Rigoberto Rodriguez, a recent graduate of University of California, Irvine, who worked for the community center and the newly formed Orange County against 187 campaign, recalled that for two full days after the story ran a barrage of hostile callers tied up the center's phone lines with complaints, demanding to know why the nonprofit organization was supporting lawbreaking "illegals." Overwhelmed by the outrage and response, Rodriguez came to the sinking realization that the callers were probably "the same people calling the elected officials and media" with similar charges, a capacity that Proposition 187 opponents simply did not have.[100]

A final challenge facing the grassroots anti-187 campaigns concerned the ongoing, sometime public disagreements that erupted with the Taxpayers against 187 campaign. These disagreements were rooted in differences over tactics as well as the types of public narratives and messages the campaigns used. The Taxpayers continued to maintain that the framework asserted by Governor Wilson and Proposition 187's proponents, which constructed a fundamental opposition between *them* (unauthorized immigrants) and *us* (the innocent taxpayers) could not be contested; it was a fixed feature of the political landscape. Therefore, the only credible response was to affirm the basic framework but argue that the initiative would cause "us" more problems without doing anything about "them."

Again, it was not only the Republican consultants who embraced the logic of this approach. Many Latino elected officials, Democratic and labor leaders, and even prominent Latino civil rights organizations recited variations of this core message. For example, John Palacio of the Mexican American Legal Defense and Education Fund wrote in an *Orange County Register* op-ed that if three hundred thousand "kids without proper documentation" were thrown "out of our schools and into our streets … some of these kids would surely become involved in committing crimes."[101]

Frank Wu, the attorney who volunteered for several months with Californians United against 187, says that he was initially persuaded by this logic, particularly after making public presentations to audiences who were extremely hostile toward any perceived defense of undocumented immigrants. But Wu says that, in retrospect, he might have favored embracing what he describes as the "moral high-ground" argument, foregrounding the human rights of the undocumented and challenging the racist suppositions of the ballot measure. Wu suggests that the attempts to appeal to the notion of self-interest by arguing "we don't like them any more than you do but if we don't provide these services we'll all suffer" might be persuasive if voters somehow considered the measure entirely through a "rational policy discourse" framework and if they employed a "strict cost-benefit analysis." But Wu concludes that if a "racial subtext is there," then voters are not "amenable to these" claims, resulting in the use of "arguments [that] just don't sound good" or ethical, like those used by the Taxpayers campaign.[102]

The grassroots and Taxpayer factions began to clash, often publicly, accusing each other of sabotaging the campaign. Many grassroots organizers felt that the Taxpayers campaign sought to muzzle them before the mainstream press, fearing their strident opposition to the measure would alienate the very voters they were targeting. As one Los Angeles organizer told the *Sacramento Bee,* "We're tired of all this scapegoating. If the people in the suburbs can't deal with it, they can't deal with it. I have my disagreements with Taxpayers Against 187 and some of the arguments they've raised, too."[103]

The Taxpayers campaign was well aware of this friction. Scott Macdonald conceded in an interview after the election that the decision to affirm the idea that undocumented immigration was a problem "drove the people who were supposed to be our allies right through the roof," and the conflict diverted the time and energy of people on both sides of the debate. But he maintained that he and his colleagues at Woodward and McDowell had the expertise regarding "how to evaluate the polling and come up with the messages" and that a campaign like theirs had to "reflect those messages and further the public's understanding of them, or it is a waste." Because grassroots activists like Californians United, he insisted, "did not concentrate on those messages" the Taxpayers campaign had developed, their efforts were a "waste and in fact counterproductive."[104]

Disputes over tactics were another main difference between the two anti-187 campaigns. The Taxpayers campaign believed the best way to reach the high-frequency voters was to use recognizable centrist or even conservative spokespersons. Los Angeles County sheriff Sherman Block thus became one of the main spokespersons for the Taxpayers campaign, in the hopes that he could credibly make the case that Proposition 187 risked increasing the threat of street crime. In addition, there was an unspoken but well-understood rule within the campaign that Latino immigrants themselves would not be persuasive representatives before the white electorate.[105]

Groups like Californians United, by contrast, felt that the initiative provided an important opportunity for immigrants themselves to get involved in political activity. Even those who could not vote could still speak to the ethnic media and join phone banks and precinct walks in their communities. And whereas Macdonald felt that any imperative other than winning on Election Day was a distraction and a waste, organizers like Jan Adams with Californians United held the opposite view. According to Adams, when she looked at the initial polling data and realized the tenor of the political debate that was unfolding, it became "clear absolutely from the get-go that we could not defeat this thing." Adams and many of her colleagues hoped to use the campaign to build the political capacity of immigrant communities beyond the election by developing networks, relationships, and skills. To focus exclusively on the (unattainable) task of winning a majority of the votes statewide while neglecting the very communities being targeted made little sense.[106]

FIGURE 3.1. March against Proposition 187, Los Angeles, October 16, 1994. Estimates put the crowd at between 70,000 and 100,000 people. Photo by Andy Scott courtesy of the *Los Angeles Times*.

This dispute erupted most forcefully a few weeks before the election when anti-187 activists called for a large march in downtown Los Angeles. On October 16, an estimated crowd of seventy thousand to one hundred thousand people marched from East Los Angeles to city hall, a four-mile trek through the heart of the city's Latino community. Newspaper coverage of the crowds fixated on the thousands of Mexican flags carried by the marchers and their strident denunciations of Pete Wilson and Proposition 187. Over the next two weeks, students at dozens of high schools across the state followed by organizing their own walkouts and marches; thousands of students, mostly Latino, participated in the loosely coordinated actions.[107]

For some, these marches represented a breathtaking display of political energy—a rejection of a deeply abusive and racist political culture that constructed Latino immigrants as fit for low-wage labor but not for basic human rights or civic recognition. Californians United, which did not organize the marches formally but attempted to channel some of the energy into the election, felt that the marches and walkouts represented an outpouring of political anger and expression that could not and should not be suppressed. As Californians United's Irma Munoz explained, "Students are extremely frustrated. They're worrying about whether their friends and neighbors are going to be able to attend school, and they want to do something about it. But they can't vote, and they don't know how to make an impact."[108] Adams believed it was pointless for organizers to fret over the impact the marches would have on broader public opinion; they were going to happen regardless of whether the organized campaigns thought they were tactically effective. Californians United tried to recruit some of the students participating in the walkouts to join phone-banking and precinct-walking efforts before the election.

The Taxpayers campaign, however, regarded the marches and walkouts as a huge tactical blunder that sabotaged much of their work during the last three months. Their entire campaign strategy had been based on avoiding explicit discussions about race, immigration, and the political status of Latinos while largely affirming the anti-immigrant sensibilities of white voters. The march represented an outright rejection of such a strategy—a refusal to remain politically invisible and silent in the midst of venomous attacks or to apologize for one's presence. From the perspective of the Taxpayers campaign, the images of thousands of Latino students marching in the streets waving Mexican flags undercut any progress made by affirming the deepest fears of white voters. Taxpayers consultant Jack McDowell described the marches and walkout as a "tragedy. [The marchers] were trying to help. But the result was, I believe, they hurt."[109] As one letter in the *Los Angeles Times* put it, "Why should Californians support a foreign welfare state on its own soil? I would like to see all those Mexican flag-wavers go back to Mexico and demand free health care, education aid to dependent children and welfare."[110]

Racial Liberalism and Proposition 187

Just as the marches were erupting in mid-October, the Taxpayers campaign opened up a second front in their attack on Proposition 187. The Taxpayers launched a series of radio ads charging that the measure was tainted by extremism through its associations with the controversial Pioneer Fund, a New York-based foundation with a long history of funding eugenic and often explicitly racist social science research. Since 1988, the Pioneer Fund had contributed at least $600,000 to FAIR, which was employing Alan Nelson as a part-time consultant when he helped draft Proposition 187. The Taxpayer ads charged that "white supremacists are behind 187" and suggested that indiscriminate profiling would result if the measure were passed.[111]

The Taxpayers decision to affirm the racialized anxieties of the electorate, while simultaneously charging that Proposition 187 was a measure that went "too far," was a familiar tactic. The same approach was used by fair employment proponents in 1946 and continued with opponents of the anti-fair housing measure in 1964, the antidesegregation measures of the 1970s, and the English Only measures of the 1980s. The Taxpayers campaign similarly argued that Proposition 187 violated the principles of tolerance, fairness, and racial liberalism more generally.

The ballot measure's proponents, however, eagerly refuted such charges, recalling an equally familiar strategy of defending racialized political claims within the same discourse of fairness, tolerance, and liberalism. Disavowing any racist intent and invoking a long tradition of racial innocence, the proponents claimed the measure had nothing to do with race; it was illegal behavior, rather than people, they sought to address. Here, narratives about the environmental and fiscal "carrying capacity" of the state—the regrettable but inevitable limits imposed by nature itself—as well as the distinction between worthy and unworthy immigrants, effectively refuted charges of extremism. Ronald Prince asked, "What is it about the initiative that's racist? It doesn't deal with race. No one is identified in the initiative by race, creed or color." To the contrary, he insisted, "We're doing this out of love; we love our country." Republican congressman Dana Rohrabacher similarly held that "people with love in their hearts and good intentions know we can't afford to take care of everybody that comes here."[112]

Pete Wilson also defended his support of Proposition 187—he finally endorsed the measure on September 18—by rehearsing the distinction between worthy and unworthy immigrants. A television ad Wilson released in late October, which ran extensively during the two weeks before the election, opened with a nighttime view of the Statue of Liberty before cutting to a proud sea of faces at a citizenship ceremony. The warmhearted narration began, "It's how most of us got here. It's how this country was built. American citizenship is a treasure beyond measure." The ad then cut to the same footage of a stampede across a border checkpoint used in the "They Keep Coming" advertisement from the spring. Turning more stern and alarmist, the narrator intoned, "But now the rules are being broken." Alternating between these two images—proud new citizens affirming their loyalty and ominous figures streaming across the border—the narration concluded, "There's a right way, and there's a wrong way. To reward the wrong way, is not the American way."[113]

Some Proposition 187 supporters did certainly embrace the measure as a deliberate expression of racial nationalism and nativist exclusion. For example, Glen Spencer, head of a San Fernando Valley-based restrictionist group, Voices of Citizens Together, declared that "illegal immigration" was a "part of a reconquest of the American Southwest by foreign Hispanics." He added, "Someone is going to be leaving the state. It will either be them or us." Another bombastic Long Beach-based activist within the California Coalition for Immigration Reform similarly declared, "I have no intention of being the object of 'conquest,' peaceful or otherwise, by Latinos, Asians, blacks, Arabs or any other group of individuals who have claimed my country."[114]

But political scientist Robin Dale Jacobson, who conducted interviews with Proposition 187 supporters after the election, concluded that her respondents dismissed any notion that they were motivated by racism or cultural chauvinism.[115] From their perspective, pragmatic notions of fiscal limitations and the rule of law motivated their support for the measure, which they believed adhered to the basic principles of tolerance, fairness, and indeed racial liberalism as they understood them. Heavy-handed restrictions on unauthorized immigrants could not be regarded as racist because un-authorized immigrants remained legally outside of the nation's protections; they were not recognized as rights-bearing subjects.

This critique and disavowal worked on the terms and terrain of a liberal national political imagi-nation. As legal scholar Linda Bosniak has perceptively argued, even progressive critics of Proposition 187 had difficulty establishing the normative grounds on which the measure could be opposed. For such progressives, the nation-state still functioned as the arbiter of rights for disenfranchised or subordinated groups. Because a nationally defined conception of political community seemed by definition to exclude unauthorized persons from its protections, progressives lacked a political vocabulary and imagination to summon a bold defense of the rights of the unauthorized. Bosniak argues that, as a result, even progressive critics of the measure primarily emphasized the *collateral* damage the measure would cause—such as violations of the rights of U.S.-born Latinos through racial profiling—rather than defending the rights' of the undocumented as such.[116]

In the imagination of many Proposition 187 supporters, nationally defined ideals of rights and protections similarly exempted them from any charge of racism or an unwarranted denial of rights. Race could still function as an absent referent in this discourse, an unstated proxy for those who resided beyond the protections of the nation. And race, gender, and nation still mediated conceptions of worthiness and unworthiness through distinctions drawn between taxpayers and "illegals." But the normative ideals of rights, equality, and nondiscrimination not only failed to offer any resources or protection against such equivalences, they actually nurtured them, supplying Proposition 187 proponents with a liberal vocabulary through which to narrate and legitimize their claims.

While I describe the political subjectivity shaping this process as political whiteness, support for Proposition 187 extended beyond white voters. The distinctions between "good" and "bad" im-migrants were also embraced by some African American, Asian American, and even Latino voters. A Latina in East Los Angeles fumed in a television interview that undocumented immigrants "know if they come over here, everything is going to be for free. They have more babies … they have it made."[117] While scholars have cited various factors for the support Proposition 187 garnered among some Latinos, the comment reveals that the gaze of political whiteness, which relies on race to help signify the boundaries of exclusion and the grounds of inclusion, can be inhabited by those who do not identify as white.[118]

Countdown to the Election

As the election approached, Proposition 187 was still only endorsed by the California Republican Party, some individual Republicans, and a network of grassroots restrictionist organizations.[119] The opposition, by contrast, won endorsements from nearly every leading news organization in the state; dozens of prominent law enforcement, health care, and religious officials; numerous corporate representatives and various chambers of commerce; and even several prominent Republicans, including Jack Kemp, President Bush's secretary of housing and urban development, and William Bennett, who served as secretary of education under President Reagan. Kemp and Bennett, summoning the figure of the good immigrant argued that the "vast majority of immigrants hold principles which the Republican Party warmly embraces: an entrepreneurial spirit and self-reliance, hostility to government intervention, strong family values, and deeply-rooted religious faith."[120]

In addition, the original proponents of the measure began openly feuding, as grassroots activists like Barbara Coe and Ronald Prince faced off with more prominent figures like Harold Ezell and Alan Nelson. The sponsoring committee largely abandoned fund-raising and waged no organized campaign. Several proponents, including Ezell and Prince, stopped talking to the media altogether, wary of the increasingly strident tone and tactics of their critics.[121]

These developments, ordinarily disastrous for an initiative effort, mattered little in the campaign's final weeks, as the terms of the debate had already been firmly set. During the preceding year, Democrats had reasoned that by taking a tough posture on some restrictionist reforms—especially increased border enforcement and limiting access to public benefits—they would forestall demands for more sweeping changes. The opposite occurred. With Democrats now fully endorsing the claim that immigrants were indeed responsible for many of the state's crises, the rationale for limiting far-reaching policy prescriptions, such as those within Proposition 187, had largely dissipated. The state GOP never directly involved itself in the racialized-ballot measures discussed in previous chapters in this book, and its support of Proposition 187 was uneven during the qualification period, as party operatives waited to see how the initiative would play. But with Democrats also advocating a crackdown on unauthorized entrants and with polls suggesting that voters believed the measure to be reasonable rather than extremist, the risks of backing the measure seemed small. The California Republican Party decided to make the ballot measure the central issue of its voter mobilization efforts, distributing slate mailers, coordinating volunteer phone banks, and delivering more than two million door hangers to mobilize voters. Wilson also aggressively promoted and backed the measure with millions of dollars after also deciding in late September that the potential benefits outweighed the risks of backlash. Wilson's focus on the measure in the weeks leading up to the campaign was relentless. According to one Wilson critic, "by the time the election rolled around, Wilson's internal tracking polls showed that more than 90% of voters knew Wilson's position on Proposition 187, more than the number of people who could identify Sacramento as the state capital." Wilson's own pollster conceded the recognition number was "amazing."[122]

The Taxpayers against 187 campaign, which fell well short of its $4 million fund-raising goal, continued attempting to convince voters that while their hostilities toward undocumented immigrants were legitimate, the unintended consequences the measure would produce would outweigh any benefits. But opinion polls taken in the closing weeks before the election seemed to confirm that many voters cared less about the specific components of Proposition 187—and their relative benefit or harm—and more about the message it would send to lawmakers and immigrants themselves that, as Wilson declared, "Enough is enough."[123] That is, they responded affirmatively to the first part of the Taxpayers message—that "illegal immigration" was indeed a problem—and remained ambivalent toward the second part—that Proposition 187 only made a bad problem worse. As Frank Wu of Californians United against 187 suggested, the effort to reach the rational and utilitarian voter who would be amenable to a "right idea, wrong solution" message was futile. With both sides affirming the proposition that there were indeed worthy and unworthy immigrants, the dispute mainly focused on the best method of containing or expelling the bad ones.[124]

A troubling irony also undergirded this strategy. Though the Taxpayers consultants concluded that the campaign must endorse the idea that many immigrants posed a somber threat to the welfare of the state, they also implicitly participated in wildly exaggerating the scale and impact of this alleged threat. As scholar David Hayes-Bautista later pointed out, beginning in the early 1990s immigration to the state had dropped considerably; in 1994 and 1995 more Latino immigrants left California than arrived, a pattern that continued for much of the decade. California's rapidly contracting labor market dimmed the prospects facing new arrivals. Yet even Senator Feinstein's reelection ads, depicting shadowy border crossings at night, insisted, "And they keep coming! Three thousand each night." Hayes-Bautista argues that if Feinstein's figures were correct, by the end of 1994 one in three California residents would have been an undocumented Mexican immigrants, and eight out of ten Latinos in Los Angeles County would have been undocumented.[125]

Hayes-Bautista also notes the flaws in the alarmist charges that "our children's classrooms" had become "over-crowded by those who are illegally in our country."[126] In fact, the overall enrollment in the Los Angeles Unified School District was actually 2.7 percent lower in 1994 than it was in 1969, and most school overcrowding could be traced to the district's decision in the early 1980s (in the wake of the ballot measures slashing property taxes and fanning public discontent over busing) to close many schools. Roughly 95 percent of Latino students in Los Angeles public schools were U.S. citizens or legal permanent residents; the "flood" of undocumented students was entirely imaginary, yet it was a problem affirmed by Proposition 187's proponents and opponents alike. Similarly, the large-scale cutbacks in public services that fueled so much of the animosity driving Proposition 187, nearly all of which could be traced to the wave of property tax-slashing measures in the late 1970s and early 1980s as well as to the increase in state prison spending, became almost singularly understood as a result of the impact of undocumented immigration.[127] But these points became largely inadmissible in the debate over Proposition 187.

The Outcome of the Election and Beyond

Proposition 187 was approved by 59 percent of the California electorate, receiving more than five million votes (see table 3.1). Exit polls suggested that the Taxpayers strategy of targeting white moderate and suburban voters largely failed. Sixty-three percent of white voters supported the measure, along with 62 percent of independent voters and 55 percent of self-described moderates.

TABLE 3.1 Proposition 187 Exit Poll Data by Race/Ethnicity, 1994

Group (% of electorate)	Yes (%)	No (%)
All (100%)	59	41
White (81%)	63	37
Black (5%)	47	53
Latino (8%)	23	77
Asian American (4%)	47	53

Source: LAT exit poll, California General Election, November 8, 1994.

Proposition 187 spawned multiple and contradictory legacies. Immediately after the election, a coalition of civil rights groups, backed by an array of unions, school boards, city councils, and religious and medical groups, filed successful legal challenges before the California Superior Court and U.S. District Court to block implementation of the measure; the suits had been readied well before election day by attorneys in anticipation of the measure's passage. Multiple legal cases were ultimately consolidated as the *League of United Latin American Citizens et al. v. Wilson*. The case took more than four years to finally adjudicate; not until activists groups pressured Democratic Governor Gray Davis, who succeeded Pete Wilson in 1998, did the state formally drop its appeal and accept the judge's ruling blocking implementation of nearly all provisions of the measure. Only the section providing for penalties for document forgery were permitted to stand, and even those had a contradictory impact, as errors in the phrasing of the initiative language meant that the new provisions actually lowered criminal penalties for some forgery infractions.[128]

Though the courts prevented the state from implementing most of Proposition 187's provisions, several of the key tenets of the measure provided the blueprint for sweeping and more far-reaching federal reforms. The Republicans' 1994 Contract with America included no mention of immigration policy reforms. But after Proposition 187, a newly organized Congressional Task Force on Immigration

Reform, chaired by Republican Elton Gallegly of California, essentially recommended federalizing much of Proposition 187. California Democrats, including Anthony Beilenson, Howard Berman, and Jane Harmon, expressed "strong support" for many of the proposals.[129] Major revisions to federal welfare law through the 1996 Personal Responsibility and Work Opportunity Reconciliation Act and immigration law through the 1996 Illegal Immigration Reform and Immigration Act prohibited undocumented immigrants from receiving most public health services and benefits. The laws further prescribed a five-year waiting period even for lawful permanent residents to receive many of these services.[130]

For their part, the grassroots restrictionist organizations responsible for bringing Proposition 187 to the ballot failed to grow significantly in size or authority after the election. Proponents like Barbara Coe promised they would successfully recall many of the elected officials who supported the court's ruling against the measure. None of these efforts were successful. Nor did these organizations succeed in multiple subsequent attempts to qualify a Son of 187 measure for the ballot after the initial court rulings. Indeed, between 1994 and 1999, restrictionist groups attempted to qualify seven different statewide measures barring unauthorized immigrants from receiving different public services or benefits; Proposition 187 was the only one to even reach the ballot. Attempts to qualify measures in 2004 and 2006 also failed to meet the signature threshold. The populist ire claimed by Proposition 187 supporters proved less reliable and enduring than imagined.[131] But the boundaries of legitimate discourse over immigration control had been firmly established; political actors who did not make their claims through appeals to an aggrieved California populace risked swift dismissal. And as the next chapter explains, Democratic Party leaders in particular would come to view such boundaries as unassailable.

For many California Latinos, both immigrant and nonimmigrant, Proposition 187 represented a singularly important political event. During and after the election, advocacy organizations noted a swift upsurge in reported incidents of anti-Latino violence and aggression; one Los Angeles group set up a hotline that recorded more than one thousand incidents in the eleven months following the measure's passage.[132] In time however, analysts would conclude that the measure would help bring about a dramatic increase in naturalization, voting, and political participation rates among many Latinos, producing a cohort of deeply politicized voters that would begin transforming the composition of the California electorate.[133] Nonprofit organizations serving immigrant communities would also increasingly come to appreciate the role of political participation in asserting the rights of their constituents.[134]

For Proposition 187's organized opponents, response to the measure's passage fell into two distinct camps. The groups affiliated with the mainstream Taxpayers against 187 reiterated their contention that the crisis posed by undocumented, largely Latino immigrants could not be fundamentally altered, at least within the cycle of any election. The Taxpayers strategists insisted that pragmatism alone should govern the messaging and framing strategies for future public debates and ballot measures over immigration policy. A postmortem memo authored by Frank Sharry, head of the Washington,

D.C.-based National Immigration Forum who worked for the Taxpayers campaign, made these points forcefully. Sharry declared that the "goal of winning 50% plus 1 of the votes on election day" was the only imperative that mattered with regard to such initiatives. Sharry emphasized that he "strongly endorse[d] the kind of messages" used by the Taxpayers campaign and that these themes should serve as the blueprint for future initiative campaigns.[135]

Organizers aligned with the Californians United against 187 effort sharply disagreed with this assessment. A postelection memo written by two of the main Californians United organizers and leaders, Ignatius Bau and Emily Goldfarb, challenged the fundamental assumption that the Taxpayers campaign strategy had any impact on the electorate or that a winning campaign must start with the concession that "something must be done to stop illegal immigration." They insisted that their "pro-immigrant/immigrant rights messages [were] sound" and that "Proposition 187 was a pretext for racism, for fear and anger about the demographic changes in California." Goldfarb and Bau conceded that their groups were "totally unprepared for an initiative campaign…. We didn't have the experience, expertise, or resources to respond."[136]

Jan Adams of Californians United also rejected the "50% plus 1" criteria asserted by Sharry. From her perspective, the anti-187 campaign had already arrived too late and with too few resources or electoral expertise to have any realistic hope of defeating the measure. She agreed that the various grassroots efforts to defeat Proposition 187 all "suffered from lack of electoral experience." In particular, the challenge of how to compete for votes within an electorate that was older, whiter, and more conservative than the populace as a whole was much different than shaping public opinion within the constituencies the groups behind Californians United typically engaged. In this Adams largely agreed with Sharry's assertion that marches and walkouts could not win elections, though she did contend that "this kind of activism was an important way for threatened communities to express perfectly justifiable outrage" and to "raise the visibility of the threat of the groups under attack."[137] However, as long as the electorate remained overwhelmingly white and expertise in electoral organizing remained the sole province of high-priced consultants who frowned upon grassroots involvement, the Proposition 187 outcome would likely be repeated in future electoral cycles.

For Adams, Goldfarb, and Bau, building the capacity to contest statewide elections and expanding the electorate more generally constituted the long-term imperative. In this regard, the Californians United campaign in San Francisco seemed to hold some promise.[138] In San Francisco County, 71 percent of voters rejected Proposition 187. Adams would insist that this outcome was not simply the bias of the state's most liberal electorate, pointing out that other liberal campaigns—including the effort to approve a single-payer health insurance initiative (Proposition 186) and to reject the Three Strikes criminal-sentencing law (Proposition 184)—did not achieve similar results. Even the most conservative districts in San Francisco rejected Proposition 187, and margins in solidly immigrant and progressive areas exceeded 80 percent.[139]

The San Francisco outcome and experience, Adams reasoned, gestured toward a new model of electoral organizing. What if, rather than ceding the capacity to run successful electoral campaigns to consultants, community organizations developed these skills and abilities themselves? What if, rather than focusing almost exclusively on the mythical white, middle of the road voter, such a project grounded itself precisely within the communities that were most often marginalized by the electoral process? And finally, what if such a project placed the battle over ideas and interests—especially regarding race and racial oppression—at the center of its aspirations and tactics, refusing to subordinate itself to the "50% plus 1" mantra?

Adams and her colleagues soon began drafting a concept paper for a new framework for electoral organizing. Their plan, they soon realized, would face an immediate test: sponsors of a sweeping proposal to abolish all public affirmative action programs promised to qualify their own ballot measure within the next eighteen months.

Notes

1. "Economy Slows Voters' Ballot Measures to a Crawl," *LAT,* January 5, 1994.
2. "Voters Approve 'Three Strikes' Law, Reject Smoking Measure Proposal for Government-Run Health Care System, Gasoline Tax to Fund Rail Projects are Also Defeated," *LAT,* November 9, 1994.
3. *Second and Third Strikers in the Adult Institutional Population* (Sacramento: Department of Corrections and Rehabilitation, Offender Information Services Branch, Estimates and Statistical Analysis Section, Data Analysis Unit, September 30, 2007), 46–51; Ehlers, Schiraldi, and Lotke, *Racial Divide.*
4. Lustig and Walker, *No Way Out.*
5. Haefele, "California Shipwreck."
6. Hood and Morris, "Brother, Can You Spare a Dime?" 194; Citrin, Green et al., "Public Opinion toward Immigration Reform," 858–81; K. Johnson, "An Essay on Immigration Politics, Popular Democracy, and California's Proposition 187," 629–73; Alvarez and Butterfield, "The Politics—The Resurgence of Nativism in California?" 167–80; Hero and Tolbert, "Race/Ethnicity and Direct Democracy," 806–18.
7. "Governor's Remarks in News Conference," November 9, 1994, box 319, folder 14, Anthony Beilenson Papers, University of California, Los Angeles (hereafter AB).
8. Wroe, *Republican Party and Immigration Politics,* 58–59.
9. "Prop. 187 Creators Come Under Closer Scrutiny," *LAT,* September 4, 1994.
10. Quoted in Wroe, *Republican Party and Immigration Politics,* 59.
11. "Figures behind Prop. 187 Look at Its Creation," *LAT,* December 14, 1994.
12. *California Ballot Pamphlet, General Election, November 8, 1994* (Sacramento: California Secretary of State, 1994), 51–53.
13. Ibid., 91.
14. Wroe, *Republican Party and Immigration Politics,* 78.
15. Gaines and Cho, "On California's 1920 Alien Land Law."
16. Wroe, *Republican Party and Immigration Politics,* 33; Simon and Alexander, *Ambivalent Welcome.*
17. "O.C. Reaction: Strong Praise, Condemnation," *LAT,* August 10, 1993.
18. Tichenor, *Dividing Lines,* 241.
19. "Immigration Bill Signed by Reagan," *San Diego Union-Tribune,* November 7, 1986.
20. Laham, *Ronald Reagan and the Politics of Immigration Reform.*

21. "Lobbyists Back Border Ditch Plan," *San Diego Union-Tribune,* March 16, 1989; "Border Protests Growing with Illegal Immigration," *Daily News of Los Angeles,* June 23, 1990; "Poway Control over Migrants, Limited," *San Diego Union-Tribune,* May 7, 1988.

22. Quoted in Wroe, *Republican Party and Immigration Politics,* 58. See also "O.C. Group Helps Fuel Anti-Immigrant Furor Viewpoint," *LAT,* August 30, 1993; and "Prop. 187 Creators Come Under Closer Scrutiny Initiative," *LAT,* September 4, 1994.

23. "Striking a Balance," *Orange County Register,* July 17, 1992.

24. In California, groups such as Zero Population Growth in Los Angeles demanded tough immigration restrictions. E. Gutiérrez, *Fertile Matters,* chapter 7.

25. Dianne Klein, "State Puts New Edge on Immigration Debate Border," *LAT,* September 6, 1993.

26. Cacho, "'People of California are Suffering'"; Santa Ana, *Brown Tide Rising;* Leo Chavez, *Covering Immigration;* Ono and Sloop, *Shifting Borders.*

27. See, for example, Almaguer, *Racial Fault Lines;* Sanchez, *Becoming Mexican American;* Deverell, *Whitewashed Adobe;* and E. Gutiérrez, *Fertile Matters.*

28. H. Johnson, *Undocumented Immigration to California, 1980–1993.*

29. See M. Davis, "Social Origins of the Referendum," For other accounts, see Mehan, "Discourse of the Illegal Immigration Debate," 249–70; and Calavita, "New Politics of Immigration."

30. For a critique of the ambivalent stance of Republicans in general during the preceding decade, see Laham, *Ronald Reagan and the Politics of Immigration Reform.*

31. Brimelow, "Time to Rethink Immigration?"

32. "Migrants Hear Buchanan Pitch a Tighter Border Speech," *LAT,* May 13, 1992; "Buchanan Sees California as Battle after War's End," *LAT,* April 4, 1992.

33. "State Puts New Edge on Immigration Debate Border," *LAT,* September 6, 1993.

34. "Immigration Ballot Initiative Possible," *San Diego Union-Tribune,* May 27, 1992.

35. John Tanton, "Immigration on the News Stands," *Social Contract* (Fall 1992): 1–2.

36. "Charting Wilson's Transformation on Immigration," *LAT,* November 2, 1994; "Wilson Urges INS to Ease Up Enforcement to Aid Growers," *LAT,* June 19, 1987.

37. Pete Wilson, "Pass More Laws, Set More Limits?" *LAT,* October 16, 1990.

38. "Wilson Backs Initiative for English-Only Law in State," *LAT,* August 21, 1986. See also Tichenor, *Dividing Lines.*

39. FAIR did praise Wilson at the time for pointing out that "illegal immigration" was a "prime contributor to California's and the nation's budget woes". "Cut Off Aid to Immigrants, Group Urges," *LAT,* November 21, 1991.

40. "Wilson to Seek Funds for Immigrant Services," *LAT,* November 22, 1991. In the same article, Democratic state senator Art Torres of Los Angeles said he was "disappointed" by Wilson's "anti-immigrant sentiment" but supported the governor's lobbying mission.

41. "Wilson's Huge Bill to U.S. Uses Sleight of Hand Budget," *LAT,* February 8, 1993.

42. "Why Governor Wants U.S. Immigrant Aid," *San Francisco Chronicle,* January 11, 1993.

43. "Welfare Rolls Reach Record Level," *LAT,* March 3, 1992. Wilson had begun attacking the state's assistance programs as "welfare magnets" in 1991, in the wake of criticism he received from Republicans for raising taxes earlier in the year, failing to cut state spending more, and supporting abortion rights. Wilson had difficulty with conservative voters and the Republican base throughout his first term in office. See George Skelton, "Wilson Backed in Welfare Cuts for Newcomers," *LAT,* December 12, 1991.

44. "Democrats and Unions Lead Prop. 165 Fight," *LAT*, October 7, 1992. See ballot arguments in *California Ballot Pamphlet, General Election,* November 3, *1992* (Sacramento: California Secretary of State, 1992).

45. George Skelton, "Beleaguered Wilson Needs a Winner on Election Day," *LAT*, November 2, 1992; "Welfare Measure That Boosts Governor's Power Sparks Costly War," *LAT*, October 25, 1992.

46. "Anti-Immigration Bills Flood Legislature," *LAT*, May 3, 1993; Eric Bailey, "Bill Would Bar Illegal Migrants at State Schools," *LAT*, January 5, 1994.

47. George Skelton, "Rational Talk on Immigrants for a Change," *LAT*, May 27, 1993.

48. Diane Feinstein, "Perspective on Illegal Immigration," *LAT*, June 16, 1993; Stein quoted in Glenn F. Bunting and Alan C. Miller, "Feinstein Raises Immigration Profile Politics," *LAT*, July 18, 1993. See also George Skelton, "Feinstein Takes Immigration Out of Closet," *LAT*, July 12, 1993; and "Immigration Foe Supporting Feinstein's Bill," *San Francisco Chronicle,* July 16, 1993.

49. John M. Broder, "Immigration Delicate Issue for Clinton," *LAT*, September 7, 1993; "Brown Endorses Proposal to Issue Tamper-Proof ID Cards," *LAT*, September 2, 1993; "State Puts New Edge on Immigration Debate Border," *LAT*, September 6, 1993.

50. Alan C. Miller, "Beilenson, Gallegly Ideas in U.S. Spotlight Politics," *LAT*, August 29, 1993.

51. Ronald Brownstein, "Polarization Marks Debate on Immigration Policy Politics," *LAT*, November 30, 1993.

52. The newspaper ads are quoted in Wroe, *Republican Party and Immigration Politics,* 44. See also "Many Obstacles to Wilson Plan on Immigration," *LAT*, August 11, 1993.

53. "O.C. Reaction: Strong Praise, Condemnation," *LAT*, August 10, 1993.

54. "Residents Call Migrants a Burden Immigration," *LAT*, August 22, 1993; "Immigration Stance Helps Wilson's Rating," *LAT*, August 21, 1993. Wilson's August approval rating grew to *22* percent, up from 15 percent in May, while his negative rating fell to 33 percent, the lowest it had been during the preceding year.

55. "Democrats' Ad Attacks Wilson on Immigration Politics," *LAT*, August 18, 1993.

56. Quoted in Chin, "Civil Rights Revolution Comes to Immigration Law," 343. See also Tichenor, *Dividing Lines,* 191.

57. Nevins, *Operation Gatekeeper,* 1.

58. Richard G. Polanco, "Cut the Rhetoric and Work on Solutions Immigration," *LAT*, August 13, 1993; George Skelton, "Straddling the Line on Illegal Immigration," *LAT*, August 26, 1993.

59. "Polarization Marks Debate on Immigration Policy Politics," *LAT*, November 30, 1993.

60. "Scope of Immigrant-Control Initiative in Dispute," *San Diego Union-Tribune,* November 21, 1993.

61. Wroe, *Republican Party and Immigration Politics,* 61–62, 67; "Immigration Opponents May Link Up with Perot," *Orange County Register,* August 20, 1993; "Backers of Anti-Illegal Immigrant Petition Deliver Signatures Initiative," *LAT*, May 17, 1994.

62. "Backers of Anti-Illegal Immigrant Petition Deliver Signatures Initiative," *LAT*, May 17, 1994.

63. Wroe, *Republican Party and Immigration Politics,* 68; Dan Schnur, telephone interview with author, October 15, 2008.

64. "Wilson Ad Sparks Charges of Immigrant-Bashing Politics," *LAT*, May 14, 1994. The ad ran for about two weeks at a cost of approximately $1 million.

65. On the role of racialized political advertisements, see Mendelberg, *Race Card.*

66. Domanick, *Cruel Justice,* 65. On the complex roots of California prison expansion, see especially Gilmore, *Golden Gulag.*

67. Based on an analysis using the keyword search term "crime" in the California Ballot Propositions Database, Hastings Law Library, http://holmes.uchastings.edu/library/california-research/ca-ballot-measures.html (accessed December 8, 2008).

68. Zimring, Hawkins, and Kamin, *Punishment and Democracy,* 17.

69. *California Ballot Pamphlet, General Election, November 8, 1994* (Sacramento: California Secretary of State, 1994), 36.

70. This was the tagline of several of Governor Wilson's campaign commercials, including one on immigration, www.youtube.com/watch?v=oof1PE8Kzng (accessed January 31, 2009).

71. "Grass-Roots Movement Pushes 'SOS' Initiative," *San Francisco Chronicle,* June 15, 1994; Wroe, *Republican Party and Immigration Politics.*

72. "Initiative to Deny Aid and Education to Illegal Immigrants Qualifies for Ballot," *LAT,* June 24, 1994.

73. "Firm Targets Illegal-Alien Proposition," *Daily News of Los Angeles* August 15, 1994; Wroe, *Republican Party and Immigration Politics,* 66.

74. Woodward and McDowell memo, "Talking Paper: Initial Survey Results and Winning Campaign Messages," July 14, 1994 (in author's possession).

75. Ibid.; Wroe, *Republican Party and Immigration Politics,* 15.

76. "Opponents Hire a Proven Winner," *Orange County Register,* November 2, 1994; "History Doesn't Favor Anti-Immigrant Initiative," *Long Beach Press Telegram,* September 16, 1994; Wroe, *Republican Party and Immigration Politics,* 75.

77. "Firm Targets Illegal-Alien Proposition," *Daily News of Los Angeles,* August 15, 1994.

78. *California Ballot Pamphlet, General Election, November 8, 1994* (Sacramento: California Secretary of State, 1994), 55.

79. "Firm Targets Illegal-Alien Proposition," *Daily News of Los Angeles,* August 15, 1994.

80. See Shultz, *Initiative Cookbook.*

81. Wroe, *Republican Party and Immigration Politics,* 76.

82. Frank Sharry, "Interested Parties" memo, December 7, 1994 (in author's possession).

83. "Taxpayers against 187 Campaign Update: Introducing the Taxpayers against 187 Staff," press release, box 319, folder 14, AB. See also Martinez, "Fighting 187."

84. On the role of nonprofits in the legalization programs of IRCA, see S. Baker, *Cautious Welcome,* chapter 5.

85. Ignatius Bau, interview with author, September 18, 2008, Oakland.

86. Jan Adams, interview with author, September 18, 2008, San Francisco.

87. Ibid.

88. Ibid.

89. "Californians United against Proposition 187: Statewide Contact List," September 6, 1994 (in author's possession).

90. "March Just a First Step, Latino Leaders Say," *LAT,* June 4, 1994.

91. Ignatius Bau, interview with author, September 18, 2008, Oakland.

92. Bau, "Immigrant Rights," 12.

93. Burt, *Search for a Civic Voice,* 319–20.

94. Mario Garcia, *Memories of Chicano History,* 314. In the early 1970s, groups such as CASA organized in undocumented communities, calling attention to abusive workplace and residential raids conducted by the INS and even calling for open borders. Pulido, *Black, Brown, Yellow, and Left.*

95. Burt, *Search for a Civic Voice,* 321.

96. Emily Goldfarb, telephone interview with author, November 6, 2008; Jan Adams, interview with author, September 18, 2008, San Francisco. For more recent organizing and advocacy work addressed toward such a framework, see the essays in Buff, *Immigrant Rights in the Shadows of Citizenship*.

97. See Simon and Alexander, *Ambivalent Welcome*.

98. "SOS Dominates California Campaign," *Migration News* 1, no. 4 (November 1994); "Feinstein's TV Attack on Immigration," *LAT*, July 10, 1994.

99. Nevins, *Operation Gatekeeper*, 1.

100. Rigoberto Rodriguez, telephone interview with author, December 2, 2008.

101. John Palacio, "Problem or Opportunity," *Orange County Register*, September 12 1994.

102. Frank Wu, telephone interview with author, November 12, 2008. For a similar position, see Park, "Race Discourse and Proposition 187," 175–204.

103. "Ardent Activism Hurting Anti-187 Effort, Some Say," *Sacramento Bee*, October 30, 1994.

104. Quoted in Wroe, *Republican Party and Immigration Politics*, 76.

105. Ibid.

106. Jan Adams, interview with author, September 18, 2008, San Francisco.

107. Wroe, *Republican Party and Immigration Politics*, 86–87.

108. "Ardent Activism Hurting Anti-187 Effort, Some Say," *Sacramento Bee*, October 30, 1994 (Munoz quote); Jan Adams, interview with author, September 18, 2008, San Francisco.

109. "Opponents Hire a Proven Winner," *Orange County Register*, November 2, 1994. The Taxpayers campaign claimed that internal polls and a Field Poll suggested the race was tightening in late October, but that the marches and walkouts sabotaged this movement. However, the largest demonstration took place on October 15, well before the polls were taken, suggesting the marches did not immediately raise support for the measure, though they certainly shaped news coverage of the campaign.

110. Quoted in Wroe, *Republican Party and Immigration Politics*, 88.

111. "White Supremacist Link Trips Prop 187," *San Francisco Chronicle*, October 13, 1994. See also "Pro-Prop 187 Group Admits It Bought Ads," *Orange County Register*, October 26, 1994. FAIR immediately sought to distance itself from Proposition 187, stating that Nelson was not working for the organization when he helped draft the measure and that FAIR had contributed no funding toward the campaign. But the Taxpayers campaign released documents showing that FAIR had arranged to purchase radio advertisements in the weeks before the election. "Both Sides Air Ads on Prop. 187," *LAT*, November 6, 1994.

112. "In Shadows of SOS," *Orange County Register*, October 21, 1994.

113. Wroe, *Republican Party and Immigration Politics*, 86.

114. "Prop. 187 Backers Counting on Message, Not Strategy," *LAT*, October 30, 1994.

115. Jacobson, *New Nativism*.

116. Bosniak, "Opposing Prop. 187," 555–619.

117. "Prop 187," aired October 16, 1994, on *Vista L.A.*, Channel 7, Los Angeles, UCLA Film and Television Archives.

118. See, for example, Newton, "Why Some Latinos Supported Proposition 187"; and Morris, "African American Voting on Proposition 187."

119. "Wilson Hasn't Decided on Controversial Prop 187," *San Francisco Chronicle*, September 10, 1994.

120. Empower America, "A Statement on Immigration," October 19, 1994, box 319, folder 14, AB.

121. "'SOS' Friends, Foes Get in Final Swings," *Orange County Register* November 6, 1994; "In Shadows of SOS," *Orange County Register*, October 21, 1994; "Prop. 187: It's Not Racist At All, Supporters Say," *Orange County Register*, November 6, 1994; "Supporters Say 'SOS' Measure also Saving Nation," *Orange*

County Register, October 29, 1994; "Prop. 187 Opponents Confront Ezell Immigration," *LAT,* October 13, 1994.

122. "For Pete Wilson, His Political Ambition Is Never Blind," *LAT,* July 23, 1995.
123. The symbolic dimensions of Proposition 187 constitute a central argument in Calavita, "New Politics of Immigration," 284.
124. Frank Wu, telephone interview with author, November 12, 2008.
125. Hayes-Bautista, *La Nueva California,* 127, 130. See also H. Johnson, *Undocumented Immigration to California.*
126. *California Ballot Pamphlet, General Election. November 8, 1994* (Sacramento: California Secretary of State, 1994), 54.
127. See Schrag, *Paradise Lost.*
128. Wroe, *Republican Party and Immigration Politics,* 96–107; "Davis Won't Appeal Prop 187 Ruling, Ending Court Battles," *LAT,* July 7, 1999.
129. Congressional Task Force on Immigration Reform, "Report to the Speaker Newt Gingrich," June 29, 1995, box 320, folder 8, AB. The committee was formed at the start of the 104th Congress.
130. For an insightful account of these developments and their impact on Asian American immigrants, see Fujiwara, *Mothers without Citizenship.*
131. Based on an analysis using the keyword search term "immigration" in the California Ballot Propositions Database, Hastings Law Library, http://holmes.uchastings.edu/library/california-research/ca-ballot-measures.html (accessed December 8, 2008).
132. The hotline group ultimately determined that 229 of these inquiries and complaints were "serious rights abuses." Cervantes, Khokha, and Murray, "Hate Unleashed," 9.
133. Pantoja, Ramirez, and Segura, "Citizens by Choice, Voters by Necessity."
134. Wong, *Democracy's Promise.*
135. Frank Sharry, "Interested Parties" memo, December 7, 1994 (in author's possession).
136. Emily Goldfarb and Ignatius Bau memo, Proposition 187 campaign, December 14, 1994 (in author's possession).
137. Adams, "Mobilizing against White Backlash," 1–6.
138. The Californians United campaign did not appear to be particularly successful at registering new voters, however. Five weekends of voter registration work in San Francisco during September only yielded four hundred new registrants, a result Adams admitted was "not gargantuan." "A Push to Get Immigrants to Vote Campaign to Defeat Prop. 187," *San Francisco Chronicle,* September 24, 1994.
139. Adams, "Mobilizing against White Backlash."

CHAPTER TWO

LOS ANGELES: CITY OF DIVERSITY, STRIFE AND PROMISE

Latino Los Angeles

The Promise of Politics

MARTIN SCHIESL, MARK M. DODGE

> REMEMBER—how we used to ask for street lights, bus transportation, play grounds, side walks, street repairs, for help in getting equal treatment in housing and employment?
> REMEMBER—how they used to cup their hands to their ears and say, "Speak louder, please. We only hear about one-fifth of what you are saying"?
> That is because only one-fifth of us had registered and voted. That is why we always ended up with one-fifth of the neighborhood improvements we needed.
> —Community Service Organization Get-Out-The-Vote flyer, 1948[1]

This 1948 Community Service Organization flier was emphatic in its message that the best way to make government responsive to the people was for the people to vote. Five decades later, history has repeated itself as a new generation of immigrants and their children experienced the consequences of powerlessness and being ignored, or worse, being blamed as scapegoats for larger socio-economic ills. In 1943, during the Zoot Suit Riots, uniformed military personnel attacked young Latinos on the streets of Los Angeles. In 1994, Governor

Pete Wilson led the campaign to pass Proposition 187, a voter initiative to deny millions of Latino children access to a public education and medical care. In both cases, the marginalized population was a group of significant size—people (by and large) whose first language was Spanish and who were not part of the political system. Each of these events also served as a catalyst that generated an intense and passionate reaction from the largely disenfranchised Latino community. Substantial numbers of eligible voters were motivated to enter the political arena (many for the first time) and elected new leaders which, in turn, resulted in the emergence of powerful new alliances. Energized by the voters' mandate, the new Latino elected leaders sought more than just ending the attacks on the community; they sought to use the power of government to improve the lives of ordinary people.

There are many similarities between the political activism of the 1940s and 1990s. The young activists of the 1940s were the children of those who had fled the violence of the Mexican Revolution of 1910 to 1917, a period during which 10 percent of the population in Mexico emigrated to the United States. The size of the community grew with additional migration and a high rate of child-birth so that in the 1940s Los Angeles was roughly 10 percent Mexican American. Comparatively, during the 1990s, many of the activists were from families escaping poverty in Mexico and the civil wars in Central America, especially El Salvador. The most notable difference is in the size of the two groups. During the Mexican Revolution, the numbers of immigrants measured in the tens of thousands. However, the wave of those escaping the poverty and civil wars of Mexico and Central America numbers in the millions. This has had a dramatic impact on Los Angeles in terms of race, class, and culture; demographic changes have corresponded to an economic restructuring as well as an outbound migration of Anglo Saxon Protestants who for decades dominated the region in terms of government and commerce. These migratory trends—into and out of Los Angeles—led to the rapid "Latinoization" of many smaller cities in Los Angeles County, effectively unseating the power from traditionally elected Anglo leaders to Latino leaders. The largest municipality, the City of Los Angeles, itself is roughly one-half Latino.

Finally, the growth among Los Angeles Latinos has occurred within the context of continued growth in California, in both total population and relative size to the rest of the United States. The growth of the state's congressional delegation illustrates these dramatic changes as well as the state's increased importance. In 1910, at the start of the Mexican Revolution, Latinos comprised only 2.4 percent of the state and California had only eight of the 435 members in the U.S. House of Representatives. The California delegation was the same as Kansas and Mississippi, and less than Minnesota. By the 1930s, when this story starts, California claimed twenty seats, the sixth largest total. In 1960, California surpassed New York to become the most populated state and was awarded 38 seats, and Latinos were roughly 10 percent of the state. Today the state's delegation has 52 seats, and Latinos are more than a third of the population.[2]

Votes, Coalitions, and Leadership

Latino Los Angeles became active in electoral politics during the 1930s, but the number of voters was small due to low rates of naturalization and the fact that only a few of the American-born children had reached voting age, which was then 21. During this era, three men captured the community's imagination: the President, Franklin D. Roosevelt, first elected in 1932; then the gubernatorial campaigns of Upton Sinclair (1934) and Culbert Olson (1938). Roosevelt's appeal was based on the fact that he "seemed to care about the poor."[3] The national Democratic Party put an emphasis on organizing the poor, blue-collar workers, and the foreign-born and their children (which then included about 25 percent of the country, mostly from Europe).

"After the 1932 election, the Democrats possessed a relatively vast coalition, in which Mexicans were numerically a modest part."[4] For this, Los Angeles Latinos were rewarded a few symbolic appointments to boards and commissions. Still, the number of eligible Mexican American voters was not sufficient to elect one of their own to the State Assembly or to the Los Angeles City Council. Even by the end of World War II, Latinos had not yet organized a collective voice comparable to the National Association for the Advancement of Colored People (NAACP), in the African American community, or the Japanese American Citizens League (JACL).

Nonetheless, with the absence of an organizational voice, in 1947 a handful of Latino businessmen encouraged 29-year-old Edward R. Roybal to run for the city council in the Ninth District. Despite his age, Roybal seemed older and more established than most other World War II veterans. Roybal was born in Albuquerque to a family that traced its roots back 400 years to the founding of Santa Fe. His parents moved to Boyle Heights from New Mexico in 1922 to start a new life following a railroad strike that had left Roybal's father unemployed. Edward Roybal graduated from Roosevelt High School, joined the New Deal Civilian Conservation Corps, attended the University of California at Los Angeles and then worked for the Los Angeles County Tuberculosis and Health Association. Roybal, his wife, and two children lived in "the flats" located on the southern edge of Boyle Heights.[5]

Roybal would run against an aging incumbent, Parley P. Christensen. Like most Angelenos of the day, Christensen was a native of another state. He became a national figure of the American Left in 1920 as the presidential candidate of the Farmer-Labor Party. In Los Angeles, Christensen successfully used progressive ideology and support from organized labor to cut across ethnic and racial lines to maintain a progressive coalition. This strategy worked for years because the Ninth District was progressive and multicultural in what was then a mostly white, Protestant, and politically moderate Los Angeles. Based in Boyle Heights, the Ninth District served as the entry point for immigrants, particularly Jews from Eastern Europe and smaller numbers of Latinos from Mexico. The district extended downtown, and included various residents from older homes on Bunker Hill to those in the cramped quarters of Little Tokyo. In addition, the Ninth District had a thriving commercial, entertainment, and office center. As the district turned south it took in part of Central Avenue, the center of segregated African American life in Los Angeles. This area had exploded in growth due to the arrival of Blacks who had escaped the serfdom of the "Jim Crow" American South. The cosmopolitan Ninth District was a cauldron of leftist political activity, residents radicalized by events in their home countries (including the Russian Revolution and the Mexican Revolution) and by the upsurge in political and labor activism during the Great Depression.[6]

In the campaign of 1947, Christensen once again utilized his labor and minority coalition to emerge victorious. Roybal finished third out of the five candidates, earning just 16 percent of the votes. However, after the election, Roybal and his small band of campaigners decided to stay together to form the Community Political Organization.

Over the next few months, a convergence of events, interests, and individuals began to unfold. Two participants from outside the community focused on helping the young activists organize into a stronger community voice. The first was Fred Ross, a talented young Anglo organizer who had previously worked with Mexican Americans in several surrounding communities and wanted to organize in Los Angeles. He sought to combine his strategic vision with the raw talent of the young activists, most of whom had learned leadership skills through service in World War II, or in unionized factories on the home front during the war. However, the main problem was money as the new group did not have the funds to hire Ross. About the same time, Saul Alinsky, the head of the Chicago-based Industrial Areas Foundation (IAF), wanted to start a new organizing project and heard of Ross. Alinsky, a Jew, had organized one of Chicago's multi-ethnic neighborhoods in conjunction with the Catholic Church and the United Packinghouse Workers union. This confluence of interests was to have an historic result. The Latino group broadened its goals beyond politics, changed its name to the Community Service Organization (CSO), and became a non-profit affiliated with the IAF. Alinsky agreed to undertake this first project focused on Latinos and to pay Ross' salary for the next year; Ross agreed to become the CSO organizer.[7]

One of the first tasks was to formalize CSO's structure. Roybal became chairman, in large part because he was widely known in the Mexican American community due to his recent campaign. He was also representative of World War II veterans and the emerging middle class. Jaime Gonzalez, a labor leader-turned-YMCA youth counselor, filled the slot of vice chairman. Emigrant Maria Duran, then a member of the executive board of the ILGWU Dressmakers Union, accepted the post of treasurer. The board also included steelworker Tony Rios and X-ray technician Henry Nava. Nava, the son of a barber, grew up in a local Spanish-speaking Presbyterian Church. Most of the twenty people coming to the CSO meetings were, like Rios and Nava, friends or co-workers of Roybal or, like Manuel, Roybal's uncle, part of the extended family.[8]

CSO decided to build from the ground up. It utilized nightly "house meetings," then an innovative process whereby members invited friends and family to their home to talk about their frustrations and to learn how by working together, through CSO, they could collectively address these concerns. Interested individuals were put to work on a committee or agreed to host a meeting of their own. At the same time, Ross moved to obtain the institutional support from the groups with the largest number of Latinos: organized labor and the Catholic Church. CSO established ties to two strategically situated unions in which core group members were already active: the AFL International Ladies Garment Workers Union (ILGWU) and CIO United Steel Workers. Each had ten to fifteen thousand members in Los Angeles and believed in organizing around labor and community issues. The Roman Catholic Church also embraced CSO. At the request of Monsignor Thomas O'Dwyer, Father William J. Barry, then an assistant pastor at St. Mary's Church in Boyle Heights, joined the CSO board. CSO also reached out to the Protestant churches, small business people, and to the large Jewish community.[9]

It became clear that elected officials were not motivated to address community concerns put forward by CSO because most of the people it represented were not registered to vote. So CSO began to focus its attention on voter registration. "All of us were voter registrars," recalled Margarita Duran, then enrolled at the University of California at Los Angeles. "That's how I met my husband. We registered people to vote. Fred [Ross] would pick you up at the house. He'd drop you off in a neighborhood. Then he'd pick you up after a few hours of work."[10] Those who agreed to register had to decide which political party to join. "Mexican Americans didn't really know the difference between the Democratic Party and the Republican Party," lamented ILGWU organizer Hope Mendoza, a World War II "Rosie the Riveter." "They would ask, 'What was Roosevelt?' You'd say, 'Democrat.' 'That's what I want to be.'"[11]

The results were phenomenal. "In a 3 1/2 month campaign by the Community Services Organization, more than 11,000 voters were registered in Los Angeles' eastside communities," announced the weekly *Belvedere Citizen* in April of 1948.[12] CSO celebrated its success in registering voters in Boyle Heights and Belvedere by sponsoring a dance at St. Mary's Church. up by running a non-partisan get-out-the-vote drive in June and November 1948. culcate the importance of voting in the newly registered. There was also a second did not vote in the 1948 presidential elections would be purged from the election pring municipal contests.

49, Edward Roybal officially made the transition from CSO President to candi- district city council seat. The campaign was based on two fundamental strategies- o voters, and then forming coalitions with other groups, most notably Jews, and anized labor, but also smaller numbers of Irish-American, Japanese-American, and African-American voters. Roybal beat out the other challenges and forced the incumbent into a runoff election. When the polls closed and the votes were counted, the extent of CSO's operation and the larger Roybal campaign became clear. Roybal received over 20,000 votes. This was more than double the *total* votes cast in the entire 1947 election. Roybal's margins were greatest in the Latino and Jewish sections of Boyle Heights.[13] The CSO-registered voters had turned out at the unbelievably high rate of 87 percent.[14] In July 1949, Roybal was sworn in as Los Angeles' first Latino City Councilman since 1881.[15]

The 1950s: Beyond Boyle Heights

Councilman Roybal authored several fair employment ordinances, delivered dozens of streetlights and sidewalks to his district, and took on the issue of police brutality, which came to a head when CSO's third president, steelworker Tony Rios, was beaten by members of the Los Angeles Police Department in 1952.[16] In all these efforts, Roybal continued to closely work with CSO, and with Jewish, Black, labor, liberal and religious allies.[17]

The new power at the ballot box was infectious and exhilarating. CSO took its message—voting makes a difference—to marginalized Latino neighborhoods around Los Angeles County. The total number of CSO registered voters climbed to 35,000 prior to the November 1950 election. CSO's influence now reached way beyond the Eastside, into the San Fernando Valley, the San Gabriel Valley, the Southeast portion of the County, and the Westside. CSO had effectively mobilized Latinos to vote.[18]

The most dramatic election was in the City of San Fernando, northwest of downtown. The city had grown up around a Spanish Mission, but was now part of the developing suburbs. Led by Hope Mendoza, CSO activists went door to door and registered hundreds in the segregated Latino sections of town. Then in April 1950, Latino activists turned out the Latino vote for a young Mexican American businessman, Albert G. "Frank" Padilla. Padilla not only became that city's first Latino councilman, but he came in first in a multi-candidate field for two seats.[19]

In the early fifties, as CSO expanded to other cities (Cesar Chávez joined in San Jose in 1952), in Los Angeles the organization enjoyed expanded political influence even as many activists started to focus on other aspects of their lives. This included getting married and having children, attending college and buying a home, usually in a developing suburb. "Housing was real scarce," recalled social worker Margarita Duran Mendez. "We had thought we'd buy a house in the City Terrace or East L.A. and stay close to the neighborhood. We couldn't find anything. And these houses [in southeast L.A. County] came really cheap. $100 down. Naturally we moved down here [to Norwalk]."[20] She added that her situation was similar to many of her friends. CSO's second president, Henry Nava, bought a house in Monterey Park. Hope Mendoza Schechter moved to the San Fernando Valley, as did Henry's brother, Julian Nava.[21]

The increasingly dispersed Los Angeles Latino community leaders began to play even more important roles in civic life as they concentrated on careers and families. This included garnering appointments to local and state boards and commissions. One of the most celebrated victories was Republican Governor Goodwin Knight's appointment of Carlos Teran to the East Los Angeles Municipal court. This made him the first Spanish-speaking judge in modern Los Angeles. Judge Teran is representative of the upwardly mobile members of the Mexican American Generation. The child of an immigrant, he was a company commander in World War II. Upon returning to the states, he used the GI Bill to go to college, graduating from the University of Southern California Law School. He was also active in the community, serving as President of the Board of Directors of the

Council of Mexican-American Affairs, and a member of the American GI Forum, a Latino veterans group.[22]

CSO spearheaded the movement that had profound and lasting consequence in Los Angeles and the state for generations to come; it successfully worked to change federal immigration law to make it easier for Latinos to become naturalized citizens by expanding eligibility and allowing the test to be taken in Spanish. In 1952 Senator Pat McCarran of Nevada was moving a major immigration bill through Congress. Hope Mendoza Schechter, the Latino liaison to Congressman Chet Holifield (D-East Los Angeles), said that Holifield persuaded McCarran to amend the bill, by using the phrase "it's politically important." Holifield also "flattered" McCarran, saying that the senator "would go down in history and this doesn't change the essence of the Act."[23] Soon thereafter, CSO also undertook organizing the first large-scale citizenship classes. In the fall of 1955, CSO sponsored a mass swearing in of 3,000 new citizens at the Hollywood Bowl.[24]

While still only a small portion of the city's population, Los Angeles Latinos continued to register voters in a city still dominated by Anglos throughout the fifties. On the city council, the only other "minority" was Roz Wyman, who was Jewish and female; there were no African or Asian American, or other women on the council. Councilman Roybal (whose district had never been majority Latino) continued to show leadership within his own ethnic community while maintaining cross-cultural, and class-based coalitions to advance the interests of his lower income constituents.

By 1958, the Mexican American generation stood on the cusp of another major breakthrough. Councilman Roybal, one of the most popular elected officials in Los Angeles, was running the open seat on the Los Angeles County Board of Supervisors. He enjoyed a broad coalition and the support of the retiring supervisor, John Anson Ford. At the same time, Los Angeles attorney Henry P. Lopez won the Democratic Party nomination for Secretary of State. The son of a Colorado beet farmer, Lopez had served in World War II, and was one of the first Latinos to graduate from Harvard Law School. Lie was active in the California Democratic Council (CDC), CSO, and the American GI Forum.[25]

Roybal and Lopez ended their symbolically powerful campaigns at Brooklyn (now Cesar Chavez) and Soto, in the heart of Boyle Heights, where the young Roybal had first won his city council seat nine years earlier. Despite well-run campaigns, the two lost in a cloud of scandal and anger that was to having last effects within the ethnic community. It initially appeared that Roybal had won the race for supervisor, but after days of recounting, and the discovery of additional voting boxes, he was declared the loser. Lopez lost his statewide race by a narrow 50,000-vote margin. It was particularly painful because he was the only statewide candidate to lose in what was otherwise a Democratic sweep. Some activists, like fellow attorney Herman Sillas, speculated his loss was due to anti-Latino bias. Lopez believed that it was the presence of a third party candidate that took anti-incumbent voters away from him.[26]

The 1960s: Congress and the State Legislature

Despite these setbacks, the Latino community experienced unprecedented victories over the next five years. In 1960, Mexican Americans played a major role in the presidential campaign of John F. Kennedy, and emerged from the experience with heightened expectations for the Latino role in politics at all levels of government. In 1961, for the first time, Latinos made the critical difference in the election of Sam Yorty as the new Mayor of Los Angeles. Mayor Poulson explained his defeat, saying, "In the districts where I won, there was a light turnout but in the Negro and Mexican districts the turnout was larger."[27] The victory was particularly sweet because *Newsweek* magazine gave Los Angeles Latinos credit for Yorty's win.[28] Sweeter still, Mayor Yorty quickly rewarded Latinos for their critical support. Yorty placed Dr. Francisco Bravo on the important Police Commission. He put Professor Julian Nava on the Civil Service Commission. More important still, Yorty placed Richard Tafoya on his personal staff where he functioned as a deputy mayor, a first for Mexican Americans.[29]

Latinos retained their momentum as 1961 rolled into 1962. Roybal was elected to Congress and Phil Soto and John Moreno were elected to the State Assembly, which was then a part-time job. Roybal, Soto, and Moreno benefited from post-Census reapportionment that created districts without incumbents. Each could campaign partly on their service as veterans of World War II, and on their city council records. All three received volunteers by virtue of their being part of the newly established Mexican American Political Association (MAPA).[30] Roybal and Soto won in districts without a majority of Latino voters. Roybal's urban district started in Boyle Heights and moved onto Hollywood. Soto, a small businessman and councilman in La Puente, represented the post-war movement of Latinos to the Southeastern Los Angeles County. He estimated that his district was 10 percent Latino. Schoolteacher Moreno was the Mayor of Sante Fe Springs and represented greater East Los Angeles. It was a majority Latino district, and should have been politically safe. However, Moreno would last only one term due to a drunken driving scandal that led Dionicio Morales to challenge him. A number of suburban elected officials backed Morales, such as Pico Rivera Councilman Frank Terrazas and Sante Fe Councilman Ernest Flores. This divide in Latino voters allowed an Anglo to beat them both in the primary. For his part, Soto survived two terms. He lost his "swing district" to a Republican as part of the landslide for Ronald Reagan in 1966.[31]

The following year, 1967, Julian Nava, became the first Latino to win a seat on the Los Angeles School Board, then a citywide race. Nava grew up on the Eastside, worked in an auto plant, and then earned a doctorate at Harvard University. Back in Los Angeles, he involved himself in the community and served as a Mayor Yorty appointee to the Civil Service Commission and helped found the American Federation of Teachers at California State College, Northridge. The campaign leadership represented his broad political support. African American City Councilman Tom Bradley Jewish AFL-CIO head Sigmund Arywitz, and Judge Leopoldo Sanchez served as campaign co-chairs. Hollywood celebrities Steve Allen and Gregory Peck lent their names, as did a host of present and former Democratic elected officials, including Senator Robert Kennedy.[32] Nava assembled a board coalition and campaigned vigorously. The San Fernando resident recalled that "University lecturing, in addition to the CSO experience, had prepared me very well to speak to all groups across town."[33]

In 1968, the Latino community played a huge role in the presidential primary victory of Senator Robert R Kennedy. That election brought Latinos into the national spotlight as never before, in part because of Kennedy's champion of the farmworkers' cause, and a massive voter registration and turnout by MAPA and the United Farm Workers. However, the election of Roybal aide Alex Garcia to represent the Boyle Heights-based Assembly District was nearly forgotten in the anguish over the assassination of Senator Kennedy. "Roybal called me and asked me to help," recalled Hank Lacayo, president of the 30,000 member United Auto Workers Local 887. "We won with Garcia because we went in with heavy fire power, with money, and all that."[34] Garcia subsequently moved to the State Senate and Richard Alatorre and Art Torres won seats in East Los Angeles, while Joseph Montoya won in the suburbs of Southeast Los Angeles in the early 1970s.[35]

From Washington, Congressman Roybal delivered federal job training programs to improve the lot of Los Angeles Latinos. He authored the amendment that created the first federal support for bilingual education, signed by President Lyndon Johnson in 1968. Roybal also helped place Latinos in appointed and civil service posts within the federal government. Likewise, Roybal helped to pass the 1965 immigration reform bill to increase the number of people from Mexico and Latin America who could enter into the United States. While no one then knew the full impact of this bill (which was the first major change in federal law since 1924), there was a definite sense of its historic value. In an image that captures both the past and the future, Roybal flew with Johnson on Air Force One to New York where, against the backdrop of the Statue of Liberty, he signed the new immigration bill that would help reshape California and the nation.

The upward trajectory of Latino political empowerment in the State Legislature, Congress, and in presidential politics was not matched on the Los Angeles City Council. The 1963 election to replace Roybal on the Los Angeles City Council exposed the weaknesses created within the Latino community by the passage of time and the demographic shifts in Los Angeles. Roybal sought to increase the chances that a Mexican American would replace him. He addressed a large gathering of activists at a MAPA called meeting at the Alexandria Hotel. "Many of you are under the false impression that the Mexican-American lives in the greater majority in this district," said Roybal. "In the last 10 years the Mexican-American population has been less than the Negro community!"[36] Holding on to the seat would require, as Roybal laid out, both Latino unity and an understanding with the African American community leaders. This might be possible because, despite the intense desire that Gilbert Lindsay get the seat, and thus become the first African American on the city council. There were also strong coalition campaigns underway for the spring 1963 municipal elections. Tom Bradley and Billy Mills were running with liberal white support in two other districts with a significant percentage of black voters. Roybal sought another meeting to decide upon a sole community representative; he could also use the time to talk with Black leaders to see if there was a Latino candidate whom they could coalesce. To Roybal the lesson from his 1949 election was clear: that in a cosmopolitan district where Latinos were a minority of the voters, they must unite behind a single candidate who had the ability to work with other groups. Unfortunately, it was not so clear to a majority of those present who proceeded to endorse three Latinos, ensuring a Latino divided electorate, and opposition from the African American community united behind former janitor Gilbert Lindsay.[37]

The problem was complicated by the fact that the strongest candidate, Richard Tafoya, Roybal's cousin, was a polarizing figure. The majority of the city council and key liberals strongly opposed his patron, Mayor Yorty, who had also angered the African American community by not following through on his promise to fire Chief of Police Parker. Moreover, Tafoy a was not seen as liberal enough for the progressive district. Meanwhile, absent an effort to find a Latino candidate agreeable to Black voters, a consensus developed among African Americans for Gilbert Lindsay, an aide to Supervisor Kenneth Hahn and a former CIO activist. Lindsay's supporters did not wait for the special election, instead getting allies on the city council to push through his interim appointment. Lindsay immediately reached out to the Latino community by hiring one of the candidates, Felix Ontiveros, to serve as his chief deputy.[38]

In the runoff, Roybal and other Eastside activists endorsed Tafoya.[39] These endorsements appear to have solidified the Latino support for Tafoya, but the candidate emphasized the reduced number of Spanish-speaking voters in the district due to the building of freeways, urban renewal, and the movement to the suburbs. "Mexican Americans went into Pico Rivera, Whittier, and Montebello. The Jewish population, which was very liberal and which could have voted for a Mexican, moved out," said Tafoya. "Who moved in? Mexicans from Mexico, primarily, who didn't vote."[40]

The anger within the Latino community over Tafoya's defeat only intensified because Lindsay's 1963 election coincided with the election of two other African Americans, Tom Bradley and Billy Mills. There were three Blacks, one Jew, and eleven Anglos on the fifteen-member city council. A sense of shock and then depression set in among Latino activists who never really considered they could lose the city council seat that for so long was emblematic of the community's political empowerment.[41]

The problem was painfully clear—there was no organization in Latino Los Angeles in the mid-sixties with the muscle exhibited by CSO in 1948–1952. Under the leadership of organizer Fred Ross, CSO made sure that Roybal was the only Latino who would appear on the ballot, it registered voters and then mobilized them with the assistance of the progressive elements of organized labor and the Catholic Church. At the same time, Roybal and CSO built alliances with non-Latinos to form a majority coalition. In response, a new form of organization emerged: the Latino political machine, that depended not on social movements, but on money and connections, in a way that had more in common with political traditions in New York and Chicago than Los Angeles.

Finally, understanding the development of California Latino politics requires a look at strategies in light of shifting demographics and changing rules. The post-Mexican American era can be broken down into three district periods: the rise of political machines in Los Angeles, the statewide Latino-business alliance, and the present Latino-labor alliance. These developments are unique to California, which never had the ethnic political machines so typical of the white ethnic immigrant period on the East Coast and Midwest. As Carey McWilliarns and others noted in the 1940s, political parties in California are weak and campaigns are candidate centered. The state's decision to place the party label on legislative candidates helped the Democrats come to power in 1958 and undoubtedly helped Latinos win seats in Congress and in the part-time State Legislature in 1962. The part-time nature of the Legislature also meant very limited staff and limited budgets to mail to constituents, making it harder to solidify a political base, and thus harder to hold on to newly won seats.

Latino Political Machines

The move to a full-time Legislature with large staffs was designed to enhance the power of the legislature relative to that of the governor and the lobbyists. But it also had major political implications because it quickened the trend toward concentration of power in Sacramento, which was possible because of the decline of volunteer-driven groups like Mexican American Political Association and the California Democratic Council. This made possible the creation of Latino political organizations with the ability to recruit candidates, direct financial and political support, and disciple members. Members of the Chicano Generation, who came to power in the early seventies, would lead these organizations. These new political forms were designed to take control politically of—and to hold on to—vast neighborhoods in Los Angeles with large numbers of Latino residents but small numbers of voters, like Boyle Heights and East Los Angeles. Assemblyman Richard Alatorre was the architect of this new organization, which also became identified with Art Torres.[42]

Alatorre became a close ally of Assembly Speaker Willie L. Brown, who developed the most powerful Speaker ship in modern state history. Key to the operation was Brown's ability to centralize power. This allowed Brown to raise huge amounts of campaign funds from a wide range of economic interests. One year he induced the United Farm Workers to turn over its half-million dollar war chest for his distribution. Brown spent liberally to protect incumbents against primary challengers as well as Republicans. He also aided legislators interested in moving up the political ladder. This was achieved, in part, through the newly created unit known as the Speaker's Office of Majority Services. For example, this unit organized an Alatorre-sponsored community event where volunteers painted over graffiti. To maximize the political benefits, they arranged for the press to cover the event and then sent copies of the resultant article, along with a letter from Alatorre, to district voters. At election time, Majority Services staff often transferred to the Speaker's campaign payroll to work on targeted legislative races. An assembly member's career was thus protected in return for his loyalty to the Speaker.[43]

Inside the Capitol, Speaker Brown named Alatorre to chair the powerful Reapportionment Committee to oversee the redrawing of the legislative boundaries following the 1980 Census. In this capacity, he helped Brown further consolidate power and he represented Latino participation in the ruling coalition. During the 1970s, the statewide Latino population had grown due to immigration and childbirth by 92 percent, from 2.37 million to 4.54 million. Latinos now constituted 20 percent of the state population but held few legislative or congressional seats. Alatorre was limited in his ability to draw districts favorable to Latinos because of the importance of votes and coalition politics. The most notable achievement of the redistricting was the creation of a second Latino congressional seat in Los Angeles County. The longtime United Auto Worker staffer and President Carter appointee, Esteban Torres, won the seat in the San Gabriel Valley. Mid-year Assemblyman Marty Martinez won an election to fill a third seat of an Anglo Congressman in Southeast Los Angeles who retired early. The general inclination to protect incumbents combined with the vested interests of other minority machines to reduce possibilities for new "Latino seats," especially in the State Legislature. Equally important, however, was the reality that few Latinos voted—and voters, not residents, decided elections. The low point was in Assemblywoman Gloria Molina's Boyle Heights-based district, where only seventeen percent were registered! This small number of voters made it difficult for Latinos to compete in areas where their proportion of residents would have otherwise made them a powerful force. Stated Brown: "They are fine people, but if they're not registered to vote they can't help you much."[44]

Legal Strategies Drive Politics

Beginning in the late 1980s a fundamental transition began to take place in the Latino community. Faced with the reality of perilously low voter participation, Latino activists sought to change the rules of the game as the best way to gain advantage at the ballot box. The most successful was the creation of "majority minority" districts that all but guaranteed Latinos election. This was achieved through a combination of federal intervention and legal action. Congress amended the 1965 Voting Rights Act and the U.S. Justice Department's subsequent interpretation had far reaching consequences. The federal government had long held that state and local government could not gerrymander district boundaries to prevent the election of a minority candidate. Now they decided that government at all levels now had the affirmative responsibility to create districts dominated by minorities even if it involved piecing together non-contiguous areas. Legal advocates pushed for district elections in cities, counties, and school districts where Latinos were having trouble winning in an at-large system. This would give Boyle Heights its own school board member, for example, reducing the need for extraordinary candidates like Julian Nava who could stitch together a citywide coalition. The strategy also reflected a dependence on an elite, top down legalism that had grown out of the later stages of the civil rights movement. It stood in stark contrast to CSO's earlier bottom-up strategy of mobilizing the masses and forming alliances with other communities. Instead, it dovetailed with the operation of the Alatorre-Torres machine then seeking to leverage its power in Sacramento to break into Los Angeles politics.[45]

The U.S. Department of Justice sued the City of Los Angeles for not creating a council district in which a Latino could be assured of winning. As a by-product of this suit, Boyle Heights City Councilman Art Snyder resigned in 1985. Assemblyman Alatorre was elected to the post with the help of Speaker Brown. Alatorre thus became the first Latino on the city council since Roybal resigned to take his seat in Congress some twenty-three years earlier. On the council, Alatorre became an ally of Mayor Tom Bradley, the city's first and only African American mayor.[46] Soon thereafter, Richard Alarcon broke another barrier and was elected to represent the eastern portion of the San Fernando Valley giving Latinos a second councilman for the first time. The Civil Rights Act was also used as the basis of challenging at large elections. This led the Los Angeles School Board to adopt district elections, making it easier to elect a Latino.[47]

Attention then turned to the five-member Los Angeles County Board of Supervisors. In 1988, the Mexican American Legal Defense Fund (MALDEF), the ACLU of Southern California, and the U.S. Department of Justice sued, claiming that the board had purposely drawn the lines to prevent the election of a Latino. After extensive maneuvering, the board created a largely Mexican American district. Assemblywoman Gloria Molina, now head of her own political machine, won, becoming the first Latina on the Los Angeles Board of Supervisors, just as she had been the first Latina in the State Legislature. At her swearing-in, Molina stating that she should not have been the first Spanish-speaking supervisor. "This victory should have been celebrated 30 years ago. That is why I want to dedicate this victory to Congressman Ed Roybal. They stole the election from him 30 years ago."[48]

Changes in the Voting Rights Act had a similarly dramatic impact on the state legislative races following the 1990 census, despite an acknowledged undercount of minorities. This was due to a second decade of unprecedented growth in the Latino population. Latinos now comprised 37.8 percent of Los Angeles County and more than a quarter of the state. When Republican Governor Pete Wilson and the Democratic-controlled Legislature failed to agree on a reapportionment plan, the issue went to the State Supreme Court. The Court—using the new interpretation of the Voting Rights Act—exaggerated the effects of the demographic changes by reducing the number of politically moderate, mixed suburban-urban districts in favor of Democratic-oriented, urban, majority-minority districts, and Republican-oriented, Anglo dominated suburban districts. Race based reapportionment thus served to reduce the lag-time between demographic change and political representation by radically changing the districts on the incumbents. The effort to create Latino districts resulted in a fourth Latino seat in Congress and the addition of legislative seats in the Eastern and Southeast portions of the county. Among those who would win a congressional seat was Assemblywoman Lucille Roybal-Allard, who took her father's seat. In so doing, she became the first Latina of Mexican heritage to be elected to Congress.[49] Another Latina with ties to the past was Nell Soto. She won a seat in the State Legislature where her husband, Phil Soto, had served from 1963 to 1967.[50]

The 1990 statewide reapportionment also produced the first large number of Latino legislators outside of Los Angeles. One Los Angeles Latino, Assemblyman Richard Polanco, an Alatorre ally, did more than anyone else to elect Latinos to the Legislature.[51] He recognized that there was a basic organizational void in the Latino community and labor had stopped being a major political player. The opportunity rested, as Polanco saw it, in raising large sums of money from business and then using it to run consultant driven and mail-oriented election campaigns in targeted seats. This Latino-business alliance produced generally conventional and moderate public policy and focused on existing voters. Moreover, there was a growing gap in thinking between more affluent third generation Latinos and the working class immigrants. Political columnist Dan Walters put it succinctly: "Anglo voters and middle-to-upper income Asians and Hispanics are identifying more strongly with the Republican Party. And while they may be outnumbered in the general population, they are the most likely to be politically active—to register and vote."[52]

Proposition 187

The Republican Party appears to have taken its growing share of the upwardly mobile Latino vote for granted as it moved to scapegoat immigrants for the state's economic malaise in 1994. Eighteen points behind in the polls just weeks before his reelection, Governor Wilson made the aforementioned Proposition 187, to deny public services to undocumented immigrants, the centerpiece of his campaign. The pro-187 campaign spent millions of dollars to air television commercials showed Mexicans illegally crossing the border while an announcer intoned, "And they keep coming." The Proposition 187 campaign served Wilson's short-term political needs because it allowed him to win reelection and for the Republicans to take control of the State Assembly and come close to winning control of the State Senate. Also dashed in the election was the hope of Senator Art Torres, the best known Latino in the state, who had sought to become the first statewide elected official. He narrowly lost the race for Insurance Commissioner.[53]

Governor Wilson had shocked the Latino community more violently than at any time since soldiers and sailors attacked unarmed Latinos in the Zoot Suit Riots during World War II. This traumatized the immigrant community and angered deep-rooted Mexican Americans. The loudest voices of support for the immigrant community came from Cardinal Roger Mahony and the Catholic Church, and a number of AFL-CIO unions. (Only a majority of Asians, Jews, and Latinos vote against the initiative.[54]) Among Latinos, Proposition 187 led to an unprecedented level of pre-election mobilization, with 100,000 people marching through the streets. But neither Proposition 187 nor Torres on the ballot substantially increased turnout. "The forecast is for rain, but there is sun behind those clouds," stated Congressman Xavier Becerra.[55]

The Republican Party continued its anti-Latino drumbeat into 1995 and 1996. This further engrained Proposition 187 in the collective memory even as it was appealed in the courts (and eventually overturned). With the November 1994 Republican takeover of Congress, Speaker Newt Gingrich adopted the anti-immigrant agenda: "House GOP Charts California Agenda," read one headline in the *Los Angeles Times*.[56] Congress proceeded to deny benefits to legal residents to undocumented and legal non-citizen residents alike. In response, an unprecedented number of Latinos—including some who had been in California for decades—-completed the process to become citizens and to register to vote. The number grew rapidly because President Clinton, recognizing the value of Latino voters, cut the time it took the federal government to process citizenship applications from two years to six months.[57]

In California, the Republicans in 1996 underscored the importance of voting for Latinos by backing Proposition 209 to end affirmative action, reducing opportunities for college and employment.[58] Worse yet, the 1996 Republican Dole for President campaign openly appealed to racial antagonisms and linked affirmative action to immigration issues. "The significance of Dole's endorsement of California's Proposition 209 is not that it was a new political strategy, but rather, by openly appealing to white racial resentment for political gain, it revived a tactic that had been considered off-limits in American politics since the [pro-segregationist] George Wallace presidential campaign in 1968."[59] As a result, 80 percent of California Latinos voted for Clinton, the best performance for any Democrat since President Johnson in 1964. Moreover, a third of the Latino voters "either naturalized or turned 18 years of age since the last election."[60] There were also changes among Anglo voters. Los Angeles County, which had voted for Ronald Reagan for president in 1980 and 1984, voted for Clinton in 1992 and 1996, allowing the Democrats to carry the state in a presidential election for the first time since 1964.[61] The increased Latino civic engagement combined with the intensity of the anti-Latino attacks produced a new interest in the plight of immigrants by progressive non-Latinos, organized labor, the Catholic Church, and by the Democratic Party. The time was ripe for a reemergence of a more activist style of Latino coalition politics as practiced by Roybal and CSO and segments of organized labor in the late 1940s.

Latino-Labor Alliance

Yet another unpredictable event was to shape the modern history of California Latino politics. James Wood, the executive secretary of the Los Angeles County Federation of Labor died in mid-1995 (about the same time as the national AFL-CIO elected new, more aggressive leadership). This opened the door to a Latino to head the Los Angeles Federation more than a decade before it would otherwise have occurred in the seniority driven institution. Miguel Contreras, the County Federation's Political Director, emerged victorious, earning the right to speak for 600,000 union members in Los Angeles County. He had assets that uniquely positioned him to tap into the political developments within the state, the labor movement, and the immigrant community.

Born into a farmworker family in Dinuba, a small town south of Fresno, in the Central Valley, Contreras saw the confluence of labor and culture and politics and its impact on workers and their families. He first met Cesar Chavez when the labor leader came to town to rally workers to campaign for Robert Kennedy in the 1968 presidential primary. After Kennedy's assassination, Contreras joined the UFW's Ranch Committee and then, in 1973, moved to Toronto. Canada to help organize the grape boycott. There he learned the art of Alinsky-style organizing that would underpin the rest of his life. He worked with labor unionists, housewives, students, as well as ministers, priests, and rabbis. Returning to California, he became an organizer for the Hotel Employees and Restaurant Employees, taking on tough projects in San Francisco, Los Angeles, and other cities. In these jobs, he worked with a multiracial workforce, but his knowledge of Spanish was instrumental in organizing the increasingly large number of immigrants in the hospitality industry (some, like himself, who had started as farmworkers). During these and other jobs, he worked with some of the best organizers of his time, including Cesar Chavez, Dolores Huerta, and their mentor, Fred Ross.[62]

Contreras immediately began to look for political opportunities. The goal for organized labor was, like for Latino Los Angeles, to demonstrate that it was relevant politically—that it could go beyond backroom deal making to mobilize its members to walk precincts and to vote in ways that it had not done for years. Contreras found a place where there were low expectations, but a high level of rewards if victory was achieved: the 1996 legislative elections. "Assembly Democrats are saying, we will win in the Salinas area … we will win in Orange County … but don't think we can win in Los Angeles," Contreras said afterwards. "We said, no, we are targeted and we are focused and we are working in conjunction with the national AFL-CIO. So we are going to put all the unions on the same page when it came to politics in November 1996."[63] The new labor movement in Los Angeles focused on "kitchen table economics" and delivered the message by mail and with 3,500 union volunteers. At the same time, SEIU and the education unions utilized their Opportunity PAC, which spent hundreds of thousands of dollars on these races. On Election Day, Los Angeles labor helped Democrats, including a Latina community college teacher, Sally Havice, win in historically Republican suburbs, and thereby take back the majority in the State Assembly. This led to the election of Cruz Bustamante as the first Latino speaker. One of his major achievements was the restoration of some programs used by immigrants that were cut by Newt Gingrich and the House Republicans in Washington, D.C.

With Los Angeles labor having demonstrated that they could deliver the winning margin between two self-selecting candidates, Contreras then sought to prove that the new labor movement could elect one of its own. The opportunity presented itself the next year in a special election for the assembly seat based in Boyle Heights, the birthplace of CSO and the historic center of progressive Latino politics. But those days seemed so far away. Louis Caldera had occupied the seat. He was a talented man, Harvard and West Point educated, but a self-identified moderate largely seen as a "business Democrat." The heir apparent was Vickie Castro, a school board member and protege of Supervisor Molina. Labor's candidate was union organizer Gilbert Cedillo. He was a product of the Eastside, with ties to the old CSO and Jewish labor. Most importantly, as the leader of the SEIU union representing county workers, he had played a pivotal role in saving the County General Hospital, where the largely uninsured Eastside residents obtain health care. He did this by putting thousands of protesters in the streets and by having national union leaders pressure President Clinton to provide a partial bailout. That campaign set a new tone for the labor and community alliance.

Cedillo, the crusading labor leader, started the campaign far behind Castro, the entrenched politician, who enjoyed a huge lead in the polls, ample financing, and a traditional résumé. Had Cedillo run a standard campaign he would have lost badly, as Roybal had against Christensen in 1947. He could win only if the campaign became a cause, and labor and its allies dramatically enlarged the number of voters. There would be three parallel and reinforcing efforts. Cedillo's campaign made the case that he would be the best person for the job. The Los Angeles County Federation of Labor had its campaign, based on economic issues, with its own mail program and a dozen full-time organizers who mobilized hundreds of others to communicate with AFL-CIO members. Equally important was the "new voter" program, led by the immigrant unions, and community allies, such as Hermandad Mexicana National, led by the aging labor and Latino activist Bert Corona. This was possible because he had mentored a number of the new labor leaders, including María Elena Durazo, and dreamed of building a new social movement. Their message was clear and passionate: immigrants needed to vote as a way to fight the attacks on their families and on their community. In their fight, Cedillo would stand and fight with them. The Latino Caucus added to Cedillo's margin when it arranged for some business groups to back Cedillo.[64]

This "new style" of campaigning was reminiscent of Roybal's initial win in 1949, when CSO brought thousands of new voters to the polls—and it worked. Cedillo won big, sending shock waves through the political establishment. (For his part, Cedillo would keep faith with the immigrant community in his fight for a driver license bill for non-citizens.) Politics in Latino Los Angeles had changed course. In the succeeding years, the County Federation of Labor has become a political machine, consciously constructing a Latino-labor alliance, as well becoming a force in other ethnic and minority communities. This is due to its unique ability to deliver thousands of campaign volunteers at a time when activists are absent from many campaigns. It is also due to the ability of organized labor to target large sums of money, spent wisely with the aid of top-flight political consultants. The ability to exercise such influence is due, in part, to the huge influx of Latinos into Los Angeles and the corresponding flight of Anglos and much of the traditional business elite. It also reflects labor's ever-present attempts to speak for working families and for immigrants beyond its own membership, and its partnerships with the faith community. Contreras and new labor received generally positive marks from the *Los Angeles Times,* for which Frank Del Olmo provided a Latino voice.[65]

The changing of the formal political rules in California, and in Los Angeles, also contributed to the lessening of the power of incumbent politicians. For the Latino community, it represented both a threat to existing Latino-held seats while holding the promise for Latino victories in Anglo-held seats.[66] Under voter-approved term limits (yet another conservative voter initiative, this one designed to drive African American Speaker Willie Brown from power), elected officials may serve only three two-year terms in the Assembly, and two four-year terms in the Senate. Los Angeles voters followed suit and imposed limits of two four-year terms on their city councilmembers. These limits have led to constant turnover in the ranks of the once entrenched politicians. Up-and-coming elected officials still need to establish name identification and to develop a fundraising base, and those in office still influence their replacement. However, there has been a fundamental shift in power away from politicians and towards the constituency groups who participate in this game of musical chairs.[67]

The new Los Angeles-based Latino-labor alliance came into its own in Sacramento with the election of Antonio Villaraigosa as the second Latino speaker, and the first from Los Angeles. A smart and charismatic leader, Villaraigosa was a former organizer for United Teachers Los Angeles. When forced out by term limits, he decided to run for mayor of Los Angeles. Early polls gave him only 4 percent support, a measure of how little press state legislators receive in the celebrity and crime-oriented Los Angeles media, far behind a number of other contestants. The County Federation of Labor decided to go all out and Villaraigosa sought to construct a coalition based on the Roybal model. In one of the memorable rises in local politics," the coalition carried Villaraigosa into the runoff and into a 47 to 47 tie in the polls just days before the runoff. "Labor, the constituency that is the linchpin of his coalition, is the single most potent anti-nationalist force in the city. Time and again over the past five years, the County Federation of Labor has opposed ethnocentric candidates backed by Polanco with class-oriented candidates of its own," opined *LA Weekly's* Herald Meyerson.[68] In the end, Villaraigosa came up short, but it was a dramatic event, with the defeated candidate's party outnumbering that of the victorious Jimmy Harm. Shortly thereafter, Villaraigosa gambled again: he defeated a city council incumbent from Boyle Heights by dramatically increasing voter turnout with the help of labor.

Cedillo and Villaraigosa were not the only ones to emerge from the ranks of Latino-labor alliance. In 2002, Cedillo moved to the State Senate, filling the seat occupied by Richard Polanco, who was forced out by term limits. This opened up the Boyle Heights based seat in the State Assembly. The progressive candidate was Fabian Nuñez. The twelfth son born to a maid and a gardener, the 35-year-old Nuñez attended college and became a labor organizer. Nuñez came to prominence in East Los Angeles fighting the passage of Proposition 187. Soon thereafter, Nuñez assumed the post as political director of the Los Angeles County Federation of Labor, AFL-CIO, where he worked with Miguel Contreras to forge a Latino-labor alliance. Nuñez then headed the governmental relations unit for the Los Angeles Unified School District.

Nuñez was opposed by a more conventional Latino candidate, Pedro Carrillo, aide to Congresswoman Lucille Roybal-Aliard, and who was backed by forces close to the California Chamber of Commerce. The business interests pumped resources into both Carrillo's formal campaign, which was very nasty, and into a series of "independent expenditures" on behalf of their candidate. However, this was a fight that labor was determined to win. The Los Angeles County Federation of Labor and the Opportunity PAC spent $500,000 on their own "independent expenditures" that included precinct walkers on release time and Spanish-language TV ads. Nuñez won and, in his freshman year, was elected Speaker of the Assembly by his new colleagues. His election as speaker was supported and encouraged by two important mentors—City Councilman Antonio Villaraigosa and AFL-CIO head Miguel Contreras.

Mayor Antonio Villaraigosa

Antonio Villaraigosa soon eclipsed Nuñez by being elected as the first Latino Mayor of Los Angeles since Cristobal Aguilar left office in 1872. Villaraigosa's election in 2005 drew national and international coverage. In its cover story, entitled "Latino Power," *Newsweek* emphasized that Villaraigosa's dramatic defeat of an incumbent mayor in the nation's second largest city was emblematic of the rise of Latinos within the political arena.[69] In this they are correct. There is no question that Villaraigosa represents a major electoral breakthrough. But even as Villaraigosa's election is an historic milestone, he is also representative of a long tradition of coalition politics in Los Angeles. For the first time, Latinos accounted for a quarter of the city's electorate. While this was a large increase over previous years, it still necessitated an electoral alliance. Villaraigosa won with a coalition that included Jews, African Americans, Asians, organized labor, and the liberal-left. It is not a coincidence that just such an alliance elected Edward R. Roybal as the first Latino to the Los Angeles City Council back in 1949 from a district in which Latino voters were likewise a minority. It was a matter of philosophy and strategy that led Villaraigosa to make history as a Latino candidate by campaigning to be the mayor "for all of Los Angeles."

Villaraigosa thematically stressed bringing the city together and injecting new energy into municipal government. He also benefited enormously from an engaging personality, government experience, and his years as a coalition builder and fundraiser and the high name identification from the previous mayoral campaign that had catapulted him to a celebrity status rare for politicians. The endorsement of U.S. Senator John Kerry (for whom Villaraigosa had been a national co-chair of his 2004 presidential campaign) served to reinforce the councilman's momentum and helped secure votes in the more politically moderate San Fernando Valley. In the final days, Villaraigosa captured the endorsement of both city's newspapers. "Villaraigosa's drive, people skills and knack for coalition-building earned our endorsement in 2001," noted the *Los Angeles Times,* before concluding: "He is the best choice to lead Los Angeles."[70]

The most fundamental change in the city's politics that made victory possible, in addition to the growing number of Latino voters, was the creation of a labor-based, progressive and multicultural network of organizations, donors, and elected officials. The architect of this new Los Angeles was labor leader Miguel Contreras, who died, at age 52, two weeks prior to Villaraigosa's triumphant election. While the Los Angeles County Federation of Labor did not campaign for Villaraigosa as it had in all his previous races (because the incumbent, Mayor Hahn, had delivered for labor), the majority of labor's dollars and votes went to the former teachers' union organizer. Contreras, more than anyone else, had helped construct the foundation for victory by increasing Latino voter registration and by restitching the pieces of progressive Los Angeles. Lie led the movement that redefined the role of local government as helping to create a livable city for immigrants and working families.[71]

On Election Day, Villaraigosa decisively defeated Mayor Hahn. The 59 to 41 percent margin represented a victory for his coalition strategy of reaching out to every group and every geographic region of the city. Latino elected officials, such as Assemblywoman Cindy Montañez of San Fernando, partnered with hundreds of farmworkers and hotel workers who helped turn out the Latino vote in the Northeast San Fernando Valley. The Villaraigosa campaign oversaw a parallel operation in its base in East Los Angeles, the political birthplace of California Latino politics. These turnout efforts reinforced the desire by many Latinos to elect one of their own. For the first time, Latinos represented 25 percent of the total city electorate; an overwhelming 84 percent voted for Villaraigosa. According to the *Los Angeles Times'* exit poll, he also enjoyed majority support from three important groups: Jewish voters, union members, and liberals, and split white voters. Among identified ethnic and racial groups, Villaraigosa won 55 percent of the Jewish voters (17 percent of the total), 48 percent of African Americans (15 percent of the electorate), and 44 percent of the Asian voters (5 percent of the total). Even though Villaraigosa narrowly missed receiving the majority of African American votes, he ran strong with Blacks under 45 years of age, which is seen as an important step in healing historic tensions. Celebrating the victory, the rainbow of multicultural Los Angeles joined Villaraigosa on stage.[72]

The Promise of Politics

The search for a Latino political voice expressed in the 1948 CSO leaflet has been realized many times over. Today, Latinos are omnipresent in Los Angeles City Hall. The large and growing number of Latino voters is a reality in many districts. The number of Latino elected and appointed officials—beginning with Mayor Antonio Villaraigosa—provides a level of influence in the corridors of power unknown in previous generations. The politically powerful Los Angeles County Federation of Labor has served an important role in electing councilmembers and in advocating for policies that benefit immigrants and working class families. Organized labor also serves as a bridge to other minority, religious, and political organizations that help reduce the political isolation and parochialism that is more prevalent with ethnocentric candidates.

Los Angeles Latinos also benefit from the statewide Latino population growth, and the fact that the Latino Caucus is now the largest group within the majority party within the State Legislature. Moreover, close to half of the Latino Caucus members are from Los Angeles County. This helps account for the fact that three of the last five Assembly Speakers have been Latinos, and two of the three—Villaraigosa and Nuñez—are from Los Angeles. Likewise, five of the seven Latino Members of Congress are from Los Angeles County; moreover, four the five are Latinas: Grace Napolitano, Lucille Roybal-Allard, Linda Sanchez, and Hilda Solis. There are also a growing number of women and men serving in local government. Gloria Molina is the County Supervisor, Rocky Delgadillo is the City Attorney, and Alex Padilla is the City Council President.

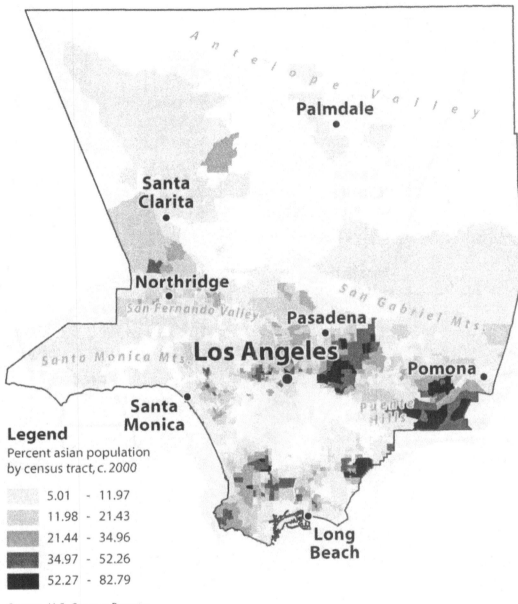

Legend

Percent asian population
by census tract, c. 2000

5.01 - 11.97
11.98 - 21.43
21.44 - 34.96
34.97 - 52.26
52.27 - 82.79

Source: U.S. Census Bureau

The fifteen-member city council includes four Latinos (27 percent), and 82 of the 344 board and commissioners are Latino (24 percent).[73] Many of the county's smaller cities are now entirely Latino-led, from San Fernando to Southgate.

The demographic and political changes over the last sixty years since the end of World War II are profound. Never again will the Latino community be so highly dependent on a single

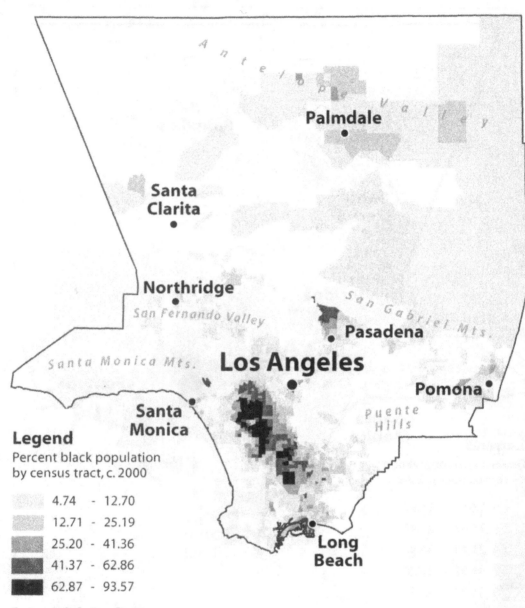

Legend

Percent black population
by census tract, c. 2000

4.74 - 12.70
12.71 - 25.19
25.20 - 41.36
41.37 - 62.86
62.87 - 93.57

Source: U.S. Census Bureau

elected official, as it was when Edward Roybal was the only major elected official in the city and the state. Yet his election and public service was an important milestone in the community's political awakening and development. Moreover, the political pioneers' realization—that votes count, coalitions matter, and leadership makes a difference—is a timeless truism. Still, politics occurs within a larger political context. This may also help explain the timing of the two big breakthroughs. The Roosevelt New Deal Democratic Party coalition and World War II changed

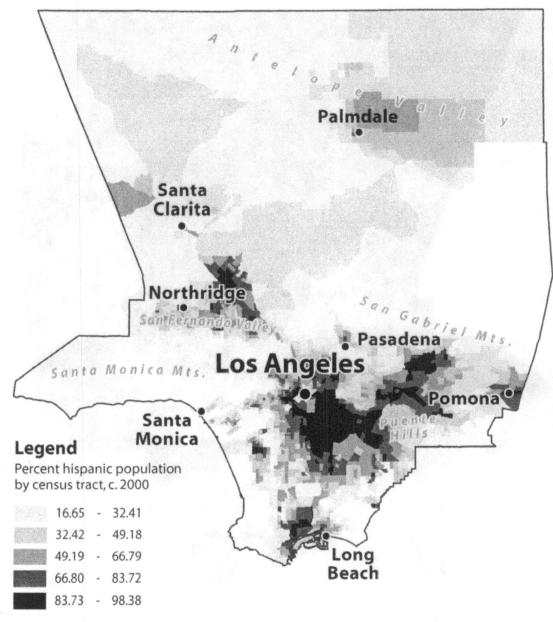

Legend

Percent hispanic population
by census tract, c. 2000

	16.65 - 32.41
	32.42 - 49.18
	49.19 - 66.79
	66.80 - 83.72
	83.73 - 98.38

Source: U.S. Census Bureau

the way Latinos saw themselves and the way the community was approached by potential allies. So today, Latinos have decided to stand up for their rights at the same time the sixties values of civil rights and equal opportunity have come to dominate cities like Los Angeles. "Today's Democrats are the party of the transition from urban industrialism to a new postindustrial metropolitan

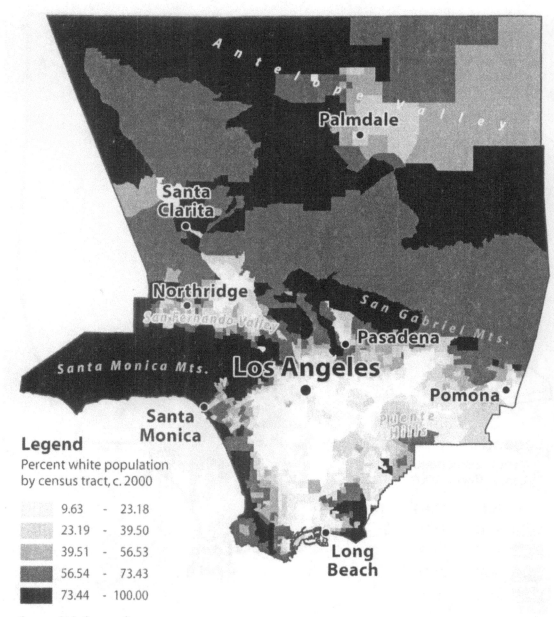

Legend

Percent white population
by census tract, c. 2000

9.63	– 23.18
23.19	– 39.50
39.51	– 56.53
56.54	– 73.43
73.44	– 100.00

Source: U.S. Census Bureau

order in which men and women play equal roles and in which white America is supplanted by multiracial, multiethnic America."[74]

Favorable context alone may not be enough to trigger a large increase in civic engagement. It may require a catalyst. This helps to explain why the two largest jumps in the percentage of Latino voter' registration in California history occurred in the years following traumatic attacks on the community. In Los Angeles, five years after the Zoot Suit Riots, the 1948 CSO driven voter registration drive netted 15,000 new voters that more than doubled the size of the Latino electorate. The momentum continued and, by 1950, the number of new Latino voters had grown to 35,000. So, too, in 2000, five years after Proposition 187, the number of new voters had doubled. In Los Angeles, this translated to 500,000 new Latino voters. What differentiates the two periods is the size of the Latino community. However, the number of residents is not enough. What counts is the number of voters, activists and elected officials. At least in the City of Los Angeles, the need for Latino civic engagement and coalition politics will continue as people from varied backgrounds continue to seek the promise of politics—and a fulfilling life—in a diverse metropolitan community.

Notes

1. CSO, "Attention Voters, We Are 16,000 Strong," 15/Mexican Groups, 1948, Jewish Community Relations Council Papers, Urban Archives Center, California State University, Northridge.

2. Mark Baldassare, *California in the New Millennium: The Changing Social and Political Landscape* (Berkeley: University of California Press, in conjunction with the Public Policy Institute of California, 2000), p. 3; David Hayes-Bautista, La Nueva California: Latinos in the Golden State (Berkeley: University of California Press, 2004), 16–17. *California Statistical Abstract*, (Sacramento: State of California, 1970), p. 11; *California Statistical Abstract*, (Sacramento: Department of Finance, State of California, 2001), p. 11; *Democracy At Work, The Official Report of the Democratic National Convention, 1948* (Philadelphia: Local Democratic Political committee of Pennsylvania, 1948), p 553.

3. Rodolfo Acuña, *Occupied America: A History of Chicanos,* Fourth Edition (New York: Longman, 2000), p. 216.

4. Juan Gomez-Quinones, *Roots of Chicano Politics, 1960–1940* (Albuquerque: University of New Mexico Press, 1994), pp. 400–401.

5. Author's interview with Edward Roybal, Pasadena, March 10, 1995; Author's interview with Roger Johnson, Hollywood, December 19, 1981; Himilce Hovas, *The Hispanic 100: A Ranking of the Latino Men and Women Who Have Most Influenced American Thought and Culture* (New York: A Citadel Press Book, 1995), pp. 81–85.

6. Author's interview with Leo Frumkin, for Japanese American National Museum, Tarzana, December 19, 2001; Roger Johnson interview; Author's interview with Margarita Duran Mendez, Norwalk, March 11, 1995; Author's interview with Hope Mendoza Schechter, Sherman Oaks, September 3, 1994; Author's interview with Tony Rios, Los Angeles, 1992–2002; Edward Roybal interview; "Parley P. Christensen," *Who's Who in California,* p. 173.

7. Kenneth C. Burt, "Latino Empowerment in Los Angeles: Postwar Dreams and Cold War Fears, 1948–1952," Labor's *Heritage,* Vol. 8, No. 1 (Summer 1996), pp. 4–25; Sanford D. Horwitt, *Let Them Call Me Rebel: Saul Alinsky—His Life and Legacy* (New York: Vintage Books, 1992), pp. 222–226.

8. Author's interview with Jaime Gonzalez Monroy, Monrovia, June 22, 1997; Author's interview with Henry Nava, Monterey Park, February 9,1995; Henry Nava interview; Tony Rios interview; Edward Roybal interview; Margarita Duran Mendez interview.

9. Author's interview with Msgr. William J. Barry, Newport Beach, November 2, 1994; Henry Nava interview; Tony Rios interview; Hope Mendoza Schechter interview; Sanford D. Horwitt, *Let Them Call Me Rebel: Saul Alinsky—His Life and Legacy*, pp. 231–332.

10. James Mendez interview.

11. Hope Mendoza Schechter interview.

12. "Latin Vote Registration Doubled, Group Announces," *Belvedere Citizen,* April 30, 1948, p. 1. See also "X-Ray Used in Registration of Voters for Tests for TB," *Los Angeles Daily News,* March 6, 1948, p. 2; "Spanish-Speaking Group Spurs Vote Registration," *Los Angeles Times,* March 15, 1948.

13. "Tabulation of Returns, City Council District 9, City of Los Angeles, 31 May 1949," Los Angles City Archives. The precincts were plotted to a precinct map of the district to develop insights in voting patterns by neighborhood. Katherine Underwood, "Process and Politics: Multiracial Electoral Coalition Building and Representation in Los Angeles' Ninth District, 1949–1962" (Ph.D. diss., University of California, San Diego, 1992).

14. Tony Rios interview; CSO, "Highlights of the Past 20 Years," author's files; Minutes, JCRC, June 14, 1949, p. 2, in 10/CSO-1948–1949, Jewish Community Relations Council Papers, Urban Archives Center, California State University, Northridge.

15. For a fuller description of the election, see Kenneth C. Burt, "The Power of a Mobilized Citizenry and Coalition Politics: The 1949 Election of Edward Roybal to the Los Angeles City Council," *Southern California Quarterly,* Vol. 85, No. 4 (Winter 2003), pp. 413–438.

16. Kenneth C. Burt, "Tony Rios and Bloody Christmas: A Turning Point Between the Los Angeles Police Department and Latino Community," in the *Western Legal History: The journal of the Ninth Judicial Circuit Historical Society,* Vol. 14, No. 2 (Summer/Fall 2001).

17. One of the requests that the CIO and the Catholic Church made of Tony Rios in 1952 is that he became a union organizer. See Kenneth C. Burt, "The Battle for Standard Coil: The United Electrical Workers, the Community Services Organization, and the Catholic Church in Latino East Los Angeles," in Robert W. Cherny, William Issel, and Kieran Walsh Taylor, eds., *American Labor and the Cold War: Grassroots Politics and Postwar Political Culture* (New Brunswick, NJ: Rutgers University Press, 2004), pp. 118–140.

18. Author's interview with Dan Luevano, Sacramento, June 22, 1996; Tony Rios interview; Hope Mendoza Schechter interview CSO, "Highlights of the Past 20 Years," author's files; Ralph C. Guzman, *The Political Socialization of the Mexican American People* (New York: Arno Press, 1976), p. 141.

19. Hope Mendoza Schechter interview; "Padilla Wins Council Seat in San Fernando," *People's World,* April 14, 1950, p. 12; "Spanish Vote Rallied in Los Angeles," *Christian Science Monitor,* May 29, 1950; CSO, "Highlights of the Past 20 Years," author's files; Minutes, City Council, April 18, 1950, Clerk's Office, City of San Fernando; Ralph C. Guzman, *The Political Socialization of the Mexican American People,* p. 141.

20. Margarita Duran Mendez interview.

21. Henry Nava interview; Hope Mendoza Schechter interview.

22. Author's interview with Leopoldo Sanchez, Los Angeles, January 4, 1982; Author's interview with George R. Sotelo, Pasadena, 1981–2002; "Carlos M. Teran," Martindale-Hubbell Law Directory, 1957, p. 164; John Anson Ford, *Thirty Explosive Years in Los Angeles County* (San Marino, California: The Huntington Library, 1961), p. 137.

23. Hope Mendoza and Harvey Schechter interview.

24. Tony Rios interview; CSO, "Highlights of the Past 20 Years," author's files.

25. Author's interview with Hank Lopez, Los Angeles, January 4, 1982.

26. *Ibid.;* Author's interview with Herman Sillas, Los Angeles, August 22, 2003.

27. Norris Poulson, Oral History UCLA, p. 441.

28. "Los Angeles: Upset," *Newsweek,* June 12, 1961, p. 38.

29. George Sotelo interview; Eddie Ramirez interview; Richard Tafoya interview; Benjamin John Bridgeman Allen, *Amigos Sam? Mayor Sam Yorty and the Latino Community of Los Angeles* (Thesis, Department of History, Harvard University, March 23, 2000), p. 48. The author wishes to thank Raphael J. Sonenshein for a copy of the thesis which provides new insights into the relationship between Yorty and Latinos.

30. Kenneth C. Bun, *The History of MAPA and Chicano Politics in California* (Sacramento: MAPA), 1992, p. 7.

31. Author's interview with Philip L. Soto, Los Angeles, March 9, 1982; Author's interview with Dionicio Morales, City of Commerce, July 29, 2003; Hispanic Link News Service files.

32. *MAPA News,* May 24, 1967, p. 8, Chicano, Subject File, Southern California Library for Research and Social Studies.

33. Julian Nava, *Julian Nava: My Mexican American Journey* (Houston: Arte Público Press, 2002), p. 72.

34. Author's interview with Henry L. Lacayo, Newbury Park, January 4, 1997, and 2000–2004.

35. Statement of the Vote, 1968–1974, California State Archives,

36. "Roybal Speaks, Interview Council Candidates at Mass Meeting," n.p., n.d., Clippings, Edward Roybal Papers, Special Collections, California State University, Los Angeles.

37. *Ibid.*

38. Clippings, Edward Roybal Papers; Raphael J. Sorenshein, *Politics in Black and White: Race and Power in Los Angeles* (Princeton, New Jersey: Princeton University Press, 1993), pp. 40–46.

39. Miscellaneous Clippings, 1962, Edward Roybal Papers.

40. Author's interview with Richard Tafoya, Montebello, May 31, 1997.

41. George R. Sotelo interview; Richard Tafoya interview.

42. Peter Skerry, *Mexican Americans: The Ambivalent Minority* (New York: The Free Press, 1994).

43. James Richardson, "The Members' Speaker: How Willie Brown Held Center Stage in California, 1980–1995," in Michael B. Preston, Bruce Cain, and Sandra Bass, eds., *Racial and Ethnic Politics in California,* Vol. 2 (Berkeley: Institute of Governmental Studies Press, UC Berkeley, 1998), pp. 137–158. For full disclosure, the author worked for the Speaker's Office of Majority Services for a number of years.

44. Richard A. Clacus, *Willie Brown and the California Assembly* (Berkeley: Institute of Governmental Studies Press, UC Berkeley, 1995); Fernando J. Guerra, The Career Paths of Minority Elected Politicians," in Bryan O. Jackson and Michael B. Preston, eds., *Racial and Ethnic Politics in California* (Berkeley: Institute of Governmental Studies Press, UC Berkeley, 1993), pp. 117–131; James Richardson, *Willie Brown* (Berkeley: University of California Press, 1996), p. 225; Peter Skerry, *Mexican Americans.*

45. Bruce E. Cain, *The Reapportionment Puzzle* (Berkeley: University of California Press, 1984), pp. 166–178. The U.S. Supreme Court subsequently restricted the Justice Department's interpretation: "Court Overturns Federal Rule for Voter Redistricting Plans," *Sacramento Bee,* May 13, 1997, p. A6; "High Court Again Bars Race-Based Redistricting," *Los Angeles Times,* June 30, 1997, p. A12.

46. Richard A. Clacus, *Willie Brown and the California Assembly,* p. 122; James Richardson, *Willie Broivn,* p. 329; Richard Skerry, *Mexican Americans,* p. 332; Dan Walters, *The New California: Pacing the 2V Century,* Edition (Sacramento, California Journal Press 1992), p. 33.

47. The legal breakthrough came in a Watsonville case. See Joaquin G. Avila, *Latino Political Empowerment: A Perspective* (self published, [1990?]), p. 21.

48. Richard Skerry, *Mexican Americans,* pp. 333–335, with "stole the election" quote on p. 334; Jaime Regalado, "Conflicts Over Redistricting in Los Angeles: Who Wins? Who Loses," in Byran O. Jackson and Michael B. Preston, eds., *Racial and Ethnic Politics in California,* pp. 373–394; Dan Walters, *The New California: Facing the 21st Century,* 2nd edition, p. 24.

49. Cuban-born Ileana Ros-Lechtinen was elected to Congress in 1988 from Florida and the Puerto Rican-born Nydia M. Velazquez was elected from New York in 1993.

50. Statement of the Vote, 1990–1992, California State Archives; Raymond A. Rocco, "Latino Los Angeles," in Allen J. Scott and Edward W. Soja, eds., *The City: Los Angeles and Urban Theory at the End of the Twentieth Century* (Berkeley: University of California Press, 1996), pp. 365–389.

51. Fernando J. Guerra,. "The Career Paths of Minority Elected Politicians," in Michael B. Preston, Bruce Cain, and Sandra Bass, *Racial and Ethnic Politics in California,* Vol. 2, pp. 450–451.

52. Dan Walters, *The New California: Facing the 21st Century,* 2nd Edition, p. 19. Richard Santillan and Federico A. Subevi-Velez, "Latino Participation in Republican Party Politics in California," in *Racial and Ethnic Politics in California,* pp. 285–319.

53. IT. Eric Schockman, "California's Ethnic Experiment and the Unsolvable Immigration Issue: Proposition 187 and Beyond," and "Nativism, Partisanship, and Immigration: An Analysis of Prop. 198," both in Michael B. Preston, Bruce Cain, and Sandra Bass, *Racial and Ethnic Politics in California,* Vol. 2, pp. 233–304.

54. IT. Eric Schockman, "California's Ethnic Experiment and the Unsolvable Immigration Issue: Proposition 187 and Beyond," p. 269.

55. George Skelton, "Straddling the Line on Illegal Immigration," *Los Angeles Times,* August 26, 1993, p. A3; "State's Diversity Doesn't Reach Voting Booth," *Los Angeles Times,* November 10, 1994, p. A1; "Prop. 187 May Show Clergy's Political Role is Dwindling," *Los Angeles Times,* November 20, 1994, p. A3; "Despite Gains, Latino Voters Still Lack Clout," *Los Angeles Times,* December 4, 1994, p. A1.

56. "House GOP Charts California Agenda," *Los Angeles Times,* November 13, 1994, p. A1.

57. IT. Eric Schockman, "California's Ethnic Experiment and the Unsolvable Immigration Issue: Proposition 187 and Beyond," in Michael B. Preston, Bruce Cain, and Sandra Bass, *Racial and Ethnic Politics in California,* p. 261.

58. See Michael B. Preston and James S. Lai, "The Symbolic Politics of Affirmative Action," Michael B. Preston, Bruce Cain, and Sandra Bass, eds., *Racial and Ethnic Politics in California,* Vol. 2 (Berkeley: Institute of Governmental Studies Press, UC Berkeley, 1998), pp. 161–198.

59. Bruce E. Cain and Karin Mac Donald, "Race and Party Politics in the 1997 U.S. Presidential Election," in Michael B. Preston, Bruce Cain, and Sandra Bass, *Racial and Ethnic Politics in California,* Vol. 2, p. 200.

60. Harry P. Pachon, "Latino Politics in the Golden State: Ready for the 21st Century?" Michael B. Preston, Bruce Cain, and Sandra Bass, *Racial and Ethnic Politics in California,* Vol. 2, p. 420.

61. John B. Judis and Roy Teixeira, *The Emerging Democratic Majority* (New York: Scribner, 2002), p. 29.

62. Author's interview with Miguel Contreras, Los Angeles, 1977–1984.

63. Miguel Contreras interview, March 28, 1977.

64. Fernando Guerra, "Latino Politics in California: The Necessary Conditions for Success," Michael B. Preston, Bruce Cain, and Sandra Bass, *Racial and Ethnic Politics in California,* Vol. 2, p. 450. The need for the three legally separate campaigns arose from a newly enacted but since discarded campaign reform law. The basic outlines of the campaign, targeted union members and newly registered immigrant voters, along with a more generalized candidate campaign would be used repeated. In terms of full disclosure, the author

served on the AFL-CIO campaign during this election as the newly hired political director for the California Federation of Teachers, a post that provided a participant-observer vantagepoint for most of the subsequent events.

65. For more on the County Federation, see Larry Frank and Kent Wong, "Dynamic Political Mobilization: The Los Angeles County Federation of Labor," *Working USA: The Journal of Labor and Society,* Vol. 8, No. 2 (December 2004), p. 154–181

66. "A significant question, especially for political incorporation theorists, is whether the incorporation of communities of color will be more difficult to achieve, and sustain, under term limits," asked Jaime Regalado. "It seems likely that, since mass-based electoral and community coalitions have historically been difficult to maintain over time, it would be difficult to consistently create/or maintain electoral coalitions to replace 'termed' councilmembers," stated Jaime Regalado, in "Minority Political Incorporation in Los Angeles: A Broader Consideration," in Michael O, Michael B. Preston, Bruce Cain, and Sandra Bass, eds., *Racial and Ethnic Politics in California,* Vol. 2, p. 393.

67. To date, Latinos and Asians have gained from the process. In Los Angeles, Contreras has worked to ensure African American representation, helping to elect Blacks supportive of Latino and working family concerns.

68. Harold Meyerson, "Getting to 50-Puls-l," *Los Angeles Weekly,* April 27–May 3, 2002.

69. Cover, "Latino Power: L.A.'s New Mayor—And How Hispanics Will Change America's Politics," *Newsweek,* May 30, 2005.

70. "Out With the Ho-Hum: L.A. Times Endorsement: Villaraigosa for Mayor," *Los Angeles Times,* May 8, 2005.

71. "Leader Who Restored Labor's Clout in L.A. Dies," *Los Angeles Times,* May 7, 2005.

72. "The 2005 Mayoral Election Compared to 2001," *Los Angeles Tunes,* May 19, 2005, p. A19.

73. City of Los Angeles website, November 26, 2005.

74. John B. Judis and Roy Teixeira, *The Emerging Democratic Majority* (New York: Scribner, 2002), p. 6. The book focuses explains the role of Latinos and California in the evolving Democratic Party coalition. Specific attention is focused on Latino Los Angeles.

The Multicultural Nature of Los Angeles Unrest in 1992

KWANG CHUNG KIM

The 1965 revision of the U.S. immigration law drastically increased the number of immigrants from Asian and Latin American countries, ending the historical pattern of numerical dominance by European immigrants (Barringer, Gardner, and Levin 1993; Reimers 1985; U.S. Commission on Civil Rights 1988). The presence of recent non-European immigrants has helped transform the United States into a complex multiracial and multiethnic society, one that goes beyond the traditional bi-racial relationship between whites and African Americans and the ethnic experiences of European immigrants and their descendants, Such a change in the composition of the U.S. population presents a great challenge to the study of recent racial and ethnic relations.

The Los Angeles racial unrest of 1992 shockingly demonstrated this complex and diverse nature of American society. African American residents in South Central Los Angeles destroyed local businesses as an angry protest against the "not guilty" verdict announced in the case against white policemen charged with beating Rodney King. Hispanic residents took advantage of the opportunity and joined the looting of local businesses (Light, Har-Chvi, and Kan 1994). All the major racial and ethnic groups in the United States were eventually involved: African Americans, whites,

Hispanics, and Asian Americans. Korean business owners emerged as the biggest victims of property loss resulting from the riots (Institute for Alternative Journalism 1992).

The Los Angeles unrest has generated numerous debates (Institute for Alternative Journalism 1992). Through these debates, two contrasting positions have emerged, both of which unfortunately regard the unrest as a type of biracial event. One position treats the unrest as a basic conflict between Korean business owners and African American residents in South Central Los Angeles. According to this position, the source of the conflict is the presence of many small Korean businesses in South Central Los Angeles, which has generated a considerable degree of racial tension. African American residents complain that Korean business owners treat African American customers rudely and exploit them economically. Local residents' hostility toward Korean storekeepers was further intensified when a Korean store owner who had shot and killed an African American customer received a lenient sentence from the court (Institute for Alternative Journalism 1992; Madhubuti 1993; *Los Angeles Times* Staff 1992).

A serious problem with this position is that it sees the Los Angeles unrest as an interminority group conflict between two minority groups. This position misses an essential feature of racial and ethnic relations in the United States, namely, that the positions and roles of minority groups in the United States are largely determined by the respective relationship of those groups to the dominant white group. For an adequate analysis of the unrest, therefore, it is necessary to examine the role of the dominant group involved in the interminority group conflict. Charles Simmons alludes to this necessity: "Although there is friction between Black consumers and Korean merchants, this issue was overstated by the media. The Los Angeles problem has much deeper historical and social roots" (1993:142–43).

Mindful of the powerful role of the dominant group, supporters of the other popular position treat the Los Angeles unrest as a biracial conflict between whites and African Americans. They argue that the conflict originated in the historical and continuing patterns of whites' exploitation and victimization of African Americans. The urban unrest was a way for African American residents in South Central Los Angeles to protest their experience as victims. If exploitation by whites were the main issue, however, one would wonder why Korean business owners turned out to be the biggest victims. This argument does not clearly define the structural position and role of Korean small business owners in the unrest; it instead often treats them merely as bystanders caught between African American rage and white power (Choi 1992).

For a satisfactory analysis of the Los Angeles unrest, it is necessary to recognize the conflict's multiracial nature (E. Kim 1992; Oliver, Johnson, and Grant 1993; Sonenshein 1993; West 1993). We aim, then, to clarify the multiple racial groups involved in the unrest and to examine the nature of their involvement based on their structural positions and roles in the United States. The diverse factors can undoubtedly be conceptualized in many different ways. For example, Melvin Oliver, James Johnson, and David Grant (1993) define the Los Angeles unrest as a multiethnic rebellion in the sense that African American and Hispanic residents in South Central Los Angeles were involved in the unrest.

We define the Los Angeles unrest as a multiracial event from the perspective of victimization. Several victimized groups are recognizable in the Los Angeles unrest. We focus on the two most severely victimized groups: African American residents in South Central Los Angeles and Korean business owners in South Central Los Angeles and nearby Korea-town. While the victimization experienced by African Americans has been much debated, and feelings of victimization, despair, and anger are said to be the major source of the Los Angeles unrest, little attention has been paid thus far to the victimization of Korean business owners. We therefore put considerable stress on the traumatic experiences of this neglected group, pursuing two questions: Why were Korean businesses in South Central Los Angeles and nearby Koreatown attacked, and what happened to Korean business owners after their businesses were looted or burned? For our analysis, we must also pay attention to the dominant white group's relationship with each of the two victimized groups. The relationship between the two minority groups needs to be examined within this context of the dominant-minority group relationship.

Figure 5.1 illustrates the multiracial currents that fed into the Los Angeles unrest. The basic source is the relationship between whites and African Americans, which has led to African Americans' victimization. A critical issue is the relationship between these two groups, particularly in urban areas during recent American history (A in Figure 5.1). However, African American residents attacked Korean businesses and victimized business owners who had filled delicate socioeconomic roles in South Central Los Angeles (B in Figure 5.1). The Korean immigrants' relationship with the dominant white group encompasses both the Korean immigrants' entry into business in the United States and the middleman minority role some Korean businessmen play in inner-city minority communities (C in Figure 5.1).

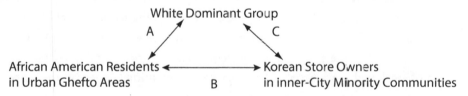

FIGURE 5.1 Multiracial Currents Underlying the Los Angeles Unrest

For our purposes, the two biracial positions illustrated above treat the role of Hispanic residents as a passive one. Although many Hispanic residents in Koreatown were resentful of Korean storekeepers and landlords and participated in the unrest, they did not initiate the disturbance and instead seem to have simply taken the opportunity to join in (Oliver, Johnson, and Grant 1993; Simmons 1993). Furthermore, most of the Hispanic residents in South Central Los Angeles and nearby Koreatown were either immigrants or undocumented workers who appeared to be motivated mainly by material gain, looting stores rather than burning them down as an expression of rage, as did African Americans (Light, Har-Chvi, and Kan 1994).

The Concept of Victims and Victimization

The concepts of victims and victimization provide important conceptual frameworks necessary for understanding the mass violence in Los Angeles. The term *victims* refers to individuals or a group of individuals who suffer harm inflicted by others, the offenders. The harm may include many kinds of loss or pain: psychological, social, cultural, economic, political, and so on. Victims are not considered responsible (either totally or partially) for this harm. If they were responsible, they could not be considered victims, no matter how enormous their suffering. *Victimization* refers to the victims' suffering, including adverse life conditions that follow from the original harm inflicted by the offenders.

In the discussion of victims and victimization, it is important to examine the nature of the relationship between the victims and offenders, as well as the sociocultural context in which their relationship exists (Elias 1986). The analysis of their relationship often includes the controversial issues of blaming the victim (victims' sharing in the responsibility for their harm) and defending the victim (proclaiming victims' innocence). In order to clarify these issues, Robert Elias (1986) suggests examining the broad social, political, economic, and cultural structures of society. Otherwise, the whole argument of victims and victimization degenerates into a debate over the symptoms of a problem rather than its sources.

African Amerians' Experiences of Victimization

African Americans have been mistreated and victimized by the dominant white group in numerous ways throughout American history. For the purpose of our study, the scope of analysis will be limited to African Americans' experiences in the recent industrial and postindustrial eras. As the U.S. economy rapidly industrialized at the end of the nineteenth century, the changing economy demanded a huge number of unskilled workers; this labor demand was initially met by the unprecedented number of immigrants arriving from European countries (Lieberson 1980). After World War I had drastically curtailed the immigration flow from European countries, African Americans in the rural South finally managed to begin a steady flow of migration to major cities, joining the urban labor force there as latecomers. In 1870, according to Douglas Massey and Nancy Denton, 80 percent of African Americans lived in the rural South. A century later, 80 percent of African Americans lived in urban areas; nearly half of them lived in urban areas outside the South (1993:18).

Owing to the racism of a white majority, these African American migrants and their descendants were forced to live in heavily segregated areas within major cities. Such residential segregation and other types of discrimination are examples of African Americans' experiences of victimization in urban areas. Massey and Denton call this residential segregation "the missing link in prior attempts to understand the plight of the urban poor" (1993:3). In these congested urban areas, African American residents have watched their job opportunities completely dry up during the steady deindustrialization of the inner city. As a result, a high proportion remain unemployed and poor. This concentrated poverty is the harm that has been inflicted upon African Americans as the victims of white racism throughout the changing context of the U.S. economy.

Massey and Denton point out that at the turn of the twentieth century, only a small number of African Americans were in northern and Midwest or West Coast cities, and they generally lived in racially integrated neighborhoods. But as more African Americans migrated to the major cities during the second decade of the new century, urban whites began to view African American mobility with increasing hostility and alarm. As a result, they started to force the migrant African Americans to live in segregated areas, gradually creating a pattern of residential segregation of major cities.

By the 1930s, the perimeters of African American settlements were well established in most cities, and the level of African American-white residential dissimilarity had stabilized at a very high level. The Great Depression drove more African Americans out of the rural South, which was economically worse off than other parts of the country. From 1930 to 1940, some four hundred thousand African American migrants left the South for major cities. Massey and Denton note that when these migrants arrived in major cities, they faced unusually bleak residential circumstances. Compounding the problems of segregation, the Great Depression had virtually ended new residential construction after 1929.

World War II further facilitated the migration of African Americans from the rural South into the major cities. After World War II, residential segregation continued to accelerate through the process of suburbanization:

> The suburbanization of America proceeded at a new rapid pace and the white middle class deserted inner cities in massive numbers. Only one-third of U.S. metropolitan residents were suburban residents in 1940, but by 1970 suburbanites constituted a majority within metropolitan America.
>
> Throughout the United States—in both southern and northern cities—the ghetto had become an enduring, permanent feature of the residential structure of black community life by 1940, and over the next thirty years the spatial isolation of African Americans only increased. (Massey and Denton 1993:43, 49)

This segregation in the major cities has been accompanied by occupational discrimination against African Americans (Kerner Commission 1968; Lieberson 1980). The two patterns of racial discrimination then reinforced each other, developing the current grim life conditions of inner-city residents. William Wilson (1987) contends that the recent inner-city deterioration also reflects several contemporary forces that operate directly against inner-city African Americans.

One of these forces is the deindustrialization of the inner-city economy. As the U.S. economy shifted from manufacturing to service-oriented industries, numerous inner-city plants were closed and low-skilled manufacturing jobs were eliminated or moved elsewhere. This trend has created a high rate of unemployment in inner-city areas, particularly affecting young male workers. Wilson (1987) stresses that joblessness among these young men is a factor in the current delay in marriage, and both these conditions in turn contribute to the high rate of out-of-wedlock births and single-parent, female-headed households.

Another contemporary force that has severely deteriorated living conditions of inner-city residents is the change in age composition. A greater proportion of young people live in inner-city ghetto areas today than ever before, and their presence contributes to such serious problems as low income, high unemployment rates, and crime. Wilson (1987) observes that inner-city areas are no longer vertical communities in which middle- and working-class African Americans live together with underclass African Americans. The middle- and working-class African Americans, who can afford to move away, have already left ghetto areas, so that only the most disadvantaged segments of the African American community remain (the concentration effect). Wilson maintains that a net result of the concentration effect is social isolation—a lack of contact or of sustained interaction with individuals and institutions that represent the mainstream society. Inner-city ghetto areas are thus plagued with what Wilson calls problems of social dislocation—joblessness, drugs, school dropouts, teenage pregnancies, poverty, out-of-wedlock births, female-headed households, welfare dependency, and serious crime. This deterioration in South Central Los Angeles has also led to an extremely high infant mortality rate there—22 per 1,000 (Hamilton 1992).

Current adverse life conditions of inner-city African American residents, then, stem from a number of historical and contemporary forces, many of which are intricately related to past racial discrimination. For example, because many African Americans have been forced by past residential discrimination to live in inner-city ghetto areas, they are more severely hit than any other racial or ethnic group by the recent deindustrialization of the inner-city economy. The current changes in the age makeup of inner-city residents and the removal of middle- and working-class African Americans from inner cities can both be traced to the bleak inner-city living conditions originally generated by past racial discrimination. The effects of all these forces may then, in part, be considered what Joe and Clairece Feagin (1986) call the side effects, or past-in-present effects, of earlier discrimination. The historical pattern of racism is, therefore, a critical factor in explaining the current victimization of African Americans in inner-city ghetto areas.

Racial Unrest in South Central Los Angeles

African American residents in South Central Los Angeles have not been excepted from this general pattern of urban degeneration. They have gone through the same kind of concentrated poverty and related victimization. They share their community with another impoverished group, Hispanics, but the two groups live in a highly segregated area as a result of the planned deurbanization of Los Angeles (Cooper 1992). In 1990, only about 6 percent of local residents in South Central Los

Angeles had a college degree, and fewer than half of them had completed a high school education (Sonenshein 1993:173). As many as 230,000 of the community's 630,000 residents live at or below the annual income poverty threshold. While only 18 percent of Los Angeles families live in South Central Los Angeles, 37 percent of the city's impoverished families are found there (Curran 1992).

Large corporations have abandoned South Central and other parts of Los Angeles in recent years, and the resulting job exodus continues to accelerate (Soja, Morales, and Wolff 1983; Oliver, Johnson, and Grant 1993). Living conditions in the community continue to deteriorate, while the underground economy takes over and various forms of vice such as theft, drug trafficking, and prostitution thrive. The whole of South Central Los Angeles has become an explosive mixture of poverty, crime, and drugs (Sonenshein 1993:163). Under these circumstances, the basic needs in the community are not being met by state, county, or city agencies. Many parts of South Central Los Angeles are physically dismantled, and the area has been written off by banks, corporations, social service agencies, and others (Hamilton 1992).

This accumulation of experiences of victimization and the accompanying sense of despair and anger has been seen as the root cause of the Los Angeles racial unrest. Eui-Young Yu observes that it "was a violent explosion of anger accumulated over years of frustration, helplessness and alienation of people of color, particularly African Americans trapped in the inner-cities of America" (1994: 137). Haki Madhubuti also views the urban unrest as stemming from African Americans' "anger for unfulfilled promises" (1993: xiv). Oliver, Johnson, and Grant (1933) argue that the Los Angeles violence reflects the frustration and alienation built up over the past twenty years among the residents of South Central Los Angeles. Dan Hazen takes the same position in his analysis of the Los Angels racial unrest: "The riots were frightening and tragic, but they gave expression to years of pent-up frustration and anger about decades of forced urban decay, steady increase in poverty, a growing exodus of jobs as corporations have fled South in search of cheap labor, enormous cutbacks in every kind of government support and exponential increase in homelessness and violence" (1992:10).

The "not guilty" verdict in the trial against officers who were videotaped beating Rodney King was the event that sparked the explosion of African Americans' anger. This verdict stood as a symbol of whites' racism and their insensitivity to African Americans' suffering, and it was taken as a terrible insult to the dignity of African Americans (Madhubuti 1993). The following reaction by members of an African American church who counseled against the residents' street violence demonstrates the shinned experiences of African American residents in South Central Los Angeles: "The mood at the First A.M.E. Church was somber. One could still see the shocks and disbelief on the faces of the church members and all who gathered to watch as the verdict was read Pounding his fist into his left hand, Rev. Cecil Murray began to cry, 'They gave no nothing, nothing, not even a bone, dear God, not even a bone'" (*Los Angeles Times* Staff 1992:59).

When even members of a moderate African American church experienced such intense shock and disbelief, it is not surprising that people on the street responded much more violently. Local residents started to loot and burn local businesses Wednesday evening, April 29, 1992, and their destructive behavior continued, with little police response, until Friday. The local residents' apparent attempts to move into white areas such as Beverly Hills and the Westside were curtailed by police forces, but mobs easily flooded into Koreatown. Along with Hispanic residents there, African Americans looted or burned small Korean businesses (*Los Angeles Times* Staff 1992). Although their anger was directed toward the white dominant group, what residents actually did was to vandalize and destroy local nonwhite businesses and other properties, including a large number of small Korean businesses that were left unprotected by the police force during the three days of unrest. Those reporting on the destruction were taken aback by the lack of police support: "By Thursday evening, Koreatown was besieged by flames and looters. Desperate calls for help to city authorities were not answered. Koreans thought they had many friends in City Hall, as they had given generously to politicians. In times of danger, however, Koreans learned that they had to stand all alone" (Yu 1993:2).

Korean Business Owners' Experiences of Victimization

As a whole, the Los Angeles unrest turned out to be the most destructive urban riot that has ever occurred in the United States (Oliver, Johnson, and Grant 1993; *Los Angeles Times* Staff 1992). During the Los Angeles violence, 58 persons died, 2,383 were injured, and over 17,000 were arrested (Sonenshem 1993:223). Total property damage has been estimated to be between $785 million and $1 billion (Oliver, Johnson, and Grant 1993); approximately 4,500 businesses were totally or partially damaged, about half of which (2,300) were Korean businesses in South Central Los Angeles and nearby Koreatown. The total estimated Korean property damage ranged between $350 million and $400 million (KAIAC 1993). Grocery stores (273 stores, with estimated damages of $67 million) and swap meet shops (336 shops, with estimated damages of $55 million) were hardest hit, followed by clothing shops (222 shops, with estimated damages of $34 million) and liquor stores (187 stores, with estimated damages of $42 million). Other types of Korean businesses damaged by the unrest included dry cleaners, electronic shops, gas stations, jewelry shops, restaurants, beauty salons, auto shops, video shops, and furniture shops (Yu 1993:4).

What adversities are faced by Korean immigrants who lost their businesses in South Central Los Angeles and Koreatown? The most immediate problem is the strong sense of despair, helplessness, and hopelessness felt by Korean business owners and their family members. Their businesses, built up through many years of hard work and sweat, were suddenly reduced to ashes. Most of the destroyed businesses (65%) were uninsured at the time of the rioting, and a survey indicates that ten months after the unrest, only one-quarter of the Korean victims (27.8%) had reopened their businesses (KAIAC 1993). Most of the businesses that reopened were those that had sustained the least amount of damage. Half of the victims (49%) viewed their chances of rebuilding as nil, and only the remaining 29 percent looked at their chances of rebuilding with any optimism (KAIAC 1993).

The victims' other immediate problem is how they can obtain the money necessary for daily living. Many of them were forced to borrow money at high interest rates in order to pay their living expenses and attempt to reopen their businesses. As a result, they could no longer pay their mortgages and many have already lost their houses or are now threatened with eviction. For Korean immigrants, home ownership is a conspicuous symbol of achieving the American dream; for them, the loss of this dream is particularly painful and jarring. The victims in the survey mentioned mortgage and rental assistance as their greatest need (KAIAC 1993).

In addition to financial problems, victims and their family members generally suffer from the psychological and physical symptoms of depression and other severe forms of shock following sudden loss:

> The majority of riot victims had portrayed moderate to severe symptoms of post traumatic stress disorder. Many of the victims have stated that they have difficulty of sleeping and continue to have frequent nightmares about their burning and/or looted businesses. Some have developed ulcers and many have not regained their lost appetite and weight. These victims suffer under extreme stress and chronic attacks of depression, anxiety, and fear. One victim's daughter became so overwhelmed [that] she attempted suicide. Clearly there is a tremendous amount of anger and guilt that desperately needs to be processed. There is evidence of an increase in family conflict, domestic violence, child abuse, and substance abuse. It is also clear that these symptoms and incidents of abuse are directly related to the riot and victim's financial difficulties. Unfortunately, although so many victims suffer from severe anxiety and poor health, a great deal of suspicion and shame attached to mental health related services inhibit them from readily receiving counseling. (KAIAC 1993:5–6)

As suggested by these observations, a severe form of victimization experienced by Korean immigrants during the rioting is a tense relationship with their immediate family members, kin, friends, and others. With the loss of their livelihood, the victims are placed in a position of desperately needing to seek help from others, while the victims themselves have little ability to help anyone. In this situation, the victims often experience their relationships with others as frustrating, even humiliating, while at the same time they often feel slighted by others; such an interpersonal difficulty is likely to be accompanied by a drastic change in the victims' self-concept, because they suffer from an enormous loss of self-confidence and respect. Self-doubt and other severe forms of personal deterioration are thus another form of the fallout Korean immigrants suffered following the unrest.

Korean immigrant entrepreneurs came to the United States to pursue the American middle-class dream (Hurh and Kim 1988). In pursuit of this dream, they had an unshakable belief in the American system, trusting that hard work would pay off here. Their faith in the whole American system was badly shaken—leaving in its place a sense of despair and anomie. Their feelings of betrayal have been intensified not just by the original harm inflicted by the minority local residents but also by the subsequent disappointing responses from various federal, state, and local government agencies (KA1AC 1993). This is another severe loss—an intangible, but extremely devastating, experience of victimization.

The Middleman Minority Role of Korean Immigrant Entrepreneurs

To analyze the experiences of victimization of Korean immigrant entrepreneurs in South Central Los Angeles and nearby Koreatown, it is necessary briefly to review their experiences in the American labor market. Like other recent Asian immigrants, Korean immigrants who came to the United States had generally enjoyed a high preimmigration socioeconomic status. Many had already completed a college education in Korea, and most of those with occupational experience in Korea had been employed either in professional and technical occupations or administrative and managerial occupations prior to immigrating (Hurh and Kim 1988; U.S. Commission on Civil Rights 1988). Like other recent Asian immigrants, their immigration may thus be characterized as a "middle-class migration."

Most Korean immigrants could not, however, utilize their Korean educational and occupational resources in the American labor market. With the exception of those college graduates who had majored in health-related fields, most discovered that their education and occupational experiences were generally not recognized in America. These college graduates were thereby excluded from the mainstream occupations for which they had been trained. The jobs available to them in America were those jobs usually available to all immigrant workers: (1) occupations with a short supply of workers; (2) occupations avoided or disdained by native-born whites; and (3) low-wage, low-skill occupations.

Currently, as in the recent past, health care jobs in the United States fall under the category of occupations with a short supply of workers. So, with the exception of those in health-related fields, immigrating college graduates generally face the stark reality of limited occupational choices. The types of occupations currently available to them are either self-employment in a small business or low-wage, low-skill service or manual occupations. Faced with this limited choice, college graduates naturally prefer self-employment, even though running a small business is probably an occupational step down for most. Even those with no college education view the employment conditions associated with low-wage, low-skill occupations as unfavorable, also preferring self-employment in a small business.

This limited occupational structure in the American labor market has compelled a high proportion of Korean immigrants without any previous business experience in Korea or any systematic business preparation in the United States to open and operate small businesses. Their business can, therefore, be considered a new phenomenon emerging from the unfavorable labor market situation facing Korean immigrants in the United States. The small business opportunities available to them are, however, also limited and tend to be of two types: an inner-city retail or service business or an extremely labor-intensive business (e.g., laundry and dry cleaning services or fruit and vegetable shops). These two types of small business are generally so risky, low-status, or difficult to manage that many native-born whites tend to avoid them.

Consistent with this summary, Ivan Light and Edna Bonacich observe that a large majority of Korean service and retail businesses in Los Angeles are located in nonwhite, low-income areas that have been ignored and underserved by big corporations (1988). Korean immigrants' entry into inner-city minority markets, therefore, stems from the interaction of two features of their relationship with the white dominant group in the United States: (1) the exclusion of Korean immigrants from the mainstream professional and technical occupations or administrative and managerial occupations, which are usually dominated by native-born whites (U.S. Bureau of the Census 1990); and (2) the availability of business opportunities in inner-city minority communities, which are usually avoided by native-born whites (Kim, Hurh, and Fernandez 1989; Light and Bonacich 1988).

Edna Bonacich and her colleagues attempted to characterize Korean small business in the United States in terms of the middleman minority theory, but they have subsequently abandoned this effort (Bonacich, Light, and Wong 1980; Bonacich and Jung 1982; Light and Bonacich, 1988). Light and Bonacich (1988) argue that the middleman minority framework is too restrictive to analyze small Korean business in the United States. They also state that the middleman minority theory stresses sojourning minorities and is oriented toward the Third World context, whereas small Korean business is found in a developed country and Korean immigrants are not generally sojourners (1988:17–18).

The middleman minority theory is indeed too restrictive a tool for analyzing small Korean business as a whole in the United States, but we find it useful for analyzing a type of small Korean business, namely, those operating in inner-city, low-income African American or Hispanic communities. Relevant here are the social conditions under which middleman minorities are likely to thrive, not their role as sojourners. As Jonathan Turner and Edna Bonacich (1980) stress, middleman minorities tend to thrive in a highly stratified society. If the socioeconomic gap between the elite (the dominant group) and the masses (the minority group) is great in a society, this gap hinders effective interaction between the two groups. The society then needs another distinct group to stand between the two groups and perform an intermediate, or mediating, role. Edna Bonacich and John Modell thus characterize middleman minority entrepreneurs as those who are socially or racially distinguished and "tend to concentrate in trade and commerce—that is, to act as middleman between producers and consumers" (1980:14).

The racial and socioeconomic gap between the white dominant group and the inner-city African American and Hispanic communities in major American cities offers Korean immigrants just such a middleman business opportunity. As retailers, Korean business owners in inner-city African American and Hispanic communities are at the end of a complex process of production and distribution of the goods needed by inner-city minority residents. Producers of these goods are mostly American corporations or international corporations located in South Korea, Taiwan, and other Third World countries (Illsoo Kim 1981; Light and Bonacich 1988). A high proportion of these two types of corporations are intimately related through the international involvement of American corporations through direct investment, transfer of capital or technology, subcontracting, and so on (Light and Bonacich 1988). The goods produced by these corporations are eventually distributed to Korean retailers through Korean and white wholesalers (Kim and Hurh 1985).

We find no evidence that major American banks, big corporations, or government agencies (white-dominated institutions) have actively helped or assisted Korean immigrants to enter small business in inner-city minority communities (Bonacich, Light, and Wong 1980; Light and Bonacich 1988). Korean immigrants have instead relied heavily on their own resources and those of their ethnic group (Kim and Hurh 1985; Light and Bonacich 1988; Min 1988). By running a business in inner-city ghetto areas and distributing goods purchased from white-dominated corporations and Third World manufacturers, these Koreans are inevitably placing themselves in the position of middleman minority, whether they are aware of it or not. What Korean retailers actually do in inner-city minority markets is "distribute the products of big businesses in hard-to-access central city markets" (Light and Bonacich 1988:23).

> As middleman retailers, Korean business owners in inner-city minority communities share their profits with suppliers (producers and wholesalers). As those who reside and spend their earnings elsewhere, Korean business owners and their suppliers contribute, to some extent, to the draining of local economic resources. They are, therefore, perceived by many inner-city residents as outside invaders who exploit local minority residents and undermine African American communities' economic autonomy by preventing local residents from establishing their own businesses in the community.

Responsibility of Korean Immigrant Entrepreneurs

Were Korean business owners in South Central Los Angeles and nearby Koreatown responsible for their losses? Most of the residents in South Central Los Angeles and in other inner-city, low-income communities are currently too poor to sustain any viable retail business in their neighborhoods. These areas have therefore largely been abandoned by those who would otherwise dominate the markets: white merchants, chain stores, and big corporations. Even those African Americans who are entrepreneurially capable have left the inner-city areas rather than set up shop there (Wilson 1987). As a result, the inner-city ghetto areas contain only the barest rudiments of retail trade (Massey and Denton 1993:135).

Under these stark conditions, Korean immigrant entrepreneurs stand out as the group that has most actively invested in these areas, which otherwise are wastelands of empty store fronts, burned-out buildings, and vacant lots (Massey and Denton 1993:137). Korean business owners have thus contributed to the development and revival of many deteriorated or abandoned neighborhoods

(Light and Bonacich 1988:6). Their business has created employment opportunities in areas with high rates of unemployment and generated earnings for local youth.

It is not surprising that Korean merchants in these abandoned markets have encountered little resistance or competition from big corporations or native-born white or African American entrepreneurs. In this respect, their business experiences are quite different from those of prewar Japanese immigrants on the West Coast (Bonacich and Modell 1980). However, because many Korean immigrants enter the same types of retail market and draw upon the same ethnic resources, most experience intense competitive pressure from other Korean business owners (Kim and Hurh 1985).

This intragroup competition forces Korean business owners to keep the prices of their goods relatively low. In order to do so, Korean retailers and their family members must work unusually long hours and maintain a frugal lifestyle. Such difficult measures are necessary to reduce the labor costs of their business and to enable them to survive commercially in the difficult low-income markets whose economy Daniel Fusfeld and Timothy Bates (1984) call "penny capitalism." Light and Bonacich characterize the long hours of Korean business owners and their family members as "a disguised form of cheap labor" (1988:23) and further explain that "the Korean entrepreneurs and their families worked longer hours to earn a lower return on their human capital than did the non-Korean entrepreneurs" (1988:176).

Because of their immigrant status, inner-city Korean entrepreneurs and their family members are desperate to secure a socioeconomic base in the United States, so they are strongly motivated to manage their business, however difficult. Furthermore, they have come from a country where the standard of labor and employment conditions are much tougher than in the United States. During the 1970s and 1980s, when most of the Korean entrepreneurs in business today came to the United States, Korea exported large quantities of goods manufactured by workers receiving low wages and working extremely long hours (Light and Bonacich 1988). This background has imbued many Korean immigrant entrepreneurs in the United States with an intense commitment to an Asian version of the Protestant ethic. Korean immigrants, therefore, seem better prepared to manage businesses in inner-city areas than native-born entrepreneurs.

It seems inevitable that the residents in South Central Los Angeles and other inner-city minority areas have come to depend, to a large extent, on outside entrepreneurs for their daily necessities. Most of the local residents are too poor to start their own business or are entrepreneurially unprepared to do so, and the inner-city markets are generally too small or too risky to entice big corporations or chain stores. Of those who are nevertheless interested in these areas, immigrant entrepreneurs seem to offer the local residents a decent retail business. Of these immigrant entrepreneurs, Korean business owners have filled the inner-city niche and created intense intragroup competition among Korean-owned businesses. Korean immigrant entrepreneurs are hardly in a position, then, to exploit local residents by charging unusually high prices, inasmuch as their prices are set by the pressure of this intense competition. Such a business climate actually benefits local consumers enormously, as prices would undoubtedly be higher under the monopolistic or oligopolistic market that might exist in the absence of competing immigrant entrepreneurs.

The concentrated poverty and suffering that led to the Los Angeles unrest already existed long before Korean immigrants started their businesses in South Central Los Angeles (Kerner Commission 1968; Oliver, Johnson, and Grant 1993). Furthermore, these Korean immigrants ran their businesses diligently and frugally under heavy pressure of intragroup competition. So why were Korean businesses attacked in South Central Los Angeles and nearby Koreatown? Two factors seem to answer this question. First with their history of victimization and their related sense of anger and frustration, African American residents in inner-city areas tend to perceive any outside business owners as part of the established system of exploitation and treat them with hostility and suspicion (Light, Har-Chvi, and Kan 1994). Inner-city residents are then not inclined to perceive the changing roles of various entrepreneurial groups in different socioeconomic contexts, even when undeniable differences are found among these groups, such as the differences observed between Korean and Jewish storekeepers (Chang 1993). For African Americans, all non-African American entrepreneurs in their communities represent the same homogeneous group of exploiters, regardless of their history or their business activities. The following statement demonstrates such a stereotypical judgment of immigrant business owners: "Ethnic groups that have made it into the American Dream have traditionally stepped on the necks of African American communities on their way up. Jews, Italians, Greeks, Chinese, Arabs, and now East Indians and Koreans have all, to greater or lesser degrees, quickly assimilated this Fundamental Law of Immigrant Upward Mobility" (Martin 1993:32).

Second, some situational elements associated with Korean entrepreneurs' middleman minority position helped facilitate the Los Angeles attacks. As an angry protest against the white establishment, local residents in South Central Los Angeles attempted to attack and destroy the targets nearest to hand; many businesses located in South Central Los Angeles were destroyed regardless of the owners' ethnicity (Institute for Alternative Journalism 1992).

Korean businesses were also somewhat more tempting targets than other businesses, because their culturally and racially different owners made them more visible and they had clearly proliferated in the area (Oliver, Johnson, and Grant 1993; *Los Angeles Times* Staff 1992). At the same time, Korean businesses located in South Central Los Angeles and Koreatown were easily accessible to African American and Hispanic residents. Furthermore, these businesses had little power to stop local residents' attacks or to retaliate. In this sense, Korean business owners are typical middleman minority entrepreneurs—economically active but politically weak or helpless. Unfortunately, their plight was worsened by the virtual absence of police protection during all three days of rioting (*Los Angeles Times* Staff 1992; Yu 1993). These three characteristics—visibility, accessibility, and vulnerability—explain the disproportipnate property loss of Korean entrepreneurs during the Los Angeles unrest. In sharp contrast, white residents in Beverly Hills and other areas were well protected by the Los Angeles police force during the same period (*Los Angeles Times* 1992). Though highly visible, these white residents were neither accessible nor vulnerable.

During the riots, then, Korean businesses were convenient scapegoats upon whom local residents could express their anger. African American residents substituted local Korean businesses as a target of hostility, exaggerating the economic conflict of interest between Korean entrepreneurs and local residents (Light and Bonacich 1988:323). In this process, Korean business owners paid a heavy toll and ended up shielding the business interests of the white establishment. These Korean store owners were, therefore, the victims of the misdirected anger of African American residents as middleman minority entrepreneurs in ghetto markets. Manning Marable expresses this position eloquently:

> One tragic outcome of this legacy is the rage directed against the Asian American community during the Los Angeles riots, during which 1,800 Korean-owned businesses were damaged or destroyed. Black young people need to understand that it is not the Korean American small business merchant who denies capital for investment in the black community, controls the banks and financial institutions or commits police brutality against blacks and Latinos. There may be legitimate complaints between the two groups. But such misdirected anger makes a unified response to race and class oppression virtually impossible. (1992:83)

One specific complaint expressed by local residents against Korean business owners before and during the unrest in South Central Los Angeles and other urban ghetto areas was that Korean business owners treat their minority customers disrespectfully (Shin Kim 1994). While it is conceivable that some Korean business owners treat their minority customers in such a way, it is equally conceivable that others do not. Unfortunately, the idea of rude treatment by Korean store owners spread, becoming a collective prejudice against all Korean business owners—a simplified, negative view applied to all members of a group. Local residents generally suggest that Korean culture is the source of such rude behavior. This expressed complaint clearly carries a victim-blaming message: Because of their culture, Korean business owners were rude to African American customers. Due to this rude behavior, Korean business owners deserved the property loss inflicted during the Los Angeles riots.

On the issue of the rude treatment of customers, one may wonder, on the one hand, whether Korean business owners are ruder than other business owners in the same areas. A preliminary study shows that a great majority of African American customers do not think that Korean business owners are much different from other business owners (Shin Kim 1994). On the other hand, if Korean culture accounts for the rude treatment of customers, Korean business owners in other areas should also treat their customers disrespectfully. Yet, no evidence has been found that customers (Korean, white, or racially mixed) in other areas single out Korean business owners for their rudeness. Cultural differences do create a definite problem of misunderstanding between Korean business owners and their African American customers, but misunderstandings should be clearly distinguished from the alleged Korean habit of treating customers rudely.

The issue of rudeness should be examined in the context of interaction between storekeepers and customers. Today, Korean business owners are gravely concerned about frequent robbery and shoplifting attempts. Korean business owners pay an extremely high price for these crimes—economically, psychologically, and physically, as many incidents have resulted in the injury or death of business owners and employees (Shin Kim 1994). In such a defensive atmosphere, an owner's behavior may be perceived as rude by African American customers. However, complaints about such rude behavior were exaggerated and were used as part of the victim-blaming logic for looting and burning Korean businesses.

Conclusion

The Los Angeles unrest was the most destructive urban riot in American history. One victimized minority group victimized another minority group. A real tragedy in the Los Angeles disturbance is that while the deprived structural conditions associated with African Americans' victimization remain basically the same, their anger has devastated another minority group, Korean immigrant entrepreneurs. As a result, the Los Angeles unrest has intensified minority sufferings as experienced by Koreans in the United States without any prospect of improving the difficult life conditions of either minority. The Los Angeles unrest demonstrates again the meaning of the lesson stressed three decades ago by the Kerner Report: "Violence cannot build a better society" (1968:2). The tense situation left in the wake of such destruction is very likely to set into motion another cycle of minority unrest in the future.

This unfortunate current state of complex racial relations in Los Angeles and other major American cities calls for a systematic analysis of the structural mechanisms of urban racial unrest. The Los Angeles unrest signals a new era of such racial relations, one that must be conceptualized in terms of multiracial events. This approach calls attention to both the relationship between minority and dominant groups and the interminority group relationships in the United States.

If applied correctly, the middleman minority theory offers a useful and coherent perspective from which to analyze the roles of multiple race and ethnic groups that are distinguished from one another economically (and racially or ethnically) in a hierarchical way. The theory also suggests that, along with other social elements, the two critical factors—race and class—are intertwined. Therefore, it is crucial systematically to examine the influences of these two factors on such multiracial relations. If one factor is stressed at the expense of the other, studies will miss some essential ingredients of these complex relations.

Reference

Barringer, Herbert, Robert W. Gardner, and Michael J. Levin. 1993. *Asians and Pacific Inlanders in the United States.* New York: Russell Sage Foundation.

Bonacich, Edna, and Tae Hwan Jung. 1982. A portrait of Korean business in Los Angeles: 1977. pp. 75–98 in *Koreans in Los Angeles,* edited by Eui-Young Yu, Earl II. Phillips, and Eun Sik Yang. Los Angeles: Koryo Research Institute and Center for Korean-American and Korean Studies, California State University.

Bonaeich, Edna, Ivan Light, and Charles Choy Wong. 1980. Korean immigrant small business in Los Angeles. pp. 167–84 in *Sourcebook on the New Immigration,* edited by Roy Simon Bryce-Laporte. New Brunswick, N.J.: Transaction Books.

Bonackh, Edna, and John Modell. 1980. *The Economic Basis of Ethnic Solidarity: Small Business in the Japanese American Community.* Berkeley and Los Angeles: University of California Press.

Chang, Edward T. 1993. From Chicago to Los Angeles: changing the site of race relations. *Amerasia Journal* 19:1–3.

Choi, Laura. 1992. Black rage and white power. In Institute for Alternative Journalism, *Inside the L.A. Riots: What Really Happened and Why It Will Happen Again.*

Cooper, Marc. 1992. L.A.'s state of siege: city of angels, cops from hell. pp. 12–19 in Institute for Alternative Journalism, *Inside the L.A. Riots: What Really Happened and Why It Will Happen Again.*

Curran, Ron. 1992. Malign neglect. pp. 24–25 in Institute for Alternative Journalism,, *Inside the L.A. Riots: What Really Happened and Why It Will Happen Again.*

Elias, Robert. 1986. *The Politics of Victimization: Victims, Victimology and Human Rights.* New York: Oxford University Press.

Feagin, Joe R., and Clairece Booth Feagin. 1986. *Discrimination American Style,* 2nd ed. Malabar, Florida: Robert E. Krieger Publishing.

Fusfeld, Daniel R., and Timothy Bates. 1984. *The Political Economy of the Urban Ghetto.* Carbondale, Ill.: Southern Illinois University Press.

Hamilton, Cynthia. 1992. The making of an American Bantustan. pp. 19–20 in Institute for Alternative Journalism, *Inside the L.A. Riots: What Really Happened and Why It Will Happen Again.*

Hazen, Daniel. 1992. Forward to Institute for Alternative Journalism, *Inside the L.A. Riots: What Really Happened and Why It Will Happen Again.*

Hurh, Won Moo, and Kwang Chung Kim. 1988. *Uprooting and Adjustment: A Sociological Study of Korean Immigrants' Mental Health.* Final Report Submitted to National Institute of Mental Health, U.S. Department of Health and Human Services.

Institute for Alternative Journalism. 1992. *Inside the L.A. Riots: What Really Happened and Why It Will Happen Again.*

Korean American Inter-Agency Council (KAIAC). 1993. Korean American Inter-Agency Council announces results of a comprehensive survey assessing situation of Korean American victims ten months after the 1992 LA riots. Unpublished report.

Kerner Commission. 1968. *Report on the National Advisory Commission on Civil Disorders.* Washington, D.C.: U.S. Government Printing Office.

Kim, Illsoo. 1981. *New Urban Immigrants: The Korean Community in New York.* Princeton, N.J.: Princeton University Press.

——. 1992. *Newsweek,* May 18.

Kim, Kwang Chung, and Won Moo Hurh. 1985. Ethnic resource utilization of Korean immigrant entrepreneurs in the Chicago minority area. *International Migration Review* 19:82–111.

Kim, Kwang Chung, Won Moo Hurh, and Marylin Fernandez. 1989. Intra-group differences in business participation: Three Asian immigrant groups. *International Migration Review* 23: 73–95

Kim, Shin. 1994. Political economy of Korean-African American conflict. Chap. 13 in *Korean Americans: Conflict and Harmony,* edited by Ho-Youn Kwon. Chicago: North Park College and Theological Seminary.

Kwon, Peter, 1992. The first multicultural riots. pp. 88–93 Institute for Alternative Journalism, *Inside the L.A. Riots: What Really Happened and Why It Will Happen Again.*

Lieberson, Stanley. 1980. *Piece of a Pie: Blacks and White Immigrants Since 1880.* Berkeley and Los Angeles: University of California Press.

Light, Ivan, and Edna Bonacich. 1988. *Immigrant Entrepreneurs: Koreans in Los Angeles, 1965–1982.* Berkeley and Los Angeles: University of California Press.

Light, Ivan, Hadas Har-Chvi, and Kenneth Kan. 1994. Black/Korean conflict in Los Angeles. Chap. 6 in *Managing Divided Cities,* edited by Seamus Dunn. London: Rybum Publishing.

Los Angeles Times Staff. 1992. *Understanding the Riots: Los Angeles and the Aftermath of the Rodney King Verdict.* Los Angeles: *Los Angeles Times.*

Madhubuti, Haki R., ed. 1993. *Why L.A. Happened.* Chicago: Third World Press.

Marable, Manning. 1992. L.A. point of view. pp. 82–83 in Institute for Alternative Journalism, *Inside the L.A. Riots: What Really Happened and Why It Will Happen Again.*

Martin, Tony. 1993. From slavery to Rodney King: Continuity and change. pp. 27–40 in *Why L.A. Happened,* edited by Haki R. Madhubuti.

Massey, Douglas, and Nancy A. Denton. 1993. *American Apartheid: Segregation and the Making of the Underclass.* Cambridge, Mass.: Harvard University Press.

Min, Pyong Gap. 1988. *Ethnic Business Enterprise: Korean Small Business in Atlanta.* Stalen Island, N.Y.: Center for Migration Studies.

Oliver, Melvin, James H. Johnson, and David M. Grant. 1993. Race, urban inequality, and the Los Angeles rebellion. In *Introduction to Social Problems,* edited by Craig Calhoun and George Ritzer. New York: McGraw-Hill.

Reimers, David M. 1985. *Still the Golden Door.* New York: Columbia University Press.

Simmons, Charles E. 1993. The Los Angeles rebellion: Class, race and misinformation. pp. 141–55 in *Why L.A. Happened,* edited by Haki R. Madhubuti.

Soja, Edward, Rebecca Morales, and Goetz Wolff. 1983. Urban restructuring: An analysis of social and spatial change in Los Angeles. *Economic Geography* 58:221–35.

Sonenshein, Raphael J. 1993. *Politics in Black and White: Race and Power in Los Angeles*. Princeton, N.J.: Princeton University Press.

Turner, Jonathan H., and Edna Bonacich. 1980. Toward a composite theory of middleman minorities. *Ethnicity* 7:144–58.

U.S. Bureau of the Census. 1990. *Statistical Abstract of the United States*. Washington, D.C.: U.S. Government Printing Office.

U.S. Commission on Civil Rights. 1988. *The Economic Status of Americans of Asian Descent: An Exploratory Investigation*. Washington, D.C.: U.S. Commission on Civil Rights, Clearing House Publication 95.

Waldinger, Roger, Howard Aldrich, Robin Ward, and Associates. 1990. *Ethnic Entrepreneurs*. Newbury, Calif.: Sage Publications.

West, Cornel. 1993. *Race Matters*. Boston: Beacon Press.

Wilson, William Julius. 1987. *The Truly Disadvantaged: The Inner City, the Underclass, and Public Policy*. Chicago: University of Chicago Press.

Yu, Eui-Young. 1993. SA-I'KU (April 29) riots and the Korean-American community, unpublished paper.

——. 1994. *Black-Korean Encounter: Toward Understanding and Alliance*. Los Angeles, Calif.: Institute for Asian American and Pacific Asian Studies, California State University.

The Folly of Presumption

Black Voters and the Los Angeles 2001 Mayoral Election

> If [Jesse] Jackson wanted to forge a Latino and black political coalition … he should have been marching in Los Angeles alongside Antonio Villaraigosa in an historic attempt to be the first Latino elected mayor of that city…. Villaraigosa lost by about 40,000 votes. Ironically, when Harold Washington was first elected mayor of Chicago, he won by roughly 50,000 votes. In November 1983, Washington addressed a gathering of Hispanic leaders, and I heard him say it was the Latino vote that put him over the top. Wouldn't it have been nice if Villaraigosa could have said that about the black vote in L.A.? But Jackson wouldn't go near L.A., not with Magic Johnson and U.S. Rep. Maxine Waters rallying blacks to support the white candidate.
>
> Juan Andrade
> President of the U.S. Hispanic Leadership Institute

In the late fall of 1999, Antonio Villaraigosa, then speaker of the California state assembly, decided, after more than a year of introspection and consideration, to run for mayor of Los Angeles. This "intense, energetic, handsome, and plain-spoken" Latino did this even though he had been advised by numerous Democratic veterans, as

Nicholas Vaca, "The Folly of Presumption: Black Voters and the Los Angeles 2001 Mayoral Elections," *The Presumed Alliance: The Unspoken Conflict Between Latinos and Blacks and What It Means for America*, pp. 85-107. Copyright © 2004 by HarperCollins Publishers. Reprinted with permission.

161

well as by some of his most fervent backers, not to run. They asked him to be a good political soldier and wait his turn, assuring him that in time conditions would be right and then he would be the candidate of choice. Villaraigosa, however, did not listen. He was accustomed to hearing such negative advice during his political career, which he would ignore and go on to prove his detractors wrong by succeeding. His career as a state assemblyman was about to end as a result of term limits, and he was eager to continue his political career by becoming mayor of Los Angeles. He was convinced that he possessed the right qualities to lead one of the country's major cities into the new millennium.

After he announced his candidacy he was assessed by the *Los Angeles Times* as being decidedly nonethnic. While in Sacramento he had advocated for school reform, health care, and open space. Nothing particularly ethnic about that, the *Los Angeles Times* wrote, observing that such issues resonated not only with Latinos and liberals but with the entire California electorate. On the negative side, the *Los Angeles Times* noted that Villaraigosa was unabashedly liberal and blunt—the latter a real liability in the world of politics where sensibility and tact sometimes spell the difference between success and failure. The concern was that his sometimes brash personality would strike a negative chord with white conservative voters. The paper also noted that Villaraigosa had low name recognition as a result of spending a great deal of time in Sacramento, California's state capital. This was not helped by the fact that his name, an amalgam of his surname and that of his wife, is nearly unpronounceable, even for some Spanish-speaking Latinos. Finally, the publication observed that while the Latino voting base was significant in Los Angeles, the time for a Latino candidate was still several years away.

Villaraigosa was also entering a crowded field that already featured a Latino candidate, Democratic state representative Xavier Becerra from Los Angeles. It also included James K. Hahn, the city attorney of Los Angeles. Not only was Hahn the only candidate to hold city office, winning five citywide campaigns over his political career, but he was also heir to a legacy that would turn out to be the difference between his success and Villaraigosa's failure in the mayoral race. Kenneth (commonly referred to as "Kenny") Hahn, James's father, was a legend among African American voters in South Central Los Angeles. If Clinton is sometimes regarded as the first African American president of the United States, Kenny was sometimes viewed as L.A.'s first citywide African American officeholder. Year after year Kenny delivered for his South Central Black constituents, and for that he was warmly regarded and repeatedly returned to office by Black voters. So when James Hahn began his campaign for mayor, he came to the game with a decided advantage. Taking the Black vote away from James would be a formidable, if not impossible, task. Challengers would not only be battling James but also vying with his father's ghost.

Villaraigosa thought from the very beginning that if anyone could do it, he could. He was Latino, a minority just like Hahn's Black voters, and he was convinced that his track record as a "coalition builder" made him the ideal candidate to draw Black voters away from Hahn's camp. Perhaps Villaraigosa did not truly appreciate the challenge he was facing. Already in January 2001,

Hahn had secured the endorsement of such Black political luminaries as Congresswoman Maxine Waters and Los Angeles county supervisor Yvonne Brathwaite Burke. He had also received the support of former basketball star Magic Johnson, as well as that of Rev. Cecil L. Murray, the senior pastor of the influential First AME Church. True, Villaraigosa would assemble his own list of Black supporters, including state assemblymen Carl Washington and Herb Wesson and state senator Kevin Murray, but, as time would prove out, Kenny's legacy ran deeper in the Black community than mere endorsements from Black candidates. Even though Villaraigosa cast himself as someone who could build a Black-Latino coalition, from the inception of the race it was clear that he was going to have a hard go of it.

As the deadline for filing papers for the mayoral race approached, Villaraigosa's friends and supporters once again beseeched him not to run. County supervisor Gloria Molina and Henry Cisneros, a former member of Clinton's cabinet, met with him several times and counseled him that if he ran against Becerra all he would do was succeed in splitting the Latino vote, thereby assuring that no Latino would win the Democratic primary or be in any runoff. Molina and Cisneros also lobbied Becerra with the same request.

Since neither Villaraigosa nor Becerra would voluntarily back away, Molina and Cisneros devised a novel plan to convince one of them to drop out. Their idea was this: Each candidate's ability to raise funds and obtain endorsements, as well as his citywide popularity, would be measured by some neutral body. The "loser" in this assessment would be asked to step down. By some accounts, Villaraigosa agreed but the proposed plan fell apart when Becerra refused to go along with it. Frustrated with Becerra's recalcitrance, Molina and Cisneros broke off all discussions.

Predicting that both candidates would fail as a result, Cisneros stated: "I think it's quite likely that neither one can make the June election runoff, if both are in the race.... That is really a shame for Latino ambitions in Los Angeles."

Early in February, the Villaraigosa and Becerra campaigns became embroiled in a scandal that revealed the effect that monetary contributions can have on the wise judgment of politicians. It would also prove to be a scandal with legs—it would stay with Villaraigosa long after its initial revelation and far into his mayoral campaign.

It was discovered that Villaraigosa and Becerra, along with Cardinal Roger M. Mahony, had written letters to President Clinton in support of Carlos Vignali Jr., a Los Angeles cocaine dealer whose sentence President Clinton commuted on his last day in office. Villaraigosa wrote his letter five years prior to the commutation. Nevertheless, he felt compelled to apologize for sending it, insisting that the letter had nothing to do with the $2,795 the Vignali family had donated to his past campaigns. This sum was only slightly less than the $3,500 the family had contributed to Becerra. The letters were viewed as clear lobbying efforts by both candidates, even though Becerra protested that all he was doing was urging the White House to make certain that justice had really been served in Vignali's case.

About the same time that the news was breaking about the Vignali imbroglio, Villaraigosa managed a significant breakthrough by winning the backing of the Los Angeles County Federation of Labor, AFL-CIO, by a single vote. It was a hard-fought battle in which Hahn worked hard to keep the union neutral. However, the union, which increasingly represented Latino workers, wanted to be responsive to its membership, and the AFL-CIO was also beginning to flex its muscle after several big electoral wins. Miguel Conteras, the unions treasurer, was positively ebullient about Villaraigosa's endorsement, making it a "bet the farm" commitment by promising to rally hundreds of volunteers to work phone banks and walk neighborhoods.

During this heated contest, Kenny's specter loomed large: Maxine Waters and Yvonne Brathwaite Burke joined Hahn in his efforts to keep the union neutral. Their argument, at least on the surface, was that the union should back a winner—someone who was certain to make the runoff. It was also an early manifestation of the problems that Villaraigosa would encounter with Harm's Black supporters.

In February Hahn launched a series of television spots that highlighted his work for Los Angeles as an insider—first as city controller and then as city attorney. Hahn, who was widely recognized as being less than dynamic, countered his milquetoast personality with an emphasis on the solid nature of his service to the city.

His television spots appeared to have the intended effect. Five weeks before the election, Hahn appeared to pull ahead of the pack. In a poll conducted by the *Los Angeles Times,* the numbers broke down like this: 24 percent of the votes favored Hahn; 12 percent for commercial real estate broker Steven Sorboroff; 12 percent for Villaraigosa; 11 percent for city councilman Joel Wachs; 10 percent for Becerra; 8 percent for state controller Kathleen Connell. Among Black voters, Hahn was favored by 58 percent.

Hahn understood that having the Black vote behind him was not enough to put him in the mayor's office. What he needed was a coalition. Coalitions are never the sole domain of minority voters—indeed, they are a thing apart from color and ethnicity. If his father's legacy helped him clinch the Black vote, then his long term as the city attorney of Los Angeles helped to guarantee the white conservative vote. In the 10 years that he had been city attorney, Hahn had doled out over $29 million to outside law firms to represent the city in a variety of cases. It was only natural, then, that some of these law firms would come to his aid. O'Melveny and Meyers, for example, contributed $25,000 to his campaign—small change compared to the $2.9 million in business that Hahn had sent their way. Other law firms contributed similarly, and several partners in some firms held their own fund-raising events. Hahn was managing to operate successfully in two entirely opposite worlds—the everyday, workingman's world of his father's Black constituents and the rarefied world of successful white businessmen.

Villaraigosa's image, on the other hand, was undergoing a severe and not too flattering remake. With the Vignali matter still dogging him, and with less than a week before the election, Villaraigosa found himself the victim of a truly diabolical plot. In a recorded telephone call to potential voters, someone who identified herself as "Gloria Morina" and who sounded surprisingly like Gloria Molina—but wasn't—announced that the call was an emergency. The caller stated that it was time to break the silence about Villaraigosa. It was time to reveal that Villaraigosa opposed increased penalties for rapists and that he twice opposed legislation to increase penalties for child pornography. The recorded message went on to say that people should vote against Villaraigosa in order to ensure the safety of women and children. Of course, all of Villaraigosa's opponents denied that they were behind the call. The call was not only disturbing in its content, it also seemed to confirm, at least to some degree, the image that Villaraigosa was acquiring among certain Los Angeles voters.

Not only was Villaraigosa being painted as soft on crime, but his stated goal of forming a coalition with Black voters was quickly slipping away. In a second *Los Angeles Times* poll released days before the election, Hahn had increased his rating among Black voters by 7 percent now 63 percent of African Americans stated they expected to vote for Hahn. What was truly startling, state controller Kathleen Connell received the next most favorable rating, with 12 percent of the Black respondents stating they favored her. Villaraigosa garnered only 7 percent in the poll. Clearly, his goal of creating a Black-Latino coalition was failing.

If Villaraigosa had accompanied Hahn on one of his frequent sojourns through South Central, he could have witnessed the true futility of his efforts to win away Kenny's legacy. "During a lunch-time program in an auditorium at the Watts Labor Community Action Committee, elderly African American women swapped stories about the Hahn family. As Hahn walked through the room, one person after another reached to clasp his hands," the *Los Angeles Times* reported. The affection that the Black residents of Watts showed Hahn also translated into support at the polls. A Black voter who approached Hahn said, "Hahn, right? I'm so appreciative of your father and the work that he did. You've got one vote."

At the same time, Villaraigosa and Becerra were fomenting tremendous excitement in the Latino community. For the first time, people believed that a Latino could be mayor of Los Angeles. But the reality was that, for all of their population numbers—which in 2001 stood at between 43 and 47 percent of the total Los Angeles population—they did not translate into votes. Indeed, in the 1997 mayors race, Latinos represented only 15 percent of the electorate. Many were unable to vote because they weren't citizens or had not registered. And a *Los Angeles Times* poll found that 37 percent of the Latinos planned to vote for one of the four white candidates.

At the eleventh hour of the election, Villaraigosa found he still could not distance himself from the Vignali fiasco, thanks to radio ads paid for by the Morongo Indians. Accusations flew as to who was really behind the ads. Parke Skelton, Villaraigosa's campaign consultant, alleged that it was Assemblyman Tony Cardenas, a supporter of Hahn. Skelton described Cardenas as the principal legislative proponent for the Morongo and other Indian tribes that had been successful in pushing to expand gaming in California. Cardenas denied the accusations and the Morongo Indians also denied that he was in any way involved in the ads, the Morongo Indians stood fast in saying that they alone were responsible for them. No matter who the instigator was, the ads did not help Villaraigosa.

On April 10, Los Angeles voters went to the polls and made Villaraigosa and Hahn the top vote getters among the pack of candidates, giving Villaraigosa 30 percent of the vote and Hahn 25 percent. Latinos swelled with pride at the fact that a Latino was so close to the highest citywide office in Los Angeles. The *Los Angeles Times* described one of the day-after celebrations: "Veterans of political struggles past, people old enough to remember the days when the idea of Chicano power was a seemingly impossible dream, all came to Villaraigosas Union Station celebration to see one of our own move one step closer to becoming mayor by making the runoff."

The "one of our own" sentiment should have been expected. Latino voters knew instinctively, if not through readings, that Los Angeles began as a Mexican town. After all, wasn't Los Angeles first named El Pueblo de Nuestra Señora la Reyna de Los Angeles de Porciuncula? A real mouthful, but one that dripped with Mexican history. And for 20 years the mayor of Los Angeles had been an African American—so wasn't it the Latinos' turn? Shouldn't it be "one of our own" sitting in that office? And shouldn't African Americans help put him there?

The level of anticipation and frustration that Latinos felt in the spring of 2001 could not be understood without an examination of modern-day Los Angeles politics and the long period of time that Latinos had stood outside the halls of power, noses pressed against the glass as they watched, unable to fully participate in the comings and goings of the political process.

Carey McWilliams, in his classic work *North from Mexico,* took great glee in deflating the myth that Los Angeles was founded in 1791 by Spanish grandees and *caballeros.* The true founders of the City of Angeles, states McWilliams, were "Pablo Rodríguez, who was an Indian; José Variegas, the first *alcalde of the pueblo,* also an Indian; José Moreno, a mulatto; Felix Villavicencio, a Spaniard married to an Indian; José de Lara, also married to an Indian; Antonio Mesa, who was a Negro; Basilio Rosas, an Indian married to an Indian; Antonio Navarro, a mestizo with a mulatto wife; Manuel Camero, a mulatto." McWilliams notes that the twelfth founder was simply identified as a *Chino,* and was probably Chinese.

Even though it could be argued that Los Angeles' founders were multiethnic, after 1848 the population took on a different complexion as white migrants began to flood into the city. In spite of the already significant Mexican and Asian populations in Los Angeles at the time of their arrival, the largely white and Protestant migrants were intent on replicating the homogeneous nature of the American heartland. To this pool of white immigrants was added white immigrants from the South. The development of a white power structure was so successful that by the 1920s the white immigrants had formed a power structure that controlled most of the public offices and closed political opportunities to minority groups.

Just as the arrival of Anglos in Los Angeles overwhelmed the existing residents, the white residents of Los Angeles soon witnessed a challenge to their own strength as a growing number of Mexicans, Asians, and Blacks left the South in search of industrial jobs in Los Angeles. Between 1920 and 1930 the Mexican population grew from 30,000 to 97,000, the Black population jumped from 15,500 to

39,000, and the Japanese population grew from 11,600 to over 21,000. Only the Chinese population remained relatively unchanged, numbering 2,000 in 1920 and 3,000 in 1930.

The flow of Blacks to Los Angeles increased significantly during World War II. Los Angeles was transformed into a major site for aircraft and shipbuilding, which necessitated a constant flow of labor. By 1960, Blacks represented 13.5 percent of the total L.A. population. By the 1950s and early 1960s, the Black community was organizing for political power. The Latino residents, also growing in numbers, proved to be less adept at exercising their political power. And the Asian community, no doubt affected by the relocation of Japanese Americans during World War II, lagged even further behind.

The growth of the African American, Latino, and Asian populations was matched by the growth of the Jewish community. Jews not only populated the downtown area and West Los Angeles, but also spilled out into the San Fernando Valley. In addition to establishing pockets of residency in areas outside of Los Angeles, Jews also created economic centers away from downtown Los Angeles.

The significance of the Jewish population extended beyond their numerical growth and business centers to the political arena. Raphael J. Sonenshein, a political science professor and longtime observer of Los Angeles politics, points out that the high literacy rate among Jews produced a higher percentage of the electorate than their population.

Despite their economic base and voting numbers, Jews were excluded from the dominant social, political, and economic life of Los Angeles. The combination of their exclusion and their liberal activism in the community led to a natural alliance with the similarly disenfranchised Blacks. In the early 1960s, this liberal ideology and shared political interest led to the formation of a political coalition, which, in conjunction with Black mobilization, led to the successful election of three Black members to the Los Angeles City Council.

Tom Bradley, a well-known Black political figure, was the focus of the biracial coalition, and he made plans to challenge Mayor Sam Yorty for office. Bradley lost his first bid for the mayoralty, but his second run in 1973 proved to be successful. As a result of Bradley's election as mayor, Blacks and Jews, the mainstay of his coalition, were rewarded with appointments to city commissions.

Bradley's coalition was based on the strong political and personal ties among Black and white activists who had worked together and learned to trust one another since the early 1960s. Any participation on the part of Latinos in the Bradley coalition was secondary to the role played by Jews and other white liberals.

It is also important to note two events regarding the Latino role in Los Angeles politics prior to the election of Bradley as mayor. The first involved the District 9 city council position, which had been occupied by Edward Roybal, the only Latino on the Los Angeles City Council. District 9 was almost equally divided between Latinos and Blacks, and because of Roybal's long tenure and visibility, that district had long been considered a Latino district. In 1962, Roybal resigned his position as city councilman and ran successfully for Congress. The City Council then faced a difficult choice in selecting a replacement: either Gilbert Lindsay, the Black deputy to then county supervisor Kenneth

Hahn, or Richard Tafoya, Roybals first cousin and aide to Mayor Sam Yorty. This was a clear zero-sum situation, with Blacks trying to obtain their first seat on the City Council and Latinos trying to retain the only seat they had.

It was the white council members from districts with Black constituencies who took the lead, championing Lindsay to replace Roybal. Joe Hollingsworth, a white council member from District 10, who had been appointed by the City Council at a time when Blacks thought that an African American should represent his district, nominated Lindsay and also ushered in a procedural move that accelerated his selection. On January 28, 1963, the City Council appointed Lindsay as one of its board members, making him the first Black to hold office in Los Angeles.

Tafoya was outraged, but the Black leadership was pleased with its success and made plans to organize a Black united front to vote for Lindsay in the upcoming municipal elections. That Lindsay, an African American, was battling with Tafoya, a Latino, for the district that had previously sent a Latino to the City Council did not appear to concern the Black leadership. They were determined to maintain the position even at the expense of going against Roybal's cousin, and even after Roybal had been the principal voice in City Council speaking out on behalf of Black representation.

In addition to running Lindsay against Tafoya, African Americans fielded candidates in two other districts—Tom Bradley in the Tenth District and Bill Mills in the Eighth District. The *Eagle*, a Black newspaper, urged the Black community to unite behind their candidates. Ceding the council seat to Tafoya did not appear to be a consideration.

On election day, Bradley won District 10, but both Lindsay and Bill Mills were forced into runoff elections. Even though Bradley's position was secured, the Black leadership did not find it necessary to change their position and support Tafoya in the runoff, thereby assuring that at least one Latino and one African American would sit on the City Council for the first time in the history of L.A. Instead, Blacks went all out to make certain that Lindsay defeated Tafoya. Bradley, who would later attempt to woo Latinos to support his mayoral bid, even sent one of his key aides to the Lindsay campaign to help him in mapping out the precincts. There would be no attempt at coalition building to save the one council seat that had historically been occupied by Latinos.

The effect of this election was devastating for Latinos in Los Angeles. It would be more than 23 years before another Latino sat on the City Council. On the other hand, it was a boon to African Americans—the three seats they won would be occupied by Blacks for the next 30 years.

Black dominance of minority politics in Los Angeles was exacerbated by the consequence of the 1965 Watts riots. The three-day riots were sparked by the arrest of two Black men and their mother by the California Highway Patrol in South Los Angeles on August 11, 1965. In all, 31 African Americans were killed, 1,032 persons were hurt, 3,438 adults and 514 juveniles were arrested, and there was $40 million in property damage.

The riots focused attention on the African American community of South Los Angeles. Black Leaders thought that the impact of the uprising would make the white power structure more attentive to the needs of this community, but Latinos and whites generally agreed that the riots would not help race relations. Both groups feared personal attacks by Blacks.

As it turned out, the riots did lead to allocation of antipoverty funds. Sonenshein notes that "Some Latino activists expressed resentment at the great attention being paid to Blacks in the wake of the riot, especially in the allocation of antipoverty funds. The obvious lack of Latino political influence was remarkable considering that Latinos outnumbered Blacks in the county."

While the riots gave Mayor Sam Yorty a platform for appealing to an existing conservative base, it inspired African Americans to push for more political representation at the local level. It also had the effect of uniting African Americans against Yorty, giving him only slightly higher ratings than police chief William Parks.

In the aftermath of the 1965 riots, divisions were created that carried forth into Tom Bradley's 1969 mayoral race. Yorty and his administration were pitted against the alliance of African Americans and white liberals. Sonenshein describes Latinos as being in the middle. Exactly what Sonenshein means is unclear, but it would appear that Latinos were not an integral part of the Black-White coalition: "Persistent attempts would be made to incorporate Latinos into this coalition, but it would be a long, frustrating process. As often as cooperation, conflict appeared between Los Angeles Blacks and Latinos over antipoverty programs, the Watts riot, police practices, and Sam Yorty."

This schism was apparent not only in the zero-sum game of antipoverty programs and the funds they distributed but in the eventual defeat of Bradley by Yorty in 1969. Sonenshein observed that coalition among Blacks, liberal whites, and Latinos had not yet formed. Not only was Jewish support for Bradley not as strong as was expected, but Latinos had voted for Yorty in numbers close to those of white conservatives.

Sonenshein explains Bradley's failure to attract Latino voters in the 1969 mayoral race by presenting a list of possible reasons for this disaffection ranging from class status to areas of residence, with poor Latinos favoring Bradley over Yorty. However, Sonenshein glosses over the level of trust that existed between white liberals and Blacks, developed as a result of their long history of working together.

Beginning with the Tafoya-Lindsay fiasco, which disenfranchised Latinos for 23 years, and followed by the conflict over antipoverty program funds, Blacks and Latinos had a substantial history of *not* working together and mistrust. Sonenshein alludes to this fact when he writes, "As far back as the battle over the Ninth District council seat in 1963, Los Angeles Blacks and Latinos had been competitors as well as allies. With three council seats for Blacks and none for Latinos, the argument that both were politically excluded rested on shaky ground. Liberal money and support had been flowing to blacks, most notably Bradley, creating resentment among even liberal Latino activists."

In 1973, Bradley finally prevailed and became mayor of Los Angeles. Like his election to City Council in 1963 and his 1969 mayoral campaign, Bradley succeeded largely on a Black-white liberal coalition. Sonenshein's attempts to explain the failure of Latinos to coalesce around Bradley during his 1973 election are somewhat ambiguous.

> On the other hand, the Latino vote may be a class vote. Los Angeles may have a basis for a Black-Latino coalition that is quite different from the sort of coalition that could be made with whites. This Latino class vote gets pulled out of voting analysis as an "ethnic vote," but it may be important in class terms. In the search for a white working-class base for black politics, observers may tend to miss it. If there is a working-class Latino base for the biracial coalition, its members probably have different priorities than those of white liberals.

Whatever meaning can be drawn from this statement, the fact remains that Latinos did not vote overwhelmingly for Bradley during his 1969 and 1973 mayoral runs, and the reasons for this reluctance can be excavated from the historical relationship between Latinos and Blades in the political and economic arenas.

Latinos also demonstrated their disaffection for other Black candidates when their votes helped defeat two Black candidates to the school board.

Approximately one year later, Bradley helped elect two Black allies to the City Council, increasing the number of Black City Council members from two to four. Bradley also invited David Cunningham, another Black candidate, to run for his now-vacant City Council seat in District 10. Cunningham ran against a Japanese American candidate, George Takei, who had been chairman for Bradley's 1969 and 1973 mayoral campaigns. Cunningham defeated Takei in December, and like the Latino community, the Asian community would not have one of their own on the council until 11 years later, when Michael Woo won the 1985 election. It was a victory, however, that would come without much Black support.

The coalition that swept Bradley into power retained its base, allowing Bradley to successfully repel opponents in 1977, 1981, 1985, and 1989. It remained, however, a largely Black-white liberal coalition, with only moderate support from Latinos. As long as Blacks and white liberals stuck together, the coalition was unbeatable. While the coalition welcomed the participation of Latinos, it was clear that their role continued to be secondary to the Black-white liberal coalition.

In time the biracial coalition came unglued. Bradley s victory in the 1985 mayoral election surpassed anything that he had experienced in his previous mayoral victories. For the first time he won all 15 council districts. The victory, however, masked changes that were occurring— changes that would eventually lead to the end of Bradley's political career.

In 1985, several events occurred that began to erode the coalition. The first was Bradley's approval of Occidental Petroleum Corporation's plan to drill in the Pacific Palisades area. The decision was apparent confirmation that Bradley had changed from someone committed to quality of life, something highly prized by a certain sector of the white liberals, to someone allied with industrial development.

Bradley damaged his Jewish alliance by not denouncing Nation of Islam leader Louis Farrakhan's anti-Semitic posture immediately when Farrakhan visited Los Angeles. A group of Black leaders had convinced him that they could get Farrakhan to tone down his rhetoric. When Black and Jewish leaders finally convened over the Farrakhan incident, "there was little common ground and much animosity."

The mayor's personal reputation as someone above reproach was tainted when it was reported that Bradley, who received an annual stipend from Far East National Bank (FENB), used his influence to restore city funds that had been removed from the bank. It was alleged that Bradley, at the behest of the FENB president, not only restored a $1 million deposit to the bank but added an additional $1 million. Proof supporting this allegation was "A notation on the treasurer's record 'per the mayor' had been whited out."

James Hahn, Villaraigosa's eventual mayoral opponent, began an investigation of the changes and subsequently issued a report that charged Bradley with ethical improprieties but did not indict him. As these facts were given wide publicity by the newspapers, Bradley's vulnerability became evident. Gloria Molina, then a member of City Council, criticized Hahn for not proceeding with criminal charges, attesting to Bradley s damaged public stature. And while the scandal eventually faded away, Bradley was never able to recover the full trust of the public.

In the 1989 mayoral race, the fracturing of the Black-white liberal coalition was further complicated by the entrance of two challengers in the nonpartisan primary: Nate Holden and Baxter Ward. Neither candidate was considered to be a real threat, not only because of Bradley s long history of success at the polls but also because both candidates did not have much money to spend on the campaign. Bradley had amassed over $1 million, and by the time the campaign ended, he had spent over $2.6 million, compared to $266,723 spent by Holden, his closest spending competitor. However, even with such an enormous expenditure, Bradley won very narrowly, with 52 percent of the vote.

Of the seven districts that Bradley carried, five were predominantly Black and two had white liberal majorities. The three districts in which Bradley was defeated were overwhelmingly white. The districts in which he broke even included two Latino districts, and one mixed Latino-white district. These numbers reaffirmed that Bradley s victory, narrow as it was, rested on his original biracial coalition—Blacks and white liberals. Latinos were almost equally divided but had low voter turnout.

The demise of the coalition, the financial scandal, and the riot that followed the beating of Rodney King in 1992 were the apparent reasons that convinced Bradley not to seek another term in 1993. This allowed Michael Woo, a onetime member of Bradley s political camp, to run against Richard Riordan, a Republican businessman. The Black-white liberal coalition that had so successfully catapulted and maintained Bradley into political prominence did not serve the same purpose for Woo, who was defeated by Riordan.

The 1997 mayoral race revealed the ethnic fault line of the Los Angeles voting public. Riordan, who had successfully created an image as a moderate, was then challenged by Tom Hayden, a Democratic state senator. During his four-year term, Riordan had successfully denned his administration not by political party affiliation but by policy issues and programs that he believed benefitted Los Angeles. President Clinton rewarded his crossover administration by providing federal funds to the city. Riordan, however, alienated Black voters when he refused to renew Black police chief Willie Williams's contract.

Riordan defeated Hayden by a 2-to-1 margin. However, the true significance of the 1997 mayor's race was the emergence of the Latino vote. In 1997, Latinos made up 33 percent of L.A.'s adult population, but only 14 percent of the registered voters. Furthermore, of this small percentage, only 8 to 10 percent of them actually voted. In comparison, even though Blacks constituted only 13 percent of the population, they represented 18 percent of registered voters. But in 1997, Latinos outvoted Blacks 15 percent to 13 percent. Not only that, whereas Blacks voted in overwhelming numbers for Hayden, Latinos voted in greater numbers for Riordan.

Now in the year 2001, Villaraigosa stood toe to toe with Hahn, battling to be the first Latino mayor of Los Angeles in modern times. He hoped it would come about with the help of African American voters. Where he got that notion was a mystery. Certainly it was not from the numbers in the April 10 primary. When all the ballots were finally counted, Hahn got 71 percent of the Black vote and Villaraigosa got only 12 percent. A political realist would have called Villaraigosa aside and advised him to forget about the Black vote—it was lost to him. But why was it lost to him? Madison Shocldey, a member of the board of directors of the Southern Christian Leadership Conference, tried to tell him. As she related in the *Los Angeles Times,* for all his willingness to work with the Black community, Blacks had a hard time "seeing a common agenda with the Latino immigrant community. Many blacks view it as a zero-sum political calculation: Their gain is our loss." Her advice to Villaraigosa was to outline to the African American community an agenda that could be shared by both groups: "Villaraigosa must show blacks a way that African American culture, community and political participation will not be destroyed by the burgeoning Latino presence." The dilemma was great for Villaraigosa. What could he do to assure Black voters that he was not going to take away what Kenny had given to them as the Latino population mushroomed before their very eyes. Nothing, as it turned out.

Earlier Sonenshein had spoken in much the same manner as Shockley. Even though Sonenshein allowed that "the most likely rainbow coalition is between Blacks and Latinos," he also observed that, upon closer examination, Los Angeles rainbow coalitions look less promising than advertised. "Ethnic conflict and economic competition significantly undermine the potential of such alliances."

During the runoff, Villaraigosa continued to pursue the Black vote. He met with the congregation of one of L.A.'s largest and best-known Black churches, announcing new endorsements from Black leaders—Bishop John Bryant of the African Methodist Episcopal Church, Bishop E. Lynn Brown of the Christian Methodist Episcopal Church, Bishop Leon Ralph of the Interdenominational Church of God of America, and J. Benjamin Hardwick, president of the Western Baptist State Convention of California—in an effort to counter Hahn's own growing list of supporters among Black religious and community leaders. Villaraigosa emphasized repeatedly his ability to create coalitions and stressed how important the Black vote was to his mayoral run.

Less than three weeks before the mayoral runoff vote, Susan Anderson, a Los Angeles writer, presented an upbeat analysis of Villaraigosa s chances for successfully wooing the Black vote. She pointed out the obvious split among Black community and religious leaders' support for Villaraigosa and Hahn as proof positive that Hahn did not have the Black vote in his back pocket. She also underlined Villaraigosa's long history of involvement with the Black community, beginning with his high school days when he was involved with the Black Students Union and continuing to his days as co-chair of the Black-Latino Roundtable during the 1980s and his long association with coalition builders such as AGENDA executive director Anthony Thingpen and Community Coalition head Karen Bass.

However, Anderson contrasted Villaraigosas potential appeal to the Black voters with Kenny's proven track record with the Black community. "Hahn's black supporters have many reasons to stick with their candidate, among them, the unmatched family legacy—'We know him,' say many...."

Anderson's somewhat academic approach to the division among Black voters was made flesh and blood in a piece written by Steve Lopez for the *Los Angeles Times. In* a scene that might have come straight out of the recent film *Barber Shop,* Lopez recounts an encounter between Kevin E. Hooks, a Black 30-year-old owner of an entertainment marketing company and supporter of Villaraigosa, and Tony Wafford, another young Black supporter of Villaraigosa, and some of the denizens of L.T.'s Barber Shop, a Black barbershop in South Central Los Angeles. Their combined attempts to win converts to Villaragosa's camp was met not so much with a virulent dislike of Villaraigosa but with a near-religious fervor in support of Hahn, based almost solely on his father's legacy. "His father didn't have no crooked in him," Hooks is told by one of the elders of the L.T.'s shop. And Lawrence Tolliver, the owner of the shop, lectures Hooks and Wafford that "The Bible tells me that the fruit don't fall far from the tree, and Ken Hahn was a strong tree!" To which Wafford responds, "You pick up fruit, you knock it, you squeeze it.... Jim Hahn's daddy's dead, I'm telling you! Is a dead white man better than a live Mexican?" The question was never quite answered, but Tolliver provides the last word. "The bottom line [is that] 90% of the black community is going to vote for Hahn ... [and] when the white man goes into the booth in the Valley and has to decide between a white man and Mexican ... " Tolliver does not complete his sentence but it is obvious to everyone in the barbershop which box will be checked by the white voter.

As Election Day approached, the generation gap between older and younger Black voters began to surface. "There is no empirical evidence on this, but we suspect that more and more younger black voters will be attracted to the Villaraigosa campaign," Michael Preston, a USC political scientist, told the *Los Angeles Times.* Preston's statement was given credence by the fact that Villaraigosa's Crenshaw district office was staffed by dozens of volunteers, two-thirds of whom were African American. Another anecdotal indication of the generational division was exemplified by Melina Reirnan, a doctoral candidate at USC, who stated that she brought young Black undergraduate and graduate students to hear Villaraigosa present his views on the mayor's race. "Every single person I've brought to hear him speak and hear what he says on the issues has become a supporter," she stated. In contrast, she pointed out that older Black voters insist that she must vote for Hahn, but few of them can give her any specific reasons why she must do so. "The only reason I would get is, 'Wasn't his daddy Kenny Hahn?'"

In the final week of the campaign Hahn revived Villaraigosa's ill-fated letter to Clinton on behalf of Carlos Vignali by running a television ad. It reinforced Hahn's attack on Villaraigosa that he was an unknown candidate who could not be trusted. The ad itself smacked of the Willie Horton commercial run by George Bush against Michael Dukakis in 1988. The Hahn ad depicted a razor blade cutting cocaine, a copy of Villaraigosa's letter to the White House, a grainy photograph of a smoking cocaine pipe and Villaraigosa. As the ad runs, a voice describes the letter and the campaign contributions and states that Villaraigosa "falsely claimed that the crack cocaine dealer had no prior criminal record." The ad ends by stating that "Los Angeles can't trust Antonio Villaraigosa."

On Election Day Hahn was carried into office on the unlikely shoulders of a Black-white conservative coalition. Hahn received 59 percent of white voters, an astounding 80 percent of the Black vote, but only 18 percent of the Latino vote. Villaraigosa received 41 percent of the white vote, 10 percent of the Black vote, and 82 percent of the Latino vote. The predictions and speculation that surrounded Hahn and his Black supporters came true.

While Hahn's father's legacy no doubt proved to be a significant factor in gaining support among Black voters, there were other reasons why Black voters came out in such astounding numbers for Harm. The *Los Angeles Times* reported, "The anti-Latino anxiety won't show up on any exit pool. But it does in candid conversations. 'I got heat from blacks,' says one African American legislator who endorsed Villaraigosa. 'They asked, Why do you support him? He'll throw us all out.'" This candid comment is understandable in the context of Black politics in Los Angeles. Tom Bradley was mayor for five terms, and during that time Blacks were able to make substantial gains when they were appointed to commissions, received public contracts, and increased their employment both in the city of Los Angeles and in the Los Angeles County public sector. Again, these gains were obtained during the reign of the Black-white liberal coalition, with Latinos and Asians playing a secondary role. This long-term relationship gave Blacks a history and a level of comfort with white liberals that they did not have with Latinos. In addition, unlike the white liberals, Latinos were now in direct competition with Blacks over jobs, housing, and educational opportunity. The interests of the Black voters conflicted directly with the interests of Latinos.

There was another unspoken reason that prevented Villaraigosa from getting the Black vote—a reflection of the candid statement translated into political terms. The fact that at the time of the election Los Angeles was 11.2 percent Black and 46.5 percent Hispanic, reflecting a 15 percent decrease of the Black population since 1990 and a 24 percent increase in the Latino population, frightened many Black politicians, who saw their voting power waning in the state. It was reportedly for this reason that Congresswoman Maxine Waters backed Hahn—"out of fear that Hispanic gains in political power come at the expense of black political power."

Congresswoman Waters had a reason to be concerned. By the time of the mayoral race in Los Angeles, Latinos had eclipsed African Americans as political players in the state, moving from 7 percent of the electorate in 1990 to 14 percent, while Blacks stayed at 7 percent. By the time of the mayoral election, Cruz Bustamante had been elected as the first Latino to a statewide office, and the new state legislature had a record 26-member Latino caucus, while the Black caucus was reduced to 6. Waters must also have been aware that approximately 20 years before, Willie Brown, now mayor of San Francisco, was speaker of the State Assembly, Tom Bradley was beginning his third term as mayor of Los Angeles, Lionel Wilson was mayor of Oakland, Wilson Riles was ending his third term as the states superintendent of public instruction, and Mervin Dymally was lieutenant governor.

In the aftermath of the election, a flood of statistics provided a glimpse of the future. Take, for example, the Los Angeles mayoral races: in 1993 Latinos cast only 10 percent of the votes; in 1997, they cast 15 percent; in the 2001 mayoral primary, they cast 20 percent; but in the 2001 runoff, they cast 22 percent of the vote. Furthermore, their registered numbers were far greater. More than 315,000 Latinos were registered to vote on Election Day, but only 128,267 actually voted, according to the William Velasquez Institute. Consider that 186,733 Latinos did not vote and Villaraigosa lost by only 40,000. Clearly, if Latinos had shown up at the polls in anything close to their registered numbers, his victory would have been assured.

What do these numbers mean for the future? A Latino optimist would argue that as the number of Latino voters continues to explode, it may be possible for Latinos to form effective alliances with the Jewish liberal vote and this alliance alone would provide a Latino candidate with the votes necessary to gain office.

While it is easy to compare the alliance that helped propel Bradley into office and keep him there with a potential Latino-white liberal alliance that could help elect a Latino mayor and keep him or her in office, such a comparison neglects the dynamics of the growing Latino population.

It is just as likely that as the number of Latinos grows in the general population and on the voter rolls, Latinos will conclude that they do not need to form alliances but can instead act on their own—a posture not unlike that advocated by Stokely Carmichael and Charles Hamilton at the inception of the Black Power movement.

From 1973 to 1993, for 20 long years, Tom Bradley, an African American, held the highest position in Los Angeles city politics. During that time, Latinos were largely excluded from the corridors of city politics.

In 2001, Villaraigosa stood on the brink of being the first Mexican American mayor of Los Angeles in over 130 years. His election would have represented a monumental moment in the history of Los Angeles politics and a sign of a new era for Latinos in California politics. In order to be ushered into that position, Villaraigosa needed the help of Black voters—the very voting block with whom Latinos ostensibly have a symbolic and ideological basis for support. When the dust settled, it was this "friendly" vote that turned against the Latino aspirant and voted in lockstep with white conservatives to deny Villaraigosa his historic moment.

What does this mean for the future of Latino-Black relations in the Los Angeles political arena? A statement from Roger Wilkins, a veteran Black civil rights leader, may be instructive. Before the mayoral race Wilkins noted, "As the Hispanic population grows, as it remembers the predominant place in the racial dialogue blacks traditionally held and remembers its feeling of exclusion, it's going to be hard for them to modulate their feeling of potency from numbers. That's going to cause real stress for blacks."[10] And so it may.

When Blacks Rule

Lessons from Compton

NICHOLAS C. VACA

> Latinos of Compton have plenty of reasons to lament. The city is being run and operated without their input and participation. Even though they represent such a large portion of the area's population they experience systemic exclusion.
>
> As a resident of 25 years in Compton, I found it very painful to know that blacks in power can be just as insensitive to minorities as whites have traditionally been toward their race.
>
> Frank M. Sifuentes
> Letter to the *Los Angeles Times*

Beginning in the late 1940s and 1950s the city of Compton, California, a hamlet adjacent to Los Angeles, began to change complexion. The largely white city began to experience an influx of African Americans who, barred from many sections of Los Angeles, found that Compton was open, if not necessarily receptive, to them. The good citizens of Compton conceded the west side of town to the newly arriving Black residents, reserving the east side to themselves. Not only did the white citizens of Compton maintain their grasp on the east side, but they also held tightly to the city's political and economic structure. The persistent attempts by African Americans to break into the corridors of power included standard tactics of the period, including frequent picketing at government offices. But for all their attempts, Blacks were unable to break the stranglehold that the white citizens had on Compton's political and economic power centers.

Things began to change in 1965 after the rioting in nearby Watts. Whites in Compton, fearful that the same thing might happen on the west side, began to flee, leaving the city in the hands of the Black residents. As the white citizens left, they were replaced by Blacks, and the political vacuum created by their departure was filled by the deserted and the newly arriving African Americans. By 1968 Blades, now with an overwhelming majority population, had gained control of the city council and the school board and also replaced most of the white employees at city hall and in the schools.

African Americans might have continued their monopoly on Compton's political, educational, and economic structures, unchallenged by any group, if the city's ethnic population had not started to change in the late 1980s. Unfortunately for the Black population of Compton, by now accustomed to holding the reins of power, Latinos started to appear in significant numbers. In 1980, the U.S. Census listed the African American population at 73.2 percent and Latinos at only 21.6 percent. However, by 1988 the Latino population had grown to 32.0 percent.

This demographic shift presented the Black power structure with a dilemma: How should they react to the growing presence of a new "minority" group who was demanding inclusion in Compton's political and economic structures? Should they recall their own experience in trying to break into the white power structure during the 1950s and early 1960s and reach out to the new group to incorporate them into the governance of the city? Or should they view Latinos as challengers to the gains they fought so hard to achieve and hold them at arm's length? As it turned out, they chose the latter, and in so doing provided valuable insights to those who believe that Black-Latino alliances are both natural and to be expected.

Three areas of conflict arose beginning in the late 1980s and continuing to the present. One battlefront was over educational resources and representation on the school board. The change in student demographics made this an early and significant issue. Between 1984 and 1989 the Latino student population in the Compton school district increased by 17 percent, while the Black student enrollment decreased by 16 percent. By the 1988–1989 academic year, 12,393 Latinos and 13,447 Blacks were enrolled—an almost equal division between the groups.

The increase in Latino student enrollment, however, did not see a concomitant increase of Latinos in the school administration. In 1989, only 3.6 percent of the 1385 teachers and administrators were Latino, while Blacks held 77 percent of those positions. Latinos also pointed out that Compton had only 30 teachers who held credentials for teaching bilingual education, while the Spanish-speaking student body of the school district numbered 7,500. Based on what they saw as an obvious disparity, and one that they did not consider to be accidental, Latinos charged Blacks with discrimination.

The second arena of conflict was public sector jobs. Latinos charged Blacks, who occupied almost all of the public sector jobs, with "systemic discrimination," pointing out that only 9.7 percent of the 514 full-time city jobs were held by Latinos while Blacks held 78 percent of the jobs. The same battle that was being fought in Los Angeles County was being replayed in Compton. The accused Blacks, unaccustomed to being in such a position but also veterans of similar battles with whites, responded with the party line that their administrators "are recruiting [Latinos] and they've done a tremendous job as far as recruiting goes."

The third turf war involved representation on the city council, where no Latino had been elected in 20 years. Latinos were severely handicapped in this area. While their numbers were increasing on a yearly basis, many of the new residents were undocumented immigrants who were unable to vote or legal residents who paid little or no attention to the political process. In 1989, Martin Chavez, a Latino candidate, acknowledged this weakness when he pointed out that of Compton's 40,000 registered voters, only 1,800 were Latino.

Even though Latinos lacked the voting numbers to effectively challenge the existing Black power structure, they still lobbied for their share of public sector jobs, bilingual personnel in city hall and schools, and city improvements to their neighborhoods. The city responded to their clamor for equal access by creating a Committee on Hispanic Affairs, which consisted of Latino leaders and city staff members who were appointed by the city council to work on Latino hiring concerns.

In April 1989, the Committee on Hispanic Affairs presented an affirmative action plan to the city council that had as one of its goals tripling the number of Latinos hired over the next five years. The city accepted the recommendation but remained noncommital on its implementation. There appeared to be two reasons for the city's lack of commitment. The first was based on bitter feelings harbored by some Black leaders who remembered a time when Latinos were in relative positions of power but allegedly refused to extend a hand to Blacks. In an interview with the *Los Angeles Times,* Maxcy D. Filer, a city councilman, pointed out that Manual Correa, the only Latino member of the Compton school board, was on the city police force when Blacks were trying to break into the employment rolls there; that Joe Ochoa, a Compton Latino activist, was on the Compton Personnel Board when Blacks were lobbying for government jobs; and that Ray Gonzales, a deceased Latino leader, was a school board member when Blacks were fighting to be hired as teachers. "I don't remember any of them fighting for Blacks. Where were they when I was walking a picket line in Compton," he told the reporter.

The second reason reflected a deeply ingrained perspective held by some Blacks and which was also expressed by Filer, when he openly conceded that there were very few Latinos working for the city of Compton. "But if you go and look at the factories between Alondra [Boulevard] and Artesia [Boulevard], 98% of those working there are Hispanic." What Filer appeared to be saying was that because Latinos were being hired in the private sector (with the implication that Blacks were being passed over by employers in favor of Latino workers), Compton was justified in discrimination against Latinos in public sector employment.

In the summer of 1989, the Compton school district was plagued with problems: low student scores on state tests; loss of teachers to neighboring Los Angeles County because of better wages offered by that district; buildings in great disrepair, leading some parents to charge that they were unsafe; and a Latino student population with special needs that were going unmet. Latinos continued to assail the school board for its failure to respond to the needs of its growing Latino population by failing to hire more bilingual teachers and Latinos in administrative positions.

Curiously enough, in the spring of 1989, Pedro Pallan, a longtime Latino activist, was removed from his position as personnel commissioner of the Compton school district on the grounds that he was not a resident of the district. Pallan was convinced that the true reason for his removal was his outspoken criticism of the district for its failure to hire sufficient numbers of bilingual teachers and its discrimination against Latinos. After consulting with counsel, Pallan filed a lawsuit to regain his position. Four years later, the court would agree with Pallan, concluding that the school district had wrongfully dismissed him. But for four years Pallan was prevented from actively working with the personnel commission to correct the discriminatory practices in which, he believed, the school district engaged.

Matters were made more difficult for the school district when in the fall of 1989 Ted D. Kimbrough, who had been superintendent since 1982, was allowed to terminate his contract with the district in order to assume the position of superintendent for the Chicago school district. It was generally agreed that Kimbrough, who in 1987 had been selected Superintendent of the Year by the Association of California School Administrators, had created order and brought professionalism to the school district. Wiley Jones, the director of the Compton teachers union, opined that before Kimbrough arrived in Compton, the schools were "deplorable" but now they are just "bad."

The summer of 1989 also saw 30 persons file as candidates for five open seats on the seven-seat Compton school board. Manuel Correa was the only Latino incumbent on the school board who was running. Gogornio Sánchez Jr. was the only Latino challenger. In November 1989, five incumbents, including Correa, were returned to the school board.

The 1990s began with a clear notice to the Black leaders of Compton of the shifting ground beneath their feet. The 1990 Census figures were out, and city wide the Black population had dropped from 73 percent in 1980 to 66 percent in 1990, while the Latino population shot up from 21 percent to 30 percent. By 1990, the number of Latino children in the Compton school district had become a majority. The 1990s, however, also began with a sobering reminder to the Latino community that even though their numbers had been increasing on a yearly basis, they remained powerless. Blacks controlled every public institution in Compton as well as the chamber of commerce and the Democratic Party machine, and they displayed no inclination to share that power with their brown brethren. "Here we are, a truly minority community and the blacks are not giving us an affirmative action committee in either the city [government] or the school district. There cannot be equal employment opportunity without an affirmative action committee," stated Pallan.

As Pallan pointed out, the affirmative action plan recommended by the Committee on Hispanic Affairs had withered and died on the vine and Latinos' calls for equal treatment by Black officials fell on unsympathetic ears. School trustee John Steward expressed his disdain for Latinos' calls for affirmative action policies, stating that such policies were "reparation" to Black Americans for their years of slavery and not for successfully crossing the "border 10 to 15 times a year."

The struggle over education resources continued unabated, indeed increasing in intensity. Latinos militated against Black teachers who were insensitive to Latino children, while Blacks fretted about having to spend an increasing amount of the school budget on bilingual education, demonstrating little sympathy for Spanish-speaking students. "I have no respect for the language issue. This is America. Because a person does not speak English is not a reason to provide exceptional resources at public expense," said John Steward.

The resignation of Ted Kimbrough, the school superintendent, and the subsequent appointment of another Black superintendent, set off another firestorm of conflict between Latinos and Blacks. Alter Kimbrough's resignation, Elisa L. Sánchez was named acting superintendent. Sánchez first came to the school district in 1983 as an acting superintendent and was later made a deputy in charge of all instructional and curricula matters. For seven months Sánchez proved her ability to successfully run the school district by steering it through difficult financial waters. Latinos thought that she would be a natural successor to Kimborough. The school board thought otherwise and instead appointed J. L. Handy, a Black educator, as superintendent.

Latinos were outraged and saw Handy s appointment as another example of blatant "systemic discrimination" by African Americans against Latinos. Joseph Ochoa, a Latino activist, went so far as to encourage Latino parents to keep their children at home for several days, which would have the effect of bankrupting the school district. Ochoa made no bones about his feeling, charging that the failure to hire Sánchez was discrimination. "What else is it?"

The Latinos' frustration over their electoral impotence continued into the 1990s. In 1991, Pallan, the sole Latino in the city council races, ran against five Black candidates for the District 1 city council seat. Pallan estimated that although there were about 2,400 registered Latino voters he believed would vote for him, they would not necessarily provide him with the more than 50 percent of votes necessary for an outright win, but could potentially catapult him into the runoff election in June. Pallan's prediction turned out to be true, and on April 16 he became the first Latino to secure enough votes to contend in the runoff. Pallan came in second with 21 percent of the vote, and Omar Bradley, a Lynwood High School teacher, secured 31.2 percent of the votes.

A newspaper account reporting the results of Pallan's historic achievement could not help adding the footnote that since 1980 the Latino population in Compton had climbed 131 percent, and that Latinos constituted as much as 44 percent of the total population.

During the runoff campaign, both Pallan and Bradley sought Maxcy D. Filer's endorsement. Filer had represented District 1 for 15 years, and had chosen not to run for reelection, instead running unsuccessfully for mayor. Given Filer's statements regarding the Latinos in Compton at the time Blacks were seeking to break into the white power structure, it was not surprising that he threw his support behind Bradley s campaign. Pallan, for his part, obtained the endorsement of Assemblyman Willard H. Murray Jr. and councilwoman Patricia A. Moore.

The runoff results confirmed the feeble voting power that Latinos exercised in Compton. Bradley won the runoff election in a landslide, garnering more than 64 percent of the vote. Pallan managed to get only 1,577 votes or only 206 more votes than he got in April. Pallan attempted to put a positive spin on the results by observing, "We are determined to be part of the political mosaic here, and we will be successful. Latinos here in Compton can sway the vote." What the numbers made clear, however, was that Latinos, in spite of their increased population, had a long way to go before they would have the votes to put "one of their own" on the city council.

Meanwhile on the educational front, matters were worsenings approaching near-critical levels. Consistently low educational scores in the Compton School District prompted Assemblyman Willard H. Murray Jr. in 1991 to introduce a bill calling for the California superintendent of schools to take over the district. The Compton school board, outraged by the bill, formally condemned the legislation, and Murray announced that the bill was not active and that in all likelihood he would not introduce it during the next legislative session. Had the bill been successful, it would have been the first time that a school district was taken over because of poor academic scores.

Murray's initial resolve not to introduce the bill in the following legislative session was severely tested by what he witnessed in the schools in Compton: a 29 percent dropout rate (40 percent higher than the statewide average), low test scores (ranked among the lowest in the state), and an overhead that appeared to drain the school budget (23 percent higher than the average for other large school districts). Murray, apparently convinced by what he had witnessed, introduced not one, but four bills that marked Compton for help, including taking it over, because of poor academic performance.

In an attempt to have improvements made to the school system, Murray wanted it examined to determine if Compton exhibited specific elements contributing to its poor performance. Handy responded to this criticism by suggesting that under his administration the school district had begun a recovery. One Compton school employee attempted to place the blame on the exploding Latino population. This argument was based on the fact that the school district witnessed the Latino student population grow from 51 percent in 1990 to 57 percent in the spring of 1992. Only 30 percent of the students had limited English proficiency; 37 percent received welfare; and 65 percent were on some form of subsidized lunch program.

In June 1992, a report prepared by the Department of Education, at the request of Assemblyman Murray, and released by the Los Angeles Office of Education, reported that the Compton school district had not done more with "a multitude of resources." The report noted that Compton students were consistently at the bottom of achievement tests. As an example, in 1989–90, Compton students rated so low on the statewide tests that 99 percent of the students taking the test scored higher. By early December 1992, the Compton school board, still worried about a takeover of the district and unhappy with Handy s administration, fired him, ending his two-year term as superintendent of the school district. The search was on for a new superintendent.

While the search to replace Handy was being conducted, the school board named Harold L. Cebrun as acting superintendent. Cebrun had been working for about a year and half as an area superintendent supervising Dominguez High, a Compton high school, as well as its feeder elementary and middle schools. The school board apparently still refused to recognize the needs of its growing Latino students by naming a Latino school superintendent.

In late February 1993, Latino students at Compton's Whaley Middle School informed school officials that they did not believe they were receiving equitable treatment at the school. The discontent among Latino students spread to other campuses, and in the spring students, parents, and activists at Walton Middle School charged at a school board meeting that the Black staff discriminated against Latino students. The grievances ranged from insulting remarks made about Latinos to the lack of Spanish-language teachers and materials.

Also in February 1993 Compton school officials revealed that the school district owed the county education office approximately $2 million in back payments for special-education services provided to the district over a period of approximately three years. This revelation was the latest in a series of financial problems the school district had faced. In November 1992, auditors discovered that the district owed approximately $1 million in tax penalties. This audit came on the heels of another that discovered that the school district had wasted millions of dollars on various construction projects and food service. It was concluded that the school district had a total budget shortfall of $4.9 million.

While Kelvin Filer, the school board president, sounded surprisingly optimistic that the matter could be resolved with help from the county, it was disclosed the following month that the school district s debt was greater than the $4.9 million announced and would force the district to request a loan from the state of between $12 million to $16 million just to keep the school in operation through the fall. If such a loan were given to the school district, the state would have the authority to take over the school district and run it. Wiliard H. Murray, already vigilant of the district's poor academic performance, offered to sponsor legislation to authorize the loan. "I was flabbergasted by this new revelation. I would characterize it as sheer incompetence," he stated upon learning of the financial condition of the school district.

Compton's school district's financial woes were exacerbated by its continuing problem with administration and oversight of the school system. In early May 1993, another report issued by the Los Angeles County Office of Education characterized the Compton school district as one rife with "political cronyism and mismanagement," where leadership was notably absent. The report found problems with almost every aspect of the school system and cited as a glaring example of the fact that the district never "developed consistent philosophy for bilingual education, even though the student population is 57 percent Latino."

In the summer of 1993, the financially strapped district was given a $10.5 million emergency loan, and Stan Oswalt, a state-appointed administrator, was put in place to take over the reins. The school board members were no longer able to vote on school district issues, use their offices, or collect their $1,000 monthly stipend.

School board members responded angrily to being relieved of their responsibilities. John Steward, a school board member, wrote to the *Los Angeles Times,* but in expressing his anger he let slip one of the true reasons for his frustration—that school funds were finally being used to address the special needs of the Latino student population. Unable to directly attack this expenditure, Steward charged the state administrator with promoting division between Latinos and Blacks by "focusing district resources on providing additional services to students who speak limited English at the expense of English-speaking students...." Steward did not make clear how meeting the needs of Spanish-speaking Latino students was divisive. He simply stated, "However, the issue here was not overcoming language barriers but divide and conquer."

The battle over representation on the city council raged side by side with the controversy of bias against Latino students in the school district. In 1993 Latinos, in a continuing bid to get some political representation, entered into what they believed was a "coalition" with Omar Bradley, the Black candidate who so soundly defeated Pallan in the city council runoff race for District 1 and who ran for mayor in 1991. Pallan, the longtime Latino activist, supported Bradley during his campaign with the apparent understanding that, if Bradley was elected, he would work to get a Latino appointed to the city council. It was a sentiment that Bradley expressed repeatedly during his campaign and one on which Pallan and the Latino community placed a great deal of faith. After Bradley was elected mayor, an opportunity presented itself for him to made good on his promise when a lame-duck city council voted to install Bradley immediately as mayor, leaving his seat empty. Pallan and other Latino leaders saw this vacancy as a rare opportunity to finally get representation for the growing Latino community. Even if they could not get a city councilman elected on their own, then their "coalition" with Bradley would allow him to appoint a Latino. It was expected that Bradley would work to get Pallan appointed.

Bradley failed to keep his campaign promise, and instead of appointing Pallan, the lame-duck city council appointed Ronald Green, a longtime Bradley supporter and ally—and an African American. Latinos were stunned. Lorraine Cervantes, a Bradley supporter and campaign worker, stated, "I feel betrayed. A few years ago the white man was doing this to the black man and now black men are doing this to brown people." Bradley defended his failure to deliver by stating that Pallan simply did not have the support of the lame-duck council members, and that the lack of support was not because he was a Latino.

The conflict between Blacks and Latinos that manifested itself in the adult world of educational policy makers and political candidates also erupted among youths in the Compton schools. On November 18, 1993, Howard Blume, a reporter for the *Los Angeles Times,* noted that "racial incidents" had occurred in three high schools in Compton—Dominguez High, Compton High, and Centennial High. At Centennial High, what should have been an insignificant incident involving an underclassman and seniors escalated into a fight between Latino and Black students with some forty combatants and onlookers. The Centennial High incident was one in a series of such confrontations. On October 25, fights erupted throughout the Centennial High campus, forcing the school to close early. The following day a fight broke out at Dominguez High, and because students were allowed to congregate in the halls, a large fight developed between Latino and Black students. In early

November, a fight between a Latino student and a Black student led to a "brawl" behind the school auditorium during which one students nose was broken, another student's jaw was fractured, and another suffered cuts. And on November 10, approximately 30 students fought in various fights that took place during the lunch hour.

Blume observed that these clashes were not restricted to Compton, but manifested themselves in Lynwood High, Jordan High in Long Beach, and various schools in the Los Angeles School District. According to Blume's report, these other fights in Compton were directly attributable to a perception that Latinos and Blacks were in competition for limited jobs and community resources and that each group saw such competition as a zero-sum game.

Some Latinos, however, placed the blame on the Black students as well as the school administration. "Most of the problems is blacks attacking Latinos, and that's the way it has always been," opined John Ortega, a Latino activist who was critical of the school district. Black activists saw the problem as one ostensibly created by Oswalt, who was white and who Blacks believed favored Latinos and discriminated against Blacks. Indeed, Amen Rahh, a school board member, repeatedly accused Oswalt of being a racist who instituted neo-Nazi policies targeting Black students and employees. Whatever the cause, it was undeniable that friction between Blacks and Latinos in the adult world had found a parallel manifestation among adolescents.

On February 4, 1994, Jerome Harris, a Black educator, was appointed by the state to replace Oswalt. As former superintendent of the school district in Atlanta, Harris had apparently demonstrated his ability to take on the task of turning the Compton school district around. In the spring of that year he promoted Cebrun from acting superintendent to superintendent of the school district.

This ongoing conflict in the educational, political, and economic arenas was exacerbated when a Latino "Rodney King"-type incident fed fuel to the fire. On July 29,1994, a videotape was taken of Michael Jackson, a Black Compton police officer, beating Felipe Soltero, a 17-year-old Latino youth who was much smaller than he. The versions of what happened between the Black police officer and the Latino boy were at odds. The *Los Angeles Times* reported that a social worker had gone to Solteros home where he lived with his mother, his mother's companion, Manuel Shigala, and five other children. The social worker alleged that Soltero interfered with her investigation and called the Compton police for assistance. From that point forward the stories diverge. Jackson alleged that Soltero threatened the social worker and attempted to take the police officer s gun when he was instructed to put his hands behind his back. Soltero alleged that Jackson knocked him to the ground as he was being arrested, and when he stood up the officer struck him in the face with a baton. The videotape, which was shown repeatedly on the local television stations, showed Jackson striking Soltero on the side of the head with his baton, striking him repeatedly with the baton after Soltero had fallen on the ground, jumping on his back, handcuffing him, and dragging him across the ground by his handcuffs.

The incident gave fodder to Latino activists who saw the videotape as yet another manifestation of their struggle against the Black power structure of Compton. Pallan charged that Soltero's beating was an example of racism by Blacks against Latinos, and Arnulfo Alatorre Jr., president of the Latino Chamber of Commerce, stated, with no small amount of hyperbole, that Latinos were treated worse than Blacks were treated by whites in South Africa.

The protest over the beating of Soltero intensified the conflict between Blacks and Latinos. Mayor Omar Bradley appeared to see no reason why Blacks should extend the benefits obtained by Blades to Latinos. Other Black community leaders saw the situation for what it was. Rev. William R. Johnson Jr., the pastor of Temple Christian Methodist Church, said, "We are today the entrenched group trying to keep out intruders, just as whites were once the entrenched group and we were the intruders."

In the wake of the Soltero beating, Latinos formed a new group, Latinos United Coalition of Compton, which called for the creation of a civil board to review police actions, federal investigation into the Black-Latino conflict, and creation of an affirmative action and job-training program for Latinos.

Bradley, for his part, argued that he was powerless to give political representation to Latinos. "What does the African American do to empower them [Latinos] when it's constitutionally illegal [for noncitizens to vote]?" he told the *Los Angeles Times*. While Bradley could hide behind this argument as it related to elected seats on the city council and the school board, it could not be used for the opening of employment with the city departments or the school district. While city officials reported that Latinos represented over 50 percent of the population, only 10.78 percent of the city's full-time employees were Latinos. Bradley had clearly set forth the only terms under which Latinos would obtain political representation—they would have to wrestle it away by voting Blacks out of power.

Friction between Latinos and the Black city council continued to escalate. In September 1994, the city council agreed to create an Office of Human Relations. Latinos wanted the office to focus exclusively on Latinos and pressed its case by presenting figures from a federal commission that showed that Latinos represented only 10 percent of the city's workforce while Blacks held 78 percent of the jobs. These figures remained constant even though between 1980 and 1990, the Black population dropped 21 percent while that of Latinos rose by 131 percent. Paul Richard, the Black assistant city manager, attempted to deflect the damning nature of these facts by pointing out that Latino employees exceeded the number of Blacks employed by some outside contractors. Latinos, predictably, were outraged at this "apples and oranges" comparison, but it also demonstrated the type of tortured logic that the African American power structure was invoking in order to justify Black overrepresentation on city employee rolls. In another move that further frustrated Latino activists, the city's promise to revise its 20-year-old affirmative action plan to reflect dates by which more Latinos would be employed was delayed.

Meantime, the Black-dominated school board demonstrated its apparent unwillingness to expand Latino representation on the school board even though half of the Compton student population was now Latino. The problem for the school board began when it ousted board member Lynn Dymally in November 1994, because of unexcused absences. The ability to appoint a replacement for Dymally was one of the remaining vestiges of power that the school board still possessed after the school district had been taken over by the state of California.

The board put out a call for applicants, and among the 13 finalists was Martin Chavez, a Latino and a human resources official at the Port of Los Angeles. Chavez had received the top rating from a screening committee, and the Latino leadership in Compton expected that he would be appointed. The school board, however, had other plans. Instead of selecting Chavez, the school board appointed Black candidate Saul E. Lankster to the vacant position. Lankster's selection was immediately mired in controversy. He had served on the Compton school board from 1977 to 1981, but he had also been convicted of felony charges for selling "false traffic school diplomas" to state investigators. His conviction resulted in a sentence of 120 days in jail and he was given three years' probation.

In addition to concerns over his criminal conviction, Lankster's appointment was challenged by Jerome Harris, the administrator appointed by the state of California to run the school district and who succeeded Oswalt, because the decision appointing Lankster was conducted in secret and thus in violation of California's public meeting laws. The school board acknowledged the procedural defect involved in appointing Lankster and scheduled another vote, to be taken on the following Friday.

Latinos, as might be expected, were outraged at what they considered another clear act of disenfranchisement by Blades and further confirmation that Blacks would not voluntarily share power. "It's time the board stops playing these racist games and hires the best-qualified candidate," Pallan told the *Los Angeles Times*.

The school board had made it amply clear that it would correct the procedural errors it had previously committed and would reappoint Lankster to the school board at its November 18, 1994, meeting. The school board was not given that opportunity, however. The meeting was canceled by William Dawson, the acting state superintendent of public instruction, after he informed the board that he would make the final determination about the secret vote.

The controversy over Lankster's appointment spilled over into the new year, and in February 1995, the California state school superintendent, Delaine Eastin, declared that Lankster could not serve on the school board because of his 1985 conviction. Eastin also found that Lankster's teaching credentials had been revoked and that he had refused to provide an explanation to state officials as to why they had been revoked. Eastin also scolded the school board for initially appointing Lankster through a secret ballot. Several of the school board members reacted with anger and indignation, frustrated at their inability to exercise the little power that they still possessed. However, Gorgonio Sánchez Jr., the only Latino school board member, agreed with Eastin's decision, stating, "If you don't have anything to hide, you should not be afraid to provide the information they ask you to. You should be trustworthy."

In 1995, three Latinos ran for city council seats: Gorgonio Sánchez Jr., Alfonso Cabrera, a five-time candidate, and Lorraine Cervantes, a longtime activist. The Latino Coalition cast its support behind Sánchez and Cervantes because it was believed that of the three Latino candidates, they had the best chance at winning a seat.

In April all three candidates lost, victims of the lack of Latino voters and an absence of Black support. Of the three candidates Lorraine Cervantes garnered the most votes, with 18.6 percent. Sánchez and Cabrera received 12.5 percent and 5.1 percent, respectively. Pallan, for his part, promised to mobilize the community and raise funds for the next attempt at placing a Latino on the city council.

The school board welcomed 1996 with a renewed attack on Jerome Harris, accusing him of failing to improve educational standards and overloading the school district with administrators. Harris countered by referring to his record, which reflected an improvement on the California Achievement Test each year that he oversaw the school district. Harris, however, had already announced that he would be leaving his post at the end of the school year. Under pressure from parents and school board members, Harris announced that he would resign early, at the end of March. He was replaced by Randolph E. Ward, a Black educator who came to the district from Long Beach.

Latinos' struggle to get representation on the city council dragged on into 1998. By then, Mayor Omar Bradley had made it absolutely clear that the only way that Latinos would get a seat on the council was if they were able to vote someone on board. There was no olive branch extended to the Latinos, no prospect of forming a coalition. After all, why did Blacks need a coalition when they held all the power? The *Los Angeles Times* reported Bradley as saying that he would "not give them [Latinos] a hand into government" and that if Pallan and other Latino leaders wanted to get Latinos elected to office, they should "get some votes, then they'll get some elected officials."

In 1998, the *Los Angeles Times* reported that academics who have studied race relations concluded that Comptons Black power structure bordered on xenophobic behavior. The *Times* further observed that Compton, in time, could share the fate of its neighbor city Lynwood, where Latinos had finally gained the political strength to sweep Blacks out of office and bulldoze the Black power structure. Indeed, within weeks of being voted into office, Latino mayor Armando Rea used his voting block on the city council to relieve various Black government executives of their titles if not their jobs.

The *Los Angeles Times* article stung Compton officials and prompted Legrand H. Clegg II, the Compton city attorney, to accuse the newspaper of being "racist." Clegg wrote, "To select Compton, one of only two black-run municipalities in this county, as a case study in Latino political under-representation is blatantly racist and mean-spirited."

Have things changed since 1986, when Latinos first started to strive for political representation? The answer is no. According to Claritas, a marketing company that provides data on demographic changes, Latinos grew from 44 percent in 1990 to 59 percent in 2001 as a percent of Comptons total population. However, according to the Southwest Voter Registration Education Project, Latinos represent only about 15 percent of the voters in Compton. This feeble voting power has allowed African Americans to retain control of the city council and school board. As of 2002, the city council was all Black and the school district had only one Latina out of five school board members.

Compton's entrenched Black power structure is an object lesson for Latinos who hold the idealized notion that African Americans not only sympathize with Latinos' history of struggle and oppression but will also voluntarily share with them the power that they have earned. What Latinos have learned is what their counterparts learned in the city of Lynwood—wait, increase the voter rolls, and when they reach critical mass, seize the power.

Inclusion and Exclusion in West Hollywood

MOIRA RACHEL KENNY

West Hollywood sits in the center of Los Angeles County, at the edge of the City of Los Angeles's wealthy Westside, nestled between Hollywood to the north and east and Beverly Hills to the west. Covering less than two square miles, West Hollywood is well known as the hub of the interior design industry. "To the trade" showrooms occupy the blocks surrounding the city's most notable architectural landmark, the Cesar Pelli-designed Pacific Design Center, known colloquially as "the big blue whale." West Hollywood is also home to the Sunset Strip, a one-mile stretch of trendy nightclubs and restaurants in a constant cycle of boom and bust. In the early 1980s, West Hollywood became a major destination for émigré Jews from the Soviet Union—an influx reflected in the Russian language signs and Jewish community centers that dominate the eastern half of the city. More recently, however, there has been evidence that gentrification and city redevelopment plans may be driving the Russian immigrants out of the neighborhood.

On the west end of Santa Monica Boulevard, the major thoroughfare bisecting the city, is the area known (either affectionately or derogatorily) as Boystown, which contains a dense concentration of gay bars and clubs, specialty shopping, and a few community institutions, most notably the

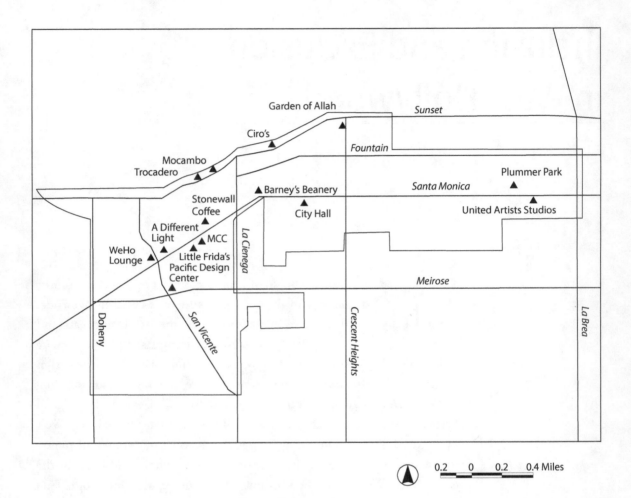

Garden of Allah

Sunset

Ciro's

Fountain

Mocambo
Trocadero

Plummer Park

Santa Monica

Barney's Beanery

Stonewall
Coffee

City Hall

United Artists Studios

A Different
Light

MCC

WeHo
Lounge

Little Frida's
Pacific Design
Center

La Cienega

Melrose

Doheny

San Vicente

Crescent Heights

La Brea

0.2   0   0.2   0.4 Miles

MAP 2 The City of West Hollywood

headquarters of the Metropolitan Community Church. Gays and lesbians throughout Southern California recognize this upscale section of town as the most visible concentration of gay culture and power in the region.

West Hollywood symbolizes gay and lesbian political strength as well, with its progressive city government leading the process of institutionalizing gay and lesbian rights in Southern California and continuing at the forefront of gay political mobilization. Since becoming an independent city in 1985, West Hollywood has been a magnet for gay businesses, and the city government has become a nationally recognized example of progressive policies. At the same time, the labeling of the area as "the gay city" by locals and the media carries multiple meanings, not all of them positive. As long as West Hollywood's image remains predominantly one of healthy, middle-class, white gay men, it is likely that the rest of the community, including lesbians, bisexuals, and people of color, will continue to view the area with suspicion. For those marginalized by the movement, West Hollywood has come to symbolize all that is problematic about the construction of sexual identity in a postliberation era:

a focus on capital accumulation, conspicuous consumption, and appearance, rather than on civil rights. Activists and apolitical gays and lesbians alike continue to debate West Hollywood's role as both a political and cultural center of the community, with the alternately welcoming or discriminatory nature of the Boystown nightlife fiercely contested. At the extreme, critics argue whether West Hollywood's status as an independent city has aided or constrained the political agendas of gays and lesbians in Los Angeles.

More than any other single location in the Los Angeles region, West Hollywood has been both the product of and constraint on the place-claiming strategies of the lesbian and gay movement. West Hollywood, like other gay enclaves in major cities, has emerged as a center for gay and lesbian business, politics, and culture because of an imperative to create a place where gay visibility is the norm rather than a daily struggle. Its presence, in turn, has shaped the access to and use of other gay and lesbian places outside the city's boundaries. The experience of building West Hollywood continues to shape place-claiming strategies and decisions around the region.

What sets West Hollywood apart from similar enclaves is the political independence of the neighborhood that in turn makes the gay political governance synonymous with a gay activist presence. This chapter frames the myths of West Hollywood and its usefulness as a point of reference for the gay or lesbian culture in the context of their activist efforts in Los Angeles. West Hollywood mirrors the complexities of Southern California urbanization as much as it reflects the processes of gay neighborhood building in other cities such as New York or San Francisco. Although West Hollywood is more residential and more suburban than these other gay enclaves, by Los Angeles standards the city is atypically dense and street oriented, with mixed commercial and residential areas. Reflecting the residential segregation of Los Angeles, however, West Hollywood—like most two-square-mile neighborhoods in the county and the city—remains ethnically and racially homogeneous. West Hollywood's development has closely followed the general patterns of Southern California's economic and urban growth, drawing its strength from the presence of the film industry with its emphasis on service jobs, many of them temporary. These regional characteristics, along with the specific history of the gay and lesbian movement in Los Angeles, have shaped the place-claiming strategies in West Hollywood.

Preincorporation West Hollywood

Ironically, West Hollywood's rise as a gay mecca rests only partly on the success of its much-heralded incorporation drive in the mid-1980s. Equally important is the earlier unincorporated status of the city, which was an overlooked and relatively ungoverned area in the middle of the county. In the first years of the twentieth century, Moses Sherman, one of Los Angeles's many railroad entrepreneurs, expanded his Pacific Railway Company into what is now West Hollywood, establishing a terminal at San Vicente and Santa Monica Boulevards (now the site of the Pacific Design Center). Although this development did not significantly transform the area, it did foreshadow the continuing use of West Hollywood as a place where the wealthier Westside could put less attractive businesses and industry.

As an unincorporated area of Los Angeles County, West Hollywood languished under government indifference for thirty years after a social heyday in the 1920s, 1930s, and 1940s. During the 1920s, when much of West Hollywood was still onion fields, the Sunset Strip emerged as a fashionable nightclub and residential district for the Hollywood silent screen crowd. This early Hollywood scene centered on the Garden of Allah, a residential hotel and bungalow colony on Sunset at Crescent Heights (now a mini mall). Russian-born silent film star Alia Nazimova built the Garden as a private residence but turned it into a hotel as the silent film industry (and her screen career) collapsed. In its earliest days, the Garden was home to many of Nazimova's fellow silent film stars, including Greta Garbo, Ramon Navarro, Errol Flynn, and John Barry-more. Later, the Garden became the West Coast retreat for New York's literary circle known as the Algonquin Table, most notably Robert Benchley, Lillian Hellman, and Dorothy Parker. Known within certain circles as a place that welcomed unmarried guests, the Garden also earned a reputation as a place for parties and was eventually targeted by early anti-Communist witch-hunts. Elsewhere in West Hollywood, the film industry expanded its influence, building numerous studios, including the headquarters of United Artists on Santa Monica at the eastern edge of the city.

At the same time, the nightclub scene along the Sunset Strip reached its heyday; the Trocadero and Ciro's (both opened by William Wilkerson, founder of the *Hollywood Reporter),* and the Mocambo all flourished in the 1940s. Money from Hollywood and the Las Vegas mob built many of the establishments, which attracted a cast of characters slightly more mainstream (and perhaps wealthier) than those at the Garden. Unlike the Garden, the nightclubs attracted tourists, oil and industry millionaires, and others outside Hollywood, creating a name for the area beyond the relatively tight Hollywood community. This shift in clientele likely affected the gay presence on the Strip, as more underground gay-only nightclubs and bars, such as the Eagle, began to open down the hill on Santa Monica Boulevard. These establishments were rarely gay owned, and were often funded by the same money (particularly organized crime) that funded the Sunset Strip clubs.

After the war, as the club scene on Sunset Strip waned (the victim of the collapse of the wartime economy and the rise of the television and other "home entertainment" industries) the upscale nightlife declined as clubs were closed and eventually torn down. In the 1960s, West Hollywood became a center of the counterculture, with the hippie movement and the rock scene moving into the clubs that the Hollywood stars had abandoned. Many of the lesbians and gay men who would later form the heart of the gay liberation movement of the early 1970s also gravitated to West Hollywood. The *Los Angeles Free Press,* which served as an unofficial headquarters for the alternative scene in Los Angeles from its offices on Sunset, was also an early site for gay organizing. The new rock scene transformed the area into a center for music publishing and sparked economic revitalization. As the Sunset Strip transformed from a relatively ritzy nightclub area to the center of the new youth culture and rock scene culture, the division between Sunset Boulevard and Santa Monica Boulevard became more distinct. Although gays were certainly part of this new incarnation, the more overt gay presence on Santa Monica Boulevard fostered an open, rather than assimilated, gay culture. Today, West Hollywood reflects all of these preincorporation cultures—hippie, rock, Hollywood star, and gay.

During the 1970s, as the Los Angeles Police Department (LAPD) stepped up attacks against gay establishments and the growing gay liberation movement brought increasing numbers of lesbians and gays out of the closet, West Hollywood gradually emerged as the visible center of this new gay presence. The unincorporated status kept the streets and bars out of the reach of LAPD while the county's disinvestment in the area created a reservoir of cheap apartments and empty storefronts that were slowly filled by gay entrepreneurs and residents.[1] The depressed real estate market of West Hollywood was crucial to the early development of the gay neighborhood. In looking at West Hollywood, the long history of real estate development and disinvestment reveal important clues about the opportunities for gay commercial and residential occupation.[2]

In this way, preincorporation West Hollywood resembled the model of the gay enclave—an area of the city abandoned by "legitimate" businesses that has attracted an agglomeration of gay businesses, bars, and other institutional organizations. In his now-classic paper on "gay ghettos," Martin Levine reported that, in the mid-1970s, 78 percent of all gay institutions in Los Angeles were located within 3 percent of the metropolitan region, in an area centered along West Hollywood's Santa Monica Boulevard. Levine describes the development of a gay ghetto in marginalized areas:

> At first gay institutions and cruising places spring up in urban districts known to accept variant behavior, resulting in a concentration of such places in specific sections of the city.... This concentration attracts a large number of homosexuals, causing a centralization of gay culture traits, turning the districts into homosexual culture areas. Tolerance coupled with institutional concentration make the areas desirable residential districts for gays. Many homosexuals, especially those publicly labeled as gay or open about their orientation, settle in these areas. At this point, the areas have become partially developed gay ghettos.[3]

In each of the areas Levine describes—West Hollywood, San Francisco's Castro district, New York's Greenwich Village, and Boston's South End—the clustering of shops, bars, and restaurants catering to a gay clientele accounts as much as residential growth in the emergence of a gay neighborhood. Levine acknowledges that these areas are highly temporal, swelling on the weekends and after work with gays who have "passed" (appeared to be straight) outside the "ghetto" during the workday. This freedom of movement and fluidity of the borders glaringly differentiates the gay neighborhood from the traditional notion of the ghetto used to describe neighborhoods of nineteenth-century Jews and twentieth-century African Americans. Finally, of course, the gentrification of these neighborhoods as they became more openly gay also distinguished them from their namesakes.

Levine describes a West Hollywood in the mid-1970s of men walking hand in hand down Santa Monica Boulevard, teenage hustlers, and gays flaunting their "look," whether it be leather, western, athlete, or drag. This daring, revolutionary behavior transformed the Boulevard into a showcase for nascent gay culture.

The term "ghettos" is used and misused often by those trying to understand the dynamics of gay geographies, and this misunderstanding underlies the need to map the boundaries and meanings of these neighborhoods with greater specificity. Esther Newton, in her history of the Cherry Grove community on Long Island, wrestles with the metaphors and uses of the term ghetto. Her attempt to define the term points to the ambivalence gays and lesbians have often voiced about the word's use:

> If Cherry Grove was a beacon towards which gays were drawn by possibility, it was also a ghetto into which they were pushed by the hatred and intolerance of straight society.... Founded in affluence rather than poverty, Cherry Grove is not exactly comparable to urban slums, but the exclusion underlying its existence is just as violent, if somewhat less effective. It has become common among younger gays in America, uneasy about an emerging model of the gay community as a minority analogous to ethnic and racial groups, to denounce the existence of gay ghettos.... Part of the feeling against "ghettoization" arises from the AIDS epidemic.... The gay meccas have become maelstroms of loss and magnets for homophobic hatred. It is not surprising that there has been a reaction against them within the gay community.[4]

As Newton obliquely suggests, the gay use of the term "ghetto" to indicate a concentration of gay businesses is counter to the more established American usage of the word to signify a high-poverty, residential concentration and place of limited mobility where ethnic and racial groups become the targets for economic and social discrimination. This is very different from the gay and lesbian experience in West Hollywood, since at least the 1970s and perhaps before. More recently, of course, this gay and lesbian use of the term has gained greater resonance as AIDS discrimination and hysteria forced gays and lesbians to reconsider their status within the majority. Most often, however, West Hollywood represents more a place to escape to than a place to escape from.

As with a whole host of terms in white urban gay lexicons, the use of "ghetto" to describe areas with high gay concentrations is not meant simply to signify connection with the oppression experienced by African Americans or Jews in their respective ghetto histories (although there may be some measure of similarity implied), but rather (often derogatorily) particular subcultures within the gay community. In this case, living in a "gay ghetto" has also come to be a way for gays and lesbians living in nongay environments to refer to the surreal quality of life in a neighborhood where there is a higher level of public comfort and awareness. Those living within an enclave such as West Hollywood are often seen as having an easier—and narrower—life than those integrated into predominantly heterosexual neighborhoods.

Perhaps the most obvious markers of the transformation of gay and lesbian communities have been the growth of clearly marked residential zones. Mickey Lauria and Lawrence Knopp's landmark article on gay community development cited the development of gay neighborhoods as a primary spatial response to gay oppression made possible by the relative openness of urban dwellers to interact with "alien groups."[5] The development of visible gay neighborhoods often begins in the context of the simultaneous process of gentrification and urban redevelopment made possible by service sector job growth in downtown districts. They tie the spatial processes of urban change to the social dynamics of gay communities with access to the capital (through service sector employment) necessary to participate in this renaissance.

> Gays have done more with space than simply use it as a base for political power. They continually transform and use it in such a way as to reflect gay cultural values and serve the special needs of individual gays vis-à-vis society at large.... In the context of a rapid commodification of space, the optimal strategy for gays with respect to the development of political and economic power is to participate in the revalorization of physical structures in a neighborhood—in other words, to emphasize exchange value.[6]

The growth of these communities has had a lasting effect on their cities, in a sense expanding gay life well beyond circumscribed boundaries. For those with adequate resources, residential neighborhoods serve as the ultimate safe space, particularly to the extent that visibility as homeowners "committed to improving their neighborhoods" translates into political power. Lauria and Knopp cite eight cities (including Washington, DC; Boston; Philadelphia; Denver; and Houston) where the gay vote was mobilized out of these gentrified neighborhoods in sufficient number to elect a gay-sympathetic straight mayor.

For the most part, this participation in the gentrification of urban neighborhoods has been a white male phenomenon. Theorist Manuel Castells, trying to make a broader argument about cultural participation in urban transformations, explains that lesbians do not participate as much because men have an innate territorial imperative, whereas lesbians, in general, have a greater "radical political agenda."[7] His argument, based on the early transformation of the Castro neighborhood, certainly reflects a general theme in the gentrification literature as planners and geographers have tried to understand the complexities of gay efforts to overcome societal disapprobation through place claiming. However, urban lesbians often do not have the residential choices of gay white males because they are poorer, are more attuned to physical danger, and are less mobile. Similarly, gays and lesbians of color have been found to place greater importance on the development of residential communities within communities of color, choosing to live outside those gay residential enclaves that exist in large cities.[8]

Not all residential enclaves, however, are easily identified. Recent research questions the ways in which the existence of a gay or lesbian neighborhood is measured, suggesting that some neighborhoods have been overlooked in the search for the gay-gentrification connection. As Sy Adler and Johanna Brenner have found in San Francisco, "there is a spatial concentration of lesbians, a neighborhood that many people know about and move into to be with other lesbians. But the neighborhood has a quasi-underground character; it is enfolded in a broader countercultural milieu and does not have its own public subculture and territory."[9]

In Los Angeles gays and lesbians recognize a number of neighborhoods as "gay or lesbian friendly" that are not immediately apparent from the outside, neighborhoods like Venice that have few openly gay or lesbian establishments and no community centers. In addition, gay enclaves within communities of color need to be understood on their own terms, as efforts to strengthen ties within ethnic neighborhoods.

Upscale commercial zones with a distinct gay or lesbian character have grown as well. Like the residential neighborhoods they abut, these commercial areas also prove important to the expansion of political capital, especially because they bring in *new* sources of sales tax and tourism revenue. They also indicate the changing boundaries of gay and lesbian influence. The recent development of the West Hollywood commercial strip, like the development of the Castro district in the mid 1970s, marked a shift of the center of the gay community away from earlier strongholds. As with the discussion of residential neighborhoods, however, there are questions of access here as well, because gay commercial zones are largely white and male.

Neighborhood place claiming in the 1970s, before the emergence of the AIDS epidemic, was more explicitly public and recreational than is the case today. Although businesses and bars catering to gays dominated Santa Monica Boulevard, many of these establishments were still owned by people outside the gay community, and therefore were not locations for political or community organizing. Edmund White, whose 1979 travelogue, *States of Desire,* chronicles many of the newly emergent gay enclaves, describes the Los Angeles scene as a mix of pleasure seekers and community activists:

> Hedonism is the governing philosophy of gay Los Angeles. With the collapse of traditional values, hedonism seems as workable as any other available code. And, since Angeleans are so career-minded, their aspirations structure their love of pleasure into long-range hedonism, always more satisfying than the melancholy search for instant sensations.[10]

White describes the other side of the West Hollywood scene as "the most active and civic minded gay movement in the country," with, charity benefits, the Municipal Election Committee (to support gay candidates), the gay Metropolitan Community Church (founded in Los Angeles in 1969 by Reverend Troy Perry), and the Gay Community Services Center, which, in the late 1970s, far surpassed community centers in other cities in terms of services, size, and outreach.

Both hedonistic and civic-minded, West Hollywood was, to outsiders like Levine and White, impossible to categorize. As Edmund White writes, gay male Los Angeles, for the most part, bypassed the gay ghetto phenomenon, moving from scattered and isolated locations to a network of neighborhoods across the city, with no one location reaching the density or intensity of the Castro or the West Village:

> The main, gay neighborhoods are West Hollywood ("Boystown") and the Hollywood Hills ("the Swish Alps"), where even little houses are in such demand they're selling for $80,000. The "Sycamore Sissies" live in Spanish Revival mansions along Sycamore Street—large cool chambers with rile floors and wrought-iron balconies overlooking tinkling fountains in shaded patios; the rents there vary between $500 and $900. Silver Lake *[sic]*, where the rents are lower, is the leather and Western neighborhood. Los Feliz, with its 1920s mansions, is becoming the Beverly Hills for gays. The nearby beach community is Venice. But Angeleans can live anywhere; the car and the freeway made the idea of the neighborhood obsolete.[11]

Here, White describes one of the enduring characteristics of gay and lesbian community life in Los Angeles. Although Angelenos identify West Hollywood as a central location, perhaps the hub of gay culture and place making, it is sustained far less by a local resident population (who might engender a more neighborhood atmosphere) than by a transient nightlife pulled from smaller gay and nongay neighborhoods around Southern California.

Political-Territorial Strategies in the Incorporation of West Hollywood

West Hollywood is important, not only because it helps us understand the transformation of Los Angeles, but also because it signals an important new strategy for gay political empowerment. West Hollywood marks the evolution of Los Angeles's gay movement from one focused on short-term responses to crises within the community to one of creating and sustaining community institutions through alliances with other local constituent groups and residents. Along the way, West Hollywood became a place that supported a broader range of gay identities—from the engaged activist to the weekend club-goer to the closeted retiree. The history of West Hollywood's incorporation, however, is not just the popular tale of gay men creating a self-affirming culture, a "gay city," but of a popular struggle on behalf of a broad and unlikely coalition of liberal activists. By most accounts, the successful incorporation drive was a campaign against the county's neglect and overdevelopment of the area rather than a crusade for a "gay city." The independence that unincorporated status had provided to West Hollywood in the 1930s and 1940s had, by the 1980s, resulted in some of the highest residential densities in the city. The cheap apartments built by speculative developers made West Hollywood a pocket of affordability as compared with its more affluent neighbors—Beverly Hills, Bel Air, the Hollywood Hills, and Santa Monica. Seniors and others on limited incomes, including intermittently employed actors and screenwriters, were drawn to these hastily built "dingbat" apartments.

In the early 1980s, a crisis involving the county's strong rent control ordinance brought to the brink a long-simmering distrust between liberal activists and local government. The county's existing rent control ordinance, passed in part through the efforts of well-organized West Hollywood senior citizen residents, was scheduled to expire at the end of 1984 and be terminated. In Los Angeles County, where the Board of Supervisors tended to reflect the wishes of homeowners on the outskirts of the city—in the San Fernando Valley and wealthy enclaves on the Westside—West Hollywood was an anomaly, with one survey showing that nearly 90 percent of all residents were renters. As an area that had managed to remain off major developers' radar screens until the early 1970s, West Hollywood was, to many observers, in danger of rapidly losing its unique character and stability.

Because residents of West Hollywood were living in an unincorporated area, this collection of neighborhoods had no locally elected governing body to press for intervention. Furthermore, the political representation West Hollywood did have was extremely fragmented, with the area divided between two U.S. Congress representatives, two state senators, and two state assembly representatives. Ron Stone, a local gay activist and founder of the 1984 incorporation drive, captured this anxiety in an *LA Weekly* article written as the campaign got underway:

> All this sub-dividing and separation makes West Hollywood a prime target for development. With no local government to turn to or take control of, citizens of the area who want to retain the village-like characteristics that attracted them in the first place have had a difficult time of it.[12]

In part because it was understood that the legacy of county indifference was useful to the gay community, the gay and lesbian leadership in West Hollywood initially opposed the idea of another incorporation drive. Both the Stonewall Gay and Lesbian Democratic Club and the Harvey Milk Lesbian and Gay Democratic Club rebuffed Ron Stone's early outreach efforts. However, when Bob Craig, publisher of the local gay magazine *Frontiers,* became convinced that supporting cityhood might be a way to increase circulation, he established himself as a vocal spokesperson for the campaign. *Frontiers,* best known for its calendar of gay nightlife and social events (and for its sexually explicit dating and phone sex ads), became an important vehicle for publicizing the campaign. Stories in *Frontiers* on a regular basis attracted the attention of both the Stonewall and Harvey Milk clubs, and incorporation slowly became identified as a "gay cause."[13] Bob Craig made one of the more catalytic statements about the new city in a speech a few weeks before the cityhood election, calling West Hollywood "a gay Camelot on the horizon."[14]

The two other groups driving the cityhood campaign—seniors and renters—were brought to the table via the Coalition for Economic Survival (CES), a tenants' rights group that had long been active in West Hollywood politics. In 1980, CES led the successful battle for the county's rent control ordinance and later tried unsuccessfully to pass a countywide proposition that would have strength-ened and extended the term of the law. Although the measure failed countywide, it won in West Hollywood by a five-to-one majority. With the coalition of gays, seniors, and renters forged, a West Hollywood Incorporation Committee was formed to do the actual work for cityhood required by the county and the state.[15]

For the gay establishment in West Hollywood, a major shift in thinking was needed before they could endorse the idea of cityhood. For the most part, the gay community in West Hollywood considered Ed Edelman, their County Supervisor, to be a friend of the community—a politician generally tolerant of gays and lesbians and concerned about the area. In 1974, when Edelman was first elected, he appointed a committee to draft a general zoning plan for West Hollywood aimed at controlling run-away development. After a slow start, the committee did manage to present a draft plan to the public in 1981. The plan set limits for building heights for every street, preserved the two remaining neighborhoods of single-story houses, closed many Santa Monica Boulevard intersec-tions to reduce traffic, and encouraged construction of off-street parking areas by local businesses. Although many residents felt that the nine years it took for the plan to reach final approval ruined most of the area forever, Edelman was seen as their only ally. Moreover, as Adam Moos (a participant in the incorporation drive) notes in his analysis of the cityhood effort, the success of behind-the-scenes politicking by the gay community was not something the gay leadership wished to jeopardize. Many feared a backlash from Edelman if the cityhood vote failed. Only when the incorporation measure was approved for the 1984 ballot did the gay leadership become more directly involved. As Moos noted,

> Now, the gay community saw that it had the potential to elect openly gay and lesbian candidates to seats of power. The question at this point was no longer one of turning the community's back on its friend, Edelman, but one of "this is our chance to determine our own fate." In this sense, the question for the gay community became one of local control—control of issues that affected and concerned gays—and having a direct voice in how those issues would be handled.[16]

Throughout the campaign the question of gay control of city politics had been a contentious issue. The anticityhood forces were attacked as being homophobic, in part for circulating a survey to senior citizens that referred to cityhood as a means to effect a "gay takeover of the city." As the cityhood measure moved to the ballot the implications of its success for gays and lesbians became more obvious. Of the forty candidates for the new city council, nineteen were openly gay or lesbian. Because each of the candidates varied widely on their support of rent control, development, and other cityhood issues, their gay or lesbian identity quickly became a background issue. However, sensitive to the possibility of an anti-gay backlash, supporters continued to paint the incorporation campaign as one driven by economic, rather than cultural, demands. An endorsement editorial in the *West Hollywood Post* reflected the argument that cityhood was more about long-term viability and fiscal responsibility than a gay agenda:

> A city is a unique business. Money—financial statements, long-range planning, cost effective decisions, understanding the profit and loss potential—That's the bottom line.... What are we going to get for our money? ... A lot has been said about the sexual preference of the candidates. That is of no importance.[17]

Perhaps because of the many agendas at work in the incorporation drive—including rent control, slowing growth, gay and lesbian rights, as well as seniors' issues—there was never a single gay platform for the campaign. Instead, gay and lesbian candidates for the new city council included, to varying degrees, each of these other agendas. Some gay candidates allied themselves directly with the rent control proponents, whereas others campaigned on the message that a "gay city" was necessary on its own merits. As Moos and others have argued, this unique situation of having enough gay or lesbian candidates to split the gay vote became a source of strength (in that sexuality was not viewed as a negative factor in the race) and a source of weakness for the new city (in that no gay slate was possible).[18] In the election, a gay/lesbian majority was elected to the council with three members—John Heilman, Valerie Terrigno, and Steve Schulte—openly identified as gay or lesbian. Of the five elected, only Schulte was not endorsed by the CES.

Although a gay or lesbian agenda had not been a centerpiece of the cityhood campaign, immediately after the election, lesbian and gay issues defined early city politics. The first official act of the city council was to pass an ordinance banning discrimination against lesbians and gays. One of the now-mythical episodes in West Hollywood's short history is the march of the entire city council and meeting audience to a local bikers hangout that sported at the entrance an antigay sign:

> The crowd stood to applaud. Some cried. Wielding this new law, council members later trooped to a restaurant [Barney's Beanery]—-with news cameras in tow—to remove a sign that had long infuriated gays: "Fagots Stay Out" [*sic*].[19]

As participants themselves quickly noted, this gesture was largely symbolic. Few accounts of actual discrimination at Barney's Beanery had been filed with the sheriff's office or reported in the media. However, this symbolic act set a tone for governance in the city—one where policies and actions were often pursued for their community-building value in establishing West Hollywood as a place of tolerance and respect.

Profiling West Hollywood

Since incorporation, the central questions for the City of West Hollywood have been the following: To what extent has a gay city been established? On what grounds? For whom? Do demographics alone constitute a city where gays predominate, or does a city (rather than a neighborhood) require some other attributes that would mark it as gay or lesbian?

More than 36,000 people live in the less than two square miles that constitutes West Hollywood. According to the 1990 census, more than half the population was between twenty-five and forty-nine years old, with a median age of just over thirty-eight. Nearly 90 percent of the residents are white, and 12 percent of the population is Russian-speaking. West Hollywood is more highly educated (with one out of three people holding a college diploma) and wealthier (average household income at roughly $53,000) than the rest of Los Angeles County. Although 32 percent of residents earn less than $25,000 per year, this figure is much lower than the county average of 42 percent. Nearly the entire city is developed, with 70 percent dedicated to residential dwellings.

West Hollywood in many ways exemplifies the image of the Westside of Los Angeles as racially homogeneous. Whites account for 90 percent of West Hollywood's residents, compared with 57 percent of Los Angeles County as a whole. However, according to the 1990 census (which generally confirms the demographic estimates from the city's own surveys), West Hollywood has a much larger percentage of elderly residents (18 percent over the age of 65) than does the county as a whole (with only 10 percent elderly residents). In addition, roughly 9 percent of the county's elderly are reported by the census to be living in poverty, while fully 11 percent of the city's elderly are considered to be living in poverty.[20]

However, attitudes toward the city and its government are more telling than demographics. According to the city's own surveys of residents, conducted every five years, West Hollywood city government and city services inspire high levels of satisfaction. This stands in contrast to public perceptions of other local municipalities, including the City of Los Angeles itself, where secessionist movements have become a regular part of the political landscape.

A sense of strong connection to the city resounds throughout the 1993 and 1998 West Hollywood Community Needs Assessment surveys by residents.[21] As the 1993 study reported, city inhabitants expressed "widespread deep affection for the City, and strong attachment to local institutions that are open to all, and that serve the needs of residents for public interactions and use of their City space."[22] These comments reflect this visceral connection between the physical space of the city and the development of the city government since incorporation. Similarly, when interviewed, local officials, activists, and business people say they want to constantly improve city life and count on the city government to be an integral part of these changes. Survey respondents stress the interconnections between government and civil society, the diversity of the city, and a strong sense of community as reasons to live in West Hollywood. Most importantly for an understanding of place claiming, gay and lesbian respondents in particular indicate they view the gay community in West Hollywood as a prime factor in the development of West Hollywood since incorporation. They also see the continued importance of the lesbian and gay community to the health of the city.

As described by the survey, the population of West Hollywood consists of three significant population groups—gay men, senior citizens (especially women), and recent immigrants from the former Soviet Union. The majority of residents live in apartments, on their own. Most likely as a result of the city's proximity to Hollywood and Burbank, rates of employment are high, with a significant proportion of workers in the entertainment industry.

Of course, most surveys of lesbians and gays in the United States and, indeed, most attempts to chart gays and lesbians demographically, are fraught with complications and inaccuracies, not the least of which are doubts about the confidentiality of the data, conflicts about labels and terms for gay men and lesbians (which may affect a respondent's participation or self-identification), and bias in sample selection.[23] Although these concerns are valid for the West Hollywood Community Needs Assessment as well, the surveys reveal information about the community that appears more interesting and potentially more accurate than similar surveys. First, West Hollywood has established itself as a gay-friendly location, something that each West Hollywood resident can be reasonably expected to acknowledge. Second, this higher degree of comfort provided by West Hollywood's openness toward gays and lesbians might have mitigated some of the issues about self-identification. Nevertheless, 16 percent of the survey respondents in 1998 refused to self-identify as gay, lesbian, bisexual, or straight, indicating the limitations of demographic research on sexuality even within an exceptionally "safe" environment.[24] Unfortunately, the Needs Assessment does not give the race or gender characteristics of those declining to respond to the sexuality question. This information would be particularly useful in understanding the dimensions of this underreporting problem. Of those who did reveal their sexual identity on the survey form, 56 percent answered heterosexual, 35 percent answered gay, 6 percent answered bisexual, and only 3 percent self-identified as lesbian. Although anecdotal evidence also suggests that far fewer lesbians than gay men live in West Hollywood, this small number of lesbians does raise questions about the completeness of the survey.

The 1998 Needs Assessment shows that there are proportionately fewer lesbians living in West Hollywood than in 1993. Although gays, lesbians, and bisexuals constitute 44 percent of the total survey population (up from 34 percent in 1993), gay men outnumber lesbians by a ratio of eleven to one (up from a ratio of seven to one five years earlier). If these numbers are indeed accurate, they suggest a reversal of a previous trend in which the ratio of gay men to lesbians had been declining throughout the years since incorporation.

As with other well-publicized surveys of gays and lesbians that have been conducted at specific venues (such as the 1993 March on Washington) or through specific channels (such as national gay and lesbians marketing campaigns), the West Hollywood survey can be reasonably expected to be biased toward upper-income consumers. Because this survey targeted a gay and lesbian population that has chosen to live in West Hollywood, a relatively small geographical area, its results cannot be extrapolated to reflect the attitudes of gays and lesbians or bisexuals in Los Angeles as a whole. As a result, they represent a particularly enfranchised group that is not excluded (in reality or in perception) by questions of access. The attitudes of gays and lesbians of color who do not live in West Hollywood (and are therefore not potential survey respondents) will be discussed further below.

Only a few marked differences appeared between the lesbian and gay population and the total population. The gay male population of the city tends to be younger and wealthier than the total residential population. A greater percentage of gay men own their houses or apartments and have completed college or graduate education. There is little overlap between the Russian and gay populations, with very few gays reporting immigrant status. Not surprisingly, the distribution of AIDS in West Hollywood (accounting for 12 percent of the city's population) centers in the gay population.

The Community Needs Assessment offers much more than a demographic analysis. The study also seeks to understand the expectations of residents concerning the growth and cultural life of the city. Many of these concerns confirm that, for residents, the physical space of the city ranks as one of the most important reasons to live in West Hollywood. During focus group discussions aimed at eliciting residents' attitudes about the city, several themes ranked high for gay men. These included the success of the city as a clearly gay space and the "gay-friendly atmosphere" of the city. One typical gay respondent characterized the positive aspects of West Hollywood life in the following way: "Small village feel, liberal views, safe for gay people, location."[25]

Gays and Lesbians as Neighborhood Activists

Because there are no exhaustive directories of West Hollywood's gay scene available for the years prior to incorporation, it is difficult to chart the concrete effect of cityhood on the number of gay businesses or residences. That the mainstream press gave attention to the gay involvement in the cityhood drive probably drew as many gays to the area as the city policies themselves. For Jodi Curlee, former director of the social services department at the City of West Hollywood and an activist in the community since the 1970s, the incorporation of West Hollywood was perfectly timed to take advantage of a new generation willing to work together and challenge discrimination with a new energy. According to Curlee, "West Hollywood emerged at a time when the movement was transforming itself and was ready to try a new kind of integration that was more about coexistence and less about hiding."[26]

As a result, the early years of incorporated West Hollywood were very much about challenging the kind of discrimination that gays and lesbians had long endured, even in that city. Gays and lesbians sought and secured representation on city boards and at city hall. In 1988 the city convened a gay and lesbian task force to review city policy, survey gay and lesbian residents, and make recommendations for community outreach and education. The task force made crucial recommendations: to create a permanent gay and lesbian advisory council to review city policy and make recommendations concerning services; coordinate with the sheriff's department to discuss active gay and lesbian recruitment in the sheriff's department; address problems with harassment and recruitment; arrange sensitivity training for city workers and the West Hollywood Marketing Corporation (an innovative public-private group responsible for city marketing) on gay and lesbian issues; include gays and lesbians in all descriptions of the city's population; develop a gay and lesbian community profile in the human services element of the city's general plan; and dedicate space for gay and lesbian community organizations.[27] Many of these concerns are echoed in the 1998 Community Needs Assessment, in particular the continued pressure on the sheriff's department concerning gay bashing.[28]

The place-claiming implications of these key recommendations underlie the feeling of security cityhood offered to gays and lesbians. The emphasis on the sheriff's department reflects the heightened attention to police harassment or unwillingness to report hate crimes that has become a central issue for the movement nationally. The emphasis on recruitment indicates a desire on the part of the community to challenge a dominant police culture and to allow for the possibility that law enforcement might be a useful ally.

The recommendations for a progay marketing strategy and greater recognition of gays, lesbians, and bisexuals in descriptions of the city's population point to a perception of the community's invisibility even in a city commonly referred to as "the gay city."

Beyond attention to specific requests and occasional friction between the gay community and other residents, the West Hollywood city government has distinguished itself with an attention to other progressive issues with no obvious reference to gays or lesbians. West Hollywood was one of the first local governments to press for sanctions on South Africa in the mid-1980s, enacted a landmark homeless services policy (which has since been replaced with a controversial anticamping ordinance that many felt reneged on the city's former commitment to the homeless and a backing away from its social justice stances), and worked to establish joint projects with African American neighborhoods following the 1992 civil unrest.

Although many of the achievements within West Hollywood have little or no relevance for those who live outside its boundaries, the city's landmark antidiscrimination policy, domestic partnership benefits for city employees, civil union registry, and close relationship with local law enforcement have become models for other cities and states. As gay and lesbian residents see that their rights are secure in West Hollywood, argues Curlee, "they can be involved in the bigger issues without fear that they are leaving their agenda behind."[29]

At the same time, however, Curlee describes an ongoing minority current of criticism against the visibility of gay issues on the city's agenda. Even while gay issues recede as priorities, some residents continue to level charges that the city favors its gay and lesbian population:

> Backlashers think that the city is a one issue city. This is so different from reality that it is scary.... They think that one queer equals one hundred queers and that is scary ... as the population becomes more integrated and casual (this is who I am and you have to deal

with it and it's not all I am) then the gays forget that that is how they are viewed by others. They don't even think about it when they are dealing with city issues but the others see it.[30]

As gays and lesbians in West Hollywood move beyond using city politics as a locus for their civil rights struggles primarily because they have succeeded, West Hollywood's role returns to one of creating a neighborhood for the gays and lesbians who live and visit there. In many ways, then, the question for the city is less how the government creates places for lesbians and gays than how the residents of West Hollywood have created a sense of community and the extent to which this enclave serves those living outside the city's borders. Since incorporation, West Hollywood has been a leader in providing services (from housing to health care) for people with HIV and AIDS. The annual gay pride parade is held in West Hollywood, and the only lesbian festival, Lesbian Visibility Week, is cosponsored with the Gay and Lesbian Center and funded by the city.

In addition to these annual events, which attract gays and lesbians across Los Angeles and emphasize the spectacle of gay and lesbian culture, the city continues to support the Lesbian and Gay Advisory Council, which serves as a shadow government to the city council, ensuring that gay and lesbian concerns are voiced and heard. The advisory council serves as a clearinghouse for events and issues in the community and coordinates with community institutions across the city and region. Thus, in recent years, the council has negotiated with the Gay and Lesbian Center to hold fund-raising events and celebrations, worked with local activists to obtain permits for demonstrations, and generally advocated the perception that West Hollywood is synonymous with gay and lesbian community and politics in Los Angeles. According to one member of the advisory council, the council acts as "the eyes and ears" of the city council members, "on the street and in the nightclubs.... We have become a sounding board for the gays and lesbians in the city, and we act as a buffer between the activist organizations and the city."[31]

The advisory council has been instrumental in the ongoing efforts of the city government to reform the attitudes of the sheriff's department toward lesbians and gays. As discussed earlier, police safety has been a constant issue in West Hollywood for gays and lesbians (as it is for gays and lesbians generally). In 1992, a ballot initiative to require the city to create an independent police force (rather than continuing to contract services from the county) was narrowly defeated after a vociferous campaign. According to one advisory council member, the police initiative provided an opportunity for a public debate on gay bashing and relations with the sheriff as well as a chance for the city to explain the measures it has instituted to improve these relations. Working with the advisory council, the city established a community board to work with the sheriff's department (to encourage gay and lesbian recruitment, provide sensitivity training, participate in a highly publicized sting operation, and monitor complaints). This community policing effort has become a model for improved community-police relations around the country, including for communities of color.

Eventually and perhaps inevitably, however, this proactive involvement of the city in these quality-of-life issues led some to argue that city hall is overinvolved in daily affairs. Although the city's policies and attitudes have contributed to the widespread perception (documented in the Needs Assessments) that its environment and lifestyle are the most important aspects of living in West Hollywood, this same engagement has some complaining that the city is overstructured. Like similarly progressive cities, West Hollywood has also been mocked by residents and the local press for its tendency to pass social justice ordinances that have little apparent effect on local life: declaring the city a nuclear-free, antiapartheid zone and opposing the military's antigay policy. As Thomas Crail, director of the Chamber of Commerce until his death in 1995 noted, "people expected mecca, but a less structured mecca" than exists today. For Crail, this backlash against the city government has to be understood in the context of gay and lesbian life outside West Hollywood:

> The question [our ambivalence about city government] begs is, can queer culture exist in a structure like that? The interesting flip side is when queers get power we overstructure.... Suddenly we are in this position where we are in control and we have never been in control of anything in our lives,... We can do something, so we do everything.[32]

This backlash also comes from straight residents, many of whom blame the city's problems on the visible gay culture. In the mid-1990s, a highly publicized conflict between the gay and Russian Jewish émigré communities erupted, first over the use of Piummer Park, which includes a community center, on the east side of town. While gay residents charged that many of the park users, (particularly the younger Russians) were harassing gays and lesbians and attempting to drive them out of the park (which is used by a number of gay organizations for meetings), the Russians countered that the gays and lesbians were equally intolerant and deliberately offended them with their visibility. Russian community leaders explained to city officials (including members of the Gay and Lesbian Community Advisory Council) that many older Russians were shocked simply by the gays passing them as they went to meetings, rather than by any overt actions or confrontations. The younger Russians, many of whom lived in the city from an early age, appeared to be motivated by a more traditional American homophobia. Attempts at negotiation have been largely successful, with many gays and lesbians involved in the negotiations admitting ignorance of the Soviet oppression from which the Russians fled and under which gay and lesbian behavior was completely unknown. Partly as a result of these new tensions, the city has embarked on a process of reevaluating the distribution of city services and the percentage of funding earmarked for gay and lesbian community uses.

Infernal Conflicts

Lesbians give many reasons why they do not live in West Hollywood in the same concentration as gay men. Many lesbians view West Hollywood as a high-rent district welcoming only professionals.

And many lesbians are uncomfortable about becoming pioneers in West Hollywood. Finally, they feel excluded because they believe that most businesses and services cater exclusively to gay men. The city and local businesses both assert that more lesbians are coming to West Hollywood on weekends, but they are not moving there. Since the mid-1990s, the number of lesbian clubs has increased. These "floating" clubs rent spaces once or twice a week from gay groups and target a young, racially diverse crowd. Rita Boyadjian, one of a new generation of lesbian entrepreneurs in West Hollywood, epitomizes the attitude of a younger generation that views this phenomenon without reference to decades of struggle and invisibility. For her, the arrival of lesbians onto the West Hollywood scene is inevitable:

> I think that there has been a commitment by lesbian entrepreneurs to create spaces for women and to create events for women in this city and dial's the major change. A lot of women promoters were just sick of having their events in these "cheesy-chivy" places and why not do it in West Hollywood? The boys have their spaces, so why not create spaces for women?[33]

Despite this interest, however, the success of lesbian spaces in Boystown has been inconsistent. Only the Palms, the lesbian bar owned by two gay men, has endured since before incorporation. Little Frida's—a coffeehouse alternative a few blocks away—has gone through at least three changes in ownership and two locations since it opened. Boyadjian recognizes that West Hollywood remains a gay male place and that lesbians in Los Angeles are not necessarily looking to develop such a place: "I don't think lesbians go out as much as gay men. They find someone and they stay home; they become condo bound." Boyadjian's goal is clear: "If more lesbians lived in West Hollywood, there would certainly be more support of lesbian retail businesses that are open seven days a week."[34]

For gays and lesbians of color, West Hollywood presents a similar paradox. Although the nightclub scene attracts a mixed crowd (and, according to many observers, grows more diverse every year), West Hollywood's racially coded atmosphere has not abated. Eric Reyes, in his master's thesis, "Queer Spaces: The Geography of Lesbians and Gay Men of Color in Los Angeles," presents diagrams and maps drawn by local activists (primarily young and all people of color) of their own understanding and use of public space.[35] Although no one he interviewed lived in West Hollywood, most of them identified the city as a key place on their maps. Compared with the positive comments in the Community Needs Assessment about West Hollywood's "spirit of togetherness," and "small town feel," or the attention of the city council to issues of access, equality, and discrimination, the attitudes expressed by self-identified queers of color are distinctly more qualified:

> West Hollywood is not an everything, just because it exists is not a reason to sing hallelujahs.[36]

> I don't really like West Hollywood. But it is one of the places where everyone is out. It's sort of like a little white boy's town, and I'm neither.... I guess West Hollywood is a token gay space.[37]
>
> West Hollywood is considered white, I feel no connection. It's too alien, foreign to me, like going to another country and I can't speak their language.... I am not free there and I choose not to deal with the comments, the looks, and everything.[38]

Despite these criticisms, West Hollywood was "mapped" by nearly all of Reyes's respondents, not solely as a place of estrangement, but also as a place to relax and meet other queers. Reyes argues that racial and ethnic experiences of discrimination complicate and bias the discussion of physical space with gays and lesbians of color. For many of his respondents, the social and mental spaces of their queer lives (represented by community networks, self-development and awareness, spaces created through temporary occupation) rank much higher than the physical spaces (in West Hollywood or elsewhere).

Reyes's work places this ambivalence about West Hollywood in the context of a white male privileging of physical space. He writes that "West Hollywood is a white-coded gay male place and to assign physical space as the only determinant of existence is to render queers of color invisible."[39] Reyes implies that the relative permanence of these physical spaces magnifies the disparity in power and access between the West Hollywood majority and communities of color. As such, these spaces are suspect. As one of Reyes's respondents described, West Hollywood reflects the norms and values of straight, rather than queer, culture: "West Hollywood is definitely not queer, it's gay. West Hollywood's gayness draws its validation from straight culture by appropriating norms, presentation, propriety and culture. The norms of society are not challenged—a normalized and assimilated gay."[40]

The Future of West Hollywood

Fifteen years after incorporation, many gays and lesbians moving to the city (and most using the city as a social escape) today know little if anything about the early struggles to create place in the city. How, then, does West Hollywood continue to assert its identity as a gay mecca beyond the attraction of the bars on Santa Monica Boulevard? Thomas Crail posed a set of three questions that reach the heart of a potential West Hollywood transformation:

> I wonder if West Hollywood *is* losing its queerness; and if it is losing its queerness what does it mean, A; and B, why is it happening; and C, is this good or bad? I don't know the answer to any of these three questions, but I think that they are valid questions that need to be addressed.[41]

Many city businesses contend that the changing demographics of the weekend crowd indicates a shift away from West Hollywood, with the social scene increasingly dominated by younger gays, most of whom do not live in West Hollywood. Although this has increased the numbers of people on West Hollywood's streets and therefore revenue for the bars and similar businesses, this emphasis on the younger, more transient crowd reflects short-term hype rather than long-term stability. As Crail explains. "It's not the same thing as having a real base that is a queer community."[42] The transient nature of the club scene, with new venues opening every few months and others losing favor and folding, creates a boom and bust atmosphere that does little to strengthen business ties to the community at large. Increasingly, these clubs, like gay organizations, are relocating to Hollywood, drawn by cheaper space and better parking.

The dynamics of diversity that have challenged the gay and lesbian movement in the past five years seem to be more critical to the future of West Hollywood than the economics of gay business. As lesbians and people of color become more visible actors in the movement, their absence in West Hollywood becomes more glaring. As long as the movement was led and staffed by white men, the demographics of West Hollywood were not necessarily surprising. As long as the movement was led and staffed by white men, the homogeneity of the city's gay population was not a public issue. Throughout the 1990s, however, a more diverse community has emerged, led in part by activists of color, and the whiteness of West Hollywood has become something of a political liability for those activists trying to broaden the movement. Initially, community institutions moved to Hollywood to find cheaper and larger spaces, but soon after new organizations located elsewhere in response to demands that the movement recognize the diversity—demographic and geographic—of the community. One of the mainstays of the Santa Monica Boulevard throughout this transition has been the local bookstore, A Different Light. After moving to West Hollywood from its original location in Silverlake, the bookstore has worked to offer literature that reflects the broader community and programs than attract people who would not otherwise visit the boulevard.

The feeling that there is a lack of community feeding the boulevard also affects the activist agenda in the city, and across local gay and lesbian politics. With little success, a few businesses (primarily coffeehouses) have opened with the intention, in part, of creating in West Hollywood a neighborhood atmosphere that would make the city more than a place to cruise on Friday night. One short-lived effort, the Six Gallery, aimed to be a community space by offering gallery space for artists and a back room for readings and meetings. During a series of massive street marches to protest the 1993 veto of a gay rights bill by the California governor, the Gallery transformed itself into an outpost of the Gay and Lesbian Center, serving as the semiofficial information central. Carter Bravmann, a founder of the Six Gallery, discovered, however, that even these popular cafes did not always benefit from the activity on the street, and that bars and clubs still defined the Boys-town environment. These bars, many of which are still not gay owned and have few ties to the community, tend to be lax with the age restriction, thus encouraging the deterioration of the boulevard:

> The Boulevard has that reputation of being loud.... Women don't want to go down there, it is not women's town, girls' town, or men's town, it is known as "Boystown" and that is exactly what it is.... The average age is probably twenty-three.[43]

Following the example set by the Six Gallery (and many similar efforts since the 1970s), new coffeehouses have opened that combine social activist agendas and aggressive outreach to the typical Boystown regulars. As chains—like Starbucks—try to cash in on the gentrification and tourist development of the city, other gay-owned establishments such as Stonewall Coffee have begun as a conscious effort to counter any mainstreaming by offering specifically gay or lesbian events, including comedy evenings to benefit local gay organizations and coffee giveaways at local gay, lesbian, and AIDS events. The first franchise is owned by Gay and Lesbian Adolescent Social Services, which provides group homes and foster care placement of gay youth as well as foster care and adoption placement for gay and lesbian families. A second store is located inside the Gay and Lesbian Center's newest location.

Even more community entrenched is WeHo Lounge, a cafe run by the AIDS Healthcare Foundation (AHF). The coffee shop designs its outreach efforts (including HIV tests) for gay men between the ages of sixteen and 21, one of the hardest-to-reach at-risk groups. The cafe, funded at start-up with a pharmaceutical company grant, also offers information about clinical trials and support groups. "It's a very in-your-face thing," said AHF president Michael Weinstein in a 1997 interview for the *Advocate*. "We share a common wall with Mickey's, one of the biggest discos in Los Angeles. We have more foot traffic on this street than anywhere west of the Mississippi."[44] Moreover, he says, the location and casual approach of the cafe aims to counter the gap between an older population accustomed to safe-sex programs and messages and younger gays who may feel ostracized from more mainstream social service locations. "Younger people are not comfortable going into official places to be tested. But people are really comfortable coming into a community establishment." The outreach to the younger generation also has attracted a crowd that is more ethnically diverse and may have otherwise seen West Hollywood as unwelcoming.

Added to these difficulties with the culture of Boystown, the physical space of the area also seems to inhibit a community ethos. The other major obstacle to the generation of community life along Santa Monica Boulevard that goes beyond barhopping is the physical layout of the area and the design impediments typical of Southern California and Los Angeles.

Bravmann described the lack of community on the Strip as resulting not only from the transient nature of the bar crowd, but also from the rigidity of the public space of Boystown:

> Physically, it just doesn't support it. Compared to the Castro, which on a day like to-day would be paradise, with people walking around, a community feeling, and a mix of

residential and commercial.... The public infrastructure cannot support more development because the Boulevard is filled up.[45]

From an urban design standpoint, the layout of the Santa Monica strip is difficult to improve. Along the busiest section of the Boulevard, across from the bookstore and a dense row of clubs and bars, is a walled-off zone containing a regional bus depot and the sheriff's substation. Together, they create a four-block obstruction to further commercial development. The sidewalks are extremely narrow, in part because Santa Monica Boulevard is a state highway, which prevents the city from widening the sidewalks that would improve pedestrian use. With four lanes of traffic, complicated intersections, and buses pulling in and out of traffic, the Boulevard has always been the most prominent feature of the neighborhood's landscape. One of the city's first major urban design projects after incorporation was the purchase of the median strip down the center of the Boulevard (a former trolley car right-of-way) to prevent the state from further widening the Boulevard. The median was lined with flagpoles flying the rainbow lambda flag. After years of planning and negotiation, the city finally undertook a major reconstruction, aiming to redesign the median and intersections to enhance city services and pedestrian safety.

The transient nature of the gay scene, however, remains the greatest obstacle to real transformation in the area. The expansion of weekend clubs on the eastern edge of Hollywood Boulevard and the emergence of new clubs in more diverse areas of the city aimed at young Latinos, Asians, and African American have shifted the geography of the community farther away from West Hollywood. Some local observers believe that the city should be concerned about this shift given the financial impact on the city's economy. The current attitude toward the gay businesses, which has been described as one of "benign neglect," is exemplified by the willingness with which the city watched the community institutions move to Hollywood. "I think," explained one local business leader, "we have had the attitude that we are the center of it all. The city gets a little arrogant about that and in the meantime your community institutions are being pulled off into other space."[46]

This concern about neglect obviously contrasts sharply with the earlier argument that the city is "overinvolved" in its residents' lives. West Hollywood's role for gays and lesbians across the larger Los Angeles area has clearly evolved. First, with incorporation came the possibility that the region could support, on its own terms, a place to rival the Castro or the West Village—a place openly committed to the needs and desires of gay men and lesbians. However, the increasing visibility of lesbians and gay men of color and the diversity of the community in Los Angeles as a whole means that no one district can hold a monopoly on gay and lesbian space. Places as ostensibly straight as East Los Angeles or the San Fernando Valley once offered little more than a neighborhood bar. Now, as evidenced by listings in the gay press and the community yellow pages (a listing of gay and gay-friendly businesses), these neighborhoods host more visible enclaves. With the greater tolerance (if not acceptance) of gays and lesbians and the possibility of alternatives to West Hollywood, the city may lose some of the advantages that made it a mecca. Crail notes,

> You can't assume that because for 40 years or 50 years you have had a monopoly on queer space you are going to have that six months later. The fact is that we are successfully creating an alternative [to West Hollywood] by putting those institutions that are the heart of our community in Hollywood.[47]

Other gay and lesbian community institutions have searched for space elsewhere in recent years, and many have moved to areas of Los Angeles not previously coded as gay or lesbian. Most notably, the International Gay and Lesbian Archives recently acquired space at the University of Southern California to allow for an expansion of its operations. Although many institutions consider a location in West Hollywood to be desirable, the attraction of affordable and permanent space outside the city may well be impossible to resist. In the summer of 1998, the Gay and Lesbian Community Services Center expanded beyond its new building on Hollywood Boulevard to additional space for educational activities elsewhere in Hollywood. This new location also offers office space for struggling gay and lesbian community organizations, filling a need that, previously, only West Hollywood has acknowledged. Clearly, West Hollywood's reputation as the only safe place for community institutions is quickly fading.

Symbolically as well as practically, West Hollywood remains the central site for activism and community celebration. When President Clinton announced the "Don't Ask, Don't Tell" policy on gays and lesbians in the military, Barbara Boxer held a meeting for community leaders to try to control whatever reaction might come from the streets. The Gay and Lesbian Advisory Committee organized a town hall meeting (cosponsored by the Human Rights Campaign Fund, a national gay and lesbian legal rights group) and march in West Hollywood, which became, in part, an official response to the new policy. The Center's California AIDS Ride, which raises more than a million dollars for the Center's AIDS services, had, until 1998, concluded its route from San Francisco to West Hollywood with a massive celebration, speeches from community leaders and city officials from both West Hollywood and Los Angeles, further solidifying the niche West Hollywood has carved out for itself.

With the new understanding of its gay identity, the city has increasingly turned to development projects and social services that have less to do with gay and lesbian culture than with the city's insistence on serving residents in all categories (straight, gay, lesbian, senior, Russian, children) as well as supporting a diversified economic base. One case in point is the ongoing revitalization of the Sunset Strip tiirough an intense planning process focusing on the use, design, and future of each building and lot on the street. Interests on the Strip range from those of the wealthy homeowners in the foothills north of Sunset Boulevard to the club owners and patrons that lend the Strip its signature character. Although there were fears of over-commercializing when the first plans appeared (including proposed celebrity statues), the plan for the area has evolved into one that balances economic development pressures and opportunities with the desires of the city's residents. At the same time, new developments on the Strip have been extraordinarily successful. This new approach to the Strip, of course, could not be more divergent from the first sixty years of development that rested on the lack of oversight and near lawlessness of the area between the 1920s and 1980s. In many ways, this approach to the area signifies one of the clearest signals coming from the gay majority city council: Overt and conscious participation in the city's development and character will have profound effects on the culture, economy, and design of the city. West Hollywood will finally achieve not just a gay enclave to rival Greenwich Village or the Castro, but also an integrated, diverse, and flourishing municipality that can be a model for cities, gay and straight, across the country.

This new burst of development has strengthened the role of gays (if not lesbians) in city government, after nearly a decade during which gays did not hold a majority of council seats. Mayor Steve Martin, the first openly gay candidate to be elected since the first election when he took his seat in 1994, sees the attention to the Sunset Strip as evidence that the city is now confident with itself as a place with a gay identity that it can now move on to other, less gay initiatives: "Developing the Strip during the 1980s was antithetical to what West Hollywood politics was all about then, and that was gay and lesbian rights, social services like AIDS information, and rent control."[48] Similarly, the revitalization of the eastern end of the city has also been a long-running attempt to improve the city's economic and cultural development. For years, the eastern edge of town languished while the westside boomed with gay development. Many of these improvements have been designed specifically for the Russian population or for the movie industry (such as postproduction houses). One consequence may well be a smoothing of relations between those who support Boystown expansion and those who feel that the city may have lost some of its original commitment to social services and livability.

In many ways, the enigma of West Hollywood is that, in an era where the focus is on national politics—from openly gay White House appointees to federal debates on gays in the military—the role of the local is not clear. Movement activists have declared that the new focus for gay and lesbian civil rights has relocated to the local level. By this they mean the cities and towns across America where the religious right is targeting gays and lesbians, not cities like West Hollywood where lesbians and gays live and work openly and without a high level of fear.

As the gay community decentralized, and the movement continues to broaden its agenda, the City of Los Angeles can claim to be responsive to gay and lesbian concerns and welcome their communities. In fact, Los Angeles increasingly steals the spotlight in the gay media with high-profile events and political accomplishments, such as the election of lesbian city councilwoman Jackie Goldberg or Mayor Riordan's public opposition to the antigay policies of fellow Republicans. But West Hollywood continues to balance its role as the gay mecca with its commitment to services for tenants, the elderly, and Russian immigrants, thus complicating the community model of identity politics. In the years since the gay "Camelot" was incorporated, one thing is clear; West Hollywood has not become a model for gay and lesbian local politics, nor is it the only platform for gay and lesbian politicians and activists. Instead, the city's influence may be waning, just as lesbians are beginning to be a visible (if small) part of the scene. The continuing challenge to the city's local gay elite from lesbians and people of color exemplifies the struggles of a community and a movement searching for a new politics and a new activism. For national gay and lesbian organizers, West Hollywood continues to represent a source of considerable wealth and power. But for those disengaged from these national politics, West Hollywood remains something much simpler—a place for escape. Like Hollywood Boulevard or Venice Beach, West Hollywood is a magnet for those seeking a version of the California myth, a place that cannot possibly deliver all that is expected. Perhaps, as suggested in the following observation, West Hollywood's most enduring lure will be the image that is created and circulated about the city, one that mingles the specific pleasures of the gay scene with the general pleasures of Southern California:

> For me, West Hollywood is an intense image that began before I arrived here—one of youthful, well-built men—a combination of surf, sand, and sun. It's our own city. It is a place where people can be open, obvious, and can be there in their gayness. It is a haven, a place to blow off the split in their lives.[49]

City officials appear to prefer to emphasize the "haven" aspect of the dream, downplaying the "sun and fun." The following description of West Hollywood, offered by the chair of the West Hollywood Lesbian and Gay Advisory Committee, expresses the heart of what the city and community leaders seek to provide and what the gay and lesbians who live in West Hollywood experience:

> It's a social base … our family, our community.… West Hollywood serves that purpose for [gays and lesbians]. Our population triples on weekends and it's not by error, it's consistently tripling as people come here to meet, to socialize.… It's validating to be among people who accept who you are, where you are safe.[50]

Critical for this perspective, however, is the often-simplistic assumption that many in the community make about what safety entails and how safety is constructed. Place claiming, for gays and lesbians in West Hollywood., has only recently begun to address these alternative visions and expectations. Although the past fifteen years of incorporation have created tangible opportunities for the most assimilated gays to build a local power base, the next decades will be a test of the flexibility of this power and the willingness of the city government and its residents to use this access for gays and lesbians outside the city's boundaries as well. For many gays and lesbians in Los Angeles, West Hollywood remains only a temporary weekend retreat. The following chapters look at the attempts of gays and lesbians without such open access to the government to claim corners of greater Los Angeles.

Reference

1. Interestingly, other businesses that flourished during the county years included animal hospitals and dry cleaning establishments. Both of these businesses are heavily regulated in incorporated sections of the county. As a result, West Hollywood now has more dry cleaners per square mile then anywhere else in Los Angeles, California Economic Development Department, *Los Angeles County Business Patterns 1992* (Sacramento, CA, 1992).

2. As discussed elsewhere, Manuel Castells's study of the Castro District in San Francisco argues that these enclaves emerge from the mismatch between increasing social acceptance and continued social repression. Through the development of "liberated zones," gays looked to create places where they could be "socialized in a new culture more suitable to their needs and behavior." Manuel Castells, *The City and the Grassroots* (Berkeley: University of California Press, 1983), 156.

3. Martin Levine, "Gay Ghetto," in Martin Levine, ed., *Gay Men: The Sociology of Male Homosexuality* (New York: Harper & Row, 1979), 201.

4. Esther Newton, *Cherry Grove, Fire Island* (Boston: Beacon Press, 1992), 9–10

5. Mickey Lauria and Lawrence Knopp, "Towards an Analysis of the Role of Gay Communities in the Urban Renaissance," *Urban Geography 6* (1985), 159.

6. Ibid.

7. Castells, *The City and the Grassroots.*

8. See longer discussion in Chapter 3.

9. Sy Adler and Johanna Brenner, "Gender and Space: Lesbians and Gay Men in the City," *International Journal of Urban and Regional Research* 16:1 (1992), 31.

10. Edmund White, *States of Desire: Travels in Gay America* (New York: E. P. Dutton, 1980), 25–26.

11. Ibid., 11.

12. Ron Stone, "Gay Pride: Will Success Spoil West Hollywood?" *LA Weekly,* 30 June 1983, 27.

13. Benjamin Forrest, "Political Territory as Symbol" (M.A. Dissertation, University of California, Los Angeles, 1991).

14. Bob Craig, Presentation to the Lesbian and Gay Advisory Council, City of West Hollywood, 14 June 1994.

15. See Adam Moos, "The Grassroots in Action: Gays and Seniors Capture the Local State in West Hollywood, California," in Jennifer Wolch and Michael Dear, eds., *The Power of Geography* (Boston: Unwin Hyman, 1989), 351–369. In short, West Hollywood needed to show sufficient tax revenues to maintain the county's level of services.

16. Ibid., 357.

17. "The Post Supports Cityhood," *West Hollywood Post,* 20 September 1984.

18. Moos, "The Grassroots in Action," 359.

19. "The 'Gay Camelot' Grows Up," *Los Angeles Times,* 27 June 1994, A18.

20. West Hollywood Community Needs Assessment, 1998, 10.

21. West Hollywood Community Needs Assessment, 1994. Using both telephone interview and mail surveys, the study elicited 832 responses, approximately 3.6 percent of all households. The report also analyzed data from the 1980 and 1990 U.S. Censuses. Given that the U.S. Census does not ask questions about sexual orientation, the telephone interview and mail survey data were most useful in analysis of the city's lesbian and gay population.

22. West Hollywood Community Needs Assessment, 1994, xvi.

23. Milton Diamond, "Homosexuality and Bisexuality in Different Populations," *Archives of Sexual Behavior* 22:4 (August 1993), 291–311.

24. West Hollywood Community Needs Assessment, 1998, 16.

25. West Hollywood Community Needs Assessment, 1998, 38.

26. Jodi Curlee, interview with author, 3 June 1994.

27. City of West Hollywood, California, "Final Report of the Gay and Lesbian Task Force" (21 November 1988), 3–1.

28. West Hollywood Community Needs Assessment, 1998, 1–7.

29. Curlee, interview.

30. Ibid.

31. Lesbian and Gay Advisory Council staffperson, interview with author, 27 May 1994.

32. Thomas Crail, interview with author, 2 June 1994.

33. Rita Boyadjian, interview with author, 8 July 1994.

34. Ibid.

35. Eric Reyes, "Queer Spaces: The Geography of Lesbians and Gay Men of Color in Los Angeles" (M.A. Thesis, University of California Los Angeles, 1993). Reyes's work is also valuable as an attempt to use cognitive mapping methods, including sketch maps by a selected group of gay men and lesbians of color.

36. SS, quoted in ibid., 99.

37. SL, quoted in ibid., 100.

38. BF, quoted in ibid., 102.

39. Ibid., 110.

40. EB, quoted in ibid., 99.

41. Crail, interview.

42. Ibid.

43. Carter Bravmann, interview with author, 31 May 1994.

44. "WeHo Lounge," *The Advocate*, 28 October 1997, 20.

45. Bravmann, interview.

46. Crail, interview.

47. Ibid.

48. *Los Angeles Times Magazine*, 15 December 1996, 24.

49. E. Michael Gorman, "The Pursuit of the Wish: An Anthropological Perspective on Gay Male Subculture in Los Angeles," in Gilbert Herdt, ed., *Gay Culture in America: Essays in the Field* (Boston: Beacon, 1992), 93.

50. West Hollywood Lesbian and Gay Advisory Committee member, interview with author.

CHAPTER THREE

CRITICAL ISSUES OF INCLUSION IN CALIFORNIA

Proposition 209 and Its Implications

PAUL ONG

n 1996, California was at the epicenter of a political tremor that has shaken the foundation of this nation's policy on how to redress the difficult, complex, and persistent problem of racial and gender inequality. As discussed in Chapter 1, affirmative action has been challenged with some success in the courts, and neoconservative administrations have weakened the enforcement of affirmative action (and equal opportunity) programs. Actors within California were party to these earlier attacks. In 1978, Allan Bakke won his case against the University of California before the U.S. Supreme Court, claiming that he was illegally denied admission to the medical school on the UC Davis campus because of preferential treatment given to minority applicants. Support for civil rights programs within the executive branch began to wane in the 1980s. As documented in Chapter 3, funding for enforcement of antidiscrimination laws declined noticeably during this period. Another indication of the antipathy toward affirmative action was a failure to conduct an analysis of California's set-aside program. Given the strict scrutiny standard set by the U.S. Supreme Court, the state had to undertake such an analysis if it wanted to continue such a program. Inaction was tantamount to letting the program wither. In 1995, Governor Pete Wilson and his appointees to the Board of Regents of the University of California pushed through two resolutions, SP-1 and SP-2, which directed the university to end the use of race, religion, sex, color, ethnicity, or national origin in its admission process, contracting, and employment.

The third front in the attack on affirmative action in California was a direct appeal to the voting public through the initiative process. In 1996, 54 percent of the voters in the Golden State passed Proposition 209, which requires the state and its local jurisdictions to "not discriminate against, or grant preferential treatment to, any individual or group on the basis of race, sex, color, ethnicity, or national origin in the operation of public employment, public education, or public contracting." Although the proposition was titled the California Civil Rights Initiative, the purpose behind it was to end the use of the more aggressive affirmative action programs.

The election result sent a shock wave throughout the nation, triggering similar campaigns in other locations, with the backers of Proposition 209 aggressively exporting their expertise. One year later, in 1997, voters in the city of Houston voted on Proposition A, which posed the question, "Shall the Charter of the City of Houston be amended to end the use of affirmative action?" Unlike California, the vote went against the initiative, by a majority of 55 percent. In the following year, Initiative 200 was placed on the Washington State ballot. It stated, "The state shall not discriminate against, or grant preferential treatment to, any individual or group on the basis of race, sex, color, ethnicity, or national origin in the operation of public employment, public education, or public contracting." The initiative passed by a majority of 58 percent. Similar initiatives and legislative efforts are being pursued in other states, including Colorado, Florida, Ohio, Michigan, Missouri, New Jersey, and Texas.[1]

The impact at the national level is a little more difficult to discern. The success of the California and Washington initiatives has encouraged some conservative members of Congress to discuss the enactment of legislation designed to have a similar impact nationally.[2] The impact on the Clinton administration appears to be one of intimidation, forcing it to lower its profile. The mend-not-end strategy already represented a middle-of-the-road approach, which is consistent with the administration's prevailing moderate political philosophy. What is intriguing, and perhaps telling, is the report from the Advisory Board to the President's Initiative on Race, in which the discussion on affirmative action is largely descriptive and noncommittal.[3]

These events raise several questions: Why did the use of direct appeal to the voting public start in California? Why are there differences in voting results on different ballots? What should be done in the wake of 209?

The California Origins

The third front in the attack on affirmative action—the initiative approach—originated in California because of an unusual set of political, social, and economic conditions. There are two defining political characteristics that provided a foundation for this Proposition 209. The first is that the 1996 campaign traveled the well-beaten path of using ballot initiatives as a form of populist politics—a path that has become increasingly dominated by special-interest groups and big money. The state's initiative process was established in 1911 as a part of the progressive movement to counter potentially corrupt and unresponsive elected officials. The relationship between race and this process is not new to California. In 1964, 55 percent of the voters passed Proposition 14, which was written to negate the 1963 Rumford Act outlawing discrimination against home buyers and apartment renters.[4] Proposition 14 did not overtly support the right to discriminate but instead couched its arguments in the rhetoric of individual rights and antigovernment. The initiative stated: "Neither the State nor any subdivision or agency thereof shall deny, limit or abridge, directly or indirectly, the right of any person, who is willing or desires to sell, lease or rent any part or all of his real property, to decline to sell, lease or rent such property to such person or persons as he, in his absolute discretion, chooses." Despite its passage, the proposition had limited impact. Decisive action by the federal government to cut housing funds to California dampened the willingness of other states to place such an initiative before their voters, and within months, California's Supreme Court ruled that the proposition violated the Fourteenth Amendment.

The potency of the initiative process as populist politics became more apparent with the 1979 Proposition 13, which was at the forefront of the "tax rebellion."[5] The passage of this proposition, which withstood court challenges, accelerated the use of initiatives in California and other states. Since that time, turning to initiatives has become a common practice, one supported by the establishment of organizations that exist to facilitate the process. While those using the initiatives still claim this avenue provides for direct democracy, much of the process has been taken over by special interest and big money.[6] Initiatives have been used by groups on both sides of the political spectrum to push narrow agendas. Success in collecting the required signatures to place an initiative on the ballot frequently depends heavily on paid petition workers, while the expense of supporting and opposing propositions often costs more than campaigns for major elected offices.

The initiative process provides any well-financed disgruntled group an avenue to seek a political solution not addressed by their elected officials. Two individuals, Glynn Custer and Thomas Wood, took advantage of the process to place 209 on the ballot.[7] Both were highly educated white males who disliked the social changes associated with minority demands. One, an anthropology professor, had become increasing disturbed by the multicultural transformation of the curriculum and faculty on his college campus, and the other felt that affirmative action denied him an academic position because of preferential treatment given to a black woman. Although the two ran an independent, populist-type operation to get the initiative process started, they eventually had to rely on funds, support, and organizational help from neoconservatives.

While the initiative process provided an opening to attack affirmative action, a second aspect of California politics—Governor Wilson's reliance on wedge issues—was a necessary ingredient. In the 1994 gubernatorial race, Wilson rebuilt his popularity and won reelection in part by using divisive issues founded on the fears of the majority of the voters, such as immigration and crime. He continued to pursue these and other hot-button issues, including efforts to weaken unions and civil rights programs. These tactics were motivated by his political ambitions to seek the presidency. His failed effort to become the GOP candidate was built in part on his claim to represent conservative interests. Attacking affirmative action was very much a wedge issue, one that the Governor supported actively.

Social changes well before Proposition 2.09 created a climate that was conducive to the initiative. California's demographic recomposition created a backlash from an increasing number of whites who felt uneasy and displaced by the changes. The demographic transformation was rooted in the liberalization of national immigration laws in the mid-1960s, which ended racially motivated quotas. The renewal of large-scale immigration in the 1960s transformed the nation, increasing the foreign-born population, from 9.6 million in 1970 to 25.8 million in 1997, and from 4.7 to 9.6 percent of the total population.[8] The dramatic growth in the immigrant population was accompanied by an ethnic and racial shift as Asian and Latin American countries replaced European countries as the primary source of immigration. By 1997, those of European ancestry accounted for only one-sixth of the immigrants, while Asians accounted for more than one-quarter and Latinos accounted for nearly one-half. Nowhere has the resulting demographic transformation been more dramatic than in California. About one-third of this nation's foreign-born population resides in California, and approximately one-quarter of the state's population is foreign-born.

This demographic change produced nativist reactions, first in the form of cities trying to stem the tide of cultural changes brought in by Asians and Latinos,[9] and later in the form of a statewide proposition. While the state's population has become ethnically diverse, non-Hispanic whites still dominate at the election polls. In 1994, non-Hispanic whites comprised 52 percent of the population[10] but an estimated 81 percent of the voters in the November 1994 election.[11] That year, the majority of the voters passed Proposition 187, an initiative designed to prevent undocumented aliens from receiving public social services, public health-care services, and public education at elementary, secondary, and postsecondary levels.[12] The proponents argued that the people of California "have suffered and are suffering economic hardship caused by the presence of illegal aliens," and "have suffered and are suffering personal injury and damage caused by the criminal conduct of illegal aliens." Although the proposition was formally aimed at undocumented aliens, there was a strong anti-immigrant undercurrent. Four years later, anti-immigrant sentiments resurfaced with the passage of Proposition 227, the English Language in Public Schools Initiative. In an effort to reassert the cultural dominance of the majority population, the initiative stated that the "English language is the national public language of the United States of America and of the State of California." Clearly, there are many backers of both Proposition 187 and Proposition 227 who are neither racist nor against legal immigrants, yet it is difficult to deny the fact that both initiatives are propelled in part by nativist sentiments.

Economic conditions also played a role by creating uncertainty and anxiety over employment and educational opportunities., particularly among white males. Starting in 1991, the state experienced a much deeper and longer recession than the rest of the nation. By mid-1993, the state's unemployment rate was over 9 percent, compared to about 7 percent for the nation. In the four months preceding the November 1996 elections—when Proposition 209 was on the ballot—the unemployment rate averaged over 7.7 percent, compared to 5.3 percent for the United States. Moreover, there was continued distress over the permanent loss of high-paying jobs, particularly in aerospace, due to cuts in the defense industry after the end of the Cold War.[13] These lost jobs were not being replaced with new high-wage jobs that could reabsorb most of the displaced workers, the majority of whom were white males. These economic problems interacted with a widely held perception that whites were losing out to less qualified minorities.[14] The dominant view, then, was one of a zero-sum game, and the gains made by some under affirmative action were perceived to have come at the expense of others. These concerns were amplified in California. Bad economic times turned the concerns over a zero-sum game into a fight to preserve shares of a shrinking pie.

The political, social, and economic factors combined into a potent force that produced a majority supporting Proposition 209. Not surprisingly, support was strongest among conservatives (77 percent for), Republicans (80 percent for), whites (63 percent for), and males (61 percent for).[15] While the specific conditions in California explain why California took the lead in opening the third front in the attack on affirmative action, subsequent events show that this form of populist politics has wider appeal. Just as in a physical earthquake, a political tremor is the product of a deep underlying tension—the confrontation of powerful and opposing ideological forces.

The Semantics of Affirmative Action

Affirmative action has created a conundrum over how this nation ought to come to terms with intergroup inequality. This strategy, which evolved out of the political history of the latter half of the 20th century, is at the heart of a debate that deeply divides this nation and the state of California. In the heat of the debate, which is often dominated by polemics rather than thoughtful discussion, it is convenient to focus narrowly on the particular strategy and forget the larger context: persistent inequality along racial and gender lines. Numerous studies, including those in this book, show that women and people of color still have far fewer employment and business opportunities than do white men. The disparities are the result of conscious and unconscious biases in hiring and business decisions, of unequal access to training and education, and of institutionalized practices, many of which are not explicitly racist or sexist. Unless these patterns and practices are altered, women and minorities will continue to be denied equal employment and business opportunities.

A consensus on what should be done eludes us. As a society, we value personal initiative and believe in an economic system that rewards people for merit and performance; therefore, it is not surprising that a majority supports eliminating overt discrimination in the workplace and the business world. Moreover, most accept the fact that discrimination has not been eliminated. For example, three-quarters of the nation agree with the statement, "Black people still face discrimination," including employment and housing discrimination.[16] In California, six out of seven believe that "discrimination is still common," and even among white males, four out of five agree with this statement.[17] These attitudes are the basis for the strong public support for antidiscriminatory policies.

For many, prohibiting discriminatory behavior is necessary but not sufficient. For them, eliminating inequality cannot be achieved simply by a promise to treat everyone the same, but rather requires attacking the systemic roots of inequality. Affirmative action has been devised as a way to counter the historical legacies of racism and sexism and to dismantle contemporary institutional barriers. Under affirmative action, concrete steps are taken to produce outcomes in employment and business that could be expected if social inequality were absent. Its very nature and logic have led to the creation of programs that target and assist minorities and women.

"For a growing number in our society, on the other hand, affirmative action goes too far. They argue that white men are bearing an unfair burden of remedying a societal problem not of their making. These opponents charge that affirmative action is merely preferential treatment that violates the goal of treating people fairly as individuals. They charge that affirmative action is based on practices that are equivalent to using quotas.

Although affirmative action programs have been refined over the years to adhere to the laws forbidding the use of quotas, the critics nevertheless raise the legitimate point that society should be cautious in using such broad measures, even to eliminate the historical legacies of discrimination.

Caution, however, is not equivalent to accepting the argument that all forms of affirmative action are unacceptable. Most Americans find the disparities produced by discrimination and prejudice unacceptable, but public support for alternative solutions varies greatly. There is great resistance to giving preferential treatment, and this creates the duality of supporting" antidiscrimination policies but opposing affirmative action."[8] The dichotomy, however, is not as simple as it appears. There are different opinions on the various forms of affirmative action. A large majority of the public support "increase[d] recruitment" and a "sincere effort to hire" fully qualified blacks in order to reach parity.[19] There is then a nuance in the support and opposition to affirmative action, and this can be seen in a survey of Houston voters prior to the 1997 election.[20] Sixty-nine percent of the respondents, including a majority of blacks, said they would support a proposition stating: "The city of Houston shall not discriminate against, or grant preferential treatment to, any individual or group on the basis of race, sex, ethnicity, or national origin in the operation of public employment and public contracting. However, support fell to 47 percent for a proposition stating: "Shall the Charter of the City of Houston be amended to end the use of Affirmative Action for women and minorities in the operation of City of Houston employment and contracting, including ending the current program and any similar programs in the future?" In the end, a majority of the voters opposed Proposition A, which stated: "Shall the Charter of the City of Houston be amended to end the use of affirmative action?" If Houston's Proposition A had been worded like those in California and Washington, it is likely that the outcome would have been different.

Given the evidence, it is clear that the appeal to direct plebiscites relies on a simplistic and undesirable reduction of the underlying concerns. This insight has not been lost on either proponents or opponents of affirmative action. Each side would like to frame the wording so as to appeal to only one of two fundamental values, the need to address inequality and the aversion to preferential treatment. The initiative process is ill suited to formulating a policy based on an acceptable compromise and pragmatic tradeoff of two conflicting principles, but this type of politics cannot be avoided. As the old saying goes, "The genie is out of the bottle." With such high stakes, the bitter political contest now revolves around semantics.

Acknowledging political reality, however, is not the same as accepting it. If the early civil rights movement hinged on winning public support, then very little progress would have been made, even over color-blind policies. Despite the trend of reductionist politics, we should elevate the debate to address as fully as possible these value-laden questions: What is the nation's obligation to correct historical wrongs? What price are we, as a nation, willing to pay for our actions or inactions? When should we adopt color- and gender-blind policies? And how strongly are we committed to racial and gender equality as an outcome?

The Effectiveness of Affirmative Action

Finding a balance rests in part on understanding what affirmative, action has accomplished in order to shed light on what would be lost if the policy were eliminated. As stated in Chapter 1, the book's contributors undertook this project with the hope of elevating the current debate through an assessment of the affirmative action programs prior to Proposition 209. As social scientists dedicated to improving This understanding, we are guided by the principle that research into the effects of government policies and programs on hiring and contracting should coincide with the geography of political discourse. While the discussion over the future of affirmative action is a national one, it is also being conducted at the state level, with California leading the way. Unfortunately, we know very little about how these programs have operated in California or any other state. The existing literature is dominated by analyses using national data. State and regional variations are at best secondary considerations, and analyses often have included only crude control variables for those variations. What is clear is that it is not possible to simply extrapolate the experience at the national level to that of the states. Each state has a different historical and demographic context that influences the nature and extent of socioeconomic inequality. Each state also has a different legislative history with regard to affirmative action, as well as a different experience in implementing programs. More information is needed on the particular impacts of affirmative action across states in order to raise our understanding of what approaches have or have not been successful and why. The studies presented in this book help fill the gap in California-specific data by analyzing the historical impact of affirmative action programs on employment and business opportunities for minorities and women. While this book provides new insights, it is far from comprehensive. It does not cover such important topics as set-aside contracting at the state level, the impact of federal regulation on the public sector, or the costs and benefits of implementing affirmative action, Even with the limited number of outcomes under study, it is difficult to isolate the effects of affirmative action programs from all the other factors that affect employer hiring practices and the viability of women- and minority-owned small businesses.

Despite these limitations, the analyses do identify the direction and the rough magnitude of changes attributable to affirmative action. Progress was made during the 1960s, 1970s, and 1980s in redressing racial and gender disparities in employment and business opportunities. State and local governments did a better job than the private sector in providing opportunities to minorities and women, and private firms covered by affirmative action programs provided more opportunities than those that were not. Yet despite the changes brought about by affirmative action programs and policies and concomitant laws combating discrimination in employment, there remains a sizable gap in economic status due to race and gender.

The findings in these studies provide glimpses into the potential consequences of eliminating affirmative action programs. As Badgett points out in Chapter 4, eliminating results-oriented requirements for public employers could reduce public-sector demand for women and minorities. Under this scenario, the number of female and minority workers who would have been employed in the public sector and could instead be readily absorbed into the private sector will depend on the strength of the labor market in the private sector. However, a shift in demand away from minority and female workers, a likely outcome of Proposition 209, may result in lower wages for these populations, given the existing wage gaps between sectors. Badgett also suggests that there could be underemployment for some female and minority employees in managerial and professional positions.

There may be similar effects on minority- and women-owned businesses that contract with the state, depending on the transitional issues they would face. Information from a recent survey of public agencies shows that Proposition 209 has already hurt minority and women contracting.[21] This is, however, only a part of the impact. As Williams notes in Chapter 6, even if these firms were to experience a significant reduction in revenue from state/local government sources, the impact of the policy change on any firm will depend on its ability to enter alternative markets and on whether there will be demand for the firm's output. Without an existing alternative market, the cost of switching to production for the private sector will determine Proposition 209's impact. In many cases, Williams suggests, it may be possible to replace sales to California state/local governments by supplying federal agencies, or by supplying state and local governments other than those in California.

The one place where the impact has been immediate and highly visible is admission to the University of California. Compared with the previous year, new registration by underrepresented minorities for the entering 1998 freshmen class fell by 30 percent at UCLA and 52 percent at UC Berkeley, the two most competitive campuses in the system.[22] As predicted by Conrad (in Chapter 8), this was offset by an increase at the other campuses, so that the total decrease was only 10 percent. Minority enrollment in law schools also decreased, and this was particularly noticeable at Boalt

Law School at UC Berkeley. None of the 14 blacks admitted to Boalt Hall registered, partly as a protest and partly because other prestigious law schools proved to be more welcoming and attractive. The impact at the medical schools, however, appears to be nonexistent, with the number of new registrants and their distribution across campuses holding fairly constant over the last three years.[23] This may be due to the modifications made by the medical schools since the landmark 1978 *Bakke* decision. The ultimate impact on minority enrollment in higher education will depend on the ability of the UC system to find alternative ways to maintain its diversity.

Intriguing as the effects hypothesized by the authors might be, one must be cautious about projecting future outcomes based on the past effects of local and state affirmative action programs. Real-world outcomes will be influenced by many other societal transformations that have taken place over the last two to three decades. Changes in public attitudes, economic transformations, and demographic shifts all share in determining who gets hired and for what jobs. There are specific federal hiring requirements that will continue to apply to state and private employers. Social conditions are also far different than they were 20 or 30 years ago. Today, there are networks for recruitment of minorities and women, and referrals that did not previously exist and will continue to function. Finally, many firms will continue to make a conscious effort to diversify their workforce to better serve an increasingly diverse consumer base. Given these complexities, statements about the effects of curtailing or eliminating affirmative action efforts remain highly speculative.

The Pursuit of Social Justice

Even the passage of Proposition 209 in November 1996 does not tell us what is permitted and what is prohibited. A federal appellate court has upheld the initiative's constitutionality, deciding that the state may limit its own authority to remedy the effects of discrimination even if it would otherwise be constitutional for it to act. The full reach of Proposition 209 still remains to be tested because eliminating "preferential treatment" as the language of the initiative states, need not be equivalent to banning all affirmative action. Programs that merely provide technical assistance to women and minorities without guaranteeing any special treatment might still be permitted. In any event, race- and gender-neutral programs aimed at assisting socially or economically disadvantaged people would still be available.

Clearly, Proposition 209 should not be turned into an excuse for denying the reality of discrimination in society or ignoring the fact that women and minorities do not currently enjoy equal access to employment and business opportunities. Affirmative action programs may be curtailed or eliminated, but there remains a national and state commitment to prohibiting racial and gender discrimination in public and private hiring. As Thomas and Garrett point out in Chapter 2, federal law imposes liabilities for employment practices having a discriminatory effect even where there is no intent to discriminate. Significantly, in a post-election editorial (*Los Angeles Times*, April 9, 1997), Ward

Connerly, one of the chief proponents of Proposition 209, reiterated the importance of guaranteeing minorities and women opportunities in hiring and contracting. Connerly stressed the need to reassure those potentially affected by eliminating preferences that they will not face discrimination or loss of job opportunities.

Although Proposition 209 does not represent a wholesale reversal of the movement to promote equal opportunity for minorities and women, guaranteeing equal opportunity is now a greater challenge. One way to meet this challenge is for state policy makers to support strong enforcement of the state's own antidiscrimination laws. Inadequate state funding for investigations of complaints, as noted in Chapter 3, is a disturbing trend and ought to be reversed. State and local officials, educators, and the public at large need to dedicate themselves to a greater effort to make quality education and training available to all individuals regardless of race or gender and to provide assistance to economically disadvantaged people and communities, possibly through new lending and technical assistance programs. If we as a society are to continue to make progress in eliminating racial and gender disparities, this nation—and this state— must pursue the goal of ensuring equality, of access to obtaining the skills and resources that people need to compete effectively in the marketplace. By addressing the various causes of social inequality more sensitively, we can improve on our efforts at achieving a just society.

This book has documented the increased opportunity, primarily in the public sphere, made possible by affirmative action policies and programs. As legislative and judicial decisions modify public policy intended to address racial and gender discrimination, the impacts of these changes on employment and business opportunities for women and minorities should be closely monitored and evaluated. This may be best done by a joint effort involving researchers and state agencies. The public and their representatives need to know what works and what does not; otherwise the continuing debate over affirmative action will simply be reduced to exchanging polemics. A better understanding of the unfolding dynamics of these processes can point to better ways to ensure social fairness.

Notes

1. American Civil Rights Coalition: *www.acrcl.org/prl00997.html*.
2. See, for example, the proposed Civil Rights Act of 1997, American Civil Rights Coalition: *www.acrcl.org/pr061797.html*.
3. The President's Initiative on Race Advisory Board, "One America in the 21st Century: The President's Initiative on Race" (Washington, DC: U.S. Government Printing Office, 1998), pp. 99–102.
4. Thomas W. Casstevens, "Politics, Housing, and Race Relations: California's Rumford Act and Proposition 14" (Berkeley: Institute of Governmental Studies, University of California, 1967).
5. David O. Sears and Jack Citrin, *Tax Revolt: Something for Nothing in California* (Cambridge, MA: Harvard University Press, 1985); Clarence Y. H. Lo, *Small Property versus Big Government: Social Origins of the Property Tax Revolt* (Berkeley: University of California Press, 1990).

6. California Commission on Campaign Financing, *Democracy by Initiative: Shaping California's Fourth Branch of Government* (Los Angeles: Center for Responsive Government, 1992); Jim Shultz, *The Initiative Cookbook: Recipes and Stories from California's Ballot Wars* (San Francisco: Democracy Center, 1996).

7. The discussion on the development of Proposition 209 is based on Lydia Chavez, *The Color Bind: California's Battle to End Affirmative Action* (Berkeley: University of California Press, 1998).

8. U.S. Immigration and Naturalization Services, "Total and Foreign-born U.S. Population: 1900–90" (*www.ins.usdoj.gov/stats/308.html); U.S. Bureau of the Census, "Foreign-born Population Reaches 25.8 Million, According to Census Bureau" (www.census.gov/Press-Release/cb98–57.html).*

9. Leland T. Saito, *Race and Politics: Asian Americans, Latinos, and Whites in a Los Angeles Suburb* (Urbana: University of Illinois Press, 1998).

10. U.S. Bureau of the Census, "Estimates of the Population of States by Race and Hispanic Origin: July 1, 1994" *(www.census.gov/population/estimates/state/srh/shms94.txt).*

11. *Los Angeles Times,* November 10, 1994, p. B4.

12. The proposition passed on the strength of the white vote, with 63 percent supporting 187. On the other hand, a majority of nonwhites voted against the proposition.

13. Paul Ong and Janet Lawrence, "Race and Employment Dislocation in California's Aerospace Industry," *Review of Black Political Economy* 23 (3): 91–101 (Winter 1995).

14. Tom Smith, "Intergroup Relations in Contemporary America: An Overview of Survey Research," in Wayne Winborne and Renae Cohen, eds., *Intergroup Relations in the United States: Research Perspectives* [Bloomsburg, PA: Hadden Craftsmen, Inc. for the National Conference for Community and Justice, 1998), p. 151.

15. *Los Angeles Times,* November 7, 1996, p. A29, Although a large majority of all minority groups opposed the proposition, they comprised only a quarter of the voters.

16. Smith, "Intergroup Relations in Contemporary America," pp. 113–115.

17. Tabulation by Michela Zonta of the Field Institute's California Poll, October 1–October 9, 1996.

18. Laurence Bobo and Ryan Smith, "Anti-Poverty Policy, Affirmative Action, and Racial Attitudes," in S. Danzinger, G. Sandefur, and D. Weinberg, eds., *Confronting Poverty: Prescriptions for Change* (New York: Russell Sage Foundation, and Cambridge, MA: Harvard University Press, 1994), pp. 365–395; Dan Morain, "The Times Poll: 60 Percent of State's Voters Say They Back Prop. 209," *Los Angeles Times,* September 19, 1996, p. Al.

19. Smith, "Intergroup Relations in Contemporary America," p. 144.

20. University of Houston Center for Public Policy and Rice University's Baker Institute for Public Policy, cited in Julie Mason, *Houston Chronicle,* October 2,1997.

21. Chinese for Affirmative Action and Equal Rights Advocates, "Opportunities Lost: The State of Public Sector Affirmative Action in Post-Proposition 209 California" (San Francisco: Chinese for Affirmative Action and Equal Rights Advocates, 1998).

22. Based on statements of intent to register as reported by the University of California, Office of the President (*www.ucop.edu/ucophome/commserv/admissions/sirtable2.html).*

23. www.ucop.edn/ncophome/commserv/medenroll/98enroll.html.

The Rebirth of Rainbow Politics in California

ROBERT STANLEY ODEN

On October 7, 2003 two distinct and historic political events occurred. One was the recall of California governor Gray Davis and the election of Arnold Schwarzenegger, which garnered the majority of the media attention. The other was the overwhelming victory of the No on 54 campaign, resulting in the defeat of the measure that would have banned the collection of racial and ethnic data in areas of health, education, law enforcement, and civil rights enforcement.

The recall election was a mobilization of the California populace from the center to the right, and the No on 54 campaign was a mobilization of the California populace from the center to the left. The recall election was fueled by the conservative forces in and out of the state, while the No on 54 campaign was led by progressive forces assisted by mainstream political consultants. Both campaigns had to define a message and frame it for media electoral consumption. For Schwarzenegger and the recall forces that message involved political change from a corrupt Gray Davis administration. For the No on 54 forces, the message focused on the defeat of the information ban on health-related data and other pertinent data in education, law enforcement and civil rights compliance. Both messages resonated with the voting populace.

However, while the recall of Gray Davis became a political tidal wave for Arnold Schwarzenegger, funded by top corporate dollars and embedded with former California governor Pete Wilson operatives, the No on 54 campaign came from out of nowhere. That campaign overwhelmingly defeated the Yes on 54 Racial Privacy Initiative that became the Classification by Race, Ethnicity, and National Origin Initiative. The final vote was impressive: 64% voted No and only 36% voting Yes. The success of the No on 54 campaign was due to its grassroots, multicultural character. Also significant was the Internet-driven campaign coordinated by Coalition for an Informed California, and Californians for Justice. And a major boost to the campaign was the infusion of $3 million plus for media publicity, funds that came from the Indian tribes who were funding Lieutenant Governor Cruz Bustamante's campaign to become governor if the effort to recall Gray Davis were to succeed. After a heated dispute over the allocation of the money, Bustamante's campaign was ordered by the state court to not use funds donated by the Indian tribes because of the fact that he had tried to keep the funds in a prior campaign fund. This money was then used to promote the No on 54 campaign in commercials featuring Bustamante. While these commercials did much to publicize the No on 54 message, it was the grassroots, multiethnic effort that was the significant factor which led to the defeat of Proposition 54. This grassroots effort was broadly based and highly inclusive, involving organized labor, non-profit organizations, racial advocacy groups from the NAACP, to MALDEF to the many Asian American organizations throughout the state.

Several major political forces were significant in defeating Proposition 54: (1) Coalition for an Informed California based in Los Angeles, and Californians for Justice out of Oakland provided literature and information through the Internet which kept progressive forces connected, (2) Organized labor particularly in Sacramento, after realizing the connection between defeating the recall and defeating Proposition 54 decided to release its resources to the No on 54 campaign, (3) Grassroots efforts by organizations that spanned the array of racial ethnicities in California and (4) Strong support in the form of media advertisements from the Indian communities through the use of gaming revenue for campaign purposes.

The forces within the No on 54 campaign articulated a discourse that was both oppositional and mainstream. These two discourses kept the Proposition 54 proponents off-guard in futile attempts to respond to these discourses, which ultimately framed the defeat of Proposition 54. The oppositional discourse was directed at Ward Connerly, one of the authors of Proposition 54. Connerly has been a lightning rod to progressive forces since his successful campaign to end affirmative action through U.C. Regent actions and passage of Proposition 209 the ballot measure ending so-called racial preferences in hiring, education, etc. It was evident to many in the progressive community that passage of the then Racial Privacy Initiative would have put the civil rights and social justice agenda up in flames. The discourse evident with the No on 54 campaign was essentially the importance of not turning back the clock on civil rights, but instead fighting for an end to the assault on group rights. The oppositional discourse was important in mobilizing and informing the base of minority and liberal and progressive supporters, for it explained the ways in which Proposition 54 was another step by the conservative right to further its agenda. In this case, the agenda would involve eliminating the basis for enforcing the equality of life chances for millions of Californians who are of color, as well as millions more who were women or individuals with specialized medical and education needs.

The focus of the No on 54 campaign on the medical implications of the passage of the "information ban" was the centerpiece of the mainstream discourse that utilized to inform Californians of the deleterious aspects of Proposition 54 as they related in health matters. The initiative stated that it would exempt "medical research" from the information ban, but at the same time left it clear that statistics kept by health authorities at the county level and state level would not be exempt. This would efficiently exclude such information as that indicating the high rate of African Americans contracting asthma because they live close to an oil refinery, or data related to breast cancer rates for women of any race but particularly those races and ethnicities that are underrepresented in health care systems. This mainstream discourse was articulated by many in the health professions, including the California Medical Association, the California Nurses Association, Kaiser Permanente, and other health care providers, as well as county and state health care officials who came out in opposition to 54. The No on 54 campaign was winning the hearts and minds of middle-class suburban Californians because the information ban was seen as going too far particularly in the area of health. This was evident in a "lobbying day" activity at the State Capitol when the author was involved in a conversation between a group of No on 54 advocates and the Chief of Staff of Republican and Minority Leader Dave Cox. The Chief of Staff stated that Assemblyman Cox was also concerned with the ban on information as it related to health because the Asssemblyman had personal issues related to the need for health information. The subsequent silence from this powerful Republican as well as from others in his party helped spell the doom of this measure.

Both of these discourses evolved as the campaign became fully engaged in those hectic three months from the time it was clear that the recall election was going to get certified and a date was established as October 7, 2003. It was, however, the force of the oppositional discourse that was most significant in the victory to defeat Proposition 54, a discourse that was well organized by multiracial and trans-ethnic cooperation. In Sacramento, as well as elsewhere, progressive forces used an oppositional discourse to energize individuals and groups in their respective communities. Each racial and ethnic group shared a similar fate if Proposition 54 passed. The information ban focused on no single color or ethnicity. In Sacramento and other communities, coalitions were forming in order to defeat 54. The oppositional discourse was that of defeating the right-wing forces that brought the state into an anti-affirmative action environment. The oppositional discourse focused on Connerly's assertion of the need for a color-blind society, and contrasted Connerly's assertion, to the risk of setting civil rights in California back to the pre 1954 days before *Brown* v. *Board of Education.*

At the statewide level, fundraising was occurring that would help build a media-focused campaign. Working alongside the Coalition for an Informed California was a group out of Oakland called Californians for Justice. They had been involved in local organizing efforts and connected directly to other social justice organizations and individuals. The statewide steering committee was directed by seasoned social movement individuals and legal minds, which included, Attorney Eva Paterson of the Equal Justice Society, who along with others directed fund-raising efforts that exceeded $4 million. Attorney Paterson also debated Connerly and proved to be an influential spokesperson for the No on 54 forces.

In Sacramento as in other California communities, the local group (United Sacramento Citizens Against the Information Ban) worked closely with the Sacramento Central Labor Council. The labor council donated office space, which included phone bank lines. Our committee, as well as others organized fundraisers and distributed information about the proposition. More than 50 volunteers came out of communities as well as from labor organizing, staffed phone banks at our locations, and there were also other phone-bank operations occurring at various sites throughout the city. There was no rivalry between organizations, only multi-racial cooperation focused on the goal of defeating Proposition 54. This occurred throughout the state, because progressive organizations in communities of color knew that this issue would affect each organization regardless of race or ethnicity. Evidence of this cooperation were demonstrated in the reports given in weekly conference call sessions sponsored by the steering committee made up of statewide activists, led by Josh Pulliam an attorney and statewide coordinator of the No on 54 campaign. It was clear that this type of multi-racial and multi-cultural cooperation happened across the state, for these calls included numerous reports of campaign efforts, ranging from voter registration to fund-raising to precinct walking to phone banking, as well as various other efforts.

Ward Connerly and his right-wing forces provided an opportunity for a rainbow coalition of interests to come together, and to succeed in defeating Proposition 54. It was the grassroots forces that turned the election around, with the assistance from the statewide steering committee. In July 2003 the polls stated that 50% of the registered population was voting Yes on Proposition 54 (*Sacramento Bee,* August 19, 2003). It also indicated that four out of five persons did not know about Proposition 54. By early September those figures changed dramatically, with No on 54 in a statistical deadheat with Yes on 54 at 40% each. During that time period there was very little statewide advertising on No on 54 campaign. Grassroots publicity and organizing against 54 was primarily conducted by local organizations such as the one in Sacramento and other groups such as the NAACP, ACLU, the National Lawyers Guild and many other local groups, which put their reputations, resources and money against this measure.

The results of the victory on Proposition 54 were stunning. The exit poll data from the *Los Angeles Times (Los Angeles Times,* October 9, 2003) provides the magnitude of the victory:

No on 54—Democrats—80%
Independents—64%
Republicans—44%
Whites—62%
Blacks—88%

Latinos—75%
Asians—75%
Union household—68%
Nonunion household—62%
White men—58%
White women—65%
First time voters—66%

An overwhelming number of California counties (54 out of 58) voted No on 54. The only counties that voted Yes on 54 were in the Sierra foothills and Lassen county. The above categories only represent a few of the categories in which a majority vote went for voting No on 54.

This was a widespread victory across the board, and represents a new beginning for racial and ethnic politics in California. While the mainstream discourse of the dangers of banning information related to health was an important factor in defeating Proposition 54, it is clear that the oppositional discourse utilized by progressive grassroots organizations and forces brought about a multi-racial, multicultural victory. This victory provides an opportunity to maintain the contacts developed during the campaign. Organizations that became energized in the fight against 54 are staying energized through the early stages of the Schwarzenegger administration. As this governor attempts to eliminate health, education, and social programs that are vital to the state's ability to enhance opportunities to communities of color and the poor in California as opposed to sharing the budget deficit with the state's wealthiest citizens, these groups are taking concerted and continued actions.

The battle for a California that will reflect the vast multicultural landscape continues to be waged. But with a victory over the Connerly-led right-wing forces by the progressive, labor and communities of color bods well for future battles in California.

Bibliography

Los Angeles Times, "Time Exit Poll Results," October 9, 2003, www.latimes.com/news/localAa-me-pagea26top-pr9oct09155420,1,855505.story

Sacramento Bee, "Proposition 54 Poll Gap Narrows," August 8, 2003, Jim Sanders, www.sacbee.com/conte...tics/recall/story/7253443p-8198484c.html

——, Backing Sags in Poll for Prop. 54," September 11, 2003, Dan Smith, p. A3.

——, "48% in Poll Back Racial Data Measure," April 23, 2003, Dan Smith, p. A4

The Third World Left
Today and Contemporary
Activism

LAURA PULIDO

P
roposition 187; Rodney King and the 1992 uprising; Justice
for Janitors; the Bus Riders' Union; the Hahn/Villaraigosa
election; Three Strikes; Black-Korean tensions; globalization...[1]
These are just some of the key events and processes that have
created the contemporary political and economic landscape of Southern
California. To what extent, if any, are these developments related to the
1960s and 1970s? What role might Third World Leftists have played
in them? While the world, and Southern California in particular, has
changed greatly over the last three decades, there are clear connections
between the past and the present, although they are not always recognized.
The media, for example, persist in portraying the sixties as the space of
radical activism, thereby erasing any connection to contemporary efforts.[2]
This is, of course, partly due to the countercultural moment of the sixties,
which marked activism with a particular aesthetic,[3] but it is also due to
political and economic changes. Activists in the New Left, Third World
Left, and New Communist movement routinely talked about revolution,
believing it was an actual possibility. In contrast, few talk about revolution
today, and communism has largely been discredited. Indeed, the very term
Third World has lost much of its currency. In short, material conditions
have changed greatly. What was possible or even regarded as possible in

the 1960s is not necessarily so today. While there are continuities with the past, including ongoing struggles against racism, poverty, U.S. militarism, and police abuse, there are also new challenges posed by the end of the Cold War, globalization, and heightened tensions between communities of color. In this chapter I examine contemporary activism in Los Angeles and assess where members of the Third World Left are today. I conclude with some general lessons to be learned from the experiences of the Third World Left.

While the participants of the Third World Left have changed a good deal, few have joined the corporate world or adopted right-wing politics. As Max Elbaum has observed, "[M]ost ex-party builders [builders of parties of the New Communist movement] did not retreat completely into private life or transfer allegiance to any antileft political trend. Rather, they gradually and almost invisibly meshed into the country's amorphous progressive milieu."[4] In terminology indicative of how things have changed, contemporary social justice activists identify as progressives rather than revolutionaries. This trend is certainly apparent in Los Angeles, where former members of the Third World Left are actively involved in politics, organizing, and community service. Even though the movement itself has collapsed, its legacy and impact can be seen in the greater empowerment of people of color, as well as in the coalitions and organizations forged out of the experiences and networks of that era.

Equally important have been the personal legacy and impact of the movement for individuals. Activists' participation in the Third World Left was also an intense process of personal transformation. Some people emerged from the process damaged and bitter, and in some cases tensions are still being played out by various factions. But many others were greatly empowered and have become highly productive members of society.

Upon the demise of the Third World Left, individuals focused on rebuilding their lives, making a living, and tending to their families.[5] This was an especially difficult time politically because the seventies were followed by the eighties, a period of intense conservatism in which the embers of the left were finally buried. However, as the eighties progressed, growing economic tensions and new forms of oppression, such as homelessness, immigrant bashing, and the rise of the prison-industrial complex, led to a new wave of grassroots mobilization. This work began bearing fruit in the 1990s. Not surprisingly, former members of the Third World Left, with their commitment to racial and economic justice, played important roles in these new projects. Such individuals, who carry with them a wealth of experience, have contributed actively to Los Angeles's rich political infrastructure, helping it to become one of the leading sites of progressive activism in the United States today.[6]

The current crop of progressive organizations differs from those of earlier times not only because this is a different historical moment but also because many activists have consciously tried to learn from past mistakes. Table 11.1 provides a partial list of contemporary Los Angeles organizations with a connection to the Third World Left, either through key individuals or, in some cases, through their emergence from previous organizations.

A review of what the former members of the Third World Left are currently doing challenges the widely held belief that radical politics is the province of the young. Though few can maintain the all-encompassing commitment that revolutionary politics requires, such thinking reduces activism to a youthful pursuit and prevents us from appreciating how political commitment and work may change over the course of a life. Although the specific outcomes and trajectories of activists' lives varied greatly, patterns can still be discerned among racial/ethnic groups. These differing patterns provide a glimpse into how Southern California's racial and class structure has evolved over time and highlight the changing political landscape.

TABLE 11.1 Partial list of contemporary Los Angeles organizations with links to the Third World Left

Action for Grassroots Empowerment and Neighborhood Development Alternatives (AGENDA)
Asian Pacific American Labor Alliance (APALA)
California Nurses Association
Coalition Against Police Abuse (CAPA)
Community Coalition for Substance Abuse Prevention and Treatment
Community Service Organization (CSO)
Community Youth Sports & Arts Foundation
Families to Amend California's Three Strikes (FACTS)
Great Leap
Hermandad Mexicana Nacional
Hotel Employees and Restaurant Employees Union (HERE)[1]
Japanese American Community Services—Asian Involvement
Labor/Community Strategy Center
Liberty Hill Foundation
National Coalition for Redress and Reparations (NCRR)
The New Black Panther Party
One-Stop Immigration
Visual Communications (VC)

Source: Compiled by author.

[1]Merged with the Union of Needletrades, Textiles, and Industrial Employees in 2004 to form UNITE HERE

The Third World Left at the Dawn of the Twenty-First Century

Although the people I interviewed for this project were engaged in a wide variety of pursuits, most were still politically active. Many were involved in full-time political work, whether as politicians, organizers, community workers, artists, or fund-raisers, in a wide range of sectors, including labor, youth, arts, civil rights, immigrant advocacy, police abuse, and ethnic-specific work. Others became teachers, civil servants, journalists, and administrators—careers that allowed them to pursue community activism on the side or as part of the job. Still others had redefined the nature of political activism and now contributed to the community through spiritual work and healing. No one was engaged in work that was antithetical to his or her earlier beliefs and practices.[7] Further, though most were aware of the limitations and weaknesses of the Third World Left, no one renounced it. Rather, most appreciated that it reflected a particular place and time and were thankful that they had been part of it.

Despite the diversity of careers and lifestyles that former activists assumed, there were clear patterns reflecting racial and class differences. For instance, Asian Americans were most likely to become professionals and continue their activist work in that capacity. In contrast, former Panthers struggled the most financially and sometimes emotionally. Not only were they, in the words of one activist, "the walking wounded," but their limited class mobility reflected the barriers that working-class Blacks still face. Members of CASA tended to have the primary objective of working for or with organized labor. Many eventually earned college degrees, and the labor movement itself became a vehicle for upward mobility.

CASA

Because of CASA's focus on workers, a significant percentage of the membership decided to concentrate on changing labor laws. According to one interviewee, "In CASA we were all committed to doing work for workers, which also meant most of us were going to go to law school, to work for the unions. That was the goal, to work for unions, and to do it from a legal standpoint." This was not idle talk. Although former members of CASA followed a variety of paths, including acting and work in academe and foundations, a highly visible contingent entered the labor movement. Some became involved with worker and immigration projects, such as Hermandad Mexicana Nacional and One-Stop Immigration, but many others worked for unions and went on to become labor lawyers and/or politicians aligned with the labor movement. Today there is a dense network of ties between former members of CASA who either are involved in labor itself or directly support it through legal services, foundations, progressive legislation, and community/worker services and alliances.

Although CASA never succeeded in functioning as the vanguard of the revolution, its members have been instrumental in the re-creation of a progressive labor movement in Los Angeles. When CASA began in the 1970s the national labor movement was spiraling downward, and it bottomed out when Ronald Reagan fired striking air-traffic controllers in 1980. Moreover, immigrant workers were still considered peripheral to any organizing effort. Thus there was limited institutional support for CASA's goals. Unions were indifferent, or even hostile, to the needs of such workers, and there was little public support for organized labor. Third World Left and especially Chicana/o organizations, despite their small size and marginality, were some of the few advocates for immigrant workers.

By the 1990s things had changed considerably. Organized labor, led primarily by the service unions, began to refocus on organizing workers and reaching out to a rapidly changing labor force increasingly composed of women, immigrants, and workers of color. As a result, low-wage service unions, led by groups such as Justice for Janitors and the Hotel Employees and Restaurant Employees Union (HERE), began winning some highly visible contracts and contributed to a growing sense of labor militancy that has profoundly affected not only workers' lives but the larger political culture of Southern California.[8]

One of the factors that contributed to this political shift was demographic change. Over the last several decades Southern California has been transformed by massive immigration from Latin America and Asia. Whereas in 1970 Latinas/os were 14.6 percent of Los Angeles County's population, they registered 45 percent in 2000 (see table 11.2). As a result, the Latina/o population is rapidly growing, while the white and Black populations are diminishing through outmigration and lower fertility rates. Such changes have profound implications for the racial and class structure of the region. Specifically, Los Angeles County has become the U.S. capital of the working poor, who are composed overwhelmingly of Latina/o immigrants. In effect, there has been a growing racial and class overlap in Los Angeles's working class: the poor are increasingly nonwhite and the wealthy are disproportionately white.[9]

TABLE 11.2 Los Angeles County population by race/ethnicity and poverty, 2000

Racial/Ethnic Group	% of Total Population	% beneath Poverty Line
Latino	45.0	24.2
White	31.0	8.5
Asian American	12.0	14.2
African American	9.5	24.4
American Indian	0.3	22.5

Source: United Way, *A Tale of Two Cities* (Los Angeles: United Way of Greater Los Angeles, 2003), 11; United Way, 2003 *State of the County Report* (Los Angeles: United Way of Greater Los Angeles, 2003), 32.

Complementing these demographic and economic changes, particularly the proliferation of low-wage work, Los Angeles boasted a contingent of labor activists who had historically focused on low-wage and immigrant labor. These people did not have to be convinced that people of color, women, and immigrants should be the focal point of any union strategy: they had been talking about and trying to promote such issues for the previous twenty years, even when organized labor had dismissed such workers as unorganizable and persisted in myopically focusing on white male workers.

One of the more prominent such activists is María Elena Durazo, the president of HERE, Local 11. After CASA collapsed she began working for the International Ladies Garment Workers Union, an experience that showed her firsthand the transformative capacity of collective action among workers. After several years there she attended the People's College of Law and worked part time at a labor law firm that represented HERE's Local 11. This connection eventually led to a job as an organizer with the local. Unfortunately, at that time Local 11 was racist and not committed to rank- and-file leadership and democracy. "In L.A. labor's prize moment of idiocy, the leadership of the Hotel Employees and Restaurant Employees Union spent $100,000 in a 1984 lawsuit to ensure union meetings would *not* be translated into Spanish for their membership—70% of whom were Latino."[10] Sensing the untapped potential of the local, Durazo ran for office and was elected president. Besides radically reorienting the organization to meet the needs of its members, Durazo has made Local 11, like Justice for Janitors, a model of the new social movement unionism, which stresses community-labor links, direct action, democracy, and worker leadership.[11]

Although Durazo is remarkable, she did not accomplish this alone. She has effected such changes partly by her participation in a series of networks and relationships focused on a shared goal: to build a vibrant and relevant labor movement that serves the needs of low-income and immigrant workers and workers of color. These networks, a history of working together, and a sense of trust are vital to the development of effective political cultures. Such political cultures do not evolve overnight but are built out of earlier organizing efforts and relationships.[12] Former members of CASA had created not only a network of like-minded people but seeds of resistance within the "old" labor movement that would blossom with the advent of greater institutional support.

East Wind

Most members of East Wind became professionals and continued their political involvement either through their occupations or in a volunteer capacity. Full-time activists were concentrated in community service, labor, and progressive Democratic politics, while those who had pursued less activist-oriented careers, including public sector work, still participated as volunteers in the above sectors, as well as alternative radio, youth work, healing, and teaching. Only one interviewee consciously chose to remain close to his working-class roots, despite a college degree. In keeping with the larger politics of East Wind, most were still involved in the Japanese American community, but they also engaged in pan-Asian work and often interracial work.

Just as CASA made a significant impact on the contemporary labor movement, East Wind was highly influential in the Japanese American struggle for redress arid reparations. The two organizations differ, however, in that members of CASA entered the labor movement because of a set of shared commitments and a clearly defined goal. In contrast, former members of East Wind joined the League of Revolutionary Struggle (LRS), which only later became involved in the quest for redress.[13] Although not all of East Wind joined, many members did, so that the activists were able to remain fairly consolidated politically. Because the LRS's political ideology emphasized working with the most oppressed nationalities and sectors, many Japanese Americans ended up working in Chicana/o labor campaigns, such as the Watsonville strike, or in Black communities. While most Japanese Americans embraced such work, over time some resented not being able to spend more time among the Nikkei population, as the LRS did not consider Japanese Americans to be among the most oppressed. However, when Japanese Americans brought the nascent struggle for redress and reparations to the league's attention, the LRS, seeing the potential significance of the issue, decided to rally behind it. As a result, former members of East Wind working through the LRS played a prominent role in the pursuit for reparations by working with the National Coalition for Redress and Reparations.

The campaign for redress and reparations was highly significant. It was a huge step forward for a community that still struggled with the shame of internment and dealt with it primarily by repressing its past. Consequently the initial struggle for redress was internal, as many mainstream Japanese Americans opposed the idea. Not only did the idea seem utterly implausible but many were uncomfortable with making such demands on society As one internee explained, "I never thought it would happen. My attitude was 'I'll believe it when I see it.' I didn't think people were sympathetic, or saw it as a hardship, or that they would even be sorry. You know, they told us that it [internment] was for our own good." This is where the leadership of revolutionary activists was so instrumental. As people used to thinking outside the box and armed with the discipline to conceive and carry out a long-term campaign, activists began shifting the discourse and attitudes of the larger Japanese American community, while at the same time making connections with potential allies. Having built this kind of base, they were then able to take the struggle to the U.S. public. At last, President Reagan, in one of his finer moments, offered a formal apology and authorized monetary reparations to internees in 1988.[14]

The Japanese American pursuit of redress and reparations was a milestone in the struggle for democracy and civil rights among U.S. people of color. This was one of the few times that the U.S. government acknowledged that it had violated the civil and human rights of a racial/ethnic minority group and offered monetary compensation. While $20,000, the amount given to internees, could never compensate for what they had lost and suffered, it was an important step in attempting to heal an open wound, as well as a move toward reconciliation and a reminder to us all of the precarious nature of freedom. The campaign for redress and reparations has become a model that other racial/ethnic groups have studied in an effort to address past grievances, including the current movement for slave reparations.[15]

While Japanese Americans continue to be active in Nikkei struggles, much of their activism has shifted toward the larger Asian/Pacific Islander (A/PI) community. This has become necessary because the A/PI population has diversified tremendously and the Nikkei continue to decline. As recently as 1970 Japanese Americans were the largest Asian American group in the region, but today they are one of the smallest. Since the 1965 Immigration Act, Chinese immigrants have been coming to Southern California in record numbers, as have Filipinas/os, Koreans, and Vietnamese, all of whom now have larger populations than Japanese Americans. Further, the Japanese American population is declining, some say vanishing, due to intermarriage, as members are marrying whites, Latinas/os, Blacks, and especially other Asians in unprecedented numbers. In addition, Southern California Nikkei have continued to prosper economically and socially so that their income now rivals that of whites. Accordingly, while Japanese American activists still take on important community issues, such as the current struggle for a recreational center in Little Tokyo, they frequently focus on other Asian American groups when it comes to issues of class and poverty.[16]

Regardless of such shifts, Japanese Americans remain extremely important to the political landscape of Los Angeles. Because of their long history in the region, Japanese Americans have one of the most established community service traditions among A/PIs. One of the results of the Asian American movement of the 1960s and 1970s was the development of a whole series of Asian American-oriented social services. Originally built primarily, but not exclusively, by Japanese Americans, these social service organizations have long since diversified to serve a more varied and immigrant-oriented population. Many of these organizations are still led by Japanese Americans, a fact that is at times the cause of resentment but also illustrates the historical significance of this population.

The Black Panther Party

The experience of former Panthers is markedly different from that of either East Wind or CASA. In general, the lives of Panthers followed more divergent paths: Some attained national prominence, others emerged as community leaders, while still others endured material, emotional, and physical hardships. At the national level this diversity of outcomes precludes any generalizations: Assata Shakur lives in Cuba; Mumia Abu-Jamal sits on Death Row; Eldridge Cleaver became a political conservative before his death; Kathleen Cleaver is a lawyer and academic; Elaine Brown married a French industrialist; Ericka Huggins teaches yoga to educators; Angela Davis is a prominent academic; David Hilliard has sought to preserve the history of the party; Bobby Seale hawks barbecue sauce; and Huey Newton was murdered in a drug deal in 1989. While a degree of sensationalism has been attached to prominent Panthers, such has rarely been the case for the rank and file. Instead, many struggle with unresolved issues stemming from betrayals on the part of the party, the collapse of the Black Panther Party (BPP) itself, and physical and emotional problems stemming from their experiences of violence. In addition, the general poverty and limited education of much of the rank and file have prevented many Panthers from entering the middle class, in distinct contrast to Chicana/o and Asian American activists.

The differing trajectories and outcomes of activists' lives constituted one of the most pronounced differences that I found in this study. This had implications for whom I was able to contact and how they responded to me For instance, given that many CASA members were associated with organized labor, they were relatively easy to track down, and many (except for some prominent politicians) consented to an interview. Moreover, as a Chicana, I knew some of the activists from before the project and was able to interview some highly visible CASA members early on, making contacts that in turn facilitated subsequent interviews. Asian American activists were fairly easy to locate, as they were embedded in relatively visible institutions. In addition, the small size and close-knit nature of the Japanese American community made it easy to identify potential interviewees.[17] But because Japanese Americans were so rooted in mainstream institutions, they were more reluctant to talk.

While some may have been wary of an outsider, others did not wish to share this chapter of their lives. Indeed, some of those who consented to an interview requested anonymity, and one actually withdrew permission to use any material from the interview upon seeing the transcript. Even accounting for my outsider status, these experiences suggest some ambivalence among Asian American members regarding their past.

And then there were the Panthers. Finding Los Angeles Panthers was a difficult task. This was partly due to my lack of familiarity with the African American community, as well as the fact that only a handful of Southern California Panthers had become famous or highly institutionalized. Although it was relatively easy to find and contact high-profile people like Michael Zinzun of the Coalition Against Police Abuse, most Panthers were more difficult to reach, as few were attached to formal institutions. I had a major breakthrough, however, when Geronimo Pratt was released from prison in 1997. To commemorate this event, UCLA convened a forum that former Panthers attended and at which I was able to make some initial contacts. Although many Panthers were initially suspicious of me—I was asked more than once if I was with the FBI—I found that although I was a Chicana with no history in their community, there was some willingness to share their stories. Rank-and-file Panthers were painfully aware that dominant narratives of the BPP were written by party leaders or outsiders and did not necessarily reflect their experiences—which they wanted known.

Equally important, however, are the Panthers that I was *not* able to interview because they were either dead or incarcerated. No organization experienced the level of political repression that the Panthers did, and the toll can be seen in the casualties. Ward Churchill, in his analysis of state repression, found that more Panthers had been killed by the police in Los Angeles than in any other city.[18] While many Panthers were guilty of a variety of crimes, both violent and nonviolent, many were also framed and imprisoned by the state in an effort to destroy the party. One of the best examples of this is Geronimo Pratt (now known as geronimo ji Jaga), who was convicted of the 1968 murder of a white, female schoolteacher on a Santa Monica tennis court. Evidence was withheld that would have exonerated Pratt, suggesting that the state had an ulterior motive in his conviction. Specifically, the FBI had a wiretap that placed Pratt in Oakland at the time of the murder, but because of the state's desire to eliminate Pratt he ended up serving twenty-seven years for a crime he did not commit.[19] Accordingly, many former Panthers are currently in prison, or have served time in prison, which greatly affects one's life chances.

While some of the Panthers I interviewed had completed college and become professionals, others were working in community service and/or full-time activism, while still others were just barely making it, trying to keep mind, body, and soul together. There are several reasons why former Panthers have had a harder time rebuilding their lives. For one, virtually all of the Panthers that I interviewed came from low-income working-class families. Many people from such backgrounds, regardless of their political involvement, have had a difficult time "making it" in the United States, as they must contend with inferior schools, high rates of unemployment, residential segregation, and police repression. However, these were not ordinary residents from South Central—they had been Panthers, and, as such, they had been in a state of war. Consequently, they bore many of the marks of those who have experienced intense conflict, including post-traumatic stress disorder, physical disabilities, shattered relationships, and a limited educational background and marketable set of skills.

Also contributing to the hardships that many former Panthers faced were racial and economic shifts. Many suspected, and there is considerable evidence to support the charge, that significantly more drugs began flowing into communities of color, especially Black communities, in the early 1980s. Some believed that this was the government's last attempt to stifle the political unrest that had been fermenting for decades, despite the fact that it was already in decline. Consequently, many poor communities were devastated by the waves of crack that hit the ghetto in the 1980s and the gangs that developed to manage its sale and distribution.[20]

In addition to the erosion of the social infrastructure that accompanied the crack epidemic, Black Los Angeles underwent increasing social, spatial, economic fragmentation. Although the process of class polarization began in earnest in the late 1960s, it accelerated greatly, exacerbated by the rise of gang warfare and the drug epidemic. Middle-class and professional Blacks found increasing opportunities in the service sector, both public and private, but low-income Blacks found fewer opportunities as the last remnants of the Fordist economy disappeared in the 1980s.[21] The subsequent "post-Fordist" economy was characterized by greater flexibility (read: less job security), a decline of the welfare state, an expansion of the service sector, heightened economic polarization, and vastly expanded incarceration Some argue that such hardships have been intensified by greater economic competition from Latina/o immigrants, who are the preferred source of low-wage labor in the region.[22]

In response to these changes, many Blacks began leaving South Central to start a new life at the edges of Southern California. Places such as Riverside, San Bernardino, and Antelope Valley promised affordable housing and the chance to escape the problems of South Central. As a result, Los Angeles's Black population is declining relative to other groups.[23] Although African Americans are still a prominent force in Los Angeles, the community is painfully aware of what the future holds: a majority Latina/o city. Not surprisingly, many Blacks, particularly the older population, seek to cling to the past. This was evident in the 2001 mayoral race between Antonio Villaraigosa and James Hahn. Villaraigosa, a pro-labor Democrat with a long history of multiracial involvement and coalition building, lost to Hahn, a mainstream Democrat. James Hahn, the son of the legendary Kenneth Hahn, a white Los Angeles politician famous for his antiracist politics, captured the older Black vote by appealing to his father's legacy. The fact that so many African Americans would vote for the candidate who seemingly did not best represent their interests—James Hahn's record is weak at best—suggests their anxiety about the future.[24]

Los Angeles, like many other places, is in dire need of a politics and leadership that marginalized low-income residents, immigrants, and communities of color can mobilize around. This is a challenge, particularly in light of recent immigration, which has been so vast and concentrated that people have not had adequate time to adjust and learn each other's stories. Without such an incorporation process, immigrant bashing becomes more likely, as does the possibility of immigrants embracing a national racial order that denigrates African Americans. In many ways, this is one of the great challenges facing the United States: How will the racial formation be reconfigured by vast numbers of nonwhite immigrants? Developing a common framework is not easy because progressive political visions and movements don't just "happen." Rather, they are cultivated by efforts at both the grassroots and leadership levels to bring diverse communities together and to articulate sufficiently broad identities so that various groups can support each other without feeling threatened. But just as Los Angeles offers many challenges to the development of a broad-based movement for social justice, it offers many possibilities. If Los Angeles is able to forge such a movement, particularly one involving recent Asian and Latina/o immigrants, it could make a real impact on the city and serve as a model for other places.

One crucial aspect of the dynamics shaping Los Angeles is globalization. Globalization, the growing integration of capital, commodities, and people across the world, has become a major concern over the past decade, as it presents both challenges and opportunities. For the most part, we have seen a race to the bottom, as many places seek to attract capital by offering conditions that maximize profits. Yet we have also seen moments when pressure is applied to bring the wages, working conditions, and legal rights of impoverished and oppressive countries up to the standards of more prosperous ones.[25] Many observers treat globalization as an unprecedented shift ushering in a new historical era. They are both right and wrong. Although a new round of globalization may be occurring, globalization itself is hardly new. Equally profound moments of globalization occurred, for example, in 1492, or when the first shipment of African slaves arrived in the United States. In addition to such historical caveats, we must consider the geographical dimensions of globalization: globalization plays out differently across space. And given that Los Angeles is considered a "global city," with elements of both the "First World" and the "Third World," it has a distinctive character.[26] For instance, in Los Angeles, as in many other "First World" cities, labor activists must contend with industries threatening to relocate to Latin America and Asia, while at the same time activists are incorporating new populations like Mixtec immigrants into their organizing work, as large parcels of the Los Angeles landscape and economy belong to the "Third World." Thus in many ways globalization has created a new framework for activism that differs markedly from that of the 1960s and 1970s. Despite the unprecedented circumstances, however, there are continuities with the past, and most importantly, lessons to be learned. On the basis of this research as well as my own activism, I have identified the following key lessons from the Third World Left that can hopefully assist in movement building in a new era.

Four Lessons of the Third World Left

Democracy and Nonviolence

Despite its commitment to forging a more humane and socially just world, the Third World Left often fell short of its goal. Instead, it was plagued by violent, undemocratic, and abusive practices.

There are many reasons for this including the youth of the activists, the romance of violence and guns, the previous street experience of some activists, and harassment from law enforcement. The lack of a democratic culture manifested itself in several ways and seriously weakened the movement. One of the most debilitating characteristics was the cult of personality, in which leading political figures (usually men) with strong charismatic personalities unduly influenced group opinion, coerced others into supporting their agenda, and sometimes became almost revered.[27] While charismatic leaders often draw additional resources and attention to an organization, they also can stifle the leadership potential of others and create resentment on the part of the larger membership.

Democracy also suffered from various practices adopted from Marxism/Leninism, including democratic centralism and self-criticism. Democratic centralism is a practice whereby decisions are openly debated but, once decided upon, are carried out by all members. Most members of the Third World Left (and the New Communist movement) adhered to some form of democratic centralism. Such a practice is useful insofar as it ensures that policies and decisions are executed and helps explain how a relatively small number of people could accomplish so much. But democratic centralism could also be problematic, particularly if the discussion had not been free and wide-ranging. Sometimes even *with* extensive debate, the leadership could and would decide on a course of action that was contrary to the desires of the membership. Such practices did not inspire confidence and helped account for high rates of turnover and disillusion.

Another potentially damaging practice was criticism and self-criticism. Again drawing from Marxism/Leninism, many organizations required individuals to identify their own shortcomings, as well as point out each others' weaknesses, which were to be reflected upon. Criticism and self-criticism were adopted to deal with a real problem: How to communicate shortcomings of comrades so that the unit might become more effective as a whole? This was a pressing issue for the Third World Left given its goal of revolution and the discipline required to achieve it. In my interviews, many indicated that though there might have been some occasional hurt feelings, criticism, carried out in the manner intended, was an effective tool. The problems began when individuals used criticism to express personal grudges and when patterns of criticism began to reflect larger group inequalities. This was most evident in terms of gender. In certain organizations not only were women more likely to be criticized than men, but, when men were criticized, they might acknowledge the concern with a mere "Yes, I hear you, sister," and no substantive change afterwards. This defeated the purpose of the exercise, contributed to resentment, and reproduced gender inequalities.[28]

Developing appropriate forms of democracy within a social change organization is no easy task, and the lack of a democratic culture was widespread throughout most movements of the time.[29] Though the Third World Left reflected the larger culture and its inequalities, it was *trying* to be better. Activists wanted to create a new and better world and saw themselves as the vehicle for doing so. This required a fairly high level of self-awareness (or at least it should have). The challenge of building more democratic, accountable, and humane organizations is something contemporary groups are still struggling with today, and some progress has been made. Many organizations now strive to develop the leadership potential of *all* individuals so that they are able to speak their minds without being cowed by more powerful figures. In addition, many recognize the necessity of open debate and collaborative decision making, as well as the need to implement mechanisms that ensure a system of checks and balances. One factor contributing to greater democracy and openness is the leadership of women, many of whom were politicized in the sixties and seventies.

Gender/Sexuality

Though I have been somewhat critical of the gender relations of the Third World Left, gender is one arena that has undergone great transformation. The Third World Left was largely patriarchal, but it nonetheless created some powerful female activists. Participation in the Third World Left empowered men and women as they learned how to organize, challenge established power structures, become leaders, and serve the community. In short, they developed a sense of themselves as effective people. Once these women came into their own and continued their political work after the demise of the movement, they not only refused to tolerate sexism but realized they had the capacity to create more democratic and participatory organizations. Even many of the men interviewed recognized the need for gender equality and had made some efforts toward that end in their current organizing work.

The shift toward greater gender equality is evident in several ways. Most apparent is the rise of female leadership. Whereas only a few organizations among the Third World Left were female led, it is now commonplace to find women serving as executive directors of progressive organizations. In some cases they started the organizations themselves, whereas in others they rose through the ranks or were subsequently hired as directors. Women have also introduced a more col that often promotes greater democracy. Indeed, research suggests that women invest in the development of the rank and file, develop more collective approa ing, and foster greater collaboration between organizations.[30] And even in m though to varying degrees, numerous men who emerged from the moveme seventies recognize the need to foster greater female participation and leadersh that patriarchy has vanished and that cases of sexual harassment and miscon within the activist community, but when they do, such behavior is understo Besides greater awareness among the leadership and a growing incorporation of gender analyses into organizational ideologies and training, young women today, who are a full generation removed from the Third World Left, are far less likely to tolerate the abuses that earlier activists did.[31]

Distinct but closely related to gender is sexuality, particularly homosexuality. Aside from declaring that it was the woman's revolutionary job to sleep with a brother, frank and open organizational discussions of sexuality were limited within the Third World Left, and homosexuality was largely taboo.[32] Ironically, just as the gay rights movement was blossoming and gays and lesbians were coming out of the closet, the Third World Left remained largely closed to such developments. In some cases homosexuals were actively shunned, as in struggles surrounding the participation of lesbians in International Women's Day, and at best they were expected to keep their sexual preferences quiet. Sexuality was certainly not seen as a struggle worth taking up.[33]

Fortunately, there has been some progress toward accepting queer activists within social justice organizations. In a few cases some groups have even developed a politics that includes the struggles of gays, lesbians, bisexuals, and transgendered persons. But these remain exceptions and there is still much work to be done. Far too often I have seen activists, especially young Latino and Black men, ridicule and dismiss queers and their struggle as irrelevant. This is not only cruel and insensitive but a political mistake. For only by building a broad united front of people who are working toward a shared set of goals will a dynamic movement for social change be created. Nationalist organizations in particular have remained ambivalent toward questions of gender, sexuality, and interethnic work.

Nationalism and Multiracial Politics

The Third World Left made significant progress in terms of interethnic cooperation. Although the relationships were not as deep as they might have been, this remains an important contribution that should be appreciated and built upon. Today many organizations in Los Angeles and nationally have created impressive models of multiracial activism, but many also resist it, preferring instead to focus on their own community.[34] The attraction to nationalism is understandable and has some merits insofar as it remains an important vehicle to politicize people, but it poses real political problems and challenges in demographically complex places like Los Angeles.

It is important to appreciate why oppressed people of color may favor nationalism as a political basis for mobilization. African Americans, especially low-income segments of the population, continue to face racism and segregation. Research and history indicate that race is still the most powerful basis for political consciousness among African Americans.[35] In addition, we must be sensitive to the fact that Black Angelenos are declining numerically and are confronting waning political power. These conditions help clarify why some Blacks may feel threatened and wish to focus on their own.

Latinas/os, namely Chicanas/os, also have a long history of nationalism, which, again, is understandable given how their identity and history have been erased by colonization, immigration, racism, and the "Americanization" process. Latinas/os' gravitation toward nationalist politics may intensify in the coming years, particularly as the children of immigrants grapple with difficult issues of identity, belonging, and exclusion in a society all too happy to dismiss them as criminals. Nationalist politics may also get a boost from the recent influx of Central American immigrants, who, understandably, wish to distinguish themselves from Mexicans.[36] These politics are especially complex in South Central Los Angeles, which has been transformed in recent years from a largely Black space to one that is half Latina/o. How the tension between nationalist and multinational politics will be resolved in such places is still uncertain.

A final factor to consider is the growing political power of Latinas/os. As Latinas/os begin to flex more political muscle, many of their politicians and activists have shown little interest in working with other communities of color, feeling secure in their ever-growing numbers—clearly a short-sighted view. The challenge for those interested in building a broad-based movement for social change is how to address the needs and fears that many people of color have, while at the same time working toward building a more integrated and ultimately internationalist movement.

Care must be taken not to dismiss nationalism out of hand. As Déborah Berman Santana has pointed out, not only are there multiple types of nationalism, but nationalism may be essential at particular historical moments and places.[37] So while nationalism may be entirely appropriate to the struggle of Puerto Ricans or native Hawaiians, I would argue it is not necessarily the most effective tool in contemporary Los Angeles, where multiple populations now share a potentially similar set of concerns and where the distribution of wealth and racial privilege will remain intact as long as those communities are divided. Anthony Thigpenn, a former Panther, explained, "Self-organization of a particular ethnicity or racial community can often be a legitimate form because the cultures and/or conditions of a particular community warrant that. But ... we cannot limit ourselves to organizing just one group of people, because our vision of society is broader than that. And, if we're trying to organize on a large scale to gain real power, I don't believe there's any one ethnicity that can do it by themselves."[38]

The need for political solidarity is particularly acute among Latinas/os and African Americans. In addition to sharing the same space and similar class positions, these two groups are most likely to be pitched against each other as they fight over political and economic crumbs. Latinas/os are fast becoming the largest group in Los Angeles (and increasingly in other major cities), yet African Americans have a deeper and more established political infrastructure. Latinas/os constitute the poorest population, but Blacks continue to face the most discrimination.[39] These two groups clearly have certain commonalities and could potentially form a powerful coalition for social change, one focused on economic justice, community development, immigrant rights, and opposition to police abuse and the prison-industrial complex. All organizations need not be actively involved in all issues, but they should be aware of and sensitive to the needs and concerns of similarly positioned groups and not view them as irrelevant or, worse, as the opposition. Fortunately, some organizations have sought to bring Blacks and Latinas/os together, including the Community Coalition for Substance Abuse Prevention and Treatment (www.ccsapt.org/), Action for Grassroots Empowerment and Neighborhood Development Alternatives (AGENDA), and the Labor/Community Strategy Center (www.thestrategycenter.org/), all of which are explicitly antiracist and have a strong class analysis. Unfortunately, these organizations are still the exception.

A/PIs and committed whites must also be part of such a coalition, but Asians present special challenges because they are a highly polarized population. Although Latinas/os and Blacks are also fragmented by class and some segments have experienced significant mobility, the two still constitute a disproportionate share of the region's poor. In contrast, because of the nature of the post-1965 immigration, there is a growing number of wealthy A/PIs, a large and prosperous middle class, and a significant working class, especially among Chinese, Vietnamese, and Filipina/o immigrants.

Accordingly, while much of the previous discussion applies to the thousands of A/PIs toiling away in sweatshops and the low-wage service sector, it does not necessarily apply to wealthy A/PIs, who have a different set of class interests. Indeed, as Yen Espiritu and Paul Ong have argued, class divisions limit the possibility of pan-Asian solidarity, let alone solidarity with other people of color. Such splits can be seen, for example, in tensions regarding affirmative action.[40] Many A/PIs are committed to affirmative action due to their continued experience with racism, as seen in the attack on Wen Ho Lee, employment discrimination, and hate crimes.[41] Moreover, they often have strong feelings of class solidarity, given their historic ties to the working class. Nevertheless, the potential for class conflict exists, as wealthy A/PIs may have interests antagonistic to those of workers and other communities of color. This is especially so for wealthy immigrants, who have not necessarily embraced an antiracist politics, given that they have had a far different set of experiences. But their children, who grow up in this society and have had to confront the reality of prejudice as well as interethnic contact, regardless of their class position, often see things differently. This is one indication of where political possibilities may lie.

The complicated racial and class positions of Asian Americans remind us that class cannot be equated with race and that racial formation is a dynamic process. Indeed, the existence of interethnic conflict and hostility is perhaps one of the greatest differences between the 1960s and the present. Because of immigration, economic shifts, and changing residential patterns, there are Black-Latina/o, Asian-Black, and even Latina/o-Asian tensions, whereas earlier conflict was centered on whites. The economic diversity of A/PIs makes the work of progressives all the more urgent if we wish to address economic justice issues without fostering anti-Asian racism. One example of this kind of work is the Korean Immigrant Workers Advocates (KIWA). Because whites and more established merchants are reluctant to operate retail outlets in poor communities of color, that space is left to relatively marginalized immigrant entrepreneurs, often known as ethnic middlemen. In Los Angeles that niche is largely filled by Korean immigrants. KIWA was established by progressive Korean American activists who realized that immigrant merchants, because they were located primarily in the ethnic economy and had relatively small establishments, often did not adhere to labor laws and codes. KIWA wished to support the workers, who were mostly Latina/o and Korean, but knew it had to be strategic in dealing with Korean merchants. As the campaign developed, the strategic location of the activists was key in the struggle for just wages and working conditions for the thousands of workers employed by Korean merchants.[42] Without KIWA, such conflicts could have been diluted into "cultural conflict" or, worse, could have contributed toward racism against Koreans.

KIWA's work shows the need to pay attention to racial and ethnic differences and the question of when and how to cross such lines. Yet the geography and demographics of Los Angeles suggest that while there is sufficient space for people to carve out their individual niches, there is a far greater need for people to come together. This is the challenge. This is meant, not to invalidate or call for the end of nationalism (not that that would make any difference), but to recognize its limitations, particularly in terms of gender equality, sexuality, and interethnic work. The real strength and potential of oppressed communities lie in the ties between them—a recognition of potential allies based on their economic and social location and their interests rather than simply their skin color. Until white privilege no longer exists and various groups are no longer singled out for state repression and economic exploitation, there will be a need for ethnic-specific politics. And if there is one thing the Third World Left did, it illustrated the possibility of developing relationships with others while still focusing on one's community. What is needed now is to take this one step further, for communities to work with each other, identifying their commonalities and differences, while not losing sight of their unique histories and struggles. All people of color are not the same, but they do have certain things in common, and those commonalities can often serve as the basis for shared mobilization.

Toward a More Humane Movement

The final lesson to be drawn from the Third World Left is the need to create organizations that recognize more fully the breadth and depth of people's humanity. By that I do not mean just kinder and gentler organizations but ones that are sensitive to the economic, social, intellectual, and spiritual needs of their members and how these change over time. While the Third World Left did address such issues, its efforts were highly varied. Some organizations were plagued with violence but provided collective housing; others stressed democratic practices but refused to offer child care. My interviews suggest the necessity of taking into account these needs and concerns if large, broad-based movements are to be created.

Important differences between the past and the present must be considered in any discussion of the culture and practices of social change organizations. Revolution is no longer in the air, and most activists and organizations work within more conventional frameworks. Likewise, contemporary organizations are much better funded, as they often receive foundation grants and hire full-time staff. This is dramatically different from organizations based solely on volunteer labor and the financial contributions of members and supporters. While the activists of the Third World Left may seem to have been more dedicated and selfless than today's paid staff (not necessarily so), it is difficult to sustain such activism. As people grow older their needs and concerns change. Although most movement organizations eventually collapsed, many people left politics because full-time activism became increasingly irreconcilable with the responsibilities of adulthood. Accordingly, many of the activists I talked to had specific suggestions for how organizational cultures could have been improved and could have better supported them as revolutionaries. This remains a central challenge for activists: How to transform political activism so that it is still vibrant and energetic (qualities that attract many people) but does not drain individuals to the point where they are forced to leave? When elders leave, organizations suffer from a loss of experience, expertise, and wisdom. While it is likely that radical activism will almost always be dominated by young people, organizations would benefit greatly if all age groups participated.

One of the most obvious things that organizations should and increasingly do provide is child care. Without regular, quality child care many people will be unwilling or unable to participate fully in the life of an organization. In the Third World Left, some organizations, such as the BPP, regularly provided child care (though of uneven quality), but others, such as CASA, did not. Throughout the left it was common for children to be brought to meetings lasting far into the night and simply left in a corner.[43] In fact, more than a few interviewees who were mothers regretted not doing better by their children. Such guilt should not fall on the mothers themselves but should be directed toward organizations and the movement culture as a whole. It is simply not acceptable to ask parents to choose between their children's well-being and political participation.

A distinct but related concern is the economic security that organizations can offer their members. Today organizations are composed of full- and part-time staff as well as volunteers. And while few individuals pursue a life of Political activism for the money, more needs to be done to provide for the material and economic security of those who give of themselves. When asked what they might have done differently, one former Panther replied, "We should have had a plan for what we were going to do after." She was referring to the fact that the Panthers went into a state of war without a plan to deal with the human toll it would take. Consequently, there are homeless Panthers. In a society that provides only the most rudimentary safety net, organizations need to be considering these issues in innovative and creative ways.

Two key security issues are health insurance and retirement. Ironically, often standard worker concerns force individuals to leave a life of full-time activism. Granted, few organizations can afford to provide what for-profit concerns do, but there is room for improvement. One option might be medical collectives, similar to the legal ones that existed in the sixties and seventies. Another innovation pioneered by the National Organizers' Alliance is a pension plan for activist organizations.[44] Perhaps these benefits could b expanded to other needs as well. Other strategies include groups of organizations buying large buildings that can be used to house retired activists so that they are not living in dire poverty. By working collectively, small non-profits and grassroots groups might be able to provide more opportunities and security for their members.

Burnout and intellectual development are also serious issues. Due to the intense nature of political work, burnout is a widespread problem, particularly after a long and arduous campaign. Fortunately, the idea of sabbaticals for activists is finally catching on. While still relatively few, a growing number of fellowships and sabbaticals available to longtime activists enable them to replenish themselves and pursue their interests.[45] This is especially important insofar as it can also provide an antidote to the anti-intellectualism which some organizations suffer from.

In addition, activists need to take seriously the business of conflict resolution *within* their organizations. Many activists are skilled at waging conflict and challenging the established powers, but those talents do not necessarily translate into effective communication and conflict resolution with their own colleagues. As a result, organizations may split, develop factions, and self-destruct. Sometimes these tensions are due to genuine political disagreement, in which case a separation may be necessary. But other times needless pain, rejection, and humiliation result from people's inability to communicate effectively and compassionately and handle differences. Fortunately, consultants are now available who offer affordable training to nonprofits so that their members can develop those skills.[46] Making these changes will not be easy, not only because they cost time, money, and effort, but also because they challenge one of the fundamentals of activist culture, focusing on the immediate crisis rather than the long term. As all activists know, there is never enough time and resources to do all the things that need to be done, let alone build principled and effective coalitions with like minded individuals. But only by rethinking basic assumptions and practices will activists be able to build a new political culture.

The need for reconciliation and conflict management brings up another somewhat difficult issue. In my conversations with activists, a small but vocal number raised a distinct and diverse set of concerns ranging from a critique of the overly materialist politics of the Third World Left to the inability of organizations to recognize their members' emotional and psychological needs. I refer to these concerns as issues of spirituality. While many interviewees were so firmly grounded in a racial and class analysis that they had never even considered these issues, quite a few others had. Whether referring to the "spiritual" or to a mind/body connection, interviewees took pains to distinguish their concerns from organized religion and even the Judeo-Christian tradition.[47] Nonetheless, many saw the need for both individuals, organizations, and political cultures to address questions pertaining to the existence/nature of souls; humans' relationship to other beings (including humans, animals, and deities); healing; peace; and the importance of creating social change from within as well as without.

It is important to acknowledge the challenges of raising such concerns within a left political context.[48] While such discussions may make activists uncomfortable, to ignore such issues would only perpetuate an abiding problem of the left: its limited ability, particularly among revolutionary elements, to entertain the possibility that humans are more than political animals. Indeed, the very nature of the political animal may be more complex than imagined. As Robin Kelley has noted, "Freedom and love constitute the foundation of spirituality … [an] elusive and intangible force with which few scholars of social movements have come to terms."[49] It is time to break this silence and begin envisioning new ways of analyzing social movements and political activism itself if the pitfalls of the past are to be avoided.

At this point it is uncertain what the future holds for left politics in the United States, but a few things should inform any serious debate. First, although communism may be dead and much of the world appears to be accepting capitalism, it is clear that millions of people are protesting the imposition of an economic system that puts the bottom line (be it corporate or state) ahead of basic human needs. It is also evident that global hunger and misery have not abated, although the geography of human suffering does shift over time. This latest round of capitalist development is creating greater economic polarization in its wake, making the contradictions between the haves and have-nots all the more visible. As long as these conditions remain, there will be a deep desire for alternative social arrangements that will reduce human suffering and enable people to live with a modicum of dignity.

In short, the *need* for a leftist politics is as great as ever. If such is the case, then a new vision will be required, and this is where the difficulty lies. Over the last few decades the right has effectively cornered the market on the "vision thing," as the left has had little to offer in response to charges of sectarianism and the collapse of communism (which proved that all left ideas were futile, right?). But without a vision of what the world might be like and how to get there, the left has little to offer people and no chance of building a broad-based movement for social change. To borrow again from Kelley's *Freedom Dreams,* the left is in dire need of dreaming.[50] Activists must dream in order to develop a vision of the kind of world they would like to live in. The visions offered must be compassionate and humane and must reach people's hearts and souls as well as their minds. Although a vision is no guarantee of successfully remaking the world, it is a necessary first step. Finally, while the content of those visions remains open and uncertain, there is a need to be wary of dogmatism, coerciveness, and sectarianism. There should be no orthodoxy. Although the U.S. left never attained the level of destruction that more institutionalized forms of Marxism/Leninism did, its character was such that it *could* have, had the power of the state been behind it. It is time for those committed to social and economic justice to come up with something new and different. I have confidence that living arrangements can be devised whereby everybody can be fed and the planet healed, but it will take a profound change and a willingness to open our hearts and minds to something entirely new and different if we wish to get there.

Notes

1. See Santa Ana, *Brown Tide Rising;* Mike Davis, "Social Origins"; Robert Gooding-Williams, *Reading Rodney King, Reading Urban Uprising* (New York: Routledge, 1993); Harold Meyerson, "The Red Sea," *LA Weekly,* April 28-May 4, 2000, 17–20; Mike Davis, "Runaway Train Crashes Buses," *Nation,* September 18, 1995, 270–74; Erin Texeira, "Generation Gap Seen in Black Support for Hahn," *Los Angeles Times,* May 5, 2001, B1, B11; David Shichor and Dale Sechrest, *Three Strikes and You're Out: Vengeance as Public Policy* (Thousand Oaks, CA: Sage Publications, 1996); Freer, "Black Korean Conflict"; Edna Bonacich et al., *Global Production: The Apparel Industry in the Pacific Rim* (Philadelphia: Temple University Press, 1994).

2. Consider, once again, *Field of Dreams,* especially the scene where Amy Madigan, delighted to be taking on a conservative school board, says with relish, "It's just like the sixties!" See also Nadel, *Flatlining,* ch. 2.

3. See, for example, Angela Davis, "Afro Images."

4. Elbaum, *Revolution in the Air,* 310. See also Jack Whalen and Richard Flacks, *Beyond the Barricades: The Sixties Generation Grows Up* (Philadelphia: Temple University Press, 1989). Important exceptions to this pattern are those who became conservative radicals. See Horowitz, *Radical Son.*

5. Whalen and Flacks found that many activists were lost after the demise of the New Left, as they had delayed key decisions regarding marriage, work, and family. *Beyond the Barricades,* ch. 4.

6. Nicholls, "Forging a 'New' Organizational Infrastructure"; Pastor, "Common Ground"; Gottlieb et al., *Next Los Angeles.*

7. This conclusion is drawn from a biased sample: I only interviewed those that either I knew to be politically active or other interviewees referred me to. Thus I did not interview those who had either closed the door on this chapter of their lives or for whatever reason declined to talk to me.

8. Meyerson, "Red Sea"; Roger Waldinger et al., "Justice for Janitors," *Dissent* 47 (Winter 1997): 37–44; Nancy Cleeland, "LA Area Now a Model for Labor Revival," *Los Angeles Times,* September 6, 1996, A1, A20; Merrifield "Urbanization of Labor"; Milkman and Wong, *Voices from the Front Lines;* Stuart Silverstein, "Going to Work in LA," *Los Angeles Times,* February 22, 1996, D1, D3; Ruth Milkman, *Organizing Immigrants: The Challenge for Unions in Contemporary California* (Ithaca, NY: Cornell University Press, 2000).

9. Allen and Turner, *Changing Faces, Changing Places,* ch. 5. Paul Moore et al., *The Other Los Angeles: Working Poor in the City of the 21st Century* (Los Angeles: Los Angeles Alliance for a New Economy, 2000); Paul Ong and Evelyn Blumenberg, "Income and Racial Inequality in Los Angeles," in Scott and Soja, *The City,* 311–35.

10. Dave Gardetta, "True Grit: Clocking Time with the Janitors' Organizer Rocio Saenz," *L.A. Weekly* 15 (1993): 23.

11. María Elena Durazo, "María Elena Durazo," in Milkman and Wong, *Voices from the Front Lines,* 11–22; Lou Siegel, "LRR Voices: Local 11 Takes on LA," *Labor Research Review* 20 (1993): 21–23; Bob Spichen, "Labor of Love," *Los Angeles Times,* March 9, 1997, E1, E8.

12. Nicholls, "Forging a 'New' Organizational Infrastructure," 24–25.

13. Elbaum, *Revolution in the Air,* 235; League of Revolutionary Struggle, *Statements;* League of Revolutionary Struggle, *Peace, Justice, Equality and Socialism* (Oakland, CA: Getting Together Publications, 1986).

14. Mitchell Maki et al., *Achieving the Impossible Dream: How Japanese Americans Obtained Redress* (Urbana: University of Illinois Press, 1999); Daniels, Taylor, and Kitano, *Japanese Americans,* part 7.

15. Eric Yamamoto, "What's Next? Japanese American Redress and African American Reparations," *Amerasia* 25 (1999): 1–17.

16. On A/PI demographics, see Allen and Turner, *Changing Faces, Changing Places,* ch. 6. On economic diversity, see Ong and Hee, "Economic Diversity"; Ong and Blumenberg, "Income and Racial Inequality." On interracial marriage, see Fong and Yung, "In Search"; Tuan, *Forever Foreigners,* 31–36; Wu, *Yellow,* ch. 7. Activism around Little Tokyo dates back to the redevelopment efforts of the 1970s. On the current struggle, see http://reccenter.ltsc.org.

17. Thanks to Tony Osumi and Jenni Kuida for help with contacts.

18. Ward Churchill, "To Disrupt, Discredit and Destroy: The FBI's Secret War against the Black Panther Party," in Cleaver and Katsiaficas, *Liberation, Imagination,* 109.

19. Olsen, *Last Man Standing.*

20. Gary Webb, *Dark Alliance: The CIA, the Contras, and the Crack Cocaine Explosion* (New York: Seven Stories, 1999); Mike Davis, *City of Quartz,* ch. 5; Cynthia Hamilton, *Apartheid in America* (Los Angeles: Labor/ Community Strategy Center, 1987).

21. Melvin Oliver, James Johnson, and William Farrell, "Anatomy of a Rebellion," in *Reading Rodney King, Reading Urban Uprising,* ed. Robert Gooding-Williams (New York: Routledge, 1993), 117–41.

22. Latina/o immigrants are routinely blamed for Black unemployment and poverty. With some notable exceptions, however, such as the janitorial industry, evidence suggests that Latina/o immigration has had a mixed impact. For instance, Ong and Valenzuela found that while Latina/o immigration affected Black joblessness (but not earnings), equally important was the role of institutional racism and employer discrimination. Paul Ong and Abel Valenzuela, "The Labor Market: Immigrant Effects and Racial

Disparities," in Waldinger and Bozorgmehr, *Ethnic Los Angeles,* 165–91. Likewise, Waldinger and Lichter argue that immigration has contributed to "African Americans being 'pulled' rather than 'pushed' out of their employment concentrations." Roger Waldinger and Michael Lichter, *How the Other Half Works: Immigration and the Social Organization of Labor* (Berkeley: University of California Press, 2003), 209. See also J. Kirschenman and K. Neckerman, "We'd Love to Hire Them, but…: The Meaning of Race for Employers," in *The Urban Underclass,* ed. C. Jencks and P. Peterson (Washington, DC: Brookings Institution, 1991), 203–32.

23. Allen and Turner, *Changing Faces, Changing Places,* ch. 4

24. James Rainey and Jeffrey Rabin, "Hahn and Villaraigosa Now Must Shift Focus," *Los Angeles Times,* April 12, 2001, A1, A17; Texeira, "Generation Gap Seen." Hahn and Villaraigosa faced off again in 2005, and once again the Black vote was pivotal. The outcome of this election was different, however, as Villaraigosa won easily. Michael Finnegan, "In Testy Debate, Hahn and Villaraigosa Appeal for the Support of Black Voters," *Los Angeles Times,* April 10, 2005, B1, B6.

25. Laura Pulido, "Restructuring and the Contraction and Expansion of Environmental Rights in the US," *Environment and Planning A* 26 (1994): 915–36; Liza Featherstone, *Students against Sweatshops* (New York: Verso, 2002); Miriam Ching Yoon Louie, *Sweatshop Warriors: Immigrant Women Workers Take on the Global Factory* (Boston: South End Press, 2001).

26. Janet Abu-Lughod, *New York, Chicago, Los Angeles: America's Global Cities* (Minneapolis: University of Minnesota Press, 2000).

27. Although far fewer, such female leaders also existed. Some have suggested that Carmen Chow of I Wor Kuen was such a figure.

28. On the culture of the New Communist movement, see Elbaum, *Revolution in the Air,* ch. 8.

29. For example, the Southern Christian Leadership Conference under Martin Luther King Jr. was less democratic than either the Student Non-violent Coordinating Committee or the Congress of Racial Equality. Akinleye Umoja, "The Ballot and the Bullet," *Journal of Black Studies* 29 (March 1999): 570.

30. Carol Mueller, "Ella Baker and the Origins of Participatory Democracy," in Crawford, Rouse, and Woods, *Women in the Civil Rights Movement,* 51–70; Pardo, *Mexican American Women Activists;* Alice Eagley and Mary Johannesen-Schmidt, "The Leadership Styles of Men and Women," *Journal of Social Issues* 57 (2001): 781–97.

31. See, for example, Emily Woo Yamasaki, "Perspective of a Revolutionary Feminist" in Ho et al., *Legacy to Liberation,* 47–51.

32. For a different perspective, see Jennifer Ting, "The Power of Sexuality," *Journal of Asian American Studies* 1 (1998): 65–82.

33. Huey Newton, "The Women's Liberation and Gay Liberation Movements," in Newton, *To Die for the People,* 152–55; Wat, *Making of a Gay Asian Community,* 93–101.

34. On the challenges of multiracial organizing, see Pulido, "Multiracial Organizing."

35. Thomas Durant, "Race and Class Consciousness among Lower and Middle-Class Blacks," *Journal of Black Studies* 27 (1997): 334–51.

36. On Central Americans, see Nora Hamilton and Norma Stoltz Chinchilla, *Seeking Community in a Global City: Guatemalans and Salvadorans in Los Angeles* (Philadelphia: Temple University Press, 2001).

37. See Deborah Berman Santana, "No Somos Unicos: The Status Question from Manila to San Juan," *Centro* 11 (Fall 1999): 127–40.

38. Anthony Thigpenn, in "The View from the Ground: Organizers Speak out on Race," *Colorlines* 3 (Summer 2000): 16–17.

39. On Latina/o poverty, see Moore et al., *The Other Los Angeles;* on Black and Chicana/o political infrastructure, see Parker, "Elusive Coalition"; on racial discrimination, see Logan, "How Race Counts."

40. David Savage, "Affirmative Action Case Splits Asian Americans," *Los Angeles Times,* March 30, 2003, A30; Yen Espiritu and Paul Ong, "Class Constraints on Racial Solidarity among Asian Americans," in Ong, Bonacich, and Cheng, *New Asian Immigration,* 295–321.

41. "Scientist Says Race Was a Factor in US Spy Case," *Los Angeles Times,* January 16, 2002, A17; Elizabeth Kelly, "Claims against Abercrombie Detailed," *Los Angeles Times,* June 18, 2003, C2; Umemoto, "From Vincent Chin"; Scott Kurashige, "Beyond Random Acts."

42. On Korean merchants, see Pyong Gap Min, *Caught in the Middle: Korean Merchants in America's Multiethnic Cities* (Berkeley: University of California Press, 1996). On KIWA, see Tram Nguyen, "Showdown in K-Town," *Colorlines* 4 (Spring 2001): 26–29. See also KIWA's Web site: www.kiwa.org.

43. Marisela Rodríguez Chávez, "Living and Breathing," 69.

44. See the National Organizers' Alliance Web site: www.noacentral.org/pension.html.

45. Innovative programs include UCLA's Community/Scholars' Program (www.sppsr.ucla.edu), the Bannerman Fellowship (www.bannermanfellowship.org), and the Vallecitos Mountain Refuge Fellowship Program (www.vallecitos.org/refuge_fellowship.html).

46. On the need for reconciliation among communities of color, see Yamamoto, *Interracial Justice.*

47. The only religion openly acknowledged by interviewees was Buddhism.

48. Indeed, one manuscript reviewer insisted that any reference to spirituality should be eliminated from this book.

49. Kelley, *Freedom Dreams,* 12.

50. Kelley, *Freedom Dreams,* 12.

CPSIA information can be obtained
at www.ICGtesting.com
Printed in the USA
LVHW01s0332110718
583301LV00001B/6/P

9 781516 510641